Agrarian Angst and Rural Resistance in Contemporary Southeast Asia

Agrarian transformations, market integration and globalization processes are impacting upon rural Southeast Asia with increasingly complex and diverse consequences. In response, local inhabitants are devising a broad range of resistance measures that they feel will best protect or improve their liveli-hoods, ensure greater social justice and equity, or allow them to just be left alone. This book develops a multi-scalar approach to examine resistance occurring in relation to agrarian transformations in the Southeast Asian region. We move the boundaries of scale from previous works to include not only micro-level resistance tactics such as those documented by James Scott in his 1985 book *Weapons of the Weak: Everyday Forms of Peasant Resistance*, but also national, regional and transnational acts of resistance and defiance against policies and activities often linked to agro-food industries, global market integration and political domination.

The contributors take a fresh look at the diversity of sites of struggle and the combinations of resistance measures being utilized in contemporary Southeast Asia. They reveal that open public conflicts and debates are taking place between dominators and the oppressed, at the same time as covert critiques of power and everyday forms of resistance. The authors show how resistance measures are context contingent, shaped by different world views, and shift according to local circumstances, the opening and closing of politi-cal opportunity structures, and the historical peculiarities of resistance dynamics.

By providing new conceptual approaches and illustrative case studies that cut across scales and forms, this book will be of interest to academics and students in comparative politics, sociology, human geography, environmental studies, cultural anthropology and Southeast Asian studies. It will also help to further debate and action among academics, activists and policymakers.

Dominique Caouette is an Assistant Professor in the Department of Political Science, Université de Montréal, Canada.

Sarah Turner is an Associate Professor in the Department of Geography, McGill University, Montréal, Canada.

Routledge ISS Studies in Rural Livelihoods
Editorial Board: A. Haroon Akram-Lodhi (Trent University), Saturnino M. Borras Jr. (Institute of Social Studies), Cristóbal Kay (Chair) (Institute of Social Studies) and Max Spoor (Institute of Social Studies).

Routledge and the Institute of Social Studies (ISS) in The Hague, The Netherlands have come together to publish a new book series in rural livelihoods. The series will include themes such as land policies and land rights, water issues, food policy and politics, rural poverty, agrarian transformation, migration, rural-oriented social movements, rural conflict and violence, among others. All books in the series will offer rigorous, empirically grounded, cross-national comparative and inter-regional analysis. The books will be theoretically stimulating, but will also be accessible to policy practitioners and civil society activists.

Agrarian Angst and Rural Resistance in Contemporary Southeast Asia

Edited by Dominique Caouette and Sarah Turner

LONDON AND NEW YORK

First published 2009
by Routledge
2 Park Square, Milton Park, Abingdon, Oxon, OX14 4RN

Simultaneously published in the USA and Canada
by Routledge
711 Third Avenue, New York, NY 10017

*Routledge is an imprint of the Taylor & Francis Group,
an informa business*

First issued in paperback 2011

Typeset in Times by
RefineCatch Limited, Bungay, Suffolk

British Library Cataloguing in Publication Data
A catalogue record for this book is available from the British Library

Library of Congress Cataloging-in-Publication Data
Agrarian angst and rural resistance in contemporary Southeast Asia /
edited by Dominique Caouette and Sarah Turner
    p. cm.
    Includes bibliographical references and index.
    1. Peasantry—Southeast Asia—Political activity.   2. Social
conflict— Southeast Asia.   I. Caouette, Dominique.   II. Turner,
Sarah.
    HD1537.A785A37 2009
    305.5′6330959—dc22   2009000385

ISBN10: 0–415–54838–1 (hbk)
ISBN10: 0–415–68195–2 (pbk)
ISBN10: 0–203–87494–3 (ebk)

ISBN13: 978–0–415–54838–0 (hbk)
ISBN13: 978–0–415–68195–7 (pbk)
ISBN13: 978–0–203–87494–3 (ebk)

Contents

Figures

Tables

Contributors

Saturnino ('Jun') M. Borras Jr is the Canada Research Chair in International Development Studies at St Mary's University, Halifax, Canada. Involved in peasant movements in the Philippines and internationally since the early 1980s, he was one of the founders of the international peasant movement La Via Campesina. His publications include *Land, Poverty and Livelihoods: Perspectives from Developing and Transition Countries* (with Haroon Akram Lodhi and Cristóbal Kay as co-editors, 2007) and *Pro-Poor Land Reform: A Critique* (2007).

Dominique Caouette is an Assistant Professor in the Department of Political Science, Université de Montréal, Canada. He has lived and worked in the Philippines and Latin America and written on social movements and lately on transnational networks and advocacy. He has recently published in *Revue Possibles* (2008), *Pacific Focus* (2007), *Kasarinlan: A Philippine Quarterly of Third World Studies* (2006), *Relations* (2006) and *Persevering Revolutionaries: Armed Struggle in the 21st Century, Exploring the Revolution of the Communist Party of the Philippines* (forthcoming).

Wolfram H. Dressler is a Lecturer in the School of Social Sciences, University of Queensland, Australia. His research examines human–environment relations in Southeast Asia, with an emphasis on conservation impacts on small-scale societies, especially those in the Philippines. His most recent articles can be found in *Conservation and Society* (2007), *Political Geography* (2006), *Development and Change* (2006) and *Human Ecology Review* (2005).

Tim Forsyth is a Reader in Environment and Development at the Development Studies Institute, London School of Economics and Political Science, UK. He is a specialist in political approaches to environmental change and international development. His publications include *Forest Guardians, Forest Destroyers: The Politics of Environmental Knowledge in Northern Thailand* (2008) with co-author Andrew Walker, and *Critical Political Ecology: The Politics of Environmental Science* (2003). He edited the *Encyclopedia of International Development* (2005).

Jennifer C. Franco is a Research Coordinator at the Transnational Institute (TNI) based in Amsterdam. Her work has focused on rural social movements and democratization in the Philippines. Her publications include *Agrarian Reform Communities and Rural Democratization in Quezon Province* (2000), *Elections and Democratization in the Philippines* (2001) and *On Just Grounds: Struggling for Agrarian Justice and Exercising Citizenship Rights in the Rural Philippines* (with Saturnino Borras Jr., editors, 2005). She has published in *World Development* (2008), *Journal of Development Studies* (2008) and *Critical Asian Studies* (2005, 2007).

Erik Martinez Kuhonta is an Assistant Professor in the Department of Political Science at McGill University, Montréal, Canada. He specializes in the fields of comparative political development, political economy and international relations, with a regional focus on Southeast Asia. He has published in *Asian Survey* (2008), *Pacific Review* (2006), *Asian Affairs* (2005), *Harvard Asia Quarterly* (2004) and *American Asian Review* (2003), and is co-editor with Dan Slater and Vu Tuong of *Southeast Asia in Political Science: Theory, Region, and Qualitative Analysis* (2008).

Jean Michaud is an Associate Professor in the Department of Anthropology, Université Laval, Québec, Canada. He is a social anthropologist whose work focuses on the highland minorities who live in the Southeast Asia massif. Key publications include *'Incidental Ethnographers': French Catholic Missions on the Tonkin-Yunnan Frontier, 1880–1930* (2007), *Historical Dictionary of the Peoples of the Southeast Asian Massif* (2006) and *Turbulent Times and Enduring Peoples: The Mountain Minorities of the South-East Asian Massif* (editor, 2000).

Lesley Potter is a Visiting Fellow in Human Geography, Australian National University. She has most recently worked on commodities, governance and decentralization, especially in Indonesia. Her publications include 'Resource periphery, corridor, heartland: contesting land-use in the Kalimantan/Malaysia borderlands', *Asia Pacific Viewpoint* (2009), as well as chapters in *Taking Southeast Asia to Market: Commodities, People and Nature in a Neoliberal Age*, edited by N. Peluso and J. Nevins (2008) and *Forest Governance and Decentralisation in Asia and the Pacific*, edited by C. Colfer and D. Capistrano (2008).

Sandra Smeltzer is an Assistant Professor in the Faculty of Information and Media Studies at The University of Western Ontario, Canada. Her research focuses on development communication; blogging, social networking sites and civil society resistance in Malaysia; and alternative media pedagogy in Canada. She has recently published in *Asia Pacific Viewpoint* (2009), *Journal of International Communication* (2008), the *Canadian Journal of Communication* (2008), *Development in Practice* (forthcoming), and in *Taking Southeast Asia to Market: Commodities,*

Nature, and People in the Neoliberal Age, edited by Joseph Nevins and Nancy Lee Peluso (2008).

Trần Thị Thu Trang is an Assistant Professor in the School of Political Studies, University of Ottawa, Canada. Her research focuses on rural development, globalization, trade, and local politics in Vietnam. Her publications include chapters in Philip Taylor (editor), *Social Inequality in Vietnam and the Challenges to Reform* (2004); in Ben Kerkvliet and David Marr (editors), *Beyond Hanoi: Local Government in Vietnam* (2004) and in Duncan McCargo (editor), *Rethinking Vietnam* (2004).

Sarah Turner is an Associate Professor in the Department of Geography, McGill University, Montréal, Canada. She is a development geographer who specializes in research on small-scale entrepreneurs, marketplace traders, and urban and rural livelihoods of people 'on the margins' in Vietnam and Indonesia. She is author of *Indonesia's Small Entrepreneurs: Trading on the Margins* (2003), and has recently published in *Development and Change* (2008), *Journal of Vietnamese Studies* (2008), *Journal of Development Studies* (2008), *Human Organization* (2007), *Professional Geographer* (2007) and *Environment and Planning D: Society and Space* (2007).

Vu Tuong is an Assistant Professor in the Department of Political Science, University of Oregon, US. His interests include the politics of Vietnam and Indonesia, and Southeast Asian comparative politics. He has recently published in *Ab Imperio* (2008), *Studies in Comparative International Development* (2007), *Journal of Vietnamese Studies* (2007), *Theory and Society* (2006), *Communist and Post-Communist Studies* (2005) and *South East Asia Research* (2003). He is the co-editor (with Erik Kuhonta and Daniel Slater) of *Southeast Asia in Political Science: Theory, Region, and Qualitative Analysis* (2008).

Andrew Walker is an anthropologist at the College of Asia and the Pacific, Australian National University. His recent work focuses on agricultural transformations, resource management and environmental politics. He is author (with Tim Forsyth) of *Forest Guardians, Forest Destroyers: The Politics of Environmental Knowledge in Northern Thailand* (2008) and editor of *Tai Lands and Thailand: Community and State in Southeast Asia* (2009). Other recent publications appeared in *Journal of Contemporary Asia* (2008), *Critical Asian Studies* (2008) and *Journal of Vietnamese Studies* (2008). He is co-editor of *New Mandala*, a weblog on mainland Southeast Asia.

Preface

Perched on the side of an iridescent green rice padi, an ethnic minority Hmong woman from Tả Văn commune in upland northern Vietnam explains what it was like in the 'old days' when the collectivization of production was promoted by the country's socialist state. With a shrug of her shoulders she comments that her family did not really change production notably during those times, but remained 'under the radar' and avoided the gaze of lowland state officials, so that they could continue working their land as they had for generations. Today, her family continues to prefer to remain away from the gaze of the state, and community members deal with any disputes internally, rather than calling on state authorities to address grievances. A few thousand kilometres away, in the highlands of Southern Mindanao, Philippines, members of the Merardo Arce Command of the New People's Army are discussing their latest operations in response to the recent military offensives of the 1001st Brigade-AFP in New Bataan. For these guerrillas, most of them from peasant origins, genuine social and political change in the country requires a full-blown revolutionary takeover. Short of such radical change, breaking down the control of large landowning family clans and multinationals based in Mindanao and implementing land reforms is impossible, while open and legal activism can only bring about short-term gains and partial reforms. At about the same time, on the small island of Penang off the coast of Peninsular Malaysia, in the Third World Network office, analysts are finalizing a new issue of *Third World Resurgence* on the recent food crisis and its effects on small-scale farmers in Asia, while colleagues in Geneva are posting a *Third World Network Info* note on the internet that describes the latest proposals made by the G20 on sensitive products in agriculture. The posting reviews and analyzes, paragraph by paragraph, the highly technical documents presented to the World Trade Organization Secretariat in Geneva.

What links such disparate peoples, places and processes? In short, agrarian transformations, market integration and globalization processes that are impacting upon the rural countryside in Southeast Asia and the resistance measures that local people engage in that they feel will best serve their cause for justice, equity or just plain 'being left alone'.

This book takes a multi-scalar approach to examine resistance occurring in relation to agrarian transformations in contemporary Southeast Asia. We move the boundaries of scale from previous works to include not only 'everyday forms of peasant resistance' at the micro level, expanding upon those that James Scott documented in 1985 in his book *Weapons of the Weak: Everyday Forms of Peasant Resistance*, an important goal in its own right as people challenge different extensions of the market economy into their lives, but also national, regional and transnational acts of resistance and defiance against policies and activities often linked to global market integration. While problematizing old ways of examining scale as bounded, we incorporate instances of resistance acts often rendered invisible at the local, micro level as well as those more organized forms of opposition and dissent that are occurring across scale through to national and transnational social movements.

Bringing together scholars working on agrarian and rural resistance activities and movements at a range of scales and shapes, this book focuses on the five countries currently at the heart of the agrarian transition in Southeast Asia, namely Indonesia, Malaysia, the Philippines, Vietnam and Thailand. The thirteen contributors, from both East and West, explore the wide range of responses by rural populations to agrarian and economic policies that are exacerbating the economic inequalities faced in different Southeast Asian countries, and their implications for resistance movements.

On the ground, this book emerges in part from a series of conversations in Montréal cafés around intuitions that there might be more in common between upland ethnic minorities in Vietnam and guerrillas in the Philippines maquis than one would first expect. The book is also the result of sharing research findings while participating in a series of panels organized for the Canadian Council for Southeast Asian Studies conference, Québec City, Canada in 2007, and a panel presented at the Association for Asian Studies (AAS) conference, Atlanta, US in 2008. We would like to thank Francois Fortier, Isabelle Beaulieu and Patricia Sloane-White who, along with our contributing authors, also gave papers in these panels. We are also appreciative of the valuable feedback Vincent Boudreau gave us as panel discussant in Atlanta. This book has also benefited from the comments of participants at two workshops held in 2007, one in association with the Social Science and Humanities Research Council Canada, Multi-Collaborative Research Grant 'Challenges of the Agrarian Transition in Southeast Asia', held in Montréal, Canada, and the other for contributors, held in Québec City, Canada. We are also indebted to Ben Kerkvliet and James Scott for their comments and kind words.

We are very grateful for the research assistance of Stephanie Coen, Laura Schoenberger, Christine Bonnin, Candice Gartner, Lindsay Anderson, Carmen Diaz, Denis Côté and Cynthia Brassard-Boudreau, who helped this book to see the light of day, and for Jean Michaud's preparation of a number of the maps. We thank the editors of the *Routledge ISS Studies in Rural Livelihoods* series Saturnino 'Jun' Borras, Haroon Akram-Lodhi, Cristobal Kay and Max Spoor for their support and encouragement. Thanks also go to the two evaluators of our initial manuscript for their insightful comments, and to Tim Forsyth for his suggestions as he wrote the conclusion based on earlier chapter drafts. Last but not least, we would like to express our gratitude to our partners in crime, Bing Arguelles and Jean Michaud, for their important academic and emotional support; and Dominique would like to thank Arca and Claude Arguelles-Caouette for their patience and good humour.

Dominique Caouette and Sarah Turner
May 2009
Montréal, Canada

Abbreviations and acronyms

ALBA	*Alternativa Bolivariana para las Américas* (Alternative trade alliance, Latin America)
AMA (AMAN)	*Aliansi Masyarakat Adat* (*Aliansi Masyarakat Adat Nusantara*) (Alliance of Indigenous Peoples of the Archipelago) (Indonesia)
AMC	Asian Migrant Center
AMCHAM	American-Malaysian Chamber of Commerce
AMRC	Asia Monitor Resource Center
AoA	Agreement on Agriculture (WTO)
AOP	Assembly of the Poor (*Samacha Khon Jon*) (Thailand)
APA	Asian Peace Alliance
APEC	Asia-Pacific Economic Cooperation
API	*Aliansi Petani Indonesia* (Indonesian Alliance of Farmers)
APRN	Asia-Pacific Research Network
ARENA	Asian Regional Exchange for New Alternatives
ASEAN	Association of Southeast Asian Nations
ASEM	Asia–Europe Meeting
BERSIH	see glossary
BN	*Barisan Nasional* (Malaysia)
BRDFI	Budyong Rural Development Foundation Inc (Philippines)
BULOG	*Badan Urusan Logistik* (Indonesian Bureau of Logistics)
CAA	Community Aid Abroad (Oxfam Australia)
CADC	Certificate of Ancestral Domain Claims (Philippines)
CALABARZON	acronym for Cavite, Laguna, Batangas, Rizal, Quezon region (Philippines)
CAP	Consumers' Association of Penang (Malaysia)
CARP	Comprehensive Agrarian Reform Program (Philippines)
CAW	Committee for Asian Women

CCA	Christian Conference of Asia
CI-ROAP	Consumers International-Regional Office for Asia and the Pacific
CMARPRP	Community-Managed Agrarian Reform and Poverty Reduction Project (Philippines)
CODE-NGO	Caucus of Development NGO Networks (Philippines)
COMPACT	Community Management of Protected Areas for Conservation (Philippines)
CPAR	Congress for a People's Agrarian Reform (Philippines)
CPP	Communist Party of the Philippines
CUSRI	Chulalongkorn University Social Research Institute (Thailand)
DAP	Democratic Action Party (Malaysia)
DAR	Department of Agrarian Reform (Philippines)
DENR	Department of Environment and Natural Resources (Philippines)
DPRD	District Legislative Assembly (Indonesia)
DTE	Down to Earth
EEI	Environmental and Ecological Investigation (Thailand)
EGAT	Electricity Generating Authority of Thailand
EU	European Union
FAO	Food and Agriculture Organization
FISO	Fast-track, Issue-based, Sweeping Organizing (Philippines)
FSPI	*Federasi Serikat Petani Indonesia* (Indonesian Federation of Farmers' Unions)
FTA	Free Trade Agreement
GATT	General Agreement on Tariffs and Trade
GDP	Gross Domestic Product
HDI	Human Development Index
HINDRAF	Hindu Rights Action Force (Malaysia)
HSL	*PT Harapan Sawit Lestari* (palm oil plantation, Indonesia)
ICARRD	International Conference on Agrarian Reform and Rural Development
ID	Institute of Dayakology (Indonesia)
IDS	Institute of Development Studies
IMF	International Monetary Fund
IPAS	Integrated Protected Areas Strategy (Philippines)
ISDV	*Indische Sociaal-Democratische Vereniging* (Indies Social Democratic Association)

JERIT	*Jaringan Rakyat Tertindas* (Oppressed People's Network, Malaysia)
KMP	*Kilusang Magbubukid ng Pilipinas* (Peasant Movement of the Philippines)
KPA	*Konsorsium Pembaruan Agraria* (Consortium for Agrarian Reform, Indonesia)
KR	*Kalimantan Review* (journal published by Institute of Dayakology (ID), Pontianak, Indonesia)
LGUs	Local Government Units (Philippines)
LL	PT Ledo Lestari, palm oil plantation (Indonesia)
LTI	Land Tenure Improvement (Philippines)
MAI	Multilateral Agreement on Investment
MAINS	Master of Arts in Inter-Asia NGO Studies
MITI	Ministry of International Trade and Industry (Malaysia)
MNR	Ministry of Natural Resources (Philippines)
MSL	Mean sea level
NATRIPAL	*Nagkakaisang mga Tribu ng Palawan*, Palawan-wide tribal federation (Philippines)
NCER	Northern Corridor Economic Region (Malaysia)
ND	National-Democrat or Nat-Dem (Philippines)
NDF	National Democratic Front (NDF)
NES	Nucleus Estate and Smallholder Project (Indonesia)
NFA	National Food Authority (Philippines)
NGO	Non-Governmental Organization
NGO-COD	NGO Coordinating Committee on Rural Development (Thailand)
NIPAS	National Integrated Protected Areas Strategy (Philippines)
North-Net	Northern Farmers Development Network (Thailand)
NPA	New People's Army (Philippines)
NPS	National Peasant Secretariat (Philippines)
NRMC	Natural Resources Management Center (Philippines)
NU	*Nahdlatul Ulama* (social organization, Indonesia)
PAN AP	Pesticide Action Network Asia and The Pacific (Malaysia)
PARRDS	Partnership for Agrarian Reform and Rural Development Services (Philippines)
PAS	*Parti Islam SeMalaysia* (Pan Malaysian Islamic Party, Malaysia)
PEACE	Philippine Ecumenical Action for Community Empowerment

PECCO	Philippine Ecumenical Council for Community Organizing
PhP	*Peso* (Philippines currency)
PKI	*Partai Komunis Indonesia* (Communist Party of Indonesia)
PKR	*Parti Keadilan Rakyat* (People's Justice Party, Malaysia)
PNP	*Perusahaan Negara Perseroan* (old name for public plantation company)
POS	political opportunity structure
PPSRNP	Puerto Princesa Subterranean River National Park (Philippines)
PPW	Protracted People's War
PSM	*Parti Sosialis Malaysia* (Socialist Party of Malaysia)
PT	*Perseroan Terbatas*, Limited Liability Company (Indonesia)
PTPN	*Perseroan Terbatas Perusahaan Negara* (Government Limited Liability Plantation, Indonesia)
PTPN XIII	*PT Perkebunan Nusantara XIII* (limited liability state plantation company No. 13; oil palm)
PT SIA	*PT Sime Indo Agro* (Malaysian-owned private palm oil plantation company)
PT SML	*PT Sumatra Makmur Lestari* (private palm oil plantation, Indonesia)
Rp	*rupiah* (Indonesian currency)
RP	Resettlement planning (Thailand)
RSPO	Roundtable on Sustainable Palm Oil
SAM	*Sahabat Alam Malaysia* (Friends of the Earth Malaysia)
SEACON	Southeast Asian Council for Food Security and Fair Trade
SI	*Sarekat Islam* (Islamic League, Indonesia)
SPI	*Serikat Petani Indonesia* (Indonesian Peasant Union)
SUNS	*South-North Development Monitor*
TAP/MPR	People's Consultative Assembly Decree (Indonesia)
TERAS	*Teras Pengupayaan Melayu* (Malay Empowerment Group)
TICKA	*Tinig Katutubo sa Cabayugan* (People's Organization belonging to the province-wide tribal federation NATRIPAL, Philippines)
TOLs	Training-Organizing Laboratories
TPS-OIC	Trade Preferential System-Organization of Islamic Conference
TRIPS	Trade-Related Aspects of Intellectual Property Rights

TWE	*Third World Economics*
TWN	Third World Network
TWNF	*Third World Network Features*
UMNO	United Malays National Organisation
UNDP	United Nations Development Programme
UNDP-COMPACT	United Nations Development Programme Community Management of Protected Areas for Conservation
UNESCO	United Nations Educational, Scientific and Cultural Organization
USAID	US Agency for International Development
USTR	US Trade Representative
UUPA	*Undang-Undang Pokok Agraria* (Agrarian Law, Indonesia)
VLSS	Vietnam Living Standards Survey
VND	*dong* (Vietnamese currency)
WAHLI	*Wahana Lingkungan Hidup Indonesia* (Indonesian Forum on Environment; Friends of the Earth Indonesia)
WTO	World Trade Organization
WWF	World Wide Fund for Nature (World Wildlife Fund)

1 Shifting fields of rural resistance in Southeast Asia

Sarah Turner and
Dominique Caouette

Since 1990 many important events have occurred in the Southeast Asian region, notably the economic crisis that began in 1997, the fall of long-time Indonesian state leader President Suharto, and the rapid development of capitalist economies in countries like Vietnam and increasingly Laos and Cambodia. Catastrophic environmental disasters have transpired, including the December 2004 tsunami, powerful landslides in the Philippines, and Nargis, the 2008 cyclone that hit the coast of Burma, while environmental pressures such as the annual smog episodes covering southern Malaysia and Singapore as a result of extended forest fires in Borneo continue. Noteworthy transformations have also taken place in rural sectors throughout the region, linked to the increasing reach of the market and the relentless commoditization of the commons, production and social relations (Nevins and Peluso 2008). Today, substantial land conversions are proceeding, oftentimes the result of private and public actors, ranging from small tenants to large transnational conglomerates, interested in taking advantage of the rising demand in globalized markets for exotic commodities, including timber, biofuels and export food products (from pineapples to prawns). These dynamics are combining to intensify and deepen the agrarian transition in Southeast Asia.

The agrarian transition is not new to the region nor to the Global South for that matter. Consisting, very generally, of a wide range of processes that link a country's agricultural sector with the market economy to a far greater extent than previously, such transformations affect not only those directly involved in agricultural production, but also have numerous consequences for the entire rural-based population of any one country, and indeed often for the country as a whole. The five major agricultural countries in Southeast Asia that form the focus of this collection have witnessed dramatic transformations in their agricultural sectors since the 1960s. While their percentage of gross domestic product based in agriculture has tended to decline from 1970 onwards (Rigg 1997; King 2008), the forces of capitalism and globalization have had critical influences in shaping different modes of agricultural production and determining the forms of outputs (Hughes 2000; Potter and Majid Cooke 2004). The region has taken on a growing export role, in part as a result of the intensive capitalization of agriculture and the rapid growth of agrifood businesses. These in turn are fuelled and supported by the processes of globalization.

In tandem with these transformations are complex local-level changes to people's rural livelihoods (Hart *et al.* 1989; Borras *et al.* 2007). With greater and deeper integration into global market exchanges, access to land, labour, financial capital and technology has been modified. This has created new rural elites and middle-class farmers and, in turn, greater disparities within rural communities. While some individuals have benefited greatly from increased commoditization and linkages to regional and global markets, others have engaged selectively in markets, while others again have been disadvantaged with increasing infringements upon indigenous rights, diminishing access to resources, and escalating cultural conflicts (Moore 1998). In some locales, the proliferation of wage labour along with the agrarian transition has resulted in increased dispossession and marginalization, especially of smaller landowners and agricultural workers. In other sites, there has been increased economic growth, with people able to form new and increasingly sustainable livelihood strategies. Such divergent outcomes have even occurred between village neighbours due to the progressively more individualized consequences of the agrarian transition.

In Southeast Asia the agrarian transition has created new sites of struggle in which counter-hegemonic movements and resistance are taking place, often in very novel ways (White 1986; Edelman 2001; Hollander and Einwohner 2004). We are witness to indigenous farmers in the Philippines reworking ideas of ethnicity so as to lay claim to natural resources, while we observe ethnic minorities in Vietnam resisting the full-scale conversion of their livelihoods into the market economy by taking a route that suits their own, culturally appropriate understandings of success. We also see small-scale farmers in Kalimantan, Indonesia and local communities in Thailand coming face to face with multinational conglomerates and advocating for change with the support of local non-government organizations (NGOs), while in Malaysia resistance to powerful US trade interests is being formed across class and ethnicity.

Such sites of struggle lie at the heart of this book. Building upon and extending James Scott's *Weapons of the Weak: Everyday Forms of Peasant Resistance* (1985) and *Domination and the Arts of Resistance* (1990), published over 15 years ago, the contributors here focus on the diversity of contemporary channels and instruments by which local individuals and communities are resisting what they perceive to be the injustices brought about by agrarian change and increasing market integration. We take an innovative multi-scalar approach, moving away from more classical academic approaches to studying the agrarian transition (discussed in Appendix 1) that are increasingly critiqued as being too unilinear and narrowly focused, as well as somewhat Eurocentric (Bernstein and Byres 2001; Wilson and Rigg 2003).

We examine not only 'everyday forms of peasant resistance' at the micro level, expanding upon those documented by Scott in 1985 to include the new ways by which people challenge different extensions of the market economy into their lives; but we dissolve the conventional boundaries of scale from previous works to account for emerging transnational acts of resistance and defiance against policies and activities often linked to global market integration (Korovkin 2000; Smith and Johnston 2002; Amoore 2005; Bandy and Smith 2005). We incorporate, compare and debate studies of more organized forms of opposition and dissent, including those based in transnational social movements and national operations and their functioning in relation to agrarian societies and change in Southeast Asia, through to more micro-scale contestations often rendered invisible at broader scales of analysis (Hart 1991; Cheru 1997; Loh 2004; Piper and Uhlin 2004).

One must be mindful, nevertheless, that scale has become increasingly problematized in the social movement literature, in particular by geographers. Traditional views of scale as 'a nested spatial hierarchy consisting of fixed, bounded, and reified levels – local, regional, national, global – have been challenged by more fluid approaches to spatial relations, focused upon connections and oppositions, and the processes that construct scale in the first place' (Schein 1997: 662). As explained by Dominique Masson, 'scale should not be thought of in a void or in the abstract, but always as a dimension of social processes' (forthcoming: 44; see also Howitt 1998; Marston 2000). With such a perspective, scale might be conceptualized as 'the focal setting at which spatial boundaries are defined for a specific social claim, activity, or behavior' (Agnew 1997: 100; Agnew 1993). As contributions to this book reveal, different scales of resistance are co-constituted by social agents; both those dominating others and those engaging in various forms of resistance.

In addition to examining multiple scales, the contributors to this book study an increasingly diverse spectrum of resistance forms. We reveal the open public interactions and debates occurring between dominators and the oppressed, as well as the hidden critiques of power brewing beneath the surface at the local level, and a diversity of approaches in between (Scott 1990). To do so, we have brought together scholars working on agrarian and rural resistance activities and movements at a range of scales and shapes, focusing on the five countries currently at the heart of the agrarian transition in Southeast Asia, namely Indonesia, Malaysia, the Philippines, Thailand and Vietnam.

This book makes three core arguments. The first is that a *multi-scalar approach* to examining resistance to the agrarian transition in Southeast Asia reveals that scales of action are becoming more and more intertwined and complex. Rather than privileging an analysis undertaken at a particular geographical scale, we argue that connections and exchanges are forged across scale, playing a vital part in contemporary opposition (Featherstone 2005). We broaden the lens of analysis from past studies to incorporate emerging transnational acts of resistance and defiance. These are increasingly central to the stories of individual farmers and rural households as agricultural policies and activities in Southeast Asia are progressively more integrated into the global market. We argue that the contemporary drivers and consequences of agrarian change are multi-scalar processes in themselves, and that categories of 'local' and 'global' are inadequate to examine and explain the forms of resistance taking place (see also Howitt 1993).

Second, forms of resistance in Southeast Asia are *numerous, rapidly diversifying, and never static*. Public conflicts and debates take place between state dominators and the oppressed, at the same time as hidden critiques of power and everyday forms of resistance stir at the local level, often in the same location, not to mention other combinations of resistance tactics occurring at intermediate scales. Resistance measures are context contingent, shaped by different world views and shift according to local circumstances, the opening and closing of access to opportunities, and the endogenous peculiarities of resistance dynamics. As such we move away from a purely Marxist interpretation of resistance and recognize that along with class come many other elements that are equally important in understanding contemporary forms of defiant collective action and more hidden critiques of power and domination measures in rural Southeast Asia, such as ethnicity, culture, gender, environmental degradation, violence and regional differentiation.

Third, and closely related to our second argument, a focus on resistance to contemporary agrarian change in Southeast Asia must *recognize agency*. Acknowledging how ordinary people are involved in, and make choices about, resistance actions from everyday struggles to high-profile protests is vital. These decision-making processes might be individual or shared; they might be contradictory, ambiguous or paradoxical. Alternatively they might be highly disciplined and well-organized. The authors in this book give voice to these often marginalized actors and their approaches are brought to the forefront in each chapter, contrasting with many standard historical interpretations.

The tensions that have appeared between classical Marxist interpretations of the agrarian transition (Alavi 1973; Bernstein 1977, 1990; Shain 1984) and those of post-structuralist writers are apparent in this book. From these have emerged more nuanced studies that identify social trends, cultural diversity and ethnic differences as a basis to inductively develop alternative approaches. These stand in contrast to former schools of thought that, broadly speaking, elaborated sophisticated theoretical models in a more deductive approach that were then applied to an even more complex reality (Hart *et al.* 1989; Booth 2000).

We suggest that there is a need for conceptual frameworks that view agrarian change as a dialectical rather than linear process. Institutional arrangements governing access to and control over resources and people are associated with larger political and economic forces, while at the same time contextual factors and agency need to be taken into core consideration. Hart *et al.* (1989) argue that greater flexibility is required in the analysis of specific rural resistance situations, and that there is no universal form or definition of rural differentiation whose dynamics can be grasped via abstract formulations. Yet we must not overreact to earlier theories such as Marxist frameworks either. Comparative reflection is vital, along with social science rigour, and the inclusion of diverse methodologies. Following Hefner (1990) we argue that combining actor-oriented methodologies with regional and historical perspectives is important to understanding the economy and society. In order to bridge the impasse in social sciences between those who use the village as a unit of analysis and those who focus on the determining power of exogenous and global forces, we need to combine regional ethnography and reflexive theorizing (ibid.), an approach built upon in this book.

In the remainder of this introductory chapter we set the scene for the chapters that follow by first detailing the main elements of the agrarian transition as it has transpired in Southeast Asia, before introducing different theoretical approaches to resistance. We conclude with a brief introduction to the book's chapters.

The agrarian transition in Southeast Asia

One of the major contributing factors behind the agrarian transition in Southeast Asia has been agricultural intensification. Often labelled the Green Revolution, this has included the development and implementation of high-yielding grain varieties, intensified cropping (such as annual double cropping of rice), an increased dependence on irrigation and improvements in its delivery, and a rise in the reliance on industrial inputs, including fertilizers, pesticides, insecticides and genetically modified crops (Pearse 1980; Carney 1988; Ross 2003). As with agricultural transformations more broadly, the Green Revolution has, on the one hand, considerably enhanced the productivity of both land and labour as well as agricultural production in general (Ross 2003). Yet, on the other hand, it has also caused tremendous upheavals in customary labour patterns and culturally accepted agricultural practices. Labourers have been displaced and gender relations have been substantially altered. Land, property and tenure structures have also been vastly transformed for the rural inhabitants involved (Scott 1985; Hart *et al.* 1989; Lipton 1989; Shiva 1989; De Koninck 1992; Yapa 1996; Gupta 1998).

The agrarian transition more generally has been the focus of much intellectual debate and contestation, reaching as far back as the late 1800s. Initial works developing theories and frameworks of the agrarian transition tended to focus chiefly on the enduring question of what happens to rural populations in the face of capitalism and increasing market integration (Borchegrevink 2001). Nonetheless, over time there has been a wide assortment of co-existing and interrelated academic theoretical approaches and frameworks for interpreting the agrarian transition and agrarian change per se. Many of these have remained focused on how agrarian populations relate to the dynamics of capitalism; an issue at the heart of much rural resistance today.

Very broadly, such studies can be classified into five groups (for a more in-depth review of these approaches, see Appendix 1 at the end of this chapter) including classical Marxist approaches, the 'peasant studies' and 'neo-populist' literature, modernization theorists, dependency and related approaches, and post-impasse conceptualizations. These bodies of literature have represented peasants or family farmers[1] in different ways: as passive (yet often unwilling) victims of the agrarian transition; as 'an exploited class' or those actively exploited by the expansion of capitalism; as those in need of modernization and 'development'; or as a mass of petty entrepreneurs with considerable agency (Harrison 2001).

Contributions from subaltern studies have challenged earlier perspectives on peasant movements and agrarian change, with their rationale being a desire to write history from the viewpoint of subalterns (peasants and workers). These subalterns are argued to be

> autonomous agents who create their own forms of oppositional culture and identity, who are not victims and/or followers, and whose ideas and actions are not to be represented (appropriated) by elite agents and discourses that claim to speak on their behalf.
>
> (Bernstein and Byres 2001: 33)

The work of the neo-populist 'everyday forms of resistance' writers such as Scott (1985) and Scott and Kerkvliet (1986) shares many of the concerns of subaltern writers, as do the contributors to this book with our focus on the importance of agency.

Actors

In the earlier literature on the agrarian transition, the main actors were usually identified as being the state, class-based actors, and revolutionary movements. In the neo-populist writings, peasants practised a multitude of everyday forms of resistance in the face of all-powerful actors (Scott 1985; Adas 1992). More recently, both a changing global world order (with the fall of the Soviet Bloc, decentralization in many developing countries, and rapid changes in technology) and evolving understandings of the agrarian transition post-impasse (including the influences of post-structural and post-colonial thought) have highlighted the importance of understanding multi-layered perspectives of change. These shifts have made it clear that both individual and household interpretations must be taken into account, as well as the roles and involvement of a wide variety of peoples and groups such as NGOs, social movements and community activists (Escobar 1995). One of the important contributions of this book is a focus on this broad range of actors, including farmers of course, but also wage-workers, unions, academics, activists, organizers and development agencies. While such an approach recognizes the importance of class, other elements such as age, gender, culture and ethnicity can all have important consequences for the outcomes and impacts of agrarian change and need to be considered (Agawal 1986; Hart *et al.* 1989; Scott 2003).

Especially relevant to many of the following chapters is the fact that ethnicity must be considered in analyses of agrarian change. Shaped not only by dominant local groups, but also by colonial discourse, in many places colonial labelling placed ethnic minorities in the uplands and labelled them as 'backwards' peoples undertaking swidden agriculture, while lowlanders were 'modern', practising intensive irrigated agriculture (Hefner 1990; Li 1999). In numerous locations, these classifications are now being challenged and restructured, such as in the Philippines where a post-colonial state and NGOs are allowing people to claim the term 'indigenous' and request the right to certain resources (see Dressler's chapter). Yet in other locations, such as Vietnam, modern states have tended to reinforce colonial attitudes by continuing to relegate ethnic minorities to second tier positions (see Turner and Michaud in this volume; Sowerwine 2004). In this book, we draw attention to states, authorities and agents that are working to normalize and standardize agrarian livelihoods in Southeast Asia, and the multiplicity of diverse actors that are challenging, disputing and resisting such forces.

Drivers and outcomes

It is difficult to clearly separate the actors, drivers and outcomes of the agrarian transition in Southeast Asia as so many are interrelated, drawing upon each other in a circular fashion. At the same time, there are diverse trajectories of agrarian change that reflect, among other factors, the different degrees of national integration in the global economy, local cultural and ethnic relationships, the position of the state, and the colonial past, as the following chapters demonstrate.

Central to the agrarian transition in Southeast Asia has been the escalation of state regulations, laws, and programmes that aim to structure how people gain a livelihood. These state decisions, often intertwined with the actions of multilateral and bilateral donors and NGOs, have dramatically reshaped resource access and continue to do so. State strategies have at times resulted in immensely uneven economic development, generating new forms of conflict, exclusion and resistance. The unrolling of Green Revolution packages is one among numerous instances of state interventions into the agrarian sector (Hart *et al.* 1989; Hefner 1990; De Koninck 1992; Hayami and Kikuchi 2000[2]). Other examples include state directed migration policies, poverty alleviation packages, land titling and property rights, and trade laws (see among others Kunstadter *et al.* 1978; Hirsch 1990; Peluso 1992; Padoch and Peluso 1996; Hirsch and Warren 1998; Kelly 2000). The ways in which the state has sought to intervene via such routes has ranged from the subtle to the highly coercive, a theme picked up in the chapters by Dressler, Potter, Smeltzer, Tran, Vu and Walker; although all contributing chapters touch on these elements in some way.

Also at the heart of the agrarian transition is the increasing market integration of the countryside. This has come about either via specific political decisions, based upon a range of formal rules and regulations; or via less formal routes, following the dynamism of new technology, diversifying trade, advancements in communications, and societal change. The livelihoods of millions of farmers in Southeast Asia have become increasingly integrated into the market through one or many of these routes. Examples include, but are not limited to, the capitalization of agriculture, land titling, the monetization of land and labour markets, and the commodification of consumption practices and lifestyles (Scott 1976; Hefner 1990; Eder 1999; Li 1999; Kelly 2000; Akram-Lodhi 2005; Turner 2007).

The resultant manifold market relations that have emerged are altering how people are implicated in different forms of exchange (Plattner 1989). Both the production and reproduction of wealth and poverty are becoming more diverse and socially and spatially fragmented. In turn, actors, based on class, gender, generation and/or ethnicity, are unequally sharing in the risks and returns of market intensification and integration (see chapters by Smeltzer, Tran, Turner and Michaud, and Walker). New forms of wealth creation and exclusion, new patterns of dependency and new dimensions of inequality are all products of the changing nature and intensity of market relations (Rigg 2006).

Emerging technologies and technological change from irrigation tools to cell phones have had noteworthy impacts on how the agrarian transition has played out in different Southeast Asian locales and across scale, as shown in the chapter by Caouette revealing the importance of the internet for transnational resistance campaigns. Linked in part to globalization patterns and the international division of labour in agricultural production, technological advancements have changed markets for agricultural products and altered forms of production in both capitalist societies and socialist ones in the process of opening up to the market (Busch and Juska 1997; Goodman and Watts 1997). However, as noted by Hart *et al.* (1989), power structures and state imperatives have a key role to play with regards to technological change and adoption.

The agrarian transition and migration are also closely intertwined. At times, migration has resulted in population growth in rural areas as the result of government sponsored or encouraged programmes such as New Economic Zones in Vietnam, or transmigration schemes in Indonesia and Malaysia (Van Der Wijst 1985; Hardy 2002). Spontaneous migration has also been important, and together such movements have resulted in a fundamental transformation of the population distribution of Southeast Asia since the 1950s (De Koninck *et al.* 2003). At the household level, migration patterns affect livelihood dynamics as migrant workers seeking urban opportunities alter rural labour equations for households and communities, and have a bearing on livelihood decision making via their remittances. In turn, rural divisions of labour, gender norms and identities are all impacted upon as demonstrated unmistakably in the chapters by Dressler and Potter (see also Wolf 1971, 1982; Trager 1984; Ong 1987; Hart *et al.* 1989; Chant and McIlwaine 1995). In rural locales that lie adjacent to expanding urban areas there can also be increasing demands for the conversion of agricultural land to more urban uses, bringing potential cash booms for some households, or resulting in the loss of livelihood means for others who lack the skills to adapt to a new way of life (Kelly 1998; van den Berg *et al.* 2003).

Resistance

From everyday forms of resistance to social movements that have become global in scale, the agrarian transition in Southeast Asia has produced and resulted in complex shapes and forms of covert and overt defiance and resistance. Briefly, conceptualizations of resistance are situated within understandings of power; power being comprised of the relational interplay of dominance and subordination (Foucault 1976; Burdick 1995; Amoore 2005). Meanings of resistance are context contingent and shaped by different worldviews (Pile and Keith 1997; Amoore 2005), while emerging hand-in-hand with understandings of dominance (Foucault 1976). Forces of resistance and dominance are mutually constitutive, their forms reciprocally and continually shaping each other (ibid.). Notions of who is subordinated, in which ways, by whom or what, and the types of accompanying resistance employed to challenge subjugation differ according to the theoretical perspective adopted.

Resistance is often more intricate than it is generally made out to be, and less obvious than commonly understood (Pile and Keith 1997; Mittelman and Chin 2000; Amoore 2005; Roberts 2008). Indeed it can be flat-out ambiguous since resistance itself is constitutive and reflective of, and embedded in, sociocultural life (Mittelman and Chin 2000). Amoore (2005) claims there is a tendency to emphasize certain forms of resistance that are more overt while overlooking others. This is one of the motivating criticisms that has brought about this book. Indeed, resistance is not always clear-cut, and may blur into what appears as compliance, a point alluded to in the contributing chapters by Turner and Michaud, and by Walker.

Resistance and dominance can be understood as relational, not separable into distinct categories or levels, but rather nuanced products of the contexts in which they evolve. Foucault (1976), for example, sees power as inbuilt in relationships constituted and defined through active negotiation of their positioning via their contestations. The particular ways in which these elements come together and interact within a relational system produce specific manifestations of these relationships, such as state supremacy or social hegemony. While not fixed in one form, since the actual combinations of these relationships are dependent upon distinct time–space contexts, relationships are always unequal. Resistance is thus context-dependent and a force that is changing relative to dominance and within a dynamic network of power which can gather strength, diminish, and shift positions.

Here we briefly discuss how resistance has been conceived by three seminal analysts before, in Chapter 2, engaging the contemporary literature as a way to develop a framework for understanding the variety and the multiple scalar dimensions of rural dynamics in Southeast Asia. Three influential thinkers, Antonio Gramsci (1971) and Karl Polanyi (1944, 1957) focusing on more open protests, and James Scott (1976, 1985, 1990) detailing more hidden forms, have laid the theoretical foundations for the ways in which we tend to conceive resistance today. These propositions differ in terms of the actors involved, the targets in question, and scales and methods of contestation (Mittelman and Chin 2000; Rigg 2007). While Gramsci and Polanyi emphasize visible resistance involving concerted collective actions, this form is challenged by Scott, who introduces acts operating 'below the radar' comprising an effective subversive strategy.

Gramsci (1971) envisions resistance as 'counter hegemony', involving a collective in opposition to the state and other dominant groups of civil society that uphold the privilege of the ruling elites while oppressing others. Resistance is overt and declared, but can take different forms, from 'wars of movement', which involve palpable actions such as labour strikes and military exploits, to non-violent sources of ongoing pressure, such as boycotts, considered to be 'wars of position'. The aim of both tactics is to control the state (Cox 1993; Mittelman and Chin 2000).

Polanyi conceptualizes resistance as 'countermovement', taking the form of collective and openly declared forms of resistance. Polanyi differs from Gramsci in that the target of resistance is industrial capitalism, hence transcending the confines of state boundaries to transnational and global scales of market forces. For every movement there is a countermovement, or 'double-movement', comprised of forces of control and subordination (Polanyi 1944; Mittelman and Chin 2000). For Polanyi, one needs to perceive the extension and deepening of capitalism as creating, in the process, a countermovement of resistance. He notes,

> while on the one hand markets spread all over the face of the globe and the amount of goods involved grew to unbelievable proportions, on the other hand a network of measures and policies was integrated into powerful institutions designed to check the action of the market relative to labor, land, and money.
>
> (Polanyi 1957: 76)

Scott diverges from both Gramsci and Polanyi in his notion of infrapolitics, or 'everyday forms of resistance', enacted individually or collectively but never openly declared as formal challenges. He focuses on actions undertaken in the course of everyday life to defend material and physical interests, while subverting the authority of oppressors, such as landlords or employers (Scott 1985). Rather than highlighting the role of broader structures as sources of domination as do Gramsci and Polanyi, Scott focuses upon those forces that intimately impact upon the tangible circumstances of everyday life at the micro level. Thus, tactics in this form of resistance, such as labourers stealing a portion of grain from a farmer's field, aim to re-align the material inequities persistent in daily life. These strategies seek to rectify exploitative practices, but do so from outside the purview of the exploiters. It is precisely this clandestine quality, the intentional masking of struggle, which is argued to make these practices effective and distinct from those undertaken visibly in the public realm (see also Kerkvliet 1990, 2005). Indeed, Scott (1990) contends that such strategies may be critical when overt action is not safe. This resistance is sustained by norms of mutual support that establish such underhanded behaviour as acceptable to those aware of it, creating a certain common consciousness of active contestation of the status quo. As such, if one person is caught, it is impossible for others to provide condemning testimony since the activity in question is a valued norm. This secrecy creates a new space for subordinated groups since dominants cannot monitor their activity. Subordinate individuals oscillate between 'public transcripts' in the public realm of domination, and 'hidden transcripts' relating to the hidden realm of resistance (Scott 1990; Mittelman and Chin 2000).

While it might seem that these projections of resistance follow a rough continuum from overt/macro to covert/micro, with Polanyi describing collective, overt resistance against transnational forces, Gramsci presenting collective, overt resistance against national forces, and Scott articulating individual and collective, covert resistances at the sub-national level, these conceptualizations are more linked than their differences would suggest, bringing us back to this book's first core argument. Scott and others (Foucault 1976; Escobar 1995; Amoore 2005; Kerkvliet 2005) concur that micro and everyday resistances form a critical foundation for the materialization of – and are key to understanding – larger-scale overt struggles. Scott suggests that through the norms of conduct cultivated through infrapolitics, these everyday resistances serve to develop a 'counter-hegemonic consciousness' which acts as a seedbed for overt movements. Amoore (2005) similarly proposes that everyday forms of resistance set in place the structures that make more formally organized resistances possible. Foucault (1976) approaches this scalar linkage through what he calls 'the rule of double conditioning', whereby a certain micro layer underpins broader dynamics within a system of power, but one level is not necessarily reducible or expandable to the other.

These key ideas are not always neatly applicable to rural resistance in Southeast Asia in the current context of globalization. It must be remembered that such formulations of resistance were tied to specific historical contexts that may not necessarily be precisely overlaid across different circumstances. Rather, these concepts provide a conceptual base from which to develop understandings specific to the parameters of newly emerging power structures in the world today. As social life changes in the context of globalization, so too do the 'agents' and 'targets' of resistance, as this book explores.

This book

During the 1970s and 1980s the future seemed rather bleak for those under-taking rural livelihoods in Southeast Asia. This was underlined by fears of 'Malthusian pressures' as limited land resources experienced growing popula-tions. At a country level, one could therefore argue that a combination of factors – some directly related to the agrarian transition, others less so – have combined to defer that eventuality. Factors such as the further development of frontier regions, technological innovations, agricultural intensification and off-farm migration have – at a broad scale – reduced the precariousness of peasant life (Rigg and Sakunee Nattapoolwat 2000; Molle and Thippawal Srijantr 2003).

Nevertheless, when one takes a more nuanced approach and looks at the complex realities of peasant livelihoods, the picture is not as rosy. For starters, rural poverty remains widespread, and inequalities across the region are increasing (Scott and Truong Thi Kim Chuyen 2004). In addition, the opening up of frontier regions has led to significant pressures on ethnic minority communities and their ways of farming; the effects of which have generated a new set of choices and power relations for swiddeners as well as new forms of pressure on local ecosystems. Indeed, ecosystems have been altered not only in the uplands, but throughout the region as the agrarian transition persists. Noteworthy environmental impacts have included water pollution and diminution, floods and land and soil degradation. Not surpris-ingly, such resource depletion has, in turn, led to numerous conflicts, clashes and other forms of resistance. At the same time, large agribusiness investors are increasingly determining the crops planted and the agricultural practices used to grow and harvest them (Brookfield 2001).

This book takes a socially constructed, multi-scalar approach to explore how people are resisting and mediating the impacts and outcomes of the agrarian transition in Southeast Asia. While literature exists on organized and overt forms of agrarian resistance (Putzel 1992; Franco 2000; Loh 2004; Loh and Öjendal 2005), as well as revolutionary movements and insur-rectionary mobilizations (Kerkvliet 1979; Jenkins 1985; Jones 1989; Hawes 1990; Weekley 2001; Kingsbury 2005), and while Southeast Asia has gener-ated a strong tradition of micro-level analyses of everyday forms of resistance including foot-dragging practices, cheating on sharecropping arrangements, and cultural expressions of passive resistance through songs, poems and so on (Scott and Kerkvliet 1986; Scott 1990; Ng, Mohamad and tan beng hui 2006), a crucial gap in our conceptual grasp of these processes remains. What is missing is an analytical and comparative framework that highlights the *spectrum of the types of resistance* from hidden, ordinary and oftentimes passive to more overt, extraordinary and actively defiant forms of agrarian collective action, that all, in their own ways, rely upon *agency*. At the same time we need to focus on the interwovenness of *different scales* of collective action across the individual and community levels to regional, national, and now transnational. By bringing together these research traditions and combining a multi-scalar approach, this book introduces an innovative view to comprehending the complexities of agrarian resistance in Southeast Asia.

The choice of case studies, illustrated in Figure 1.1, is not random. Since the 1960s Indonesia, Malaysia, the Philippines, Thailand, and more recently Vietnam, have been at the forefront of intensive agrarian change in Southeast Asia. Combined, these countries are a key source of agricultural exports to the world's markets. Yet all have experienced different degrees of economic and financial liberalization, and various forms of political liberalization (Taylor 1996; Anderson 1998; Boudreau 2004), the distinct trajectories of which affect the modes and forms by which the agrarian transition is occurring.

The Philippines can be considered as an example of a country in the midst of a fragile and incomplete process of democratic transition involving the persistence of neo-patrimonialism marked by undefined and arbitrary rule of law, as illustrated in Franco and Borras's chapter (see also Sidel 1999; Rocamora 2004; Quimpo 2005). The consequences of this process can be frustrating to say the least for indigenous groups, as Dressler's chapter dem-

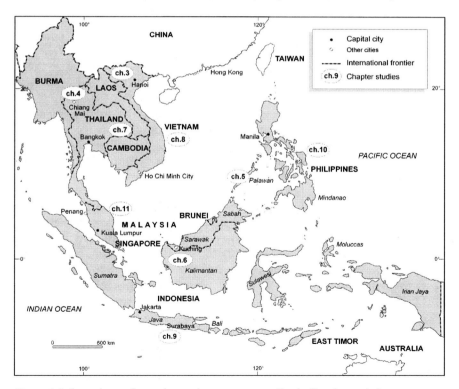

Figure 1.1 Locations of agrarian resistance case studies in Southeast Asia.

Map credit: Jean Michaud

onstrates. Similarly, in Indonesia, the democratic consolidation remains fragile and internal political dynamics unstable as observed in Vu's chapter. The country's recent decentralization policies, and intensified use of natural resources, have generated both a range of localized responses and different international advocacy campaigns. This can be seen especially in the push for palm oil plantations, as Potter's chapter details, as well as in the cases of mining and indigenous land rights (Milich 2001; Heryanto and Hadiz 2005; Hervouet 2007). In Thailand, the process of democratic consolidation that might have been hoped for in the 1990s has seen several reversals since the ousting of Prime Minister Thaksin, while the economy has opened further following the 1997 financial crisis. The diversity of responses from local farmers to these shifts is clearly depicted in Walker's chapter. As a result, Thailand is now confronted with new forms of political activism as well as expanding types of local–global activism as Kuhonta's chapter highlights.

Malaysia remains a paradox: on the one hand it is still a semi-authoritarian regime with strict control and monitoring of social dissidence, as reflected in the chapter by Smeltzer, and yet, on the other hand, it stands as a hub of a number of regional and transnational activist networks which are oftentimes less rooted in local issues (Loh 2004). Together, Bangkok, Manila, Penang, and increasingly Jakarta, host a wide range of regional and transnational NGOs and networks, many acting locally and across borders, as noted by Caouette's chapter on social movements at the transnational scale (see also Clarke 1998; Silliman *et al.* 1998; ANGOC 2001; Hillhorst 2003; Loh 2004; Piper and Uhlin 2004). Yet, the legitimacy of connections and links with local rural communities continues to be, to say the least, frequently tested (Hewison 2000, 2001). For example, in Indonesia the establishment of independent peasant and indigenous organizations is relatively recent and the local–global connections are still tentative (Li 2000; McWilliam 2006).

Vietnam, economically opening its doors to capitalism, while remaining rooted in socialist politics, offers a contrasting example where resistance has tended to remain at a more local level. Here, covert forms are the norm rather than large-scale demonstrations that are likely to result in swift reactions by the state and the prompt silencing of organizers and disputers. Nonetheless, as explored by Tran, times are slowly changing and subtle new resistance forms are beginning to see the light of day. Concurrently though, other groups living within Vietnam's borders, such as upland ethnic minorities, do not share the same sense of optimism for increasingly overt gestures of resistance, and instead work to remain 'below the radar' as they shape new means of gaining a livelihood, as detailed by Turner and Michaud.

This range of cases and variations allows for rich comparison. Moreover, they illustrate different scales of actions – from the cautiously organized covert to the more noisily overt – and how these are intertwined to different degrees, often building complex relationships and indeed, uneasy partnerships. What might appear on the surface as well-intended interventions by external actors, such as the urban Thai elite coming to the aid of 'those poor farmers', can actually hide broader narratives about social movements and stereotypes (see Kuhonta chapter). Similarly, what might appear to be the Philippine government's positive adoption of Western environmental agendas, supported by international social movements, can cause angst for local ethnic minorities and very specific resistance tactics, as shown in Dressler's chapter. Transnational movements and networks might develop policy advocacy proposals according to international campaigns but, as noted in Caouette's chapter, in the process they might be homogenizing and aggregating a range of situations and conditions under broad generic categories and themes, such as 'peasant', landless, food sovereignty, and so on.

These chapters show that scales of action are becoming more and more tangled, shifting according to local circumstances, depending on the opening and closing of opportunity structures, but also according to the endogenous peculiarities of resistance dynamics. Rural resistance measures often result from nuanced micro processes involving variables such as solidarity, identity and social networks that are intertwined with shifts in the political opportunity structure at the society level. Just how these play out in different countries, with different power politics, democratic formations (or not), local opportunities, ethnic and class relations, and international and global interconnectivity is at the core of this book.

Notes

1 The terms peasants and farmers are used interchangeably in this book to denote family-labour and small scale farmers who are engaging with the commercial economy to some degree. As Brookfield (2008: 111) has argued – before going on to treat peasants and family farmers as equivalent terms – 'in English-speaking countries, present-day family farmers are never described as peasants, whatever the scale of their operation; peasants are inhabitants either of history or of the developing countries. This terminological quirk in our language is responsible for a good deal of misunderstanding.' See his work for a more in-depth discussion of these terms in past and current day literature (Brookfield 2008). This book also discusses resistance of farm labourers, those who are often unable to own land themselves.

2 It should be noted that Hayami and Kikuchi's (2000) analysis was a broader interpretation of agrarian change, rather than a specific Green Revolution study.

3 The central premise of modernization theory rested on the assumption that traditional ways of making a living would ultimately be subsumed into the modern capitalist economy of societies as they evolved towards full industrialization (McGee 1979). Small-scale 'traditional' activities and livelihoods were considered relics of traditional society, consequently deemed 'backwards', insignificant, marginal and destined to disappear. Building on the neoclassical economics work of W.W. Rostow (1960), who coined the term 'take-off' in his highly influential schema of economic development as a progression through a set of five predetermined stages, followers proposed that all societies would eventually pass through such a sequence, or unilinear path towards full modernization, such as that observed in the developed 'West' (McGee 1979).

References

Adas, M. (1992) 'From avoidance to confrontation: peasant protest in precolonial and colonial Southeast Asia', in N. Dirks (ed.) *Colonialism and Culture*, Ann Arbor: University of Michigan Press, 89–126.

Agarwal, B. (1986) 'Women, poverty and agricultural growth in India', *Journal of Peasant Studies*, 13: 165–220.

Agnew, J. (1993) 'Representing Space: space, scale and culture in social science', in J. Duncan and D. Ley (eds) *place/culture/representation*, New York: Routledge, 251–71.

—— (1997) 'The dramaturgical horizons: geographical scale in the Reconstruction of Italy by the new Italian political parties, 1992–95', *Political Geography*, 16 (2): 99–121.

Akram-Lodhi, A.H. (2005) 'Vietnam's agriculture: processes of rich peasant accumulation and mechanisms of social differentiation', *Journal of Agrarian Change*, 5: 73–116.

Alavi, H. (1973) 'Peasant classes and primordial loyalties', *Journal of Peasant Studies*, 1: 23–62.

Amoore, L. (2005) 'Introduction: global resistance – global politics', in L. Amoore (ed.) *The Global Resistance Reader*, London: Routledge, 1–11.

Anderson, B. (1998) *The Spectre of Comparisons: nationalism, Southeast Asia and the world*, London: Verso.

ANGOC (2001) 'Overcoming hunger through community Actions', *Development*, 44: 113–6.

Bandy, J. and Smith, J. (eds) (2005) *Coalitions Across Borders: transnational protest and the neoliberal order*, Lanham: Rowman and Littlefield.

Bernstein, H. (1977) 'Notes on capital and the peasantry', *Review of African Political Economy*, 10: 60–73.

—— (1990) 'Taking the part of peasants?', in H. Bernstein, B. Crow, M. Mackintosh and C. Martin (eds) *The Food Question*, London: Earthscan, 69–80.

Bernstein, H. and Byres, T.J. (2001) 'From peasant studies to agrarian change', *Journal of Agrarian Change*, 1: 1–56.

Boeke, J.H. (1953) *Economics and Economic Policy of Dual Societies*, New York: Institute of Pacific Relations.

Booth, A. (2000) 'Rethinking the role of agriculture in the East Asian model: why is Southeast Asia different from Northeast Asia?', *ASEAN Economic Bulletin*, 19: 40–51.

Borchegrevink, A. (2001) 'Review essays. Agrarian questions and enduring peasants: a classic debate enters the age of globalisation', *The European Journal of Development Research*, 13: 181–92.

Borras Jr., S.M., Kay, C. and Akram-Lodhi, A.H. (2007) 'Agrarian reform and rural development. Historical overview and current issues', in A.H. Akram-Lodhi, S.M. Borras Jr. and C. Kay (eds) *Land, Poverty and Livelihoods in an Era of Globalization*, London: Routledge, 1–40.

Boudreau, V. (2004) *Resisting Dictatorship: repression and protest in Southeast Asia*, Cambridge: Cambridge University Press.

Brass, T. (1991) 'Moral economists, subalterns, new social movements and the (re)emergence of a (post-)modernised (middle) peasant', *Journal of Peasant Studies*, 18: 173–205.

Brookfield, H. (2001) *Exploring Agrodiversity*, New York: Columbia University Press.
—— (2008) 'Family farms are still around: time to invert the old agrarian question', *Geography Compass*, 2 (1): 108–26.
Burdick, J. (1995) 'United theory and practice in the ethnography of social movements: notes towards a hopeful realism', *Dialectical Anthropology*, 20: 361–85.
Busch, L. and Juska, A. (1997) 'Beyond political economy: actor networks and the globalization of agriculture', *Review of International Political Economy*, 4: 688–708.
Buttel, F.H. and McMichael, P. (1988) 'Sociology and rural history: summary and critique', *Social Science History*, 12: 93–120.
Carney, J.A. (1988) 'Struggles over crop rights and labour within contract farming households in a Gambian irrigated rice scheme', *Journal of Peasant Studies*, 15: 334–49.
Chant, S. and McIlwaine, C. (1995) *Women of a Lesser Cost: female labour, foreign exchange and Philippine development*, London and Easthaven: Pluto Press.
Chayanov, A.V. (1966) *The Theory of Peasant Economy*; trans. D. Thornton, R.E.F. Smith and B. Kerblay, Glencoa: Irwin.
Cheru, F. (1997) 'The silent revolution and the weapons of the weak: transformation and innovation from below', in S. Gill and J.H. Mittelman (eds) *Innovation and Transformation in International Studies*, Cambridge: Cambridge University Press, 153–69.
Clarke, G. (1998) *The Politics of NGOs in South-East Asia: participation and protest in the Philippines*, London and New York: Routledge.
Cox, R.W. (1993) 'Gramsci, hegemony and international relations: an essay in method', in S. Gill (ed.) *Gramsci, Historical Materialism and International Relations*, Cambridge, Cambridge University Press, 49–66.
De Koninck, R. (1992) *Malay Peasants Coping with the World: breaking the community circle?* Singapore: ISEAS.
De Koninck, R., Miller, M. and Gendron, B. (2003) 'Cartographier l'évolution de la population de l'Asie du Sud-Est: 1950–1995', *Mappemonde*, 71: 1–6.
Edelman, M. (2001) 'Social movements: changing paradigms and forms of politics', *Annual Review of Anthropology*, 30: 285–317.
Eder, J. (1999) *A Generation Later: household strategies and economic change in the rural Philippines*, Honolulu: University of Hawai'i Press.
Escobar, A. (1995) 'Imagining a post-development era', in J. Crush (ed.) *Power of Development*, London and New York: Routledge, 211–27.
Featherstone, D. (2005) 'Towards the Relational Construction of Militant Particularisms: or why the geographies of past struggles matter for resistance to neoliberal globalisation', *Antipode*, 37 (2): 250–71.
Foucault, M. (1976/98) 'Method' in *The Will to Knowledge: the history of sexuality, volume 1*, London: Penguin; reprinted in Amoore, L. (ed.) *The Global Resistance Reader* (2005), Oxon: Routledge, 86–91.
Franco, J.C. (2000) *Campaigning for Democracy: grassroots citizenship movements, less-than-democratic elections, and regime transition in the Philippines*, Quezon City: Institute for Popular Democracy.
Geertz, C. (1963) *Agricultural Involution*, Cambridge: Cambridge University Press.
Goodman, D. and Watts, M. (1997) *Globalising Food: agrarian questions and global restructuring*, London: Routledge.
Gramsci, A. (1971) *Selections from the Prison Notebooks of Antonio Gramsci*, trans. and ed. Q. Hoare and G. N. Smith, New York: International Publishers.

Gupta, A. (1998) *Postcolonial Developments: agriculture in the making of modern India*, Durham: Duke University Press.

Hardy, A. (2002) *Red Hills: migrants and the state in the highlands of Vietnam*, London: Curzon and NIAS Monographs, No. 93.

Harrison, G. (2001) 'Peasants, the agrarian question and lenses of development', *Progress in Development Studies*, 1: 187–203.

Hart, G. (1991) 'Engendering everyday resistance: gender, patronage and production politics in rural Malaysia', *Journal of Peasant Studies*, 19: 93–121.

—— (1996) 'The agrarian question and industrial dispersal in South Africa: agro-industrial linkages through Asian lenses', *Journal of Peasant Studies*, 23: 245–77.

Hart, G., Turton, A. and White, B. (eds) (1989) *Agrarian Transformations: local processes and the state in Southeast Asia*, Berkeley: University of California Press.

Hawes, G. (1990) 'Theories of peasant revolution: a critique and contribution from the Philippines', *World Politics*, XLII (2): 261–98.

Hayami, Y. and Kikuchi, M. (2000) *A Rice Village Saga: three decades of Green Revolution in the Philippines*, Basingstoke: Macmillan.

Hefner, R. (1990) *The Political Economy of Mountain Java: an interpretive history*, Berkeley and Los Angeles: University of California.

Hervouet, G. (2007) 'Indonésie', *L'Encyclopédie de L'état du monde 2008: dictionnaire historique et géopolitique du XXe siècle*, Paris: Éditions La Découverte.

Heryanto, A. and Hadiz, V.R. (2005) 'Post-authoritarian Indonesia: a comparative Southeast Asian perspective', *Critical Asian Studies*, 37 (2): 251–76.

Hewison, K. (2000) 'Resisting globalization: a study of localism in Thailand', *Pacific Review*, 13: 279–96.

—— (2001) 'Nationalism, populism, dependency: Southeast Asia and responses to the Asian Crisis', *Singapore Journal of Tropical Geography*, 22: 219–36.

Hilhorst, D. (2003) *The Real World of NGOs: discourse, diversity and development*, Quezon City: Ateneo de Manila University Press.

Hirsch, P. (1990) *Development Dilemmas in Rural Thailand*, South-East Asian Studies Rural Monographs, Singapore: Oxford University Press.

Hirsch, P. and Warren, C. (eds) (1998) *The Politics of Environment in Southeast Asia: resources and resistance*, London: Routledge.

Hollander, J.A. and R.L. Einwohner (2004) 'Conceptualizing resistance', *Sociological Forum*, 19 (4): 533–54.

Howitt, R. (1993) ' "A world in a grain of sand": towards a reconceptualisation of geographical scale', *Australian Geographer*, 24 (1): 33–44.

—— (1998) 'Scale as relation: musical metaphors of geographical scale', *Area*, 30, 49–58.

Hughes, A. (2000) 'Retailers, knowledges and changing commodity networks: the case of the cut flower trade', *Geoforum*, 31: 175–90.

Jenkins, J.C. (1985) *The Politics of Insurgency: the farm worker movement in the 1960s*, New York: Columbia University Press.

Jones, G.R. (1989) *Red Revolution: inside the Philippine guerrilla movement*, Boulder: Westview Press.

Kautsky, K. (1899) 'Die Agrarfrage [The Agrarian Question]'; partial trans. J. Banaji (1976) 'Summary of Selected Parts of the Agrarian Question', *Economy and Society*, 5: 1–49.

Kelly, P.F. (1998) 'The politics of rural-urban relations: land use conversion in the Philippines', *Environment and Urbanization*, 10 (1): 35–54.

—— (2000) *Landscapes of Globalization: human geographies of economic change in the Philippines*, London: Routledge.

Kerkvliet, B.J.T. (1979) *The Huk Rebellion: a study of peasant revolt in the Philippines*, Quezon City: New Day Publishers.

—— (1990) *Everyday Politics in the Philippines: Class and Status Relations in a Central Luzon Village*, Berkeley: University of California Press.

—— (2005) *The Power of Everyday Politics: how Vietnamese peasants transformed national policy*, Ithaca, NY: Cornell University Press.

King, V.T. (2008), *The Sociology of Southeast Asia: Transformations in a Developing Region*, Honolulu, University of Hawai'i Press.

Kingsbury, D. (2005) *South-East Asia: a political profile*, 2nd edn, Oxford: Oxford University Press.

Korovkin, T. (2000) 'Weak weapons, strong weapons? Hidden resistance and political protest in rural Ecuador', *Journal of Peasant Studies*, 27: 1–29.

Kunstadter, P., Chapman, E.C. and Sabhasri, S. (eds) (1978) *Farmers in the Forest*, Honolulu: East-West Center and the University of Hawai'i Press.

Lenin, V.I. (1899a; 1965) *The Development of Capitalism in Russia*, Moscow: Progress Publishers.

—— (1899b) 'The differentiation of the peasantry'; reprinted in J. Harriss (ed.) (1982) *Rural Development: theories of peasant economy and agrarian change*, London: Hutchinson.

—— (1899c) 'Book Review: *Die Agrarfrage*. Karl Kautsky', *Nachalo*, No. 4; reprinted in *Lenin Collected Works* (1964), vol 4, Moscow: Progress Publishers, 94–9. Online. Available HTTP: <http://www2.cddc.vt.edu/marxists/archive/lenin/works/1899/mar/kautsky.htm> (accessed 11 February 2009).

Lewis, W.A. (1955) *The Theory of Economic Growth*, London: Allen and Unwin.

Li, T.M. (1999) 'Marginality, power and production: analyzing upland transformations', in T.M. Li (ed.) *Transforming the Indonesian Uplands: marginality, power and production*, Amsterdam: Harwood Academic Publishers, 1–46.

—— (2000) 'Constituting tribal space: indigenous identity and resource politics in Indonesia', *Comparative Studies in Society and History*, 42: 149–79.

Lipton, M. (1989) *New Seeds and Poor People*, Baltimore: Johns Hopkins Press.

Loh, F. (2004) 'Les ONG et les mouvements sociaux en Asie du Sud-Est', in L. Delcourt, B. Duferme and F. Polet (eds) *Mondialisation des résistances: L'état des luttes*, Paris: Centre Tricontinental, Forum mondial des alternatives et Éditions Syllepse, 41–55.

Loh, F.K.W. and Öjendal, J. (eds) (2005) *Southeast Asian Responses to Globalization: restructuring governance and deepening democracy*, Copenhagen: NIAS.

McGee, T.G. (1979) 'The poverty syndrome: making out in the Southeast Asian city', in R. Bromley and C. Gerry (eds) *Casual Work and Poverty in Third World Cities*, Chichester: John Wiley and Sons, 45–65.

McWilliam, A. (2006) 'Historical reflections on customary land rights in Indonesia', *Asia Pacific Journal of Anthropology*, 7: 45–64.

Marston, S. A. (2000) 'The social construction of scale', *Progress in Human Geography*, 24 (2): 219–42.

Masson, D. (forthcoming) 'Transnationalizing feminist and women's movements: Towards a scalar approach', in P. Dufour, D. Masson and D. Caouette (eds) *Transnationalizing Women's Movements: solidarities without borders*, Vancouver, University of British Columbia Press (pages unknown to date).

Milich, L. (2001) 'Civil society breakdown: food security in the "new" Indonesia', *Development*, 44: 93–6.

Mittelman, J.H. and Chin, C.B.N. (2000) 'Conceptualizing resistance to globalization', in J. H. Mittelman, *The Globalization Syndrome: transformation and resistance*, Princeton: Princeton University Press, 165–78.

Molle, F. and Thippawal Srijantr (2003) *Thailand's Rice Bowl: perspectives on social and agricultural change in the Chao Phraya Delta*, Bangkok: White Lotus.

Moore, D.S. (1998) 'Subaltern struggles and the politics of place: remapping resistance in Zimbabwe's eastern highlands', *Cultural Anthropology*, 13: 1–38.

Nevins, J. and Peluso, N. (eds) (2008) *Taking Southeast Asia to Market: commodities, nature, and people in the neoliberal age*, Ithaca: Cornell University Press.

Ng, C., Mohamad, M. and tan beng hui (2006) *Feminism and the Women's Movement in Malaysia: an unsung (r)evolution*, London: Routledge.

Ong, A. (1987) *Spirits of Resistance and Capitalist Discipline: factory women in Malaysia*, Albany: State University of New York Press.

Padoch, C. and Peluso, N. (1996) *Borneo in Transition: people, forests, conservation and development*, Kuala Lumpur: Oxford University Press.

Pearse, A. (1980) *Seeds of Want, Seeds of Plenty: social and economic implications of the Green Revolution*, Oxford: Clarendon Press.

Peluso, N. (1992) *Rich Forests, Poor People: resource control and resistance in Java*, Berkeley: University of California Press.

Pile, S. and Keith, M. (eds) (1997) *Geographies of Resistance*, London: Routledge.

Piper, N. and Uhlin, A. (2004) *Transnational Activism in Asia: problems of power and democracy*, London: Routledge.

Plattner, S. (1989) 'Markets and marketplaces', in S. Plattner (ed.) *Economic Anthropology*, Stanford: Stanford University Press, 171–208.

Polanyi, K. (1944) *The Great Transformation. The political and economic origins of our time*, Boston: Beacon Press.

—— (1957) 'The economy as instituted process', in K. Polanyi, C.M. Arensberg and H.W. Pearson (eds) *Trade and Market in the Early Empires: economies in history and theory*, New York: Free Press, 243–70.

Potter, L. and Majid Cooke, F. (2004) 'Introduction: negotiating modernity, themes and ideas', *Asia Pacific Viewpoint*, 45: 305–9.

Putzel, J. (1992) *A Captive Land: the politics of agrarian reform in the Philippines*, London and New York: Catholic Institute for International Relations and Monthly Review Press.

Quimpo, N.T. (2005) 'Oligarchic Patrimonialism, Bossism, Electoral Clientelism, and Contested Democracy in the Philippines.' (Review Article), *Comparative Politics*, January, 229–50.

Rigg, J. (1997) *Southeast Asia: the human landscape of modernisation and development*, London: Routledge.

—— (2006) 'Land, farming, livelihoods, and poverty: rethinking the links in the rural south', *World Development*, 34: 180–202.

—— (2007) *An Everyday Geography of the Global South*, London: Routledge.

Rigg, J. and Sakunee Nattapoolwat (2000) 'Embracing the global in Thailand: activism and pragmatism in an era of deagrarianisation', *World Development*, 29: 945–60.

Roberts, J.M. (2008) 'Public Spaces of Dissent', *Sociology Compass*, 2 (2): 654–74.

Rocamora, J. (2004) 'Formal democracy and its alternatives in the Philippines: parties, elections and social movements', in J. Lele and F. Quadir (eds) *Democracy and Civil Society in Asia, Volume 2: democratic transitions and social movements in Asia*, Hampshire: Palgrave Macmillan, 196–221.

Ross, E.B. (2003) 'Malthusianism, capitalist agriculture and the fate of peasants in the making of the modern world food system', *Review of Radical Political Economics*, 35: 437–61.

Rostow, W.W. (1960) *The Stages of Economic Growth*, Cambridge: Cambridge University Press.

Schein, R.H. (1997) 'The Place of Landscape: a conceptual framework for interpreting an American scene', *Annals of the Association of American Geographers*, 87 (4): 660–80.

Scott, J.C. (1976) *The Moral Economy of the Peasant*, New Haven: Yale University Press.

—— (1985) *Weapons of the Weak: everyday forms of peasant resistance*, London: Yale University Press.

—— (1990) *Domination and the Arts of Resistance: hidden transcripts*, New Haven and London: Yale University Press.

Scott, J.C. and Kerkvliet, B.J.T. (eds) (1986) *Everyday Forms of Peasant Resistance in South-East Asia*, London: Frank Cass.

Scott, S. (2003) 'Gender, household headship and entitlements to land: new vulnerabilities in Vietnam's decollectivization', *Gender, Technology and Development*, 7: 233–63.

Scott, S. and Truong Thi Kim Chuyen (2004) 'Behind the numbers: social mobility, regional disparities and new trajectories of development in rural Vietnam', in P. Taylor (ed.) *Social Inequality in Vietnam: challenges to reform*, Singapore: Institute of Southeast Asian Studies (ISEAS), 90–122.

Shain, T. (1984) *Late Marx and the Russian Road: Marx and 'the Peripheries of Capitalism'*, New York: Monthly Review Press.

Shiva, V. (1989) *The Violence of the Green Revolution*, Dehra Dun: Research Foundation for Science and Ecology.

Sidel, John. (1999) *Capital, Coercion, and Crime: bossism in the Philippines*. Stanford: Stanford University Press.

Silliman, G., Noble, S. and Noble, L.G. (eds) (1998) *Organizing for Democracy*, Quezon City: Ateneo de Manila Press.

Smith, J. and Johnston, H. (eds) (2002) *Globalization and Resistance: transnational dimensions of social movements*, Landham: Rowman and Littlefield.

Sowerwine J.C. (2004) 'The political ecology of Yao (Dzao) landscape transformations: Territory, gender and livelihood politics in highland Vietnam', unpublished PhD thesis, University of California, Berkeley.

Taylor, R.H. (ed.) (1996) *The Politics of Elections in Southeast Asia*, Cambridge: Cambridge University Press.

Trager, L. (1984) 'Family strategies and the migration of women: migrants to Dagupan City, the Philippines', *International Migration Review*, 18: 1264–77.

Turner, S. (2007) 'Trading old textiles: the selective diversification of highland livelihoods in northern Vietnam', *Human Organization*, 66: 389–404.

van den Berg, L.M., van Wijk, M.S. and Pham Van Hoi (2003) 'The transformation of agriculture and rural life downstream of Hanoi', *Environment and Urbanization*, 15 (1): 35–52.

Van Der Wijst, T. (1985) 'Transmigration in Indonesia: an evaluation of a population redistribution policy', *Population Research and Policy Review*, 4: 1–30.

Wallerstein, I. (1974) *The Modern World-System: capitalist agriculture and the origins of the European world-economy in the sixteenth century*, New York: Academic Press.

—— (1980) *The Modern World System, II: mercantilism and the European world-economy (1600–1750)*, New York: Academic Press.

Weekley, K. (2001) *The Communist Party of the Philippines 1968–1993: a story of its theory and practice*, Quezon City: University of the Philippines Press.

White, C.P. (1986) 'Everyday resistance, socialist revolution and rural development: the Vietnamese case', *Journal of Peasant Studies*, 13 (2): 49–63.

Wilson, G.A. and Rigg, J. (2003) 'Post productivist agricultural regimes and the south: discordant concepts?', *Progress in Human Geography* 27: 181–207.

Wolf, E. (1966) *Peasants*, Englewood Cliffs: Prentice Hall.

—— (1971) *Peasant Wars of the Twentieth Century*, London: Faber.

—— (1982) *Europe and the People Without History*, Berkeley: University of California Press.

Yapa, L. (1996) 'Improved seeds and constructed scarcity', in R. Peet and M. Watts (eds) *Liberation Ecologies: environment, development and social movements*, London: Routledge, 69–85.

Appendix 1

Background to theorizing the agrarian transition

Setting the ball rolling for a brief review of the agrarian transition theoretical literature are the classical Marxist approaches to agrarian change including such renowned figures as Lenin (1899a,b) and Kautsky (1899). In their attempts to establish what would happen to peasants in the face of capitalist expansion, they focused on how agriculturalists, rural communities and rural areas become subordinated to large-scale modernizing forces, with the penetration of capitalism in agriculture shaped principally by forces of urban industrial capitalism (Buttel and McMichael 1988; see also Shain 1984). Lenin's line of reasoning of a progressive subordination of agriculture to industrial capitalism was then reworked by Kautsky (1899), who argued that the distinctiveness of agriculture modified the way in which capitalism unfolded in rural areas. Peasant households could therefore retain their shape while entering complementary relationships with larger units of capital, mediated by commodity and labour relations (Lenin 1899c; Buttel and McMichael 1988).

Distinct from the above approaches are those working in the field of 'peasant studies' and the so-called 'neo-populist' literature. Important contributors here include Chayanov (1966), Wolf (1966), and Scott (1976, 1985). Contrasting with Lenin and Kautsky, Chayanov (1966) developed a model of the peasant economy that focused on the particular characteristics of the 'middle peasants'. Arguing that the economic calculations of peasants are rooted in subsistence needs rather than profit, he claimed that peasant households therefore increase their labour output and intensity when faced with difficult circumstances (Chayanov 1966). This 'rational peasant' approach would mean that the middle peasant household could survive under difficult circumstances, while more favourable conditions would not see a change in their class characteristics nor lead to an accumulation of wealth (Brass 1991; Borchegrevink 2001; see further details in Chapter 2).

In contrast to the classical Marxist and neo-populist approaches, modernization theorists[3] argue that through increased industrialization – including Green Revolution technologies – and increased urbanization, 'development' à la the West would be reached. As such, their arguments formed a central part of the logic behind the Green Revolution. As modernization theory was enjoying popular support, neoclassical economist W.A. Lewis (1955) introduced a dual economy model which became one of the most influential models for state development planning and subsequent development debates during the 1960s (Escobar 1995). Also drawing on modernization theory, sociologists and anthropologists such as Boeke (1953) and Geertz (1963) saw development as encompassing not just economic but also social and cultural change. Therefore, an additional prerequisite to modernization theory's transformations was argued to be the presence of rational, self-interested, profit-maximizing economic behaviour. Development was thus seen to be hampered by the perseverance of traditional, pre-capitalist communalism that occurred when economic and non-economic motives overlapped and economics fell subordinate to morality and religion (Boeke 1953).

Since the modernization approach imposed a universal and narrowly deterministic model of change on the non-Western world, criticism was quick to follow. Its inappropriateness also became apparent through case studies showing that development often worked to reinvigorate extant social structures rather than simply replacing them with new more specialized institutions (Hefner 1990). In addition, charges of ethnocentrism were laid, and modernization theory waned as the 'orthodox consensus' that underlay its programme was challenged (Hefner 1990: x).

Taking a different route are the dependency, modes of production, and world systems literatures. Harrison (2001) has argued that radical theories of development such as dependency theory and underdevelopment approaches that emerged in the late 1960s onwards focused on peasants as being actively exploited by the expansion of capitalism into the agricultural realm. This argument has been elaborated upon through two separate models of agrarian development, each of which, though, remains loosely tied to dependency theory, namely the modes of production approach and the petty commodity production approach. Also attempting to understand how world economic and political dynamics operate in conjunction with those endogenous to national societies to alter the course of agrarian historical change, were supporters of Wallerstein's world systems/world economy perspectives (1974, 1980). Following Wallerstein's interpretations, Buttel and McMichael

(1988: 105) suggest that 'instead of understanding rural history as integral to the rise of national urban-industrial complexes, it has now to be understood in global terms, as integral to the rise of metropolitan urban-industrial centres of an emerging capitalist world-economy'. From this view, agrarian systems were located within the semi-peripheries, peripheries and the core hierarchical divisions of world labour. While a contentious theory of the capitalist world economy, Wallerstein's work motivated a considerable array of academic literature that has challenged assumptions regarding the independence of nation states (Buttel and McMichael 1988).

2 Rural resistance and the art of domination

Dominique Caouette and
Sarah Turner

The literature on rural resistance is extensive (Edelman 2005). Within it, one can observe two broad approaches: the first emphasizes the role of hegemony, domination and the moral economy that often leads to more covert forms of daily resistance. Such a school of thought is probably best represented by James Scott's works (1976, 1985, 1990) and his collaborators, in particular Benedict Kerkvliet (1990, 2005). The second stream covers an even larger body of literature concerned with various forms and scales of open collective action, ranging from local riots and protest to transnational social movements and advocacy networks, such as Third World Network, GRAIN, Asia Pacific Food Sovereignty Network, and *Via Campesina* (Borras *et al.* 2008). What these two bodies of work reveal – as touched upon in the introductory chapter of this edition – is a dichotomous typology that has tended to typecast forms of resistance as inherently opposite. Yet recent writers reflecting on earlier work are now showing how these perspectives overlap and inform one another in understanding contemporary resistance (cf. Amoore 2005), an angle that we aim to build upon here.[1]

In this chapter we critically review a range of writings on resistance, moving from subdued forms of resistance to more radical, extreme approaches, such as rural guerrilla movements, in order to bring to the fore the wide range of resistance practices occurring not only at these extremes, but also in between. In doing so, we hope to demonstrate how various forms of resistance cannot be divided into this long-standing binary opposition, the overt and defiant forms of resistance versus the more covert and everyday forms. Rather, the globalization of markets and their extended reach within even isolated areas, accelerating the process of agrarian transition, has important consequences for how to conceptualize and write about rural resistance. We suggest that there is much to be gained by taking an interactive and constructivist standpoint. From this approach local, national, regional or even global resistance has as much to do with how the actors themselves define their field of collective protest as with the specific nature of their targets, be it a corrupt local official, a national state agency, a contract grower, a national enterprise or a global agribusiness firm. Boundaries between scales are soon found to be much more murky and flexible than is usually assumed, a notion supported by the chapters in this book.

The argument, as detailed in the previous introductory chapter, is that rural collective action is often the result of micro processes involving agency variables such as solidarity, identity and social networks, as well as shifts in multi-scalar political opportunity structures. Local, national or transnational acts of resistance, whether open and defiant or everyday acts of covert resistance, are the consequence of a particular set of conditions, both objective and co-constituted by peasants and peasant organizers acting as social movement entrepreneurs. Extraordinary moments of open contentious resistance are intertwined with everyday forms of more hidden individual acts.

Conceptualizing rural resistance: foot dragging, engaging the market or taking arms

Contemporary analyses of rural resistance have been influenced by three prominent authors: Antonio Gramsci (1971), Karl Polanyi (1944, 1957), and James Scott (1976, 1985, 1990, 1997), introduced in Chapter 1. Yet grounded research and social movement theories have increasingly enriched the field of rural resistance studies. In the next sections, we critically review the main tendencies in this literature, highlighting the respective contributions of various intellectual perspectives.

Everyday forms of peasant resistance

Inspired by Chayanov's writing on peasant economy (1966), authors including Wolf (1966, 1969), Alavi (1973) and Scott (1976, 1985) have focused their research on the nature and logic of peasant agriculture and the coexistence of peasant/household farmers and capitalism (Buttel and McMichael 1988). Often described as 'neo-populists', these authors have examined how political resistance to modernization and capitalism is practised using the lens of the peasant 'moral community' (Bernstein and Byres 2001). They suggest that 'peasants (and others) who are subjected to social and cultural subordination create continuous, mundane and hidden ways of resisting oppression (inequality, hierarchy) – in effect, through avoidance, ridicule and acts of petty revenge' (Bernstein and Byres 2001: 33). The cumulative effects of these actions are considered to be more effective than other more drastic, organized actions might be.

Turning to Southeast Asia, Scott, writing on Malaysia (1985) and Vietnam and Burma (1976), suggests that the market presents the peasant subsistence economy, as well as traditional social relations, with a number of risks. Scott argues that peasants will often resist the market, being risk-averse, concerned predominantly with survival. Rather than seeking profits as their primary goal, they want instead to retain their subsistence capacity and maintain or restore moral relationships. In the Malaysia case, Scott (1985) explores how peasants do this through an attention to infrapolitics that includes striking against the introduction of combine harvesters, participating in petty theft, perpetuating gossip, and the killing of adversaries' animals. Turning to Vietnam, Ben Kerkvliet in his book, *The Power of Everyday Politics: How Vietnamese Peasants Transformed National Policy* (2005), gives a rich account of how difficulties in the agrarian cooperatives under socialist rule led to peasant resistance and how this resistance ultimately forced the government to embark on reforms. Writing on the Philippines, Kerkvliet (1996) also underlined how dominant views of rural electoral politics tended to emphasize patron–client relations (see also Landé 1965, Novak and Snyder 1974). Additionally, oligarchic power and elite control (Hutchcroft 1991) – also figuratively referred to by Anderson as 'cacique democracy' (Anderson 1998) – and even the neocolonial character of Filipino politics were considered (Shalom 1986). Nevertheless, these approaches failed to take into account the various forms of contestations and resistance of the rural poor against different traditional forms of control. According to Kerkvliet, such forms of resistance, expressed in a range of instrumental tactics around vote buying, kinship relations, and even outright boycott, are rooted in a 'democratic sense of proper elections' (Kerkvliet 1996: 163).

The neo-populists – and their attention to everyday forms of resistance – have not been without critics. White (1986), Hart (1991) and Korovkin (2000) in part disagree with the neo-populists' tendencies to aggregate a wide range of peasant practices and treat them all as resistance. White (1986) instead sees important differences between those peasants who have strategies rooted in petty commodity production and others whose positions have been strengthened by land reform and, in the case of Vietnam, revolution (Bernstein and Byres 2001). Another influential critic, Samuel Popkin (1979), developed a model of rational self-interested and utility-maximizing peasant behaviour which he contrasted with the moral economy view which prioritizes maintaining subsistence levels and minimizing risk. Popkin argued that peasants are constantly motivated to raise their subsistence level through long and short-term investments, and that this investment logic applies to both market and non-market exchanges. While some moral economists have interpreted peasant protests that accompany state building and the commercialization of agriculture as a reaction to the loss of subsistence, security and welfare – thus suggesting that peasants may be anti-market and operate on a safety-first principle – Popkin contends that participation in revolution is a calculated, rational attempt to improve one's future situation rather than an effort to restore or maintain a past way of life.

Recent permutations of the everyday resistance approach include ethnographic works such as those of Peluso (1992) working in Indonesia, Isager and Ivarsson (2002) in Thailand, Rigg mainly based in Thailand and Laos (2006, 2007), Li in Eastern Indonesia (2007), and Forsyth and Walker in Thailand (2008). These works use the lens of everyday resistance, subaltern strategies and globalization to problematize mechanical approaches to local resistance in Southeast Asia. These recent additions also come in the wake of growing attention to and use of civil society discourse and analyses, notably the works of Prasetyo *et al.* (2003), Alagappa (2004), Boudreau (2004), Loh and Öjendal (2005), Hedman (2006), and Weiss (2006). The common threads here are the importance of moving beyond linear class analyses to direct attention towards contextual elements such as local politics and culture, democratic space and transition, identity politics, and a plea for more nuanced approaches in theorizing how globalization might impact various forms of resistance.

Defiant collective action and open protest

Coming from a quite different perspective, one concerned with open acts of resistance such as riots, strikes, and even armed insurrections, analyses of collective action in the 1950s emphasized the extremism of mass mobilization, especially the dangerous and irrational character of the crowd (Arendt 1951; Hoffer 1951; Selznick 1952). This school of thought was largely influenced by the emergence of totalitarian and fascist movements during the interwar period. During a slightly later time period, another dominant perspective, 'relative deprivation', attributed the rise of activism to the perceptions of individuals that, by belonging to a certain social group, they were unfairly deprived in relation to a reference group (Davies 1963; Aberle 1966; Gurr 1970).

In 1965 Mancur Olson made what was considered an important breakthrough in the understanding of resistance and social movements by proposing a rational choice account of collective action, in his book *The Logic of Collective Action*. He argues that human beings are rational and self-interested and, as such, would not engage in collective action for a collective good since this good could be obtained, whether they participate or not, because of the collective action of others. This situation became known as the collective action problem or social dilemma situation.[2] Olson argues that collective action is likely to develop only in small groups because in a larger group it is rational to 'free-ride'. Two other conditions are also required for collective action: selected incentives that increase the rewards of participation, and sanctions for non-participation. Large collective actions, maintained over an extensive period of time, are therefore very unlikely to follow Olson's framework.

The history of many social movements, including labour, peasant, pacifist and environmentalist movements, in which a large number of individuals have been involved has, over time, challenged an Olsonian conception of collective action. In fact, since his 1965 book there have been numerous alternative explanations as to why large social movements can develop, discussed next.

The bases of collective action

In the 1970s, in reaction to Olson's work and confronted by the continued existence of large social movements, several scholars began to develop alternative explanations for their existence. The first issue raised was that there may be individual benefits derived from engaging in a collective action itself. For example, Hirschman (1982) suggests that the possibility for individuals to engage in group action represents something exciting and new from which pleasure can be derived. Secondly, the role of social movement organizers has been emphasized, namely the ability of movement entrepreneurs to transform existing collective grievances into social movement organizations (McCarthy and Zald 1973, 1979). Tarrow (1994) adds that social movement entrepreneurs are able to generate collective responses by transforming 'external opportunities, conventions and resources into movements' (1994, 23; see also Snow and Benford 1988, 1992).

Furthermore, McCarthy and Zald (1979) point out that these leaders usually have access to resources such as organizational structures, finance and communication, which help generate collective participation. However, as Edelman (2001: 290) notes, since not all entrepreneurs have such access to resources, a resource mobilization approach fails to explain why social movements 'usually of the very poor, emerged with few resources'. In fact, several scholars have examined movements where the risks of repression are high and chances of success low, arguing that one needs to go beyond the surface and search for alternative forms of collective action ranging from 'hidden forms of resistance' (Scott 1990), to 'shadowy' (Piven and Cloward 1977) and 'submerged' forms (Melucci 1989), a point we return to later.

Another alternative explanation for the development of social movements is that the psychology of individuals may be something other than Olson's depiction of self-interested rational maximizers. For example, analysts of the Philippine rural insurgency movement have highlighted the importance of culture and identity in understanding how the participants themselves might conceive rural resistance (Abinales 1996; Rutten 1996; Weekley 1996).[3] Such an emphasis on the role of culture and identity was previously highlighted by Ann Swidler (1986) and David Laitin (1988). For Swidler (1986: 273), culture exerts a causal influence on action not 'in defining ends of actions, but in providing cultural components that are used to construct strategies of actions'. Applying such an analytical lens, Roxane Rutten suggests in her study of sugar workers' mobilization and support of the revolutionary movement in the Philippines that in order to understand such decisions, one needs to examine

> the interplay between peoples' own perceptions, experiences, solidarities, and actions on the one hand, and, on the other, new ideas, opportunities and constraints, organizational forms and collective actions, introduced by mobilizers.
>
> (Rutten 2000: 151)[4]

In their research on social dilemmas, Dawes *et al.* (1988) found that group interactions can generate solidarity and identity through cooperation or even just promises of cooperation. Individuals do not exist in a vacuum; rather they are part of existing social networks and communities. Such belonging is seen to create collective incentives for collective action as opposed to Olson's view of individual incentives. These social networks are referred to as structures of solidarity incentives (Fireman and Gamson 1979).[5] As will be discussed, acknowledging the importance of agency and subjectivities has enriched previous structure-driven accounts of open and radical forms of protest.

Agrarian revolution and revolutionary movements

Turning to the most visible forms of dissent and collective action, the literature on rural revolutions and revolutionary movements as a whole is imposing, and we do not review it all here. As Eric Selbin (1993: 1) wrote, 'revolution remains endlessly fascinating to scholars and activists alike'. In fact, until the end of the Cold War, leftist guerrilla movements commanded widespread interest (Goldstone 1980, 1991; Boswell 1989; Parsa 2000). Timothy Wickham-Crowley, in his book *Guerrillas and Revolution in Latin America: A Comparative Study of Insurgents and Regimes since 1956* explains:

> Interest in guerrillas had grown apace with the successes of Fidel Castro in late-1950s Cuba; it latter ebbed with the death of Ché Guevara in the Bolivian jungle in 1967, and then waned further with the fall of Saigon in 1975. The 1979 overthrow of the Somoza government in Nicaragua and the recent revolutionary upsurge in Central America revived such interests, but certainly not to the levels of the 1960s.
>
> (Wickham-Crowley 1992: 4)

Wickham-Crowley (1992) identifies five conditions that made Latin American revolutionary movements successful between 1965 and 1990: first, the rural-based nature of guerrilla movements with strong support from the peasantry; second, a significant level of military strength; third, a patrimonial and authoritarian regime; fourth, the possibility of establishing cross-class alliances; and fifth, the withdrawal of American support to the authoritarian regime. This work is a rich complement to earlier works on peasant rebellions (cf. Wolf 1969; Migdal 1974; Scott 1976; Popkin 1979) and social revolutions (cf. Moore Jr. 1966; Goldfrank 1975, 1979; Tilly 1978; Skocpol 1979; Goldstone 1991). Yet, except possibly for Vietnam, these five conditions have not materialized in Southeast Asia. As such, what remain to be explored in greater detail are the internal dynamics and choices of strategic and tactical actions of revolutionary movements, including local and regional peasant mobilizations. That is, while structural conditions and social processes such as class alliances, resource mobilization, relative deprivation, international support, unequal trade and dependency are all important, a clearer under-standing of the agency of the 'movement' itself is also warranted, a point we discuss next.

Bringing 'agency' in

Writings on agrarian revolutions that followed Wickham-Crowley's 1992 paradigmatic study sought to understand the trajectory of rural insurgent movements. Concerned with the 'agency' of revolutionaries, Selbin suggests that authors following structural approaches have poorly understood the number of choices and actions made by revolutionaries themselves. He explains that 'the conscious choices and intentional actions of people have played clearly critical roles in the revolutionary process' (Selbin 1993: 3). Selbin continues that 'structuralist theories are poorly equipped to explain the even minor cross-class alliances present in some of these cases and largely deny the importance of leadership in the first generation revolutions' (ibid.: 3).[6] Therefore, there is a need to go beyond structuralist approaches of revolution since, in many instances, 'scholars have largely ignored the strongly voluntarist aspect of social revolutions: People make revolution' (ibid.: 27).[7] For Selbin, existing structural theories of revolutions are essential to capture broader social processes at play – driven by the state, class relations and the international economic and political arena – but they cannot account for the very specific actions and processes that characterize the day-to-day conduct of a revolutionary struggle (as illustrated in Figure 2.1).[8]

Published soon after Selbin's book, Forrest Colburn's *The Vogue of Revolution in Poor Countries* (1994) sheds further light on the dynamics of

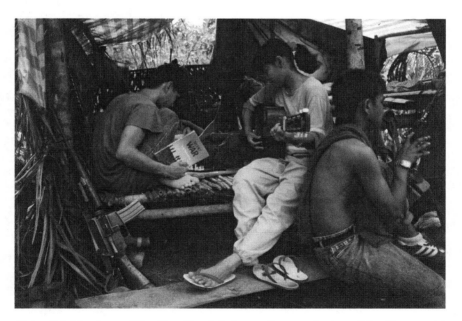

Figure 2.1 Members of the New People's Army, the armed wing of the Communist Party of the Philippines, reading *Silent War*, by Victor N. Corpus.

Photo credit: Dominique Caouette

social movement agency. Comparing Third World rural revolutions that took place between 1945 and 1990, Colburn argues that existing theories of revolutions have not paid enough attention to the role of ideas, especially those held by 'revolutionary elites', and the capacity of those elites to influence history (Colburn 1994: 5). More specifically, he argues that

> while the origins of contemporary revolutions are rooted in social, political, and economic conflict, the outcomes of these revolutions have been determined by the political imagination of revolutionary elites, an imagination that came to be surprisingly similar throughout the poorer regions of the world.
>
> (Colburn 1994: 6)

Following Colburn, we argue that to date, in the mainstream literature on revolution, it has been nation states and struggles within national borders that have acted as units of analysis. This has had the analytical consequence of not only under-theorizing local dynamics, but also missing how non-armed resistance has become an increasingly cross-border phenomenon, especially following the end of the Cold War.

The role of opportunity structures

The previous review of recent writings on social movements and revolution suggests that besides endogenous factors such as the ideas, ideology and intellectual culture of activists, there are important exogenous elements that warrant further examination. These include, for example, the role of elections, changing agrarian regulations, public policies, rural development projects, and the availability of influential political allies. In addition, broad and diffuse changes in the international context also require further discussion, a theme addressed in the chapters by Caouette and Smeltzer. While framing is clearly illuminative as to how collective action comes about, a framework for understanding rural resistance movements must also encompass the contextual components relevant to the changing nature of agrarian livelihoods.

In order to make sense of this diversity of factors, we suggest the use of Tarrow's concept of political opportunity structure (POS). Tarrow defined the domestic POS as 'consistent – but not necessarily formal, permanent or national – signals to social or political actors which either encourage or discourage them to use their internal resources to engage in collective action' (Tarrow 1994: 18). More specifically, these signals can take the form of an increasing access to power, changes in ruling alignments, the possibility of establishing linkages with influential allies, and the existence of divisions within and between the elites (oftentimes triggering open forms of protest as shown in Figure 2.2, where Philippine opposition parties and social movements mobilized during the President's State of the Nation address).[9]

Figure 2.2 Open protests in the streets of Manila, the Philippines.
Photo credit: Milagros P. Arguelles

Significant changes can also come from trans-border phenomena such as foreign intervention, international development agency projects and the arrival of multinational or other forms of investment, including foreign direct investment.

These exogenous elements create shifting political terrains of struggles for rural movements in Southeast Asia. Yet these new conditions alone cannot explain the stands and actions of a rural movement; rather, one needs to examine how these new conditions are perceived and acted upon. In making such an argument, we contend that while changes in the domestic political opportunity structure and in the international context are factors that can affect and influence the forms and shape of rural resistance, it is the movement's own experience of struggles and internal dynamics that condition the specific form of response and decisions taken by different movements.

Transnational resistance

Today, transnational resistance and its ties with globalization are complex and fluid. Beginning in the late 1980s, and especially with the 'Battle of Seattle' in 1999 during the World Trade Organization (WTO) Ministerial Meeting, parallel forums and protests have been occasions for those involved with national and transnational rural movements and networks to gather and act collectively to protest against decision-making processes deemed undemocratic and exclusionary, especially with regards to agricultural policies (O'Brien *et al.* 2000; Smith and Johnston 2002; Bandy and Smith 2005). For these movements, trade liberalization in agriculture, as embodied in the WTO agenda, constitutes a global challenge that calls for cross-border collective action to shift current neoliberal economics (Walker 1994; Keck and Sikkink 1998; Prokosh and Raymond 2002; Clark 2003).

Transnational activism can be simply defined as 'social movements and other civil-society groups operating across state borders' (Piper and Uhlin 2004: 1). Della Porta and Tarrow further refine this definition by referring to transnational collective action as 'the coordinated international campaigns on the part of networks of activists against international actors, other states, or international institutions' (2005: 7).

Recent theoretical works on transnational collective action – notably those of Risse-Kappen (1995), Risse (2002), Della Porta and Tarrow (2005) and Tarrow (2005) – suggest that three variables explain the rise and outcomes of contemporary transnational activism. These include the current complex internationalization (growing density of international institutions, regimes and contacts among state officials and non-state actors), and the multiplication of linkages among local, national and international issues (Della Porta and Tarrow 2005). Similarly important are the multi-scalar political opportunities created by the interactions between complex internationalization and domestic structures. As such, there has also been the emergence of a stratum of activists described as rooted cosmopolitans, defined as 'a fluid, cosmopolitan, but rooted layer of activists and advocates' (Tarrow 2005: 34).

In reality, transnational activists seldom work exclusively at the global scale. Instead, they tend to be 'rooted' at local and national scales, simultaneously engaging different government institutions. Many have remained involved in national struggles, arguing that advocacy and policy engagement at one scale does not deter activism at another one (Borras 2004; Desmarais 2007). Transnational activists are thus able to create linkages and coalitions among various types of actors operating across different scales in order to respond to various political contexts, each offering a different range of political opportunities (Slater 1997; Risse *et al.* 1999; Price 2003).

In Southeast Asia, transnational activism emerged largely as a response to socio-economic and political processes associated with economic globalization and agrarian transformations, and the limited political liberalization that has characterized a number of Southeast Asian countries (Loh and Öjendal 2005; Caouette 2006). For instance, in 1997, the financial crisis that shook the region pushed several countries to facilitate and accelerate access to natural resources and resource-rich areas (Andrews *et al.* 2003; Samdup 2007). At the same time, greater integration into the global economy has resulted in an intensification and thickening of organizational density of social movements and transnational networks in the region. In fact, the past ten years have witnessed an acceleration in the number and intensity of contacts between social movements, NGOs and transnational networks throughout Southeast Asia (Hainsworth 2000; Mulder 2003; Schak and Hudson 2003; Lee 2004; Loh 2004; Piper and Uhlin 2004; Loh and Öjendal 2005; Weller 2005). Unsurprisingly, transnational activist organizations tend to establish themselves in countries where relative political space exists or at least has allowed for global organizing, such as the Philippines and Thailand.

Transnational rural advocacy networks expanded in the 1990s at a time when various other social sectors (workers, migrants, women and students) were increasingly organizing and seeking alternatives to the export-oriented growth model (Loh 2004; Piper and Uhlin 2004). Two themes interconnected with rural change – along with the issue of labour migration – have become prominent lately for transnational organizing: food sovereignty, and the rights of indigenous peoples to natural resources and their ancestral domains (Sandbukt 2000; Brysk 2002; Bolinguet 2003; DuPuis *et al.* 2005; Maiba 2005; Scott and Tebay 2005; Yashar 2005, 2007; Weiner and Glaskin 2006; Morgan 2007). These themes have been at the heart of a range of campaigns launched by global networks such as Via Campesina, Friends of the Earth – International, Greenpeace, World Rainforest Movement, GRAIN, Oxfam International, Indigenous Environmental Network, Third World Network, Asia Pacific Food Sovereignty Network, and Forest Peoples Programme.

In most cases in Southeast Asia, transnational activists are interested in creating linkages and coalitions among diverse types of actors operating across different scales in order to respond to various political contexts, each offering a different range of political opportunities. In certain instances one might argue that transnational advocacy efforts produce shared identities and a common understanding of issues while also generating common campaigns and proposals that can be put forward during regional and international gatherings and implemented both regionally and nationally. However, there are a number of dilemmas and choices when transnational networks seek to weave local issues into regional and global scales of advocacy. In fact, this weaving is often more problematic than described. Exploring the micro processes at work when local issues and struggles become part of regional activism constitutes a key analytical challenge to the growing literature on transnational activism in Southeast Asia. As Kelly notes, 'speaking of "local" resistance to the "global" is an overly simplistic representation' (2000: 158; see also Hewison 2000, 2001).

Conclusions: contemporary rural resistance across multiple scales

Building on previous approaches to resistance and collective action, we suggest that more nuanced understandings are now required, with greater attention paid to the complexities and inconsistencies rooted in resistance and the multiplicity of identities represented within such struggles. Social movement perspectives or even countermovement approaches, à la Polanyi (1957), often assume that action is collective and unified and do not account for intra-group fragmentation and divisions. Indeed, Mittelman and Chin (2000) offer several critiques of such an approach. First, building on the work of Gramsci (1971), they point out that resistance today is not always bound within states, and is not always enacted towards the state. Indeed, altering state power might not be the solution to changing the power structures at the root of the problem. Rather, resistance can traverse national boundaries, even reaching the global scale via technology, easier and cheaper possibilities for international travel, shared norms, and transnational advocates able to link disparate rural struggles into global action frames. As a consequence, current understandings of counter hegemony must account for such emerging spaces.

At the same time, a number of authors, building upon Scott (1976, 1985, 1990), emphasize the ongoing importance of less blatant forms of resistance. De Goede (2005) contends that resistance does not have to be global and coherent; it can be obscure and less straightforward, as in the case of laughter and comedy in challenging norms and the status quo. De Goede stresses that these common forms of daily dissent in the form of 'the strange' and the comical, have power to transform understandings of money and finances and call attention to values underlying economic globalization. De Goede also argues that resistance to rural change, and its connections to global capital, is extremely diverse and associated understandings should be open to alternative interpretations. Examples that highlight this diversity include Turner and Michaud (2008, and chapter in this book), who argue that Hmong upland ethnic minorities in northern Vietnam are part of a flexible society that resists economic and cultural changes imposed from the outside, using their own home-grown tools to adapt through diversified livelihoods, engaging only when and how individuals and households see fit with the global economy, while sustaining their local identity and ensuring social reproduction. Similarly, Escobar (2004) suggests that resistance is the negotiation or struggle against dominant cultures in everyday life, and that understandings of social movements need to be underpinned by how meanings come about through daily practices. Only then is it possible to comprehend more concerted efforts to cope with or redress oppressive circumstances (Jung 2008).

'Everyday forms of peasant resistance' are often cited as 'non-political' and non-threatening to the status quo, not considered consequential until they erupt into more visible forms. Yet they are powerful forces of change in their own right (Scott 1990; Cheru 1997; Kerkvliet 2005). Local actors such as peasants enact a number of strategies outside the reach of the state to improve their life circumstances, such as reviving previous practices to uphold subsistence livelihoods and undertaking ingenious activities in the informal economy – strategies that at once earn them a living while providing services to other poor where the government has failed. These activities in themselves have an economic impact as people withdraw from formal avenues in order to safeguard their material welfare (Cheru 1997).

Yet Mittelman and Chin (2000) assert that infrapolitics, as supported by Scott (1990), do not give sufficient consideration to structures at the scale of the state, which often enable and shape relations of resistance and dominance and influence how these are manifested and reproduced on a daily basis. They furthermore argue that Scott presents class as a unitary identity, while multiple identities exist within social groups and resistance may be based on power relations rooted in aspects of identity other than class. As such, we argue that it is important to recognize that resistance is context-specific and linked to meanings constructed in everyday life, as well as to global-scale ideologies. This reflects Foucault's (1976) proposition in his 'rule of variations' that a greater focus on the processes and shifts in how power relationships are constantly transforming, and the processes involved, is needed, rather than concentrating narrowly on who/what is powerful and who/what is not.

In sum, together with a multiplication and diffusion of structures of dominance has come a growth and spread of forms of resistance. This involves a greater variety of resistances than traditionally considered, with more undeclared and less obvious brands existing alongside vocally declared ones. Resistance to rural change now connects actors across a wider variety of spatial scales than ever before. Individuals with a range of resources are becoming increasingly interconnected, with transnational social movements at times supporting and encouraging local 'hidden transcripts'. It follows that researchers must now grapple with new ways of conceptualizing resistance, in a world where the targets and scales of resistance are multiplying rapidly, and the politics of alliances are frequently shifting. This transcendence across scales is not just a case of local, everyday forms of resistance becoming open and public or vice versa. More subtle processes are at play, with social movements having their own political agendas and alliances, not always allowing the voices of others to be heard.

In line with a more flexible and multi-scalar analysis, the authors gathered in this book seek to amalgamate elements of more classical interpretations of resistance, adapt central concepts to the current global context, and extend consciousness to new actors, multiple scales and different medians of action. In turn these are intertwined with global–local connections brought about by expanding capitalist markets, manifold forms of commoditization, global flows of information and people, and the diffusion of experiences of rural processes and transnational rural movements. As such, studying and understanding rural resistance opens a rich and kaleidoscopic research agenda that can help shed light on what James Rosenau (2003) has called 'distant proximities'.

Notes

1 This chapter expands upon the discussions in Turner and Caouette (2009).
2 Concrete cases of such dilemmas, for example, include whether or not to donate to public radio or ride a bicycle rather than a car during a pollution alert (Dawes *et al.* 1988).
3 We are using the term collective identity as Melucci does; that is, as 'an interactive and shared definition produced by several individuals and concerned with the

orientation of action and the field of opportunities and constraints in which the action takes place'. As he later specifies by 'interactive and shared', it implies 'a process, because it is constructed and negotiated through a repeated activation of the relationships that link individuals' (1989: 342; see also Escobar and Alvarez 1992).

4   See also Gerlach and Hines (1970) and Bolton (1972) on prior contact with a movement member; Orum (1972), and Barnes and Kaase (1979) on participation in existing organisations; Gamson, Freeman and Rytina (1982) and Lofland (1977) on history of prior activism; and McCarthy and Zald (1973), among others, on biographical availability.

5   McAdam, McCarthy and Zald explain that these structures are expected to solve or 'at least mitigate the effects of the "free rider" problem' (1988: 710).

6   Forrest Colburn also makes a similar observation, stating: 'The two major interpretive schools, modernization and Marxism, share a preoccupation with the long-term origins and outcomes of revolution. And in explaining both origins and outcomes, discourse and explanation center on impersonal social structures. Modernization and Marxist analyses alike deny the importance of who the revolutionaries were or what they thought they were doing. As a result, political innovations by revolutionaries seem to be either predetermined or accidental, and their consequences seem to be irrelevant' (Colburn 1994: 9).

7   The issue of agency and its relation to structures is not new to social sciences (see Callinicos 1988). Thompson's writings on history are solid examples of historical analysis that places an emphasis on an understanding of agency (see for example, Thompson 1978).

8   As Selbin notes, the works of Eric Wolf (1969), James Scott (1976), and – to a certain extent – the works of Jeffrey Paige (1975) and Charles Tilly (1978) are partial exceptions because of their focus on peasant mobilization and resistance. However, less emphasis is placed on the critical choices and day-to-day calculations and alliances made by revolutionaries.

9   These four variables represent a synthesis of the works of various social movement analysts who in the past emphasized one or several of these variables. The origin of the concept can be traced back to Peter Eisenger (1973) who also discussed the importance of partial opening in the power structure. Hobsbawn (1974), for his part, looked at the importance of unstable alignments, while the role of influential allies was previously studied by Gamson (1992).

References

Aberle, D. (1966) *The Peyote Religion Among the Navajo*, Chicago: Aldine.

Abinales, P.N. (ed.) (1996) *The Revolution Falters: The left in the Philippine politics after 1986*, Southeast Asia Program Series No. 15, Ithaca: Southeast Asia Program Publications, Cornell University.

Alagappa, M. (ed.) (2004), *Civil Society and Political Change in Asia: expanding and contracting democratic space*, Stanford: Stanford University Press.

Alavi, H. (1973) 'Peasant classes and primordial loyalties', *Journal of Peasant Studies*, 1: 23–62.

Amoore, L. (2005) 'Introduction: global resistance – global politics', in L. Amoore (ed.) *The Global Resistance Reader*, London: Routledge, 1–11.

Anderson, B. (1998) *The Spectre of Comparisons: nationalism, Southeast Asia and the world*, London: Verso.

Andrews, T.G., Nartalin Chompusri and Baldwin, B.J. (2003) *The Changing Face of Multinationals in Southeast Asia*, London: Routledge.

Arendt, H. (1951) *The Origins of Totalitarianism*, New York: Harcourt, Brace.

Bandy, J. and Smith, J. (eds) (2005) *Coalitions Across Borders: transnational protest and the neoliberal order*, Lanham: Rowman and Littlefield.

Barnes, S.H. and Kaase, M. (1979) *Political Action*, Beverly Hills: Sage.

Bernstein, H. and Byres, T.J. (2001) 'From peasant studies to agrarian change', *Journal of Agrarian Change*, 1: 1–56.

Bolinguet, W. (2003) 'Asserting indigenous peoples' rights is not an act of terrorism', *Indigenous Affairs*, 3: 10–17.

Bolton, C.D. (1972), 'Alienation and action: a study of peace group members', *American Journal of Sociology*, 78: 537–61.

Borras Jr, S.M. (2004) 'La Via Campesina: an evolving transnational social movement', TNI Briefing Series No. 2004/6, Amsterdam: Transnational Institute.

Borras Jr, S.M., Edelman, M. and Kay, C. (2008) 'Transnational agrarian movements: origins and politics, campaign and impact', *Journal of Agrarian Change*, 8: 169–204.

Boswell, T. (1989) *Revolution in the World Systems*, New York: Greenwood.

Boudreau, V. (2004) *Resisting Dictatorship: repression and protest in Southeast Asia*, Cambridge: Cambridge University Press.

Brysk, A. (ed.) (2002) *Globalization and Human Rights*, Berkeley: University of California Press.

Buttel, F.H. and McMichael, P. (1988) 'Sociology and rural history: summary and critique', *Social Science History*, 12: 93–120.

Callinicos, A. (1988) *Making History: agency, structure and change in social theory*, Ithaca: Cornell University Press.

Caouette, D. (2006) 'Thinking and nurturing transnational activism in Southeast Asia: global advocacy through knowledge-building', *Kasarinlan: a Philippine quarterly of Third World studies*, 21: 3–33.

Chayanov, A.V. (1966) *The Theory of Peasant Economy*, trans. D. Thornton, R.E.F. Smith and B. Kerblay, Glencoa: Irwin.

Cheru, F. (1997) 'The silent revolution and the weapons of the weak: transformation and innovation from below', in S. Gill and J.H. Mittelman (eds) *Innovation and Transformation in International Studies*, Cambridge: Cambridge University Press, 153–69.

Clark, J. (ed.) (2003) *Globalizing Civic Engagement*, London: Earthscan.

Colburn, F.D. (1994) *The Vogue of Revolution in Poor Countries*, Princeton: Princeton University Press.

Davies, J.C. (1963) *Human Nature in Politics: the dynamics of political behaviour*, New York: John Wiley.

Dawes, R.M., Van de Kragt, A.J.C. and Orbell, J.M. (1988) 'Not me or thee but we: the importance of group identity in eliciting cooperation in dilemma situations: experimental manipulations', *Acta Psychologica*, 68: 83–97.

De Goede, M. (2005) 'Carnival of money: politics of dissent in an era of globalizing finance', in L. Amoore (ed.) *The Global Resistance Reader*, London: Routledge, 379–91.

Della Porta, D. and Tarrow, S. (2005) 'Transnational Processes and Social Activism: An Introduction', in D. Della Porta and S. Tarrow (eds) *Transnational Protest and Global Activism*, Lanham: Rowman and Littlefield, 1–17.

Desmarais, A.A. (2007) *La Via Campesina: globalization and the power of peasants*, Halifax: Fernwood Publishing.

DuPuis, E., Goodman, M. and Goodman, D. (2005) 'Should we go "home" to eat?: toward a reflexive politics of localism', *Journal of Rural Studies*, 21: 359–71.

Edelman, M. (2001) 'Social movements: changing paradigms and forms of politics', *Annual Review of Anthropology*, 30: 285–317.

—— (2005) 'Bringing the moral economy back in . . . to the study of 21st-century transnational movements', *American Anthropologist*, 107 (3): 331–45.

Eisenger, P. (1973) 'The conditions of protest behavior in American cities', *American Political Science Review*, 67: 11–28.

Escobar, A. (2004) 'Beyond the Third World: imperial globality, global coloniality and anti-globalization social movements', *Third World Quarterly*, 25 (1): 207–30.

Escobar, A. and Alvarez, S.E. (eds) (1992) *The Making of Social Movements in Latin America : Identity, Strategy, and Democracy*, Boulder: Westview Press.

Fireman, B. and Gamson, W.A. (1979) 'Utilitarian logic in the resource mobilization perspective', in Z.N. Mayer and John D. McCarthy (eds) *The Dynamics of Social Movements, Resource Mobilization, Social Control and Tactics*, Cambridge, MA: Winthrop Publishers, 8–44.

Forsyth, T. and Walker, A. (2008) *Forest Guardians, Forest Destroyers: the politics of environmental knowledge in northern Thailand*, Seattle: University of Washington Press.

Foucault, M. (1976/98) 'Method', in *The Will to Knowledge: the history of sexuality, volume 1*, London: Penguin; reprinted in Amoore, L. (ed.) *The Global Resistance Reader* (2005), London: Routledge, 86–91.

Gamson, W. (1992) *Talking Politics*, Cambridge: Cambridge University Press.

Gamson, W., Freeman, B. and Rytina, S. (1982) *Encounters with Unjust Authority*, Homewood: Dorsey.

Gerlach, L.P. and Hines, V.H. (1970) *People, Power and Change: movements of social transformation*, Indianapolis: Bobbs-Merrill.

Goldfrank, W. (1975) 'World system, state structure, and the onset of the Mexican Revolution', *Politics and Society*, 5: 417–39.

—— (1979) 'Theories of revolution and revolution without theory: the case of Mexico', *Theory and Society*, 7: 135–65.

Goldstone, J. (1980) 'Theories of revolution: the third generation', *World Politics*, 32: 425–53.

—— (1991) *Revolution and Rebellion in the Early Modern World*, Berkeley: University of California Press.

Gramsci, A. (1971) *Selections from the Prison Notebooks of Antonio Gramsci*, ed. and trans. Quintin Hoare and Geoffrey Nowell Smith, New York: International Publishers.

Gurr, T.R. (1970) *Why Men Rebel*, Princeton: Princeton University Press.

Hainsworth, G.B. (ed.) (2000) *Globalization and the Asian Economic Crisis: indigenous responses, coping strategies, and governance reform in Southeast Asia*, Vancouver: Centre for Southeast Asia Research, Institute of Asian Research, University of British Columbia.

Hart, G. (1991) 'Engendering everyday resistance: gender, patronage and production politics in rural Malaysia', *Journal of Peasant Studies*, 19: 93–121.

Hedman, E.-L. E. (2006) *In the Name of Civil Society: From Free Election Movements to People Power in the Philippines*, Honolulu: University of Hawaii Press.

Hewison, K. (2000) 'Resisting globalization: a study of localism in Thailand', *Pacific Review*, 13: 279–96.

—— (2001) 'Nationalism, populism, dependency: Southeast Asia and responses to the Asian crisis', *Singapore Journal of Tropical Geography*, 22: 219–36.

Hirschman, A.O. (1982) *Shifting Involvement: private interest and public action*, Princeton: Princeton University Press.

Hobsbawn, E.J. (1974) 'Peasant land occupations', *Past and Present*, 62: 120–52.

Hoffer, E. (1951) *The True Believer: thoughts on the nature of mass movements*, New York: New American Library.

Hutchcroft, P. (1991) 'Oligarchs and cronies in the Philippine state: The Politics of Patrimonial Plunder,' *World Politics*, 43 (3): 414–50.

Isager, L. and Ivarsson, S. (2002) 'Contesting Landscapes in Thailand: Tree Ordination as Counter-territorialization' *Critical Asian Studies*, 34 (3): 395–417.

Jung, C. (2008) *The Moral Force of Indigenous Politics: critical liberalism and the Zapatistas*, Cambridge: Cambridge University Press.

Keck, M. and Sikkink, K. (1998) *Activists Beyond Borders: advocacy networks in international politics*, Ithaca: Cornell University Press.

Kelly, P.F. (2000) *Landscapes of Globalisation: human geographies of economic change in the Philippines*, London: Routledge.

Kerkvliet, B.J.T. (1990) *Everyday Politics in the Philippines: class and status relations in a central Luzon village*, Berkeley: University of California Press.

—— (1996) 'Contemporary Philippine leftist politics in historical perspective', in P.N. Abinales (ed.) *The Revolution Falters: the Left in the Philippine politics after 1986*, Ithaca: Southeast Asia Program Series No.15, Southeast Asia Program Publications, Cornell University: 9–27.

—— (2005) *The Power of Everyday Politics: how Vietnamese peasants transformed national policy*, Ithaca: Cornell University Press.

Korovkin, T. (2000) 'Weak weapons, strong weapons? Hidden resistance and political protest in rural Ecuador', *Journal of Peasant Studies*, 27: 1–29.

Laitin, D. (1988) 'Political culture and political preferences', *American Political Science Review*, 82: 589–97.

Landé, C.H. (1965) *Leaders, Factions and Parties: The Structure of Philippine Politics*, New Haven: Council on Southeast Asian Studies, Yale University.

—— (1981) 'Philippine Prospects After Martial Law,' *Foreign Affairs* (Summer): 1147–68.

Lee, H.G. (ed.) (2004) *Civil Society in Southeast Asia*, Singapore: Institute of Southeast Asian Studies.

Li, T.M. (2007) *The Will to Improve: Governmentability, development and the practices of politics*, Durham: Duke University Press.

Lofland, J. (1977) *Doomsday Cult*, New York: Irvington.

Loh, F. (2004) 'Les ONG et les mouvements sociaux en Asie du Sud-Est', in L. Delcourt, B. Duferme and F. Polet (eds) *Mondialisation des résistances: L'état des lutes*, Paris: Centre Tricontinental, Forum mondial des alternatives et Éditions Syllepse, 41–55.

Loh, F.K.W. and Öjendal, J. (eds) (2005) *Southeast Asian Responses to Globalization: restructuring governance and deepening democracy*, Copenhagen: NIAS.

McAdam, D. (1982) *Political Process and the Development of Black Insurgency, 1930–1970*, Chicago: University of Chicago Press.

—— (1986) 'Recruitment to high risk activism: the case of freedom summer', *American Journal of Sociology*, 92: 64–90.

—— (1988) 'Micro-mobilization contexts and recruitment to activism', in B.

Klandermans, H. Kriesi and S. Tarrow (eds) *From Structure to Action: social movement participation across cultures*, Greenwich, CT: JAI Press.

McAdam, D., McCarthy, J.D. and Zald, M.N. (1988) 'Social movements', in N.J. Smelser (ed.) *Handbook of Sociology*, Newbury Park: Sage, 695–737.

McCarthy, J.D. and Zald, M. (1973) *The Trend of Social Movements in America: professionalization and resource mobilization*, Morristown: General Learning Press.

McCarthy, J.D. and Zald, M. (eds) (1979) *The Dynamics of Social Movements: resource mobilization, social control, and tactics*, Cambridge, MA: Winthrop.

Maiba, H. (2005) 'Grassroots transnational social movement activism: the case of Peoples' Global Action', *Sociological Focus*, 38: 41–63.

Melucci, A. (1989) *Nomads of the Present: social movements and individual needs in contemporary society*, Philadelphia: Temple University Press.

Migdal, J.S. (1974) *Peasant, Politics and Revolution: pressures toward political and social change in the Third World*, Princeton: Princeton University Press.

Mittelman, J.H. and Chin, C.B.N. (2000) 'Conceptualizing resistance to globalization', in J. H. Mittelman, *The Globalization Syndrome: Transformation and Resistance*, Princeton: Princeton University Press, 165–78.

Morgan, R. (2007) 'On political institutions and social movement dynamics: the case of the United Nations and the Global Indigenous Movement', *International Political Science Review*, 28: 273–92.

Moore Jr, B. (1966) *Social Origins of Dictatorship and Democracy*, Boston: Beacon Press.

Mulder, N. (2003) *Southeast Asian Images: towards civil society?* Chiang Mai: Silkworm Books.

Novak, T.C. and Snyder, K.A. (1974) 'Clientelist politics in the Philippines: Integration or instability?' *American Political Science Review*, 68 (3): 1147–70.

O'Brien, R., Goetz, A.M., Scholte, J.A. and Williams, M. (eds) (2000) *Contesting Global Governance: multilateral institutions and global social movements*, Cambridge: Cambridge University Press.

Olson, M. (1965) *The Logic of Collective Action*, Cambridge, MA: Harvard University Press.

Orum, A.M. (1972) *Black Students in Protest*, Washington: American Sociological Association.

Paige, J. (1975) *Agrarian Revolution*, New York: Free Press.

Parsa, M. (2000) *States, Ideologies and Social Revolutions: a comparative analysis of Iran, Nicaragua and the Philippines*, Cambridge: Cambridge University Press.

Peluso, N. (1992) *Rich Forests, Poor People: resource control and resistance in Java*, Berkeley: University of California Press.

Piper, N. and Uhlin, A. (2004) *Transnational Activism in Asia: problems of power and democracy*, London: Routledge.

Piven, F.F. and Cloward, R.A. (1977) *Poor People's Movements: why they succeed, how they fail*, New York: Pantheon.

Polanyi, K. (1944) *The Great Transformation: The political and economic origins of our time*. Boston: Beacon Press.

—— (1957) 'The economy as instituted process', in K. Polanyi, C.M. Arensberg and H.W. Pearson (eds) *Trade and Market in the Early Empires: economies in history and theory*, New York: Free Press, 243–70.

Popkin, S.L. (1979) *The Rational Peasant: the political economy of rural society in Vietnam*, Berkeley: University of California Press.

Prasetyo, S.T., Priyono A.E., Törnquist, O. and contributors (2003) *Indonesia's Post-Soeharto Democracy Movement*, Jakarta: DEMOS.

Price, R. (2003) 'Transnational civil society and advocacy in world politics', *World Politics*, 55: 579–606.

Prokosh, M. and Raymond, L. (2002) *The Global Activist's Manual: local ways to change the world*, New York: Thunder's Mouth Press/Nation Books.

Rigg, J. (2006) 'Land, farming, livelihoods, and poverty: rethinking the links in the rural south', *World Development*, 34: 180–202.

—— (2007) *An Everyday Geography of the Global South*, London: Routledge.

Risse, T. (2002) 'Transnational actors and world politics', in W. Carlsnaes, T. Risse and B. Simmons (eds) *Handbook of International Relations*, London: Sage, 255–74.

Risse, T., Ropp, S. and Sikkink, K. (eds) (1999) *The Power of Human Rights: international norms and domestic change*, New York: Cambridge University Press.

Risse-Kappen, T. (ed.) (1995) *Bringing Transnational Relations Back In: non-state actors, domestic structure and international institutions*, Cambridge: Cambridge University Press.

Rosenau, J. N. (2003) *Distant Proximities: dynamics beyond globalization*, Princeton: Princeton University Press.

Rutten, R. (1996) 'Popular support for the revolutionary movement CPP-NPA: experiences in a hacienda in Negros Occidental, 1978–1995', in P. Abinales (ed.) *The Revolution Falters: the left in the Philippine politics after 1986*, Ithaca: Southeast Asia Program Publications: Cornell University, 110–53.

—— (2000) 'High-cost activism and the worker household: interests, commitment, and the costs of revolutionary activism in a Philippine plantation region', *Theory and Society*, 29: 215–52.

Samdup, C. (ed.) (2007) *Études d'impact des investissements étrangers sur les droits humains*, Montréal: Droit et Démocratie.

Sandbukt, Ø. (2000) 'Deforestation and the people of the forest: the Orang Rimba or Kubu of Sumatra', *Indigenous Affairs*, 2: 39–47.

Schak, D.C. and Hudson, W. (eds) (2003) *Civil Society in Asia*, Aldershot and Burlington: Ashgate.

Scott, J.C. (1976) *The Moral Economy of the Peasant*, New Haven: Yale University Press.

—— (1985) *Weapons of the Weak: everyday forms of peasant resistance*, New Haven: Yale University Press.

—— (1990) *Domination and the Arts of Resistance: hidden transcripts*, New Haven: Yale University Press.

—— (1997) *Seeing Like a State: how certain schemes to improve the human condition have failed*, New Haven: Yale University Press.

Scott, C. and Tebay, N. (2005) 'The West Papua conflict and its consequences for the island of New Guinea: root causes and the campaign for Papua, Land of Peace', *The Round Table*, 94: 599–612.

Selbin, E. (1993) *Modern Latin American Revolutions*, Boulder: Westview Press.

Selznick, P. (1952) *The Organizational Weapon*, New York: McGraw-Hill.

Shalom, S.R. (1986) *The United States and the Philippines: a study of neocolonialism*, Quezon City: New Day Publishers.

Skocpol, T. (1979) *States and Social Revolutions*, Cambridge: Cambridge University Press.

Slater, D. (1997) 'Spatial Politics/Social Movements. Questions of (b)orders and resistance in global times', in S. Pile and M. Keith (eds) *Geographies of Resistance*, London: Routledge, 258–76.

Smith, J. and Johnston, H. (eds) (2002) *Globalization and Resistance: transnational dimensions of social movements*, Landham: Rowman and Littlefield.

Snow, D.A. and Benford, R.D. (1988) 'Ideology, frame resonance, and participant mobilization', in B. Klandermans, H. Kriesi and S. Tarrow (eds) *From Structure to Action: comparing social movements research across international social movements*, vol. 1, Greenwich, CT: JAI, 197–218.

—— (1992) 'Master frames and cycles of protest', in A.D. Morris and C. McClurg Mueller (eds), *Frontiers in Social Movement Theory*, New Haven: Yale University Press, 133–55.

Swidler, A. (1986) 'Culture in action: symbols and strategies', *American Sociological Review*, 51: 273–86.

Tarrow, S. (1994) *Power in Movement*, Cambridge: Cambridge University Press.

—— (2005) *The New Transnational Activism*, Cambridge: Cambridge University Press.

Tarrow, S. and Della Porta, D. (2005) 'Conclusion: "Globalization", Complex Internationalism, and Transnational Contention', in D. Della Porta and S. Tarrow (eds) *Transnational Protest and Global Activism*, Lanham: Rowman and Littlefield, 227–46.

Thompson, E.P. (1978) *The Theory of Poverty*, New York: Monthly Review Press.

Tilly, C. (1978) *From Mobilization to Revolution*, Reading: Addison-Wesley.

Turner, S. and Caouette, D. (2009) Agrarian angst: rural resistance in Southeast Asia. *Geography Compass*, 3.

Turner, S. and Michaud, J. (2008) 'Imaginative and adaptive economic strategies for Hmong livelihoods in Lào Cao province, Northern Vietnam', *Journal of Vietnamese Studies*, 3 (3): 158–90.

Walker, R.B.J. (1994) 'Social movements / world politics', *Millennium*, 23 (3): 669–700.

Weekley, K. (1996) 'From vanguard to rearguard: the theoretical roots of the crisis in the Communist Party of the Philippines', in Abinales, P.N. (ed.) *The Revolution Falters: the Left in the Philippines, after 1986*, Southeast Asia Program Series No.15, Southeast Asia Program Publications, Cornell University: 28–59.

Weiner, J. and Glaskin, K. (2006) 'The (re-)invention of indigenous laws and customs', *Asia Pacific Journal of Anthropology*, 7: 1–13.

Weiss, M.L. (2006) *Protest and Possibilities: Civil Society and Coalitions for Political Change in Malaysia*, Stanford: Stanford University Press.

Weller, R.P. (2005) *Civil Life, Globalization, and Political Change in Asia: organizing between family and state*, London: Routledge.

White, C.P. (1986) 'Everyday resistance, socialist revolution and rural development: the Vietnamese case', *Journal of Peasant Studies*, 13 (2): 49–63.

Wickham-Crowley, T. (1992) *Guerrillas and Revolution in Latin America: a comparative study of insurgents and regimes since 1956*, Princeton: Princeton University Press.

Wolf, E.R. (1966) *Peasants*, Englewood Cliffs: Prentice Hall.

—— (1969) *Peasant Wars of the Twentieth Century*, New York: Harper and Row.

Yashar, D.J. (2005) *Contesting Citizenship in Latin America: the rise of indigenous movements and the postliberal challenge*, Cambridge: Cambridge University Press.

—— (2007) 'Resistance and identity politics in an age of globalization', *The Annals of the American Academy of Political and Social Science*, 610: 160–81.

3 'Weapons of the week': Selective resistance and agency among the Hmong in northern Vietnam

Sarah Turner and Jean Michaud

Over centuries, members of the Hmong[1] ethnic minority in the northern highland Vietnam province of Lào Cai, in spite of their relative political weakness in the face of numerous and powerful kingdoms and empires surrounding them, have managed to have their say concerning when and how they accept to engage with the local and regional economy (Figure 3.1). This group has resisted transformations that do not fit with their line of thinking and reasoning, while adapting to others that they found appropriate. In making these choices, they did not necessarily follow the rational norm of liberal economic thought, but instead lived by – just like they still do today – the needs and culturally embedded judgments of their households and lineages. This is a lineage-based, acephalous ethnic group that has dealt with the hegemonic power of dominant civilizations – Han, Siamese, Lao and Kinh (lowland Vietnamese) to name a few – and which has not only survived to this day, but has also learnt ways to deal successfully with these uneasy partners over the long term.

While the Hmong in Vietnam are aware that they do not have the power to significantly alter the larger economic shifts occurring in the country – especially as Vietnam opens up to increasing global forces with the introduction of the economic renovation in the mid-1980s – they are nevertheless anything but the passive, ignorant and powerless actors that many states in the region relentlessly portray them as. The Hmong have worked with an array of economic opportunities that have come their way through time, from opium production in the colonial era, to transforming textiles for tourism as the country opened up to foreign visitors, to cultivating cardamom for a rising Chinese market demand. As such, they are adept at modulating their economic balance and their activities to tap the demands of the moment in order to gain extra cash income to supplement the subsistence side of their livelihoods.

Hmong decisions regarding which choices to implement and which to discard depend on a particular blend of local agents, cultures, history and the opportunities that arise at any precise moment. This flexibility and adaptiveness leads them to short- and mid-term strategies which we have nicknamed their 'weapons of the week' in a tongue-in-cheek reference to James Scott's

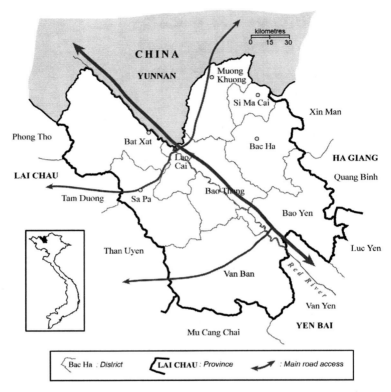

Figure 3.1 Lào Cai province, Northern Vietnam.

Map credit: Jean Michaud

book title (1985). It leads us to ask the following questions. How have Hmong become active in contemporary trade networks in these highlands? How do they utilize their culture and experience to modulate their involvement in these and, by extension, in the local and regional economy? Given these trade opportunities, how do they avoid – perhaps even resist – unwanted levels of dependency on the market? In this chapter we examine the trade of two goods in the province more closely, namely textiles and medicinal cardamom. We argue that the Hmong selectively decide the degree of their market integration, thus resisting in their own, original ways unwanted levels of dependency on the market.[2]

Hmong in northern Vietnam

About five centuries ago Han Chinese started migrating en masse to the mountain ranges of China's southwest (Giersch 2006). This advance, along with major social turbulence in southern China in the eighteenth and nineteenth centuries, caused many minorities from the mountains in the Chinese provinces of Sichuan, Guizhou, Hunan, Guangxi and Yunnan to migrate further south. Among these, many Hmong settled in the ranges of the Indochina Peninsula to practise subsistence agriculture, often in combination with opium poppy cultivation (Culas and Michaud 2004). Among their new homes was present-day northern Vietnam, where it has been demonstrated that they settled from at least the late 1700s (Michaud and Turner 2003).

In the first half of the 1800s, just before the beginning of the French conquest, northern Vietnam could be broadly schematically divided into three habitat zones (Condominas 1978). First, at the highest levels on the mountain peaks and ridges bordering China, forming the stratum above 1,000 metres, lived members of the Hmong and Yao societies. The political organization of these highlanders, who were partially sedentary, was based on kinship and, to a lesser extent, neighbourhood. Second, there was an intermediary zone of well-irrigated plateaus, foothills and high river valleys. These were inhabited by groups from the Tai linguistic family, linked together in a weakly centralized feudal system, with local chiefs maintaining a great deal of political latitude. Third, in the tier below 500 metres, comprising the Red River delta and its fertile plains, lived the majority of the country's population, namely the Kinh, who defined and formed the imperial Nation. The Kinh lived under a strong, centralized, imperial regime equipped with an extensive administration of Chinese tradition run by an educated elite, the mandarins.

What is interesting for our case here is the fact that the most numerous and most powerful direct neighbours of the Hmong and Yao highlanders were Tai-speaking sedentary peasants living in the intermediary stratum, today's Thái, Tày, Nùng and Giày, plus a few smaller groups. Organized into feudal, *muang*-style chiefdoms, the Tai-speaking lords of the middle region had numerous reasons to let new populations settle in the highlands, and perhaps even invited them to do so (Condominas 1976). In terms of economic complementarity, Hmong and Yao highlanders provided Tai-speaking merchants with highland forest products, which the latter then resold for a profit in the midland markets or sold to wholesalers from the lowlands. In terms of security, the highlanders filled a useful role on the outskirts of the Tai fiefdoms where they served as a first line of defence. These terms of trade show interesting parallels to recent commercial activities, as we will see shortly.

During the colonial period in Tonkin (1883–1954), as the French called the Red River Delta and its periphery, a number of Hmong opted to join the Vietnamese nationalists and the communists, while others tended to side with the French (McAlister 1967). Consequently, after the Việt Minh victory, a number of pro-French Hmong migrated to Laos and South Vietnam, while those remaining had to accept to live under socialist rule. Since 1954, and with renewed enthusiasm since the country was reunified in 1975, the Vietnamese state has been dedicated to incorporating all highland societies into the Việt Nation, the communist state, and the national economy (Michaud 2000). This has been undertaken in part by extending infrastructure, providing national education in the Vietnamese language, and reorganizing the economy of the highlands, all trends that are perceptible in Lào Cai province.

Today, the northern provinces of Vietnam are home to the largest populations of highland 'minority nationalities' (*các dân tộc thiểu số*) in the country. According to the 1999 national census, in Lào Cai province exactly two-thirds of the population are ethnic minorities, namely 395,000 individuals out of a total provincial population of 594,000 (Socialist Republic of Vietnam 1999). Of this number, 123,778 Hmong form one of the largest single non-Kinh groups.

Even though the Kinh make up only 15 per cent of the population in Sa Pa district (Socialist Republic of Vietnam 1999), they far outnumber the highland minorities on the local People's Committees.[3] Consequently, local political decisions infrequently convey highlander opinions. This reflects, in part, an ongoing highland/lowland ideological divide characterized by the Kinh generally considering the ethnic minority inhabitants of the highlands to be 'backward' (Hickey 1993; van de Walle and Gunewardena 2001; Sowerwine 2004). As a consequence, there exists a two-tier local economy in which Kinh traders, supported by the local authorities, dominate a growing commercial scene, while the culturally distinct highlanders, without any real support in the state apparatus, tend to maintain food production to meet their domestic needs, with complementary commercial exchanges.

Indeed, historically, the majority of Hmong in northern Vietnam were horticulturists, practising pioneering and rotational swiddening, with only a residual number taking up wet rice agriculture.[4] Commerce played a necessary, albeit secondary role in their general livelihoods that focused instead on agriculture, hunting and the gathering of forest products; in addition, from the 1800s, opium production became an important commercial part of Hmong livelihoods. Under pressure from the Vietnamese state, most Hmong have now become sedentarized and are integrating into commercial circuits via selected modern agricultural practices, such as using chemical inputs in their fields and selling some of their produce on the market. The Hmong in Sa Pa district today tend to practise what could be called composite agriculture, a mixture of permanent rice paddy fields, rotating swidden plots and tree gardens (Leisz *et al.* 2004).

Đổi mới, the economic renovation that was decreed in 1986 and implemented over the following years, ended 30 years of collectivization in the north of the country (also discussed in Tran Thi Thu Trang's chapter). Nevertheless, even lowland Vietnamese officials admit that collectivization in the highlands was only ever partially successful due to this area's remoteness. Yet the gradual removal of the cooperative system was accompanied by two other transformations in the region's economic balance that impacted directly on the highland economy in Lào Cai. First, the state introduced a ban on forest cutting to sell wood or to set up new farming areas. Second, there was a nationwide ban introduced on the growing of opium for commercial purposes. Both decisions were formulated in 1992 and decreed in 1993 as part of a larger debate that led to the implementation of the 1993 Land Act, which gave back a partial right to peasants to own land and its products. In tandem, these events caused a noteworthy decrease in the commercial revenues able to be obtained by Hmong, reducing the vitality of the monetary segment of their livelihoods that had until that time relied for the most part on the sale of opium and wood. Nonetheless, there are now a few new channels that a small but significant number of Hmong have chosen to draw upon to maintain access to cash incomes. These include textile production and medicinal cardamom cultivation, the focus of our chapter.

Two highland trade networks

A variety of examples could have been used here to make our point regarding Hmong market integration dynamics and resistance. Alcohol production from rice and corn, flower growing, forms of wage work and so on, are rich in explanatory potential. Opium production and sale, for instance, although now a thing of the past, was a quasi-universal cash crop – nearly a currency – with far-reaching implications and it could have also supplied enlightening answers. For the purposes of this chapter, however, we have selected the more local, small-scale activities of textile reproduction and cardamom cultivation because both are instructive in illuminating key elements of contemporary Hmong market involvement that we wish to focus upon here. Namely, in their current shape, these evolving commercial endeavours help highlight both a sense of economic opportunism and a capacity among the Hmong to adapt to new trade relationships and rules. They also draw attention to the resistance that Hmong involved in these trades have to becoming further involved in ways that go 'against the grain' of their own culturally embedded livelihood practices.

Hmong textile (re)production

As well as the agricultural and household activities that dominate their time, Hmong women in Sa Pa district, Lào Cai province customarily produce hemp clothes, shown in Figure 3.2. Dyed dark blue with home-grown indigo and embroidered by themselves, the creation of these clothes for family members is a time and labour intensive activity. After planting and harvesting the hemp, the women process, spin and then weave it. This was historically done on a back-strap loom, while now a portable loom is sometimes used. The final additions to these clothes are intricately embroidered symbolic motifs that often represent traditional activities and daily life (Mai Thanh Son 1999).

Since international tourism has begun to develop again in the Northern highlands after restrictions were removed in 1993 (Lloyd 2003), there has been a growing demand in Lào Cai district – and especially in the market towns of Sa Pa and Bắc Hà – for textiles produced and embroidered by

Figure 3.2 Hmong women, wearing indigo-dyed, hemp clothes, trading goods on the streets of Sa Pa.

Photo credit: Sarah Turner

Hmong women, particularly from overseas tourists. While there are now at least three different textile trade networks incorporating both Hmong and others into their flows to meet these growing tourist demands (see Turner 2007; Turner and Michaud 2008), the one that we concentrate on here is that which brings together Hmong and Kinh traders in the greatest numbers, for the most closely knit interactions. This network has, as its final product, the creation of 'ethnic' wall hangings and cushion covers, textile products that include small patches of Hmong – and sometimes Yao – embroidery sewn onto larger pieces of backing fabric, shown in Figure 3.3.[5] This trade network begins when Kinh and Tày shopkeepers in Sa Pa town recruit Hmong women who are walking to the nearby market, to complete some embroidery for them. The women who take up this offer then embroider small patches of cloth as per their own designs (shown in Figure 3.3) while keeping to the general shape required by the shop owners. The highlander women are provided with the threads and fabric to do this by the shopkeepers, who obtain supplies from central sources in the lowlands. When the patches are complete – it takes about two days for a Hmong woman to finish the embroidery of five

Figure 3.3 Kinh shopkeeper and Hmong negotiating over small embroidery patches, with finished pieces decorating the shop, Sa Pa.
Photo credit: Sarah Turner

patches – these are then returned to the shopkeepers and the Hmong are paid, the rate in 2009 being VND 30,000 (just under US $2) for five small patches of about five square centimetres each. At times, the Hmong women also ask for an advance from the shopkeepers to buy small goods in the market-place. These loans are commonly repaid within two to three days with the completion of a set of patches.

The shopkeepers in turn hire female Kinh and sometimes Tày sewers to complete the finished goods, sewing the patches on to cotton backings to make wall hangings or cushion covers. These labourers are located not only in Sa Pa, but also in Hà Nội. The owner of one such wholesaling operation, Anh, a Tày woman from Văn Bàn district to the south of Sa Pa, has three wholesale locations in Sa Pa, and has Tày and Kinh women sewing the goods together in Sa Pa as well as about fifteen more women working in Hà Nội. From Hà Nội these goods are then distributed to shops around the city as well as to other urban locales further afield including Hué and Hồ Chí Minh City. Anh also has customers from overseas, usually tourists, who come to her store about once a year to purchase large amounts of these goods to then resell them in overseas locations including Thailand, the United States and France.

Since no Hmong keep accounting records and their semi-subsistence livelihoods introduce a range of complex factors, it is virtually impossible to determine the *profits* that they make from this trade, but we can say something about their *income*. As noted above, in 2009 women embroidering these patches were being paid about VND 30,000 for completing five small patches, about two days' work. In contrast, the completed commodities – usually including five or more of these patches sewn on heavy cotton backgrounds – are sold by Kinh and Tày shopkeepers for anywhere between US $20 and US $40. While shop rents are considered high in Sa Pa town (US $200–300 a month) compared to the local standard, this still results in an important difference when we compare the financial rewards obtained by the Hmong embroiderers and those of the shopkeepers selling the final products.

One should note though, that the Kinh and Tày shopkeepers remain reliant on these Hmong women's skills, as the former do not have the talent to embroider the patterns that attract tourists' eyes as carefully or as quickly, nor are they willing to be paid so little. One would therefore think that the Hmong women had the ability to negotiate prices – and indeed they do maintain some leeway – but overall, this is slim as there are usually other Hmong women interested in trying their hand at this trade, albeit not always for long. Consequently, the Tày and Kinh shopkeepers maintain control over prices and, at the end of the day, these shopkeepers add the largest profit margin to the price of the final goods. Thus, while actively involving highlanders, this trade network has been initiated, organized and controlled by Tày and Kinh entrepreneurs who are in an advantageous position regarding easier access to spatially diverse trading networks, infrastructure and financial capital (cf. Long and Villarreal 1998). The involvement of Tày entrepreneurs here – historically powerful direct neighbours and overlords of the Hmong – has interesting historical parallels.

Do the Hmong women embroiderers want to become more involved in these trade network opportunities? Do they wish to increase their production or enter into more regular arrangements with the Kinh and Tày entrepreneurs? Or are they resisting becoming more involved in this economic opportunity; and if so, why? We will return to these questions shortly . . .

Cardamom cultivation

The second trade network we investigate here concerns cardamom (*Amomum aromaticum*), an understory, rhizomatous herb used for medicinal purposes, primarily by the Chinese. Increasingly since the mid-1980s – although there is evidence that such trade existed during colonial times between Yao cultivators and the French in Sa Pa (Sowerwine 2004) – Hmong households with the resources to be able to, have begun to cultivate cardamom for not only their own use, but for sale as well. Those who undertake this cultivation tend to live in areas closer to mature forests which provide the cardamom with the shade and other conditions necessary to reach maturity. Hmong are now not only harvesting wild cardamom but are increasingly cultivating it by maintaining more intensively planted plots in the forest. This cultivated cardamom yields much greater returns than that collected from the wild, with one hectare of cultivated cardamom yielding up to 50 kilograms (kg) of dry fruit (Aubertin 2004).

Cardamom harvesting occurs from September to October each year. It is at this time that many Hmong will be visited by Kinh and a few Giày intermediaries who will ask if they wish to sell their crop to them.[6] At times, promises of crops to be delivered in the future mean that Hmong households can obtain credit in advance from such intermediaries, a practice that is taken up by poorer households running short on rice just before the cardamom harvest. This, however, does not necessarily work to the Hmong households' advantage in the long term as they tend to receive low prices for their harvests. These intermediaries are sometimes shopkeepers who live in the predominantly Hmong villages, who are therefore in a strong position to gain crops from local Hmong due to their familiarity.[7] Other intermediaries come from Sa Pa to visit a number of hamlets or, when harvest time occurs, will wait on the access roads close to Sa Pa town to entice Hmong – heading to wholesalers in Sa Pa – to sell to them instead.

These wholesalers form the third node of this trade network, purchasing cardamom either directly from Hmong who come to town, but more commonly from the Giày and Kinh intermediaries. They then transport the cardamom to further wholesalers in Lào Cai City on the Chinese border, with only a small amount of cardamom staying in Sa Pa town to be sold by local shopkeepers in the market, predominantly to lowland Kinh tourists. Kinh wholesalers in Lào Cai city then transport the cardamom across the border to Chinese wholesalers in the border town of Hekou. From there the cardamom commonly travels on to processors in Kunming, the capital of Yunnan province. The cardamom is then sold to traders within China, as well as exported to predominantly East Asian consumer countries (see Schoenberger and Turner 2008; Tugault-Lafleur and Turner 2009).

As with the textile trade networks, it is difficult to unravel the financial rewards gained by different individuals in these cardamom trade networks. Between 2006 and 2009, the market price for cardamom averaged VND 60,000–80,000/kg (US $4–5/kg).[8] While some Hmong households reported selling small quantities of cardamom, around 20 kg each year – with one Hmong man stating that he was really only keeping the cardamom plots active for his son to inherit – a few were cultivating up to 150 kg a year. The average yearly crop for those interviewed however, was approximately 70–100 kg, equivalent to about VND 5.6 million (US $350) per family.

In turn, Kinh and Giày village-based intermediaries reported collecting between 1 and 5 tons of cardamom from Hmong cultivators in one season. They worked to earn a return of VND 5,000 (or US $0.30) a kilogram, and were therefore earning approximately VND 5 million (or US $312) per ton of cardamom bought and sold, minus transportation costs.[9] Kinh cardamom wholesalers based in Sa Pa town, buying cardamom from various intermediaries, demonstrated even higher financial returns. These wholesalers annually collected between 20 and 35 tons of cardamom. Working with the same returns as the intermediaries of VND 5,000/kg (US \$0.30), they could make up to US \$10,500. From this income, however, the wholesalers deducted costs associated with transportation and other transaction outlays. Nevertheless, some wholesalers have been able to purchase a jeep after a few years in this business, a commodity that Hmong cultivators have yet to think possible from their own returns.

In sum, Kinh cardamom wholesalers derive the greatest returns from this trade, with an average income at least ten to twenty times greater than that earned by Hmong cultivators. Yet do the Hmong want to become further involved in these trade networks? Do they wish to take up the international trade opportunities this commodity offers? We turn to such questions next.

Selective resistance and agency

What do these case studies reveal of the selective resistance and agency of the Hmong individuals and households involved? Focusing on the Hmong women textile embroiderers, what is directly relevant to our argument here is the fact that those women whom we interviewed were *not* keen to become involved further in these operations. They did not wish to embroider more often, nor did they want to have more formalized arrangements with the shopkeepers. The women explained to us that they were sewing these pieces because it gave them something to do as they sat on the side of the road attempting to sell goods to passer-by tourists, or in the Sa Pa town market if they had a stall there. The returns gave them extra funds with which they could make small purchases of household consumption items such as salt, monosodium glutamate, cooking oil, sesame seed cakes and medicine. This type of work was also a welcome change from back-breaking labour in their fields, often in climatic extremes. Nevertheless, these women made it clear that when the periods of more intensive agricultural labour demands came, they would always turn to these first, with work in the rice fields always being given priority. Additionally these women noted that, while they could continue this embroidery in their hamlets, if changing family circumstances such as a child's illness were to occur, then they would forgo these economic returns if necessary. Certainly the Kinh and Tày shopkeepers complained of unreliable supplies, often trying to stockpile embroideries.

Such decisions suggest to us that the Hmong women involved in these textile trade networks are being selective in their decision-making regarding whether to enter this trade or not, and to what degree if they do, often making choices that would seem economically unsound according to Western ideals of commercial success. While this group of Hmong women embroidering patches has become increasingly involved in a commercial activity in the town, theirs is a selective involvement. Many of the women stated that they thought their current levels of involvement in this trade were sufficient, and they had no desire to get involved in the more complex interactions that were available to them. These women repeatedly explained to us that they believed that any greater involvement would result in the shopkeepers coming to have greater expectations that the Hmong women would work to more specific standards, as well as increasing pressure to complete the goods within specified time periods. The Hmong women, rather strategically, were not interested in these types of negotiations, preferring their current ways.

By the same token, despite the fact that there are important cash returns to be gained from cardamom cultivation for Hmong compared to other cash sources available to them, not all families were interested in becoming involved in such a relatively lucrative trade. Time and again what stood out in interviews was the importance, above all else, of rice production in their livelihood portfolios, followed by having one or more buffalo to plough their rice fields. Cardamom production never outranked or came close to these as a priority (although it could certainly be an asset towards the purchase of a buffalo if cardamom returns were especially good in a certain year). Furthermore, cardamom cultivation is physically demanding work, requiring long periods away from the hamlet during the harvest period, which not all Hmong men were willing or necessarily able to do.[10] In addition, many of the plots where interviewees harvested cardamom were within the boundaries of the Hoàng Liên National Park, established in 2002. This area, patrolled by local park authorities, is legally off-limits for the harvesting of any forest product, as well as the chopping of timber, which Hmong cardamom cultivators do to prepare fires to dry the fruit *in situ* since the dried product is far lighter to transport. As such, the Hmong were well aware of the risks that they faced in this trade, some deciding for the better against it, while others maintained a limited involvement that suited their broader livelihood portfolio needs.

All told, within the Hmong package of livelihood diversification strategies are a multitude of reasons to engage in (or disengage from) specific approaches at one time or another. The perspectives of these Hmong support Long's argument that

> producers and agricultural workers sometimes fear that, if they become too heavily committed to outside markets and institutions, then critical interests can be threatened or marginalised. People may show strong allegiance to existing lifestyles, and to the defence of local forms of knowledge.
>
> (Long 2001: 228)

Thus, while a group of Hmong women and men had decided to take up certain trade opportunities, they were also content to 'give it a miss' when responsibilities they judged more fundamental called, when other activities were prioritized, or when the risks seemed too great. They maintained a selective involvement in trades that comprised only a few elements among the pluriactivity of their livelihoods. They resist in their own, innovative ways, becoming involved in the market beyond an extent that meets their own culturally rooted judgements.

If we place these decisions into an historical perspective, we notice that these trade networks and flexible livelihood approaches have known earlier embodiments. These include the growing of the opium poppy and trading of the raw product to European colonial powers from the late eighteenth century, the selling of rare timber and specific forest products to the Chinese and Vietnamese, and the trade of hemp textiles to French colonial visitors in northern Tonkin from the late nineteenth century. In turn, these reflected a niche strategy based on the particular ecosystem they inhabited and the specialist 'know-how' they had developed there.

Opium trading and rare timber extraction are no longer legally possible. Yet we contend – based on evidence from oral histories and interviews – that the same niche strategy at play historically has been remembered and is today taking new forms, among which are the sale of reconstituted textiles and cardamom, as Hmong adapt creatively to the market openings available to them. What is interesting to note here is the iterative nature of these decision-making processes. By putting their customary skills to work in new economic niches, such as embroidery for tourist crafts, and cultivating a non-timber forest product in response to growing overseas demand, we can unveil adapted, short- or mid-term actions and strategies – the so-called 'weapons of the week' mentioned in our title – that feed on those of the past and adapt in a creative, reactive way to current opportunities against the backdrop of tradition. As in the past, Hmong are taking up opportunities as they see fit. Yet the point here is that they have also previously coped with such opportunities disappearing again and have remained resilient, moving on to new livelihood strategies. This is a pattern that provides hope for future livelihood diversification, if, for instance, the tourist market for embroidered goods was to decline.

Conclusions

But can we conclude that such strategies constitute a form of active, concerted resistance? There have been lively discussions about the notion of 'peasant resistance' in the last three decades. It has been suggested – this time in reaction to the dominant, socio-evolutionary paradigm known as globalization which postulates inexorable economic progress via planetary economic integration – that the reticence of peasants to be caught up in the machine of development could be interpreted not as inertia but rather as a strategy. One of the leading authors of this perspective, Arjun Appadurai, observes that: 'Those social orders and groupings that were apparently passive victims of larger forces of control and domination were nevertheless capable of subtle forms of resistance and "exit" . . . that seemed to be not primordialist in any way' (1996: 145). In other words: resistance as a constructed strategy rather than an atavistic rejection. Indeed, despite the possible economic opportunities, many Hmong in Sa Pa say that they have no desire or need to turn away from largely subsistence-based agricultural activities in order to invest in market-oriented production. As Rigg (1997) has noted, developing on Scott (1976), peasant households of Southeast Asia generally prefer to develop a mixed economy based on agricultural production complemented by a few subsidiary business activities rather than to abandon agricultural production altogether for sudden business opportunities, even if the latter seem promising (Michaud 1994, 1997). In the same vein as Popkin (1979: 9) noted when observing Vietnamese peasants, trade expansion is often considered a last resort for Hmong farmers, deemed to be less reliable than the customary means of reproduction. One conclusion that can be drawn from our discussions with the Hmong in Sa Pa district therefore is that there appears to be a concerted refusal to become too committed to commercial activities.

Clearly, this should not be interpreted as meaning that the Hmong are not interested in taking up innovations that could contribute to improving their livelihoods. Technological novelties for agriculture such as new crops, improved seeds and chemical fertilizers, electricity in the house, better roads, or acquiring motorbikes for easier and faster transportation to the marketplace all have much appeal to them. Our point here is not so rudimentary as to suggest that material improvement is plainly turned down in order to protect cultural integrity; it is rather that the *process of selection* of these novelties seems to be infused with a will to maintain, protect and promote cultural integrity, not merely to improve one's capacity to show wealth and consume goods. Some apparently irrational choices such as persisting in producing one's carefully embroidered hemp clothes, a time-consuming activity when cheap cotton and nylon alternatives are readily available on the market, are not the result of a poor understanding of the market economy. Such actions nicely drive home the point that it is not only profit generation that guides economic strategies and livelihoods.

Wolf (1955), defending the thesis of commerce as a last resort some 50 years ago, observed that production based on market demands was only developed in peasant societies when they could no longer meet their economic and cultural needs through customary institutions. If this affirmation is true, it would seem that the Hmong in Sa Pa district have not yet reached the point of no return. This refusal can be seen as peasant resistance on a micro scale, what Scott (1985) referred to in the title of his book as 'The weapons of the weak: everyday forms of peasant resistance', a concept that was also suggested by Tapp (2001: 25, 37) in his analysis of modernization among Chinese Hmong.

Likewise, Pile and Keith (1997) contend that

> the term resistance draws attention not only to the myriad spaces of political struggles, but also to the politics of everyday spaces, through which political identities constantly flow and fix. These struggles do not

have to be glamorous or heroic, about fighting back and opposition, but *may subsist in enduring, in refusing to be wiped off the map of history.*

(Pile and Keith 1997: xi, emphasis added)

The resistance of the Hmong in Vietnam is based on centuries of proximity, quarrels, political and economic exploitation, rebellion, invasion, war, genocide and flight. It is entirely possible that societies that have been put to the test in these ways have reacted by forging an attitude of resistance to assimilation and domination, a form of collective self-defence rooted in their knowledge of their comparative political weakness. Their resistance is not one of force, since this has demonstrated its futility when faced with opponents who are much stronger, but rather is one of a more or less explicit refusal to cooperate. As Scott describes for the village of 'Sedaka' in Malaysia, here too in Lào Cai province we find 'forms of resistance that reflect the conditions and constraints under which they are generated' (Scott 1985: 242).

As is so often the case, however, local wisdom can expertly shrink complex equations into remarkably lucid statements. Bee, a young Hmong woman, explained to us in Sa Pa: 'Hmong People are concerned with having a good number of rice fields, a nice house and lots of animals rather than money. That's what's important to us. And money can bring you trouble anyway' (30 March 2007). Reflecting upon Bee's comment, we would suggest that the 'failure' of the Hmong to become even more involved in the trades explored here should be interpreted as confirmation of a devotion to a selective livelihood model driven more by cultural and social imperatives than by 'the fetishism of the market and the commodity' (Harvey 1990: 423).

Notes

1 Ethnonyms used in this text follow the most widely accepted international usage, based on ethnolinguistic divisions. In Vietnam, however, the Hmong are officially named 'H'mông'; while the Yao are named Dao.

2 This study into the market integration processes and resistances of Hmong individuals and households in Sa Pa district, Lào Cai province, builds upon information gathered from a diverse range of sources over the past 11 years. Informants include traders of Hmong, Yao (Dao), Giày and Vietnamese ethnicities; People's Committee representatives at a range of hierarchical levels and with different ethnic backgrounds, both in Sa Pa district and in the provincial capital, Lào Cai city; and a number of long-term residents in and around Sa Pa including male and female Hmong and Vietnamese. This chapter describes the state of the trade networks as of May 2009.

3 The People's Committee is the local state administration and operates at the province, district and commune levels in rural areas (a different hierarchical structure operates in urban areas). It is responsible for implementing the Constitution, the law, the formal written orders of superior state organizations and the resolutions of the People's Council (see Socialist Republic of Vietnam 1992).

4 For further information on Hmong economic organization and its historical rooting in and around Vietnam, see the collective *Hmong/Miao in Asia* (Tapp *et al.* 2004).

5 While we will focus on Hmong women here, the trade networks for Yao women who do similar embroidery in the same commercial relationship mirror this one.
6 Again here, we see interesting historical parallels with Giày, a group of Tai-speaking sedentary peasants, maintaining a powerful intermediary role.
7 This parallels Scott's (1985) description of seasonal credit practices of shopkeepers in the Malay village of 'Sedaka' before the rice harvest.
8 These prices relate to dried cardamom.
9 The main transportation cost was fuel for their motorbikes, sold at approximately US $0.75 a litre, with about 3 litres to fill up a Honda Dream, a commonly used motorbike in the highlands, alongside Minsks or Chinese copies thereof.
10 This is in part due to cultivators being concerned about the possible theft of their cardamom crops, a factor that results in some sleeping in their fields near harvest time, while others harvest their crops earlier than the optimum growing time (Tugault-Lafleur and Turner 2009).

References

Appadurai, A. (1996) *Modernity at Large: cultural dimensions of globalization*, Minneapolis: University of Minnesota Press.

Aubertin, C. (2004) 'Cardamom (*amomum spp*) in Laos PDR: the hazardous future of an agroforest system product', in K. Kusters and B. Belcher (eds) *Forest Products, Livelihoods and Conservation: case-studies of non-timber forest products systems*, Bogor: CIFOR, 43–60.

Condominas, G. (1976) 'Essai sur l'évolution des systèmes politiques Thais', *Ethnos*, 41: 7–67.

—— (1978) 'L'Asie du Sud-Est', in J. Poirier (ed.) *Ethnologie Régionale 2*, Paris: Gallimard Encyclopédie de la Pléïade.

Culas, C. and Michaud, J. (2004) 'A contribution to the study of Hmong (Miao) migrations and history', in N. Tapp, J. Michaud, C. Culas and G.Y. Lee (eds) *Hmong/Miao in Asia*, Chiang Mai: Silkworm Books, 71–96.

Giersch, C.P. (2006) *Asian Borderlands. The transformation of Qing China's Yunnan Frontier*. Cambridge, MA and London: Harvard University Press.

Harvey, D. (1990) 'Between space and time: reflections on the geographical imagination', *Annals of the Association of American Geographers*, 80: 418–34.

Hickey, G. (1993) *Shattered World: adaptation and survival among Vietnam's highland peoples during the Vietnam War*, Philadelphia: University of Pennsylvania Press.

Leisz, S.J., Nguyễn thị Thu Hà, Nguyễn thị Bích Yến, Nguyễn Thành Lâm and Trần Đức Viện (2004) 'Developing a methodology for identifying, mapping and potentially monitoring the distribution of general farming system types in Vietnam's northern mountain region', *Agricultural Systems*, 85: 340–63.

Lloyd, K. (2003) 'Contesting control in transitional Vietnam: the development and regulation of traveller cafés in Hanoi and Ho Chi Minh City', *Tourism Geographies*, 5 (3): 350–66.

Long, N. (2001) *Development Sociology: actor perspectives*, London, New York: Routledge.

Long, N. and Villareal, M. (1998) 'Small product, big issues: value contestations and cultural identities in cross-border commodity networks', *Development and Change*, 29: 725–50.

McAlister Jr, J.T. (1967) 'Mountain minorities and the Viet Minh: a key to the

Indochina War', in P. Kunstadter (ed.) *Southeast Asian Tribes, Minorities and Nations*, Princeton: Princeton University Press, 771–844.

Mai Thanh Son (1999) *Craft Tradition and Practice: the Hmong of Ta Phin, Sa Pa, Vietnam*, Vietnam: Vietnam Museum of Ethnology and Craft Link.

Michaud, J. (1994) 'Résistance et flexibilité: le changement social et le tourisme dans un village hmong de Thaïlande', unpublished PhD thesis, Université de Montréal.

—— (1997) 'Economic transformation in a Hmong Village of Thailand', *Human Organization*, 56 (2): 222–32.

—— (2000) 'The Montagnards in northern Vietnam from 1802 to 1975: a historical overview from exogenous sources', *Ethnohistory*, 47 (2): 333–68.

Michaud, J. and Turner, S. (2003) 'Tribulations d'un marché de montagne du nord-Vietnam', *Études rurales*, 165: 53–80.

Pile, S. and Keith, M. (1997) 'Preface', in S. Pile and M. Keith (eds) *Geographies of Resistance*, London: Routledge, xi–xiv.

Popkin, S.L. (1979) *The Rational Peasant: the political economy of rural society in Vietnam*, Berkeley: University of California Press.

Rigg, J. (1997) *Southeast Asia: the human landscape of modernization and development*, London: Routledge.

Schoenberger, L. and Turner, S. (2008) 'Negotiating Remote Borderland Access: Small scale trade on the Vietnam-China border', *Development and Change*, 39 (4): 667–96.

Scott, J.C. (1976) *The Moral Economy of the Peasant: rebellion and subsistence in Southeast Asia*, New Haven: Yale University Press.

—— (1985) *Weapons of the Weak: everyday forms of peasant resistance*, New Haven, CT and London: Yale University Press.

Socialist Republic of Vietnam (1992) *Constitution of the Socialist Republic of Vietnam*. Online. Available HTTP: <http://home.vnn.vn/english/government/constitution/> (accessed 12 February 2009).

—— (1999) *Census of Vietnam*, Hanoi: General Statistics Office of Vietnam.

Sowerwine, J.C. (2004) 'The political ecology of Yao (Dzao) landscape transformations: territory, gender and livelihood politics in highland Vietnam', unpublished PhD thesis, University of California, Berkeley.

Tapp, N. (2001) *The Hmong of China: context, agency, and the imaginary*, Leiden: Brill.

Tapp, N., Michaud, J., Culas, C. and Lee, G.Y. (eds) (2004) *Hmong/Miao in Asia*, Chiang Mai: Silkworm Books.

Tugault-Lafleur, C. and Turner, S. (2009) 'The Price of Spice: Ethnic Minority Livelihoods and Cardamom Commodity Chains in Upland Northern Vietnam', *Singapore Journal of Tropical Geography* 30 (3).

Turner, S. (2007) 'Trading old textiles: the selective diversification of highland livelihoods in northern Vietnam', *Human Organization*, 66 (4): 389–404.

Turner, S. and Michaud J. (2008) 'Imaginative and Adaptive Economic Strategies for Hmong Livelihoods in Lào Cai Province, Northern Vietnam', *Journal of Vietnamese Studies*, 3 (3): 154–86.

van de Walle, D. and Gunewardena, D. (2001) 'Sources of ethnic inequality in Viet Nam', *Journal of Development Economics*, 65: 177–207.

Wolf, E.R. (1955) 'Types of Latin American peasantry: a preliminary discussion', *American Anthropologist*, 57: 452–71.

4 'Now the companies have come': Local values and contract farming in northern Thailand

Andrew Walker [1]

Over the past five years the farmers of Baan Tiam, a small lowland village in northern Thailand, have participated in a rapidly changing agricultural sector. By far the most important change has been the adoption and rapid expansion of contract farming. Farmers who previously grew crops on their own account are now commonly entering into contracts with companies to grow crops according to predefined schedules and techniques. The primary driver of this transformation has been the reduction in garlic production, which farmers in Baan Tiam grow independently and sell to traders in an open and non-contractual market. In recent years garlic cultivators have fallen victim to reduced yields and low prices. Yields have suffered as a result of soil nutrient depletion and unfavourable weather, while prices were temporarily depressed by the 2003 bilateral trade agreement between Thailand and China which resulted in an influx of cheap Chinese garlic. The decline in garlic yields and prices have left many farmers with burdensome debts, given that garlic production requires substantial household investment in inputs. In brief, contract farming in Baan Tiam has emerged in a context of environmental and economic uncertainty.

In this chapter I examine the ways in which farmers in Baan Tiam have participated in and responded to this agricultural transformation. Outright resistance to what might be portrayed as a process of rural proletarianization is not on display here. Overall, the arrival of contract farming in Baan Tiam has been welcomed as providing a range of low-risk agricultural alternatives for cultivators. Farmers have actively participated in what is often clumsily described by academic commentators as the 'penetration' of capital into the countryside. Yet the farmers' agency and enthusiasm is not unqualified. Far from it. Farmers draw on an array of values to evaluate and critique their new forms of agricultural practice, and the role of corporate actors in agricultural transformation. Like the chapter by Turner and Michaud in this volume, what we see here are 'subtle transcripts' of resistance, as farmers debate and contest certain elements of agrarian change. The new phase in the commercialization of agriculture intersects with local perceptions about appropriate (and inappropriate) forms of economic activity and ongoing farmer commentary about their changing relationships with the corporate sector. Acts of resistance, as evident in Baan Tiam, need to be understood in terms of a broader 'experimental' orientation to agricultural change.

Baan Tiam is a lowland northern Thai village located about one hour's drive from Thailand's northern 'capital' of Chiang Mai. The village is located in a narrow intermontane valley a few kilometres to the west of the district centre of Pad Siew.[2] In this chapter I focus on about fifty of Baan Tiam's 126 households. These are the households that are actively involved in cash-crop farming. These cash crops are predominantly grown on irrigated paddy fields during the dry season (December to April), while during the wet season most farmers grow a subsistence rice crop. Baan Tiam's residents are also heavily reliant on other economic activities, especially wage labour, government employment and private enterprise.[3]

Transformations in dry-season agriculture

During the dry season of 2002, two crops predominated in Baan Tiam's paddy fields: garlic (56 per cent of the area) and soybeans (33 per cent). A range of other crops were grown on the remaining area: sweetcorn, cabbage, egg-plant, peas and watermelon. Garlic has been cultivated in Baan Tiam for many years, but in the past production was considerably lower. Farmers recall that thirty or so years ago, less than one *rai*[4] in three was planted with garlic. This was because the work was much more labour intensive (ploughing with buffalo rather than using hand-held tractors) and also because a large por-tion of the dry-season fields was devoted to raising cattle. Since then, the extent of garlic production has increased steadily. Many farmers recollect that around ten or fifteen years ago, garlic became the basis for Baan Tiam's relative prosperity. Revenue from garlic funded houses, pickup trucks and children's education. Soybeans have a somewhat more recent history (prob-ably introduced during the 1980s) but, despite their relatively low return, have become a popular crop because of their low input costs, the ease of cultiva-tion, and their soil-restoring properties. Both garlic and soybeans are grown by Baan Tiam farmers on their own account: they purchase all the inputs, manage the cultivation schedule, and sell the produce to private traders. Garlic is often stored in drying sheds behind the farmers' houses while they wait for a favourable price.

However, the 2002 season represented a turning point in dry-season agri-cultural practices. The main factor was the poor garlic yield. Garlic production that year was widely reported to be a failure, and almost all farmers consulted indicated that they had lost money on their crop: 'the heads were small, the leaves were short and the crop developed slowly,' one farmer lamented as he explained his 10,000 baht loss.[5] 'The heads were this big,' a more cheerful farmer joked, holding his hand as if grasping an enormous garlic head. 'But that's five heads,' he added, pointing to each finger in turn to show that the heads were actually little bigger than a fingertip. When surveyed later and asked to subjectively rate their garlic yields, farmers indicated that 70 per cent of plots were 'bad' or 'very bad'. Only one plot was described as returning a 'very good' yield with only two others rated 'good'.[6]

Farmers explained the failure of the garlic crop in various ways. One important reason was climatic variability. Farmers in Baan Tiam have a strong perception that the weather is now departing from its usual patterns. One farmer, Noot, told me that in the past the weather used to be good for agriculture but now it was too unreliable. 'One minute it's cold, then it's raining and then it's hot,' she explained. 'And now hot means very hot, cold is very cold and wet is very wet.' Anan, another garlic farmer, had a different take on climate change. He recalled that ten or twenty years ago it used to be cool in Baan Tiam, unlike in Chiang Mai, where it was unpleasantly hot. 'But now', he said, 'it is hot here too, just like the city.' The cooler weather that was good for garlic could no longer be relied upon, and Anan thought that 'perhaps it is because the forest is all gone'. Farmers' concerns about climatic unreliability were compounded by the unseasonable rainfall in late December 2002. This very unusual dry-season rainfall had resulted in the flooding of low-lying areas of the paddy fields, flattening the garlic and resulting in a negligible yield from the most waterlogged sections. Even in fields above the clearly visible flood line farmers felt that the excessive moisture, combined with unusually warm weather, had reduced yields.

These concerns about unreliable climate were combined with even more potent concerns about the state of Baan Tiam's soil. By the time the garlic crop was harvested, poor soil fertility – rather than excess rain earlier in the season – had become the main talking point. The emerging consensus was that the soil was no good, probably as a result of excessive chemical use over the years, coupled with the low use of natural manure. The relatively long history of intensive garlic production in Baan Tiam – with increasingly heavy inputs of fertilizer, herbicide and pesticide – meant that the paddy soil was now spoilt. The presence of an unknown small red soil mite in some of the plots was, for some, a disconcerting sign of the soil's decline, as was the tendency of many of the garlic plots to take on an unhealthy yellowish hue. As a result of the decline of this basic resource in Baan Tiam, one farmer commented that the agricultural prospects for the village were very bad and the farmers would have to make do with a 'sufficiency economy'.[7]

An external economic factor also contributed to uncertainties about garlic production. In 2003, Thailand entered into a bilateral trade agreement with China which abolished the 30 per cent import duty on agricultural products. In the months leading up to the agreement coming into force there were reports that it would result in a flood of Chinese garlic into the Thai market. It was widely rumoured that this duty-free garlic would be sold in Thailand at a price lower than local production costs. The status of these reports was considerably enhanced when the Thai government announced an adjustment scheme that would make cash payments to farmers who switched their dry-season production from garlic to other crops. Given the trade agreement's 'direct impact' on Thailand's garlic production sector, farmers were asked to register with district agriculture officials, indicating their intention to switch from garlic to other crops (Government of Thailand 2003).[8]

These environmental and economic uncertainties resulted in a significant change in farmers' intentions. In late 2003 I surveyed farmers about which crop they planned to grow in the coming dry season. The move away from garlic was strongly signalled. Almost 40 per cent indicated that they would grow sweetcorn and 15 per cent nominated tobacco. One of the reasons for the popularity of sweetcorn was that two farmers had grown it in 2002 and they had achieved good yields and a reasonable price. A persuasive and well-connected local broker (who was also the assistant village headman) assisted in promoting the new crop, with contracts offering what was seen as a very attractive 3 baht per kilogram. Sweetcorn was also seen as a crop that was easy to grow, requiring minimal labour input or supervision. Tobacco was also attracting some local interest. In part, this was due to the fact that a number of older farmers had grown tobacco in the 1950s and 1960s when there had been a tobacco-drying factory in the district. Oriental, a company from one of the region's major tobacco processing areas, was now seeking tobacco growers to fill orders for export to Europe. Oriental's local extension efforts were managed by a skilled and personable extension agent who had established an elaborate seedling nursery in a village about ten kilometres from Baan Tiam. He had a local production quota of 130 *rai* and was keen to fill it. In addition to those shifting to sweetcorn and tobacco, smaller numbers of farmers indicated that they would grow cabbages, peas, maize, potatoes, eggplants and soybeans under a variety of contract and independent arrangements. Only 9 per cent indicated that they would persevere with garlic.

These intentions were borne out when actual planting decisions were made in the 2003 dry season. As farmers had forecast, there was a strong move to sweetcorn with it taking up 47 per cent of the cultivated area. The second most popular crop was tobacco (24 per cent). Garlic rated a distant third (13 per cent), followed by potatoes (8 per cent), soybeans (5 per cent) and a few plots of cabbages, beans and Chinese parsley. The newfound popularity of sweetcorn was underlined when 14 farmers grew it as a second dry-season crop.

However, the experiment in sweetcorn produced mixed results. Twelve farmers considered the yield to be 'bad' or 'very bad', nine considered it to be 'average' and only six thought it was 'good' or 'very good'. Apart from the yield, farmers also complained about the low price paid by the company as a result of the low grade of the corn. The story for tobacco was rather different. Only one farmer considered the yield to be 'bad', nine considered it 'average' and four considered it 'good'. This did not amount to a strong endorsement but the returns were sufficiently attractive to consolidate interest in tobacco as a contract crop. Interestingly, the picture for garlic was also relatively positive. One farmer considered the yield 'bad', eight considered it 'average' and two considered it 'good'.

The dry season of 2004 showed signs of both reversion and innovation. After the experiments of the previous year, contract farming of sweetcorn was completely abandoned. This year the major crop was tobacco, which covered 42 per cent of the cultivated area. Baan Tiam had become Oriental's most important production site in the district, filling about 60 per cent of the company's local quota. The next two most popular crops in Baan Tiam were the old favourites: garlic (29 per cent) and soybeans (19 per cent). Reversion to garlic was encouraged by the improved yields of 2003 and also by indications that the price impact of the trade agreement with China would be short-lived. The balance of 10 per cent was made up of a diverse range of crops: cabbages, chillies, eggplants, strawberries, tomatoes and peanuts. One farmer even grew a dry-season crop of rice, given that he had lost much of his wet-season due to flooding.

The patterns that had emerged in 2004 were consolidated in 2005. Garlic continued its comeback, becoming once again the most popular crop. As the village headman commented to me, 'No crop has a good price like garlic.' Yet with 37 per cent of the cultivated area, it was less dominant than it had been in 2002 (56 per cent). Furthermore, it is unlikely to attract this level of interest again given the contract farming options that have now won considerable local acceptance. Tobacco also maintained its importance, though the area cultivated (23 per cent) was less than in the previous year. Soybeans remained a valued standby for farmers wanting a low-cost, low-input and soil-restoring crop (19 per cent). There was also ongoing experimentation with other crops, in particular cabbages (8 per cent), Japanese melons (4 per cent) and eggplants (3 per cent). The area devoted to eggplants was small, but it was a high labour input and high value contract crop that was attracting the interest of some of the village's most influential farmers. The areas of land devoted to minor crops such as those shown in Figure 4.1 may appear economically insignificant but these are important testing grounds for what might be 'the next big thing'.

An alternative to debt

Within the academic community contract farming has attracted mixed reviews. A strong body of critical literature points to its negative social and environmental impacts (see, for example, Carney 1988; Clapp 1988; Little and Watts 1994; Miller 1995; Dolan 2001, 2002; Shiva 2004; Ortiz and Aparicio 2006). For these critics contract farming often amounts to a barely disguised form of proletarianization, whereby the seemingly reciprocal agreement of the contract masks the extraction of surplus and the extension of capital's control into the agricultural labour process. As corporate agriculture inserts farmers into global commodity markets, local social and economic systems are strained to breaking point: contract farming undermines the production of subsistence crops; intra-household conflict erupts as members compete for contract revenue, unbound from pre-existing norms governing the distribution of subsistence crops; resource rights of vulnerable household and

Figure 4.1 Applying fertilizer to a contract bean crop. Small areas of land devoted to minor crops are important testing grounds for what might be 'the next big thing'.

Photo credit: Andrew Walker

community members are undermined as land and labour is drawn into new spheres of production; and inequality increases when companies contract with more affluent farmers who have capital to invest in the production process. Environmental degradation is said to be another of contract farming's legacies as it promotes chemical intensive mono-cropping and reduces farmers' ability to plan independently for sustainable land use.

While not necessarily denying some of these impacts, other commentators adopt a more benign, and even favourable, view of contract farming (see for example, Netting *et al.* 1989; Key and Runsten 1999; Warning and Key 2002; Ornberg 2003; Sununtar *et al.* 2005; Finnis 2006). This alternative perspective tends to situate contract farming, and the expansion of cash-crop agriculture more generally, within a framework of household adaptation. As households respond to demographic pressures, market uncertainty and environmental change, contract farming represents a livelihood option that can result in guaranteed access to market outlets, enhanced local incomes and higher levels of agricultural employment. Contract farming can also make up for institutional deficiencies in the agricultural sector, providing farmers with more accessible (albeit often relatively high-cost) forms of credit and insurance against the risk of crop failure. Agricultural corporations and their local brokers can also be important sources of technical advice and innovation in production techniques. While accounts of rural proletarianization may suggest labour force deskilling, in fact the technical demands of corporations and increasingly specific consumer preferences can increase the complexity and sophistication of the agricultural labour process.

It is not my intention in this case study to make an objective assessment of the impact of contract farming in Baan Tiam. I am primarily concerned with farmers' subjective responses to it. It is useful, however, to spend some time focusing specifically on the economic motivations for the adoption of contract farming. To the extent that there is any agreement emerging from the ongoing debate about contract farming it is that both the reasons for contract farming's adoption and its socio-economic and environmental impacts are location specific (Porter and Phillips-Howard 1997). Some sense of this specificity can be gained from examining the key driver of the adoption of contract farming in Baan Tiam.

At the heart of recent agricultural transformations in Baan Tiam is the problem of agricultural debt. A common statement summing up the recent economic dilemma of garlic production is 'the more we work the poorer we get'. Garlic is a high-cost crop. Part of the reason for this is that new seed stock has to be purchased each year. Farmers consistently claim that using their own garlic production as a source of seed stock results in very low yields. On top of this initial cost, garlic production has increasingly required substantial applications of fertilizer, pesticide, and sometimes fungicide. If yields are good these costs are readily covered, but declining yields in the early 2000s left many farmers with substantial debts. Of course, garlic production is not the only source of indebtedness but it has been a very significant contributing factor. It is not uncommon for dry-season cultivators to report debts of between 50,000 and 100,000 baht, with some notable cases reporting debts over 200,000 baht. Baan Tiam's headman, who had compiled some data on the issue for an official poverty alleviation scheme, told me that there was a total of around 10 million baht of debt within the village (an average of about 80,000 baht per household). In an economy where the average payment for one day's employment is around 120 baht, these debts represent very substantial financial challenges and they are a key source of anxiety, and some resentment.

One farmer eloquently recounted his tale of impoverishment (leaving out the minor detail of the busy rice mill located behind his house). When he first came to Baan Tiam to marry a local woman about twenty years ago he grew garlic and made good profits. Eventually he saved enough to buy a pickup with a 'cab', but his profits started to decline and he sold the large vehicle and bought a more modest standard pickup. Still further economic troubles, combined with a rather expensive extramarital liaison, forced him to sell the pickup and now he is reliant on a motorbike. He added that so many villagers are in debt that a system of rotating debt (*nii mul wian*) had developed whereby farmers borrow from the agricultural cooperative to pay the bank, borrow from the bank to pay the cooperative, and borrow from local money-lenders to pay both.

The primary attractiveness of contract farming for these farmers is that they do not have to pay the crop's input costs. Farmers regularly state that they have become interested in contracts because they do not have to invest their own capital (which is usually borrowed): 'We are growing for the companies because at least they are willing to invest the capital, we don't have to hurt ourselves with debt, we don't have to get stressed or tired. Investing labour is not as stressful as investing money.' Almost all the contracting companies provide the farmers with seedlings (or seed) and agrochemicals. The cost of these inputs is then deducted from the selling price of the crop. If the crop fails the loss is borne by the company. Of course, crop failure is still regarded as something of a disaster, but farmers regularly assert that their only loss is the time they have invested in the crop and that their debt situation is not worsened. Given that they have grown a subsistence rice crop in the wet season they still have a very basic level of subsistence security and many have other sources of income from wage labour, government employment and local enterprise.[9] Farmers also acknowledge, not without some resentment, that the input prices charged by the company are often higher than market rates, but the fact that the company is bearing the risk of investment is generally regarded as outweighing this disadvantage. One farmer, Jakrit, summed up the common view of the benefit of contract farming:

> The companies have been coming for a long time but people were not interested because people just wanted to grow garlic. People only really became interested in the past few years. The first person to grow peas for a company was the headman. The first year, he grew 15 *rai* and made about 200,000 baht. The second year he could not rent so much land so grew a lot less. This year I tried out less than one *rai* and I made 6,000 baht from just that little bit. The company is good, the inputs just arrive – seeds, fertilizer and chemicals. If it is not Saturday or Sunday you can just ring up the broker and the fertilizer and chemicals just come. And the extension officers come and check on what we are doing and give us advice if we need to change anything. And if the crop fails there is no cost and no problem. The company does not want us to invest our own money because they are afraid we will sell to other companies. There are several of them that would want to buy. New Asia Food has a quota of about 500 *rai* for the whole district. So why not grow for them? If you

grow your own crops you have to go and borrow from the cooperative and if the crop fails you are in debt and the interest just mounts up and up and up. And you get more and more into debt. But there is no problem with the company. All you lose if it fails is your labour.

(Jakrit, 23 May 2004)

Jakrit's comments nicely capture the economic rationale for contract farming, while also reflecting the pragmatism and adaptability that farmers bring to their agricultural decisions. There is a strong sense in Baan Tiam that the advent of contract farming has introduced a wider range of agricultural alternatives into the village and these alternatives have been enhanced by some degree of revival in the yield and price of garlic. As I have indicated, although many farmers ultimately adopt one of the major crops, this adoption is accompanied by careful observation and vigorous discussion of the numerous experiments that are going on at the margin.

Keeping good company

There is no doubt that as individual economic agents the companies are much more powerful than the farmers. As accounts of corporate proletarianization rightly point out, the seemingly reciprocal contracts gloss over substantial disparities in economic resources and sociopolitical influence; but relationships of power are not simply determined by structural position. In the everyday exercise of power, contracting companies have to operate in an environment where there is considerable competition for the land and labour of farmers. A vibrant national and international agro-commodity trade means that companies are keen to secure contracts with farmers who own land in suitable agro-ecological zones. As rural households increasingly adopt diverse livelihood strategies, companies recognize that agriculture is not the sole, or even most important, source of local income. In this climate of economic diversity and choice, companies cannot simply impose their will. They have to be careful to fit within locally valued systems of economy and sociality.

Companies usually introduce themselves to Baan Tiam's farmers by organizing a public meeting, either in the hall next to the village temple or at the cooperative in the district centre. The formats of the meetings vary but the overall content is generally similar: an overview of the crops that the company is interested in; discussions of likely yields; pricing policies; production techniques; and possible problems. There are often vigorous question and answer sessions in which the company representatives try to deal with farmer scepticism about the promised rewards. Promotional meetings may be accompanied by other gestures of goodwill which signal a willingness to become engaged in local systems of exchange. A free lunch may be provided at the meeting or the company representative may supply calendars, agricultural inputs, or even T-shirts for the village soccer team. Shrewd company representatives will also make a point of attending local ritual events (such as temple festivals and funerals) and making informal social visits to opinion leaders, such as the village headman or leaders of the irrigation groups.[10]

The mutual engagement of companies in local systems of sociality is evident in two key aspects of contract farming: the nature of the contracts themselves and the use of local brokers. Initially most of the companies use formal written contracts. These contracts take the form of a legalistic agreement between the 'seller' (the farmer) and the 'buyer' (the company). The seller agrees to plant a specified crop on a specified area and to sell it to the company. Contracts may include provisions about the timing of the planting and harvesting of the crop, and the timing and rates of application of agrochemicals. The company agrees to purchase the crop (often with certain quality provisions specified) at an agreed price with payment made within a defined period. The company also agrees to provide inputs and to deduct the specified cost of inputs from the contract payment for the produce. Some contracts are made with individual farmers while others are made with a local broker who then informally subcontracts individual farmers. These written contracts provide a formal institutional underpinning for the relationship between company and farmer. However, once relations between the companies and farmers become well established, formal written contracts often give way to informal verbal agreements. When I asked about this, farmers indicated to me that contracts soon become unnecessary as they and the company now 'understood each other' or had achieved a degree of 'solidarity'. They also said that the detailed specification of techniques was unnecessary as they were now completely familiar with the production technique. In brief, contracting becomes immersed in the everyday language of cooperation and mutual understanding.

This embedding of contract arrangements in local systems of sociality is facilitated by the use of brokers. Brokers play a key role in recruiting farmers, coordinating production schedules, distributing inputs, training in cultivation techniques, and facilitating communications between farmers and the company. Some companies use local farmers to act as brokers. Often these are village leaders (headmen or assistant headmen) and they are usually active and skilled farmers who have been early innovators and adopters of new crops. Local brokers may also be recruited on the basis of kin relations. Somsak, for example, has emerged as Baan Tiam's key tobacco broker mainly due to the fact that his father-in-law is also a company broker in the village where the company's local nursery had been established. Typically local brokers will get a small percentage of the total sale price as a reward for their services. This additional income is likely to attract gossip and some resentment but there is also grudging acknowledgement that being a broker involves a considerable amount of work and expense that warrants some reward. As an alternative to – or in addition to – these local brokers, some companies also base company employees in the district, where they can manage company assets and maintain close relations with farmers. Almost inevitably these employees are drawn into local social networks, not infrequently forming sexual liaisons with women in the district. In one much discussed case, a company broker had established a second family in the local area, a particularly strategic liaison given that his 'minor wife' held an official position in the district's agricultural administration.

This corporate embedding in local systems of sociality means that companies are subject to the critical commentary that emerges from local value systems. Most farmers have a clear idea about what constitutes appropriate corporate behaviour. The ideal mode of company behaviour runs something like this: companies will provide clear instructions for the production of the crops; company extension agents and brokers will visit regularly and provide guidance on all the stages of production; agricultural inputs will be provided promptly; company representatives will be accessible and respectful and 'talk well' with farmers; agricultural produce will be collected as close to the field as possible; financial records will be clear and transparent; payments will be prompt; and companies will not be overly strict about quality regulations. Of course no company, or individual representative, can live up to all these provisions on all occasions and it is inevitable that company behaviour is subject to local critique, and sometimes outright anger.

Local critiques of company behaviour focus on several key issues. One of the most important sources of discontent is late payment for produce. Income from cash cropping is important for many farmers to meet basic living expenses: electricity and telephone bills, fuel, education and health expenses, ritual obligations and a wide range of day-to-day consumer items. Notwithstanding companies' provision of agricultural inputs there are also costs associated with cultivation, in particular the employment of supplementary labour for intensive periods of workload, such as harvesting. Carrying considerable debts, most farmers have very limited cash reserves and prompt payment for crops is important in maintaining cash flow. More generally, delayed payment can also underline the social distance and administrative illegibility of the companies. Delayed payments are a common feature of exchange within the local economy but companies are not yet sufficiently socially embedded – or their sometimes ponderous procedures sufficiently understood – to be given the benefit of the doubt. These anxieties are compounded by stories from other villages about companies that have collected the produce and then 'disappeared', never returning to make payment.

In 2004 a number of farmers who had grown peas for a Chiang Mai-based cannery were increasingly anxious about their non-receipt of payment. When one of the company's extension officers came to the village he was harangued about the delay. Particular concern was expressed about the non-appearance of the company's local broker (who lived in a neighbouring subdistrict): 'We haven't seen his face for a long time; it's like he's scared of meeting a tiger in the fields.' The extension officer told the farmers that the issue of payment was not his responsibility and that they should talk to someone in the company's finance department. His bureaucratic response underlined the persistent social distance between company and farmer. Another group of farmers in Baan Tiam also experienced long-standing problems in relation to their payment for eggplants. In this case the extension officer was somewhat more diplomatic, sympathizing with the farmers and complaining that he had not been paid his salary in three months. Nevertheless, the company's credibility declined further when only some farmers were paid (those who were owed the smallest amounts) and later when part payments were made in bulk to growers' groups without any indication of how the payment should be distributed to individual farmers; an inevitable recipe for local conflict.

Quality standards enforced by companies are another source of discontent, complaint and occasional dispute. These standards give companies considerable leeway in the observance of the price guarantees set out in the (formal or informal) contracts. Companies regularly pay lower than the guaranteed payment by insisting that the produce does not meet quality standards. Claims about quality can be made in relation to chemical residue; damage by disease or insects; and produce being under- or over-size (zucchinis, for example, have to be between four and six inches long). Quality standards, which strictly schedule the application of agrochemicals and often require a prolonged period of non-application prior to harvest, can undermine farmers' sense of being able to adaptively manage the production of the crops. Chemical application schedules may be surreptitiously ignored but farmers run the real risk of rejection of the crop if residues are detected. Residue detection is a highly technical issue on which farmers have little ability to respond. Some companies have developed a reputation for being unreasonably strict in relation to these standards and in one particularly egregious case the agent rejected all the crops of one farmer on the basis that one portion of one of his crops was deemed to be below standard. In another case one farmer exploded with rage when his eggplant harvest was downgraded, which resulted in a substantial reduction in income. What particularly annoyed the farmer was that the extension officer had inspected the crop shortly before harvest and had made no adverse comment about its quality. 'Why did you let me harvest it?' the farmer protested. 'I have wasted my time, and I have wasted money hiring people to help me harvest.' With that he struck out, aiming a punch at the agent's face, in a display of open defiance. The agent managed to evade the punch but, according to the local gossip, he would have to be very careful in his future dealings in the village. By contrast, one of the reasons for the popularity of tobacco is that quality standards are relatively liberal and the company even knowingly turns a blind eye to the common practice of harvesting the leaves very early in the morning when their moisture content is highest. Farmers, such as those shown in Figure 4.2, do this to increase the weight and, as a result, the price of their crop, thus arrangements are constantly being renegotiated and experimented with.

A number of other operational issues can also attract farmers' ire. The location where the companies come to collect the crop is one common source

Figure 4.2 Harvesting tobacco. Farmers maximize the weight by harvesting in the morning when the moisture content is higher and, as a result, the price of their crop increases.

Photo credit: Andrew Walker

of complaint. Few companies are willing to collect the produce direct from the farmers' fields. Not only would this be overly time-consuming, but company representatives also claim that the rough tracks down to the paddy fields are not suited to their trucks and pickups. Farmers accept these practical reasons, though the refusal of some company agents to bring their vehicles into the fields is sometimes interpreted as a reluctance to share in the inconveniences that Baan Tiam's farmers face every day. Some farmers also interpret it as unwillingness on the part of company agents to mix with the 'hoi polloi' in the hot, dusty and unmistakably rural context of the paddy fields. Complaints are likely to become explicit when companies insist that farmers transport their produce to central collection points in villages closer to the district centre.[11] Many farmers are reluctant to incur this additional inconvenience and cost, especially when they have to pay inflated transport costs to the few farmers in the village who own pickup trucks (some of whom are also company brokers). Again, the Oriental tobacco company displayed admirable sensitivity to local concerns when it changed its collection point from the agricultural cooperative (about six kilometres from Baan Tiam) to a large concrete pavilion that had been erected at the centre of the village for the conduct of rituals relating to the village tutelary spirit.

There is another, much less frequently expressed, line of critique of contract farming. This is not so much directed at the companies as at the arrangement more generally and even at the farmers who enter into contracts. Some residents of Baan Tiam, including the locally influential subdistrict head (a shopkeeper), argue that the village has become overly reliant on contracts and has lost its sense of agricultural independence and entrepreneurship. While the difficulties of garlic production are acknowledged, a view is held in some quarters that the farmers need to make more effort to help themselves. On the occasion of a local festival, one of the farmers was harangued by his son, a schoolteacher who had returned home for the occasion. 'Baan Tiam has become too lazy,' he claimed. 'Why should farmers wait for companies to bring the market to them? They have to go and out and find a market for themselves.' In some cases this critique is accompanied by claims about the undesirable environmental impact of some of the contract crops. A former village headman, who is still an influential figure, was vocal in his opposition to sweetcorn cultivation. He claimed that it depleted the soil completely of nutrients and used too much water. No doubt his motivation was partly political (the sweetcorn broker was a newly appointed assistant headman and represented the new generation of leadership in the village), but it expressed the potential for local environmental uncertainties to become implicated in local assessments of agricultural transformation.

Resistance and 'experimental consensus'

Since James Scott's classic *Weapons of the Weak* (1985) it has been commonplace to discuss responses to agrarian transformation within the framework of resistance. Scott documents the reaction of farmers in a Malaysian village (which he calls 'Sedaka') to the double-cropping of rice and the introduction of mechanized harvesting. These 'Green Revolution' changes resulted in the economic and ritual marginalization of the poor: they had less access to rental land, they suffered a sharp reduction in labouring income, and they received less charity and ritual munificence from the rich. How did the poor react to these changes? Certainly, as some of Scott's more strident critics (for example, Gutmann 1993) have been keen to point out, resistance in Sedaka did not involve an attempt to overthrow the new socio-economic order. The response of the poor was nostalgic rather than revolutionary. Farmers adversely affected by the changes in Sedaka drew on a pre-existing moral order to stage a symbolic and practical 'rearguard action' (Scott 1985: 183) against the rich. They accused the rich of exploitation, stinginess, arrogance, callousness, and of failing to meet the moral expectations and obligations associated with their social position. At times this symbolic struggle translated into more direct action such as the collective withdrawal of labour, sabotage and theft (Scott 1985: 248–72). The ideological reference point for this repertoire of resistance was a selectively remembered pre-capitalist (and pre-Green Revolution) moral order in which the rich and poor were linked 'in a symbiosis of dependency and exploitation' (Scott 1985: 180). In Sedaka's traditional agricultural economy, labour was scarce and land was abundant. More successful farmers and local political leaders had to moderate their demands and provide practical and symbolic benefits to the poor in order to maintain and mobilize their labour forces and entourages. As material conditions changed, this pre-capitalist moral order provided a rich stock of ideological weaponry that the poor could use both to defend their own rights and dignity and to undermine the social standing of the rich.

Similar strategies of everyday resistance are evident in the response of Baan Tiam's farmers to the·decline in garlic cultivation and the emergence of contract farming. Farmers complain bitterly about late payment for their crops and the seemingly unreasonable quality standards that companies enforce; they harvest their crops in ways that maximize their weight; they sometimes neglect to follow the strict production schedules insisted on by the companies; they circulate cautionary tales about companies who have failed to appear when crops are harvested; and they gossip about the private lives of company representatives. They also resist the intrusion of commercial agriculture into the subsistence sector, maintaining a clear separation between the cultivation of rice in the wet season and cash crops in the dry season.

So, Scott's 'weapons of the weak' are undoubtedly present in Baan Tiam, yet some caution is warranted in interpreting their meaning and assessing their cultural significance. There is a risk of oversimplifying the intentions underpinning these various acts and statements and framing them within the reassuringly familiar narrative of a local community resisting the incursion of the capitalist market. This simplifying tendency is what Ortner (1995: 173) refers to as the 'problem of ethnographic refusal' in many resistance studies. She argues that political complexity, cultural richness and the diversity of subject positions can be lost when resistance studies provide ethnographically 'thin' accounts that are organized in terms of a dyadic relationship between dominant and subordinate groups (see also Mittelman and Chin 2000: 173; Sivaramakrishnan 2005: 348–49). Ortner's arguments are well made and it is worth taking up her challenge and exploring some of the nuances in Baan Tiam's response to agricultural transformation.

A useful starting point is to compare the 'resistance' of Baan Tiam's farmers with that observed by Scott (1985) in Sedaka. The most obvious similarity is the importance of a moral dimension. Scott's major contribution is to show that economic and technological changes are experienced via a prism of cultural orientations. In shaping responses (resistant or otherwise), these orientations are as important as the material changes themselves (Scott 1985: 138–41). This cultural framing of economic change is equally evident in Baan Tiam's farmers' assessment of contract farming. This assessment is often expressed in terms of relatively idealized statements of appropriate behaviour. Company representatives are praised or criticized according to their willingness and ability to behave in culturally appropriate ways: speaking well with farmers; providing support at levels consistent with agreements and expectations; participating in village festivals and rituals; and managing economic transactions in a fair and open manner. These expectations comprise what might be called, following Scott (1976), a 'moral economy' that ideologically regulates transactions in the agricultural sector. In the more explicitly political context of local and national elections I have referred to this set of moral expectations as a 'rural constitution' to challenge the view that the regulation of political behaviour is the sole prerogative of those who draft (on a regular basis!) Thailand's formal constitutions (Walker 2008). Whatever we call it, the key point is that rural people are not merely impacted upon by wider economic or political forces but have moral orientations which provide a broad framework – not a straitjacket – for evaluating and regulating the personal interactions that characterize those forces at a local level.

I also see an important difference between the responses of farmers in Sedaka and Baan Tiam.[12] In Baan Tiam the ideological point of reference is experimentation rather than nostalgia. Discussions of commercial agriculture in Baan Tiam are permeated by the language of experimentation. Farmers often comment that they are experimenting (*thot long*) on a new crop or technique or that they are trying it out (*long du*). In a very typical discussion, a woman planting eggplants under contract told me that she had no idea what the return from the crop would be but that she was just trying it out, largely because she had insufficient capital to grow garlic on all her land. Another farmer described his contract farming venture as 'a rat nibbling at the grass', suggesting that this was a relatively small and exploratory venture. Sometimes the verb 'to play' (*len*) is used to suggest that this 'experimental' activity is, in a sense, separate from mainstream farming. One farmer commented that he had been 'playing with organic farming' (*len insi*) in response to company expectations of a chemical-free crop. This experimental orientation is also explicitly comparative. Walking through the paddy fields farmers regularly and spontaneously comment on the state of the various crops they pass, speculating about the inputs and techniques that may have caused various outcomes: 'The garlic on that plot is beautiful because they used 1:14:12 [fertilizer]'; 'She has a good tobacco crop because she planted soybeans last year'; 'The company only paid them 2 baht [per kilogram] for those cabbages, I would want 10 baht before I was interested.' On trips outside the village, similar comparative comments are made: 'The garlic in this village is good because they have only been growing it for a few years'; 'They make a good profit on eggplants because they are very diligent and produce good quality';

'This village grew a lot of sweetcorn but the company never came to collect it.' This experimental and comparative orientation provides farmers with a rich stock of scenarios against which involvement in contract farming can be evaluated.

In suggesting that farmers' ideological orientation to agricultural transformation is experimental rather than nostalgic I am not suggesting that the past is irrelevant. Clearly, the evaluation of new economic relationships involves some reference to long-standing (and idealized) sentiments of village solidarity, ritual cooperation and benevolent patronage. There is a real attempt to draw new economic actors into these 'traditional' webs of meaning. Yet, in relation to commercial agriculture there is no ideological privileging of the past nor of traditional modes of behaviour. There are other points of reference. In an experimental orientation there is no particular moral value placed on pre-existing arrangements. Baan Tiam's farmers' contemporary ideological frameworks also draw on the importance of expert knowledge from external sources; the role of corporate investment in contributing to local development; the desirability of contract administration that is transparent (*prongsay*) and fair (*yutitham*); and the importance of fairly sharing the windfall benefits of buoyant markets. Most generally, the commercial agricultural market is ideologically valued as a potential contributor to local livelihood improvement. In complaining, for example, about overly strict enforcement of companies' quality standards, Baan Tiam's farmers are drawing to some extent on a pre-market ideology of mutual support and reciprocity, but they are also experimentally deploying a new language of equitable and transparent market access. In the petty cheating that sometimes characterizes their dealings with company brokers they are not seeking to disrupt or subvert corporate intervention in local agriculture in favour of more local or traditional forms of resource management. Instead, their ideological goal is to draw the companies into more lucrative and reciprocally balanced forms of livelihood support.

Recognizing the experimental orientation of Baan Tiam's farmers raises debates about the appropriateness of the term 'resistance'. Without diminishing the sophistication of some discussions of resistance, there is the persistent sense that it is necessarily oppositional. Even in Scott's highly nuanced accounts of everyday resistance there are no clearly demarcated battle lines – much resistance being expressed in 'offstage' contexts – but there remains an underlying distinction between the 'weapons of the weak' and the dominant ideological transcripts of the rich and powerful. An experimental orientation is rather different. It is, to some extent at least, open-minded about the possibility of success and the potential benefits of collaboration. It seeks to explore alternatives rather than to defend a particular position. This is nicely illustrated by High (2005) in her account of farmers' response to collectivization and mechanized irrigation in southern Laos. High (2005: 216–22, 228–30) does not shy away from the negative impacts of these state-imposed schemes. She vividly documents the climate of fear in which the Lao state operates, but she describes villagers' involvement in these schemes in terms of an 'experimental consensus . . . where policy is consented to, but as a basis of ongoing renegotiations and manoeuvrings':

> . . . consensus arrangements are entered into on the understanding of their malleable, contingent and experimental nature. They are thus not a final agreement, not an end-game, but an opening scene, a basis upon which ongoing renegotiation is commenced. By consenting to engage with state projects such as irrigation and collectivisation, farmers gain a toe-hold from which they can manoeuvre to a more advantageous position.
>
> (High 2005: 234–5)

This notion can help deepen our understanding of Baan Tiam's 'resistance'. Like the farmers in southern Laos, the contract farmers of Baan Tiam cannot avoid underlying structural constraints: state power (though their relationship with the state is considerably more amiable than that documented by High), corporate expansion and trade liberalization. Yet these constraints are experienced in the form of everyday transactions, and this interpersonal realm opens up spaces for experimenting with livelihood options. Of course, these are complex and uncertain experiments and, inevitably, there are problems and cases of outright failure. Not surprisingly, farmers respond to these failures with frustration, anger, gossip and condemnation. To set these particular responses apart as 'resistance', however, is to divorce them from the broader experimental context in which they are embedded. The overall results of this broader experiment are relatively positive. Baan Tiam's farmers readily acknowledge that contract farming has provided a range of relatively low-risk agricultural alternatives. What is most appreciated is that the high risk of debt associated with the independent farming of garlic is largely mitigated. Of course, this may change as broader trends in the Thai and international economy alter the terms of exchange between farmer and company. In the future, for example, farmers may have to bear the burden of some input costs in the case of crop failure, but – as High points out – an '*experimental* consensus' does not involve a one-off agreement. It is an ongoing process of culturally informed evaluation.

The concept of experimental consensus also invites a discussion of the issue of hegemony. In *Weapons of the Weak*, one of Scott's key objectives was to challenge the view that the poor are subject to some form of ideological mystification about the 'true' nature of their circumstances. He writes, and I strongly agree, that 'the concept of hegemony ignores the extent to which most subordinate classes are able, on the basis of their daily material experience, to penetrate and demystify the prevailing ideology' (Scott 1985: 317). But for some academic observers (who, presumably, are confident that they themselves have escaped it) the notion of hegemony has an enduring allure. Some have argued that the everyday resistance documented by Scott fails to puncture a broader modernist hegemony that naturalizes rural stratification, promotes the consolidation of the modern state, and asserts the inevitability of economic development. Similarly, some may argue that Baan Tiam's farmers are also encapsulated within a broader hegemonic frame that promotes 'neoliberal' values of rational experimentation and the pursuit of individual self-improvement. They may argue that Baan Tiam's experimental consensus contributes to a 'neoliberal' agenda that promotes the liberalization of trade, the commercialization of agriculture, and the steady erosion of traditional livelihoods.

There is little that can be done, empirically or conceptually, to counter such claims. For each local ideological orientation – short of outright revolution – there will be a broader hegemonic framework that can be proposed to encapsulate it. If Baan Tiam's farmers experimentally embrace contract farming they are participants in a hegemony that naturalizes commercialization. If they reject it, they are victims of a hegemony that naturalizes uneven development, valorizes community, and condemns them to the provision of low-cost labour in Thailand's commercialized urban centres. We can quickly end up in a hegemonic cul-de-sac from which there is no escape. Ultimately the choice of conceptual orientation is political and ethical. I am convinced by Scott's core message that a genuine understanding of broad-scale transformation requires a respectful engagement with local people's subjective, culturally informed and idiosyncratic experiences of it. To insist on an overarching hegemonic frame is to deny the authenticity of these experiences. Ultimately, this results in conceptual frameworks, political positions and policy responses that are detached from the aspirations of those with whom we conduct our research.

Notes

1 This chapter has benefited enormously from the patient and diligent research assistance of colleagues in Thailand. Nicholas Farrelly also contributed to the crucial early stages of field research and Sarinda Singh compiled useful background reading on contract farming. Of course, particular thanks are due to the farmers of 'Baan Tiam' who have accepted my various research projects with patience, good humour and generous hospitality. Government officials and company representatives in 'Pad Siew' district also assisted by providing data and insights into the local agricultural sector.

2 I have been undertaking ethnographic fieldwork in 'Baan Tiam' since late 2002. During this period I have made 12 short research visits to the village. I have been assisted by local research assistants who have stayed in Baan Tiam for more extended periods. The paper draws on qualitative ethnographic data as well as the results of five household surveys undertaken between 2003 and 2006.

3 Out of Baan Tiam's 126 households, 54 do not undertake any independent farming activity, most commonly because they do not own agricultural land. For some, this reflects affluence and a voluntary disengagement from agriculture to pursue more lucrative pursuits. Seven households, for example, nominated shopkeeping as their first or second most important source of cash income; but for most, non-participation in farming is a product of landlessness. Some, including more recent

migrants into the village, have never owned land while others have sold it or lost it through foreclosure. Many of these households are heavily dependent on wage labour: within Baan Tiam 33 households indicated that wage labour is their primary source of cash income while for another 12 it was their second most important source.

4 One *rai* equals 0.16 hectares.
5 During the period covered by this article the value of the Thai baht ranged from about 43 baht to the US dollar (December 2002) to 36 baht to the US dollar (December 2006).
6 Farmers were asked to subjectively rate the yield of their crop as 'very bad', 'bad', 'average', 'good', or 'very good'.
7 'Sufficiency economy' is a philosophy promoted by the Thai king that emphasizes agricultural self-reliance as a basis for development (UNDP 2007).
8 Thailand is reported to be the world's ninth largest garlic producer. Within Thailand, Chiang Mai province is one of the largest producers of garlic. Most garlic produced in Thailand is used for domestic consumption (Government of Thailand 2003, 2007).
9 Many of these farming households are also involved in an array of off-farm pursuits. Seven of these cash-cropping households indicated that wage labour was their primary source of cash income while 23 others indicated that wage labour was a secondary source.
10 There are three irrigation groups in Baan Tiam, corresponding to the three irrigation dams that service the village. Groups are made up of all the farmers who receive water from the dam. The leader is elected from the members of the group. He plays a key role in organizing maintenance of the irrigation infrastructure and coordinating irrigation schedules, especially when there is an acute water shortage.
11 This is an interesting twist on what Scott found in 'Sedaka', Malaysia regarding local transportation disputes (Scott 1985: 213).
12 An entire paper could be devoted to exploring the reasons for this different orientation. One reason for the difference may lie in the fact that Scott's accounts of resistance were focused on relatively poor (and often landless) residents of Sedaka. In this study I have focused on the subjective responses of a somewhat more affluent stratum of rural society (though relatively few of the farmers I am discussing could be described as 'rich'). A more important reason lies, I suspect, in the much greater degree of economic diversity in Baan Tiam. Sedaka was primarily a rice-growing village, whereas the agricultural and non-agricultural economy in Baan Tiam is much more diverse. Finally, Baan Tiam has a well-established history of dealing with external commercial agents including timber firms, tobacco processors and traders.

References

Carney, J. (1988) 'Struggles over crop rights within contract farming households in a Gambian irrigated rice farming project', *Journal of Peasant Studies*, 15: 334–49.
Clapp, R. (1988) 'Representing reciprocity, reproducing domination: ideology and the labour process in Latin American contract farming', *Journal of Peasant Studies*, 16: 5–39.
Dolan, C.S. (2001) 'The "good wife": struggles over resources in the Kenyan horticultural sector', *Journal of Development Studies*, 37: 39–70.
—— (2002) 'Gender and witchcraft in agrarian transition: the case of Kenyan horticulture', *Development and Change*, 33: 659–82.

Finnis, E. (2006) 'Why grow cash crops? Subsistence farming and crop commercialization in the Kolli Hills, South India', *American Anthropologist*, 108: 363–9.

Government of Thailand (2003) 'Impact on garlic of the Thai–China free trade agreement' (in Thai), Bangkok.

—— (2007) 'Garlic situation in Chiang Mai province in 2007' (in Thai), Chiang Mai.

Gutmann, M. (1993) 'Rituals of resistance: a critique of the theory of everyday forms of resistance', *Latin American Perspectives*, 20: 74–92.

High, H. (2005) 'Village in Laos: an ethnographic account of poverty and policy among the Mekong's flows', unpublished thesis, The Australian National University.

Key, N. and Runsten, D. (1999) 'Contract farming, smallholders, and rural development in Latin America: the organization of agroprocessing firms and the scale of outgrower production', *World Development*, 27: 381–401.

Little, P. and Watts, M. (1994) *Living Under Contract: contract farming and agrarian transformation in Sub-Saharan Africa*, Madison: University of Wisconsin Press.

Miller, L. (1995) 'Agribusiness, contract farmers and land-use sustainability in north-west Tasmania', *Australian Geographer*, 26: 104–11.

Mittelman, J.H. and Chin, C.B.N. (2000) 'Conceptualizing resistance to globalization', in J. H. Mittelman, *The Globalization Syndrome: transformation and resistance*, Princeton: Princeton University Press, 165–78.

Netting, R.M., Stone, M.P. and Stone, G.D. (1989) 'Kofyar cash-cropping: choice and change in indigenous agricultural development', *Human Ecology*, 17: 299–319.

Ornberg, L. (2003) 'Farmers' choice: contract farming, agricultural change and modernisation in Northern Thailand', paper presented at The Third International Convention of Asian Scholars (ICAS3), Singapore, 2003.

Ortiz, S. and Aparicio, S. (2006) 'Contracts, control and contestation: The harvest of lemons for export', *Journal of Peasant Studies*, 33: 161–88.

Ortner, S. (1995) 'Resistance and the problem of ethnographic refusal', *Comparative Studies in Society and History*, 37 (1): 173–93.

Porter, G. and Phillips-Howard, K. (1997) 'Comparing contracts: an evaluation of contract farming schemes in Africa', *World Development*, 25: 227–38.

Scott, J.C. (1976) *The Moral Economy of the Peasant: rebellion and subsistence in Southeast Asia*, New Haven: Yale University Press.

—— (1985) *Weapons of the Weak: everyday forms of peasant resistance*, New Haven: Yale University Press.

Shiva, V. (2004) 'The future of food: countering globalisation and recolonisation of Indian agriculture', *Futures*, 36: 715–32.

Sivaramakrishnan, K. (2005) 'Some intellectual genealogies for the concept of everyday resistance', *American Anthropologist*, 107: 346–55.

Sununtar, S., Leung, P.S. and Cai, J. (2005) *Contract Farming and Poverty Reduction: a case of organic rice contract farming in Thailand*, Tokyo: Asian Development Bank Institute.

UNDP (2007) *Thailand Human Development Report 2007: sufficiency economy and human development*, Bangkok: UNDP.

Walker, A. (2008) 'The rural constitution and the everyday politics of elections in northern Thailand', *Journal of Contemporary Asia*, 38: 84–105.

Warning, M. and Key, N. (2002) 'The social performance and distributional consequences of contract farming: an equilibrium analysis of the Arachide de Bouche Program in Senegal', *World Development*, 30: 255–63.

5 Resisting local inequities: Community-based conservation on Palawan Island, the Philippines

Wolfram H. Dressler

Introduction

Park managers across the developing world have increasingly relied on community-based conservation measures to transfer authority to the indigenous poor for the management of natural resources (Kellert *et al.* 2000). Replacing past coercive forms of conservation, park managers have often 'granted' indigenous peoples the responsibility to access, use and manage resources for poverty reduction and biodiversity conservation. However, in cases when community-based conservation has overlapped with rural people experiencing rapid agricultural change, the devolution of authority has frequently reinforced social disparities. Those who implement devolved conservation have often exacerbated local inequalities by upholding older stereotypes of people and agriculture as binary constructs of 'modern' and 'traditional' (see Hobsbawn and Ranger 1983).

In the Philippines, the assumption has held that the viability of indigenous livelihoods depends directly on maintaining the traditional and sustainable character of upland farming 'systems'. Any hint of cultural change affecting the integrity of 'traditional' practices has called for projects that reinvest in 'sustainable', traditional subsistence production. By classifying indigenous livelihoods as subsistence-based, practitioners have often delivered low-capital, small-scale support on the premise that it revitalizes subsistence, failing to realize that such farmers have long required productive resources (for instance, secure land holdings) to buffer the risks of agricultural intensification. Upholding such constructs in both policy and practice has neglected the reality that the livelihood multiplicity of uplanders does not conform to specific typologies of agricultural production (cf. Rigg 2005). By interpreting livelihoods in such absolute terms, the poverty of indigenous uplanders has been further reinforced and their ability to negotiate and respond to the impacts of the agrarian transition has been limited. In many locales this has resulted in local, 'everyday forms' of resistance to community-based conservation (Agrawal and Gibson 1999; Slater 2002; Goldman 2003).

In the Philippine uplands rapid demographic shifts and agricultural change have made it increasingly difficult to implement community-based conservation in an equitable manner. Perhaps the most enduring challenge has been dealing with the flow of lowland migrant settlers to upland areas where they have co-mingled and competed for resources with indigenous peoples near protected areas. Although the practice of coercive conservation, which criminalizes extensive agriculture (for example, swidden), has given way to community-based conservation that should pertain equally to 'the poor', devolved governance has reinforced power structures rooted in specific agricultural and ethnic ideals. In particular, as Ancestral Domain Claims have been incorporated into the devolved management structures of national parks, indigenous peoples have been granted new rights and responsibilities over resources that further define group membership.

At the same time as allowing indigenous peoples to coexist with national parks by integrating ancestral lands into park management, their livelihood strategies have been subject to projects that have reinforced the markers of 'tradition' and 'sustainability'. In contrast, cast as 'modern' and 'productive', migrants have received support for commercial agriculture (for example, intensified paddy farming). Despite the reality of migrant–indigenous distinctions being a matter of degree based upon length of residence, livelihood practices and impoverishment, state land managers have continued to allocate public lands and private holdings to citizens closest to the state's conceptions of modernity: lowland Christian Filipinos being linked to modern agriculture (Hirtz 1998). As dominant members of society have defined conservation policy on the basis of such distinctions, policies have continued to deny indigenous uplanders access to the same productive resources that are often allocated to lowland farmers (Lopez 1987). As a result, differing indigenous and migrant interests over land and forest resources have produced conflicting outcomes.

On Palawan Island, community-based conservation has served to classify and constrain livelihoods at the Puerto Princesa Subterranean River National Park (PPSRNP) when shifts in conservation and agricultural production have arisen (see Figure 5.1).[1] Rather than facilitate conservation and reduce poverty, the national park's history of management and settlement has ensured that the practices of community-based conservation have reinforced long-standing social divisions embedded in livelihood practices. As devolved management approaches have built on stereotypes, most livelihood support has tended to reflect and reinforce indigenous people's 'cultural' role in traditional practices. Project managers have built on these ideas, offering support through projects that have assumed indigenous uplanders lack any desire or need for financial capital or other productive resources. Such extension services have, in turn, constrained their livelihood choices. As livelihood projects led by government and/or non-governmental organizations (NGO) have come and gone, they have offered the indigenous poor few, if any, opportunities to negotiate livelihood change, particularly the onset of agricultural intensification by migrants. Rather than fulfil the dual objective of conservation and poverty reduction, the influx of 'community-based'

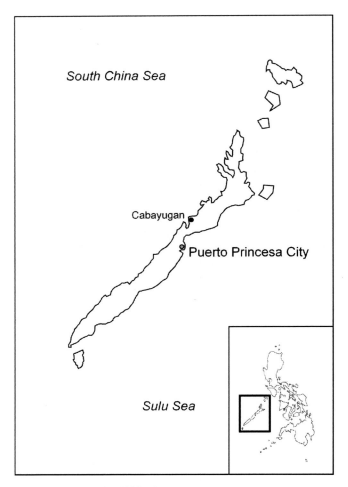

Figure 5.1 Palawan Island, the Philippines.

Map credit: Jean Michaud

conservation has perpetuated poverty among indigenous peoples by tying into and driving the disparities of agrarian change.

In recent years on the island, however, many indigenous Tagbanua have resisted such 'layered' subordination by speaking out against devolved conservation, in part by articulating their ethnicity as a form of indigeneity, being *katutubo* (innate). Such a position is considered as an expression of 'cultural belonging' among Tagbanua; one that is often used for sociopolitical leverage. This resistance has occurred as the Tagbanua – a people of Malayo-Polynesian ethnicity of central Palawan – have seen their livelihoods and social status reaffirmed by both migrants and park authorities (Fox 1982). In contrast, the migrant community (of Barangay Cabayugan, central

Palawan) has become a mixed group of about thirteen different ethnicities, has been 'formally' educated and 'integrated' into local affairs, and has retained its wealth through intensive paddy farming and conservation initiatives. The fact that outsiders have defined and controlled Tagbanua livelihoods has limited the latter's ability to manage the negative aspects and consequences of the agrarian transition in central Palawan.

This chapter will show that, in their own way, the indigenous Tagbanua on Palawan Island, the Philippines, have worked to resist the marginalizing effects of agrarian change in their local context, drawing on 'hidden transcripts' as they resist the labels that external powers have imposed on them, stressing instead their unique rights of indigeneity and cultural belonging. To begin, I provide the historical context needed to help answer how and why the practice of community-based conservation has classified and constrained indigenous livelihoods in Palawan. I then introduce the case study, exploring how park management transitions have reinforced disparities between migrants and Tagbanua in Barangay Cabayugan, Puerto Princesa City, Palawan Island. Third, I examine why social and economic disparities have persisted due to agrarian change, changes in land-use classification, and devolved conservation initiatives. In conclusion, I suggest that as park managers and non-governmental organizations (NGOs) have applied projects based on their own perceptions of pre-existing social constructs, they have constrained the ability of Tagbanua to manage the impacts of agricultural intensification, which has consequently reinforced local disparities. I discuss how reinforced perceptions of 'insider' and 'outsider' have caused Tagbanua to begin to assert their claims to land and to articulate indigeneity in resistance to migrants and park managers' efforts to subordinate them.

Colonial and post-colonial classifications of land and people

The historical impacts of Spanish (1521–1898) and United States (1898–1945) land-use laws that draw on certain social constructs has exacerbated the migrant–indigenous dichotomy of the past on Palawan, and continue today to reinforce stereotypes of land uses, identity and production (cf. Eder 1994). Spanish rule introduced the legal classification of lands and people in the Philippines. New land laws and the colonial rulers' perception of local society brought about the ethnic and spatial bifurcation of the Philippine population into a Christianized, nominally westernized majority residing in the lowlands, and a 'non-Christian tribal' minority in the uplands. The American and post-colonial administrations adopted this conception and its related legal mechanisms to inform the status of livelihoods in the Philippines to this day (Scott 1982; Hirtz 1998).

From 1521 onwards, Spanish colonizers imposed the Regalian Doctrine, holding that all lands not registered as private title were vested in the Crown as public domain. After the Spanish-American war in 1898, the American colonial government upheld this principle by classifying parts of the public domain under its claim as national parks in 1899 (Pinchot 1903). The government declared that public lands were 'reserved and withdraw[n] from settlement [. . . to preserve . . .] panoramic, historical, scientific or aesthetic values' (National Parks Act 1932: 2). This transplanted and formalized American-style 'fences and fines' park management in the Philippines. These changes meant that anyone without private title prior to the zoning of national parks – that is, most indigenous uplanders – could not legally occupy and/or secure a livelihood from state forestlands and/or public domain, effectively limiting their access to productive lands. As the state expanded national park territory in the uplands, those indigenous peoples who worked swidden plots without land titles could not defend themselves against the state's view of such cultivation being unproductive and damaging to forests.

After Philippine independence in 1946, extensions of the Regalian Doctrine remained in the Philippine Constitution (1987), forcing subsequent laws to consider all lands with over 18 per cent slope as public forest land (Republic of the Philippines (RoP) 1987). As a result, the Philippine state retained full control over many forests, minerals and water – the 'public domain' – while classifying gently sloping and flat areas in the lowlands as 'alienable and disposable', lands potentially released for settlement. While private title could be tendered on the latter land, usufruct holdings in upland areas under state control could not be held as legal property. In theory, all lands under or pending title had to be limited to the gently sloping 'lowlands', namely valley areas, plains or coastal zones. Hence land titles and legitimacy were reserved for lowlanders, while upland residents were deemed squatters, without legal tenure and subject to eviction. Ethnic differences were thus 'naturalized and essentialized', not only in terms of cultural markers, but also in terms of agriculture and forest use at different elevations (cf. Vandergeest 2003: 21 for a similar case in Thailand). Lowland peoples continued to be seen as those practising productive paddy rice cultivation, while upland 'tribes' were considered to be engaged in unproductive swidden that, unless small-scale and traditional, was destructive to forest reserves (see Yengoyan 1991).

From the 1960s onwards, the Philippine government upheld policies for forest conservation that controlled the clearing and burning of forest in national parks for swidden use by uplanders. State conservationists believed that swidden 'robbed' government treasuries of valuable timber and forest aesthetics (Scott 1979). Such policies criminalized the forest-based livelihoods of indigenous populations, while upholding migrant lowlanders' increasingly intensified agriculture that relied on capital-intensive technologies such as hybrid seeds, hand tractors, water pumps and so on.

Fences and fines to community-based conservation in the post-colonial Philippines

The discussion above reflects how the Philippine government's efforts to sustain a North American park ethic grew out of colonial laws restricting indigenous people's access to forest resources in national parks (Nash 1982). In 1975, Marcos's Presidential Decree No. 705 set out to classify public forests such that national parks became a category of forest reserve from which 'forest occupants' could be evicted (Natural Resources Management Center (NRMC) and Ministry of Natural Resources (MNR) 1983: 9). It was only after the first People Power Revolution ousted Marcos and restored democracy to the Philippines in 1986 that the softening of such strictures occurred. NGOs quickly set out to expose human rights abuses and the extensive logging of the nation's rainforests (Vitug 1993, 2000; Eder and Fernandez 1996). Building on community-based policies, campaigns arose to stabilize swidden-induced deforestation through secure tenure and livelihood support under devolved conservation (Department of Environment and Natural Resources (DENR) 1996). Rather than being directly criminalized, new 'people-oriented' policy controls governed swidden by ensuring that cultivation was customary and sustainable. In such circumstances, community-based initiatives sought to contain heavily used swiddens by introducing agroforestry at field edges while, at the same time, supporting paddy farming as an alternative.

On Palawan, environmental campaigns soon grew to protect the island's high biodiversity value, with many closely watching how farmers cultivated swidden. In the mid-1980s, the NGO Haribon Society successfully lobbied for a 25-year logging ban, a Strategic Environmental Plan with management zones, and funding for park management through a Debt-for-Nature Swap initiative (Haribon Society 1983; Clad and Vitug 1988). Backed by the Aquino government (1986–92), the Debt-for-Nature Swap programme supported an integrated protected areas (IPAS) initiative that provided infrastructure and management support for the Puerto Princesa Subterranean River National Park. The system that arose from this initiative, the National Integrated Protected Areas Strategy of 1992 (NIPAS Act), supported both forest conservation and the recognition of ancestral lands at the park (RoP 1992).

The Local Government Code of 1991 further supported community-based conservation for indigenous livelihoods and biodiversity (Sibal 2001). The Code devolved resource management authority from national agencies to Local Government Units, and further advocated for the involvement of NGOs and People's Organizations in local governance. As a result, the position of indigenous peoples vis-à-vis the state supposedly improved through alliances with NGOs under land rights frameworks. The Departmental Administrative Order No. 2 (DENR 1993) and the Indigenous People's Rights Act of 1997 (RoP 1997), for example, both recognized the rights of indigenous peoples to their ancestral lands. The former Order granted Certificate of Ancestral Domain Claims (CADC) for conditional rights to use resources and to exclude migrants from ancestral domains, while the latter law provided for the conversions of ancestral domain claims to communal domain titles.

Coercive to community-based conservation at Puerto Princesa Subterranean River National Park

For several decades, population pressure, poverty and a lack of security of tenure has driven landless migrants to settle on and transform forests into permanent agricultural fields in frontier areas such as Palawan (Kerkvliet 1977). Palawan is one region that has experienced substantial in-migration of poor farmers and fisher-folk seeking to escape marginal conditions in their homelands; areas where land holdings have become sparse or depleted of nutrients due to agricultural or fishery intensification. Once reputed to be an extensive frontier with 'vacant' lands and forests, the uplands of Palawan have come to represent a filled 'post frontier' area (Eder 2006: 150), where indigenous uplanders have diversified and specialized production, despite narratives suggesting otherwise.

Since the 1950s, several waves of migrants from other provinces (such as Pangasinan) have gradually settled in the Cabayugan area, the case study site. While often commencing with subsistence livelihoods similar to those of Tagbanua, migrants have combined swidden and forest extraction with the acquisition of land for private title. Securing flat swidden plots with private titles soon facilitated increases in agricultural intensification on the ancestral lands of Tagbanua, particularly for paddy rice and copra farming. Moreover, in the 1970s, concessions for non-timber forest products (almaciga and rattan) soon overlapped with ancestral lands (McDermott 2000). With the area's forest landscape being transformed into a site of permanent agriculture held by migrants, unequal social and economic relations persisted, effectively limiting Tagbanua access to productive resources. While past and present intermarriages between Tagbanua and migrants have partly muddied 'blood-lines', many Tagbanua remain destitute because of a lack of access to farming capital. Farming capital was (and still is) required by Tagbanua farmers in order to buffer the impacts of agricultural intensification under the control of migrants (such as debt and servitude). Since the initial waves of migrants in the 1950s, the difficulties Tagbanua have had in negotiating unequal production due to agrarian change have been exacerbated by substantive changes in park management in the 1970s.

Palawan Island has retained considerable tracts of primary rainforest, with Puerto Princesa Subterranean River National Park protecting large proportions of old-growth forest. Lush forest and Kegel karst landscapes surround the park, beneath which flows a navigable underground river, now a major tourist attraction (Ganapin Jr 1992; Madulid 1998). Yet much of the 'original' forest around the park has been partly cleared for swidden, and with stronger commodity markets since the 1960s, commercial logging, tree crops and paddy rice cultivation have surfaced and continue to intensify (Kummer 1992; Eder 1999, 2006). At the same time, Tagbanua continue their swidden cycles around the national park, including the case study site of Cabayugan, where they harvest non-timber forest/marine products, and occasionally cultivated paddy rice. Migrants now outnumber Tagbanua and intermarriages have risen (see Figures 5.2 and 5.3).

Phase I: the advent of coercive conservation

The boundaries of Puerto Princesa (then St Paul) Subterranean River National Park were instituted under Presidential Proclamation No. 835 of

Figure 5.2 Tagbanua swidden in Cabayugan (April–May 2002).

Photo credit: Wolfram Dressler

Figure 5.3 Migrant paddy rice field in Cabayugan (Summer 2001).

Photo credit: Wolfram Dressler

1971 (RoP 1971). In a few short years, the zoned boundaries claimed 3,901 hectares (ha) of the central karst and ancestral lands of Tagbanua as a national park. As migrants were busy clearing Alienable and Disposable lands in Cabayugan – public lands 'released' for permanent homesteading and agriculture – the remaining upland forests fell inside the national park boundaries. The state then used the park territory to control a large upland area by 'conserving' it, while migrants settled and cultivated low-lying areas flanking the park, forcing Tagbanua swidden further upland. The convergence of migrant property claims and binding state laws constrained Tagbanua access to and use of productive resources.

During this time, state officials believed that migrant paddy farmers could produce rice surpluses biannually without needing to clear additional swathes of forest. This impression was clearly apparent during the early days of park management in the 1970s, when foresters detailed the park boundary. Considering all swidden as destructive to forests, foresters often placed elderly Tagbanua swidden farmers in jail. In contrast, viewing paddy rice as lucrative and 'permanent' forest-friendly agriculture, foresters turned a blind eye to migrant farmers continuing to cultivate paddy fields that encroached upon old-growth forest. Because migrant paddy farmers offered a valuable supply of rice to the National Food Authority (Bureau of Forest Development 1978), foresters did little to deter the expansion of paddy rice. Early park enforcement thus added an additional layer of control over resource access and use to that which was already experienced by Tagbanua from migrant control over intensified agriculture and commodity markets.

By the late 1970s, the Bureau of Forest Development institutionalized new management procedures and a migrant staffing structure for regular enforcement around the national park. This began with the Bureau recruiting early migrant settlers as forest rangers, while politically prominent migrants secured senior positions at the national park. Migrant rangers soon formed an enforcement network grounded in kin-ties and political connections, which targeted swidden cultivation by Tagbanua near park boundaries. The fact that migrant farmers were now employed at the park soon supported their pursuit of clearing lands for paddy rice cultivation, an option not available to Tagbanua. Underlying the power to confiscate and apprehend, the initial migrant rangers – and eventually the next generation – used their positions to influence the use of forest resources and land for paddy farming near the national park. For example, because rangers were also paddy farmers and the government supported such cultivation, the fact that several hectares of paddy land overlapped with the park remained unchallenged. By owning stretches of paddy rice and being linked with managers, migrants controlled paddy rice harvests, trade relations and management, further diminishing Tagbanua access to productive resources. Wedged between coercive conservation that criminalized their swidden-base and the denial of access to productive resources, Tagbanua continued to cultivate swidden irrespective of sanctions. Tagbanua were effectively 'locked' into swidden agriculture.

With the overthrow of Marcos in 1986, the number of NGOs increased dramatically on Palawan, with many adopting 'hybrid' approaches to conserving forests by promoting indigenous rights and alternative livelihoods (Dressler and Turner 2008; Novellino and Dressler forthcoming). The 1988 Debt-for-Nature Swap gave new support to such causes, financing the park's enforcement capabilities and environmental programme in 1992 (WWF 1991). These funds supported the park's expansion from 3,901 ha to 5,753 ha, the construction of ranger stations in 1988, and new patrols around the boundaries. In time, the control of the reorganized Department of Environment and Natural Resources (DENR) extended beyond swidden to include the use of non-timber forest products, a task which NGO-led community-based conservation supported.

Phase II: the shift from coercive to community-based conservation

The Philippine state's move to decentralize and devolve park management during the early 1990s further shaped the management of Puerto Princesa Subterranean River National Park. Concurrent to the Debt-for-Nature Swap programme and local NGO initiatives, management now emphasized safeguarding biodiversity, culture and the well-being of indigenous peoples (WWF 1991). This emphasis integrated livelihood concerns into park planning to produce the ambiguous practice of 'community-based conservation'.

Community-based conservation initiatives soon became entangled in broader feuding between the City Government of Puerto Princesa ('the City') and the national Department of Environment and Natural Resources over the right to control the park. Each argued its claims based on a national law. The City sided with the Palawan Council of Sustainable Development and the Strategic Environmental Plan for Palawan, whereas the national Department of Environment and Natural Resources believed its rights were based in the National Integrated Protected Areas Strategy Act, which applied across the nation. In 1992, the City Mayor and the Palawan Council of Sustainable Development used the Strategic Environmental Plan for Palawan to devolve management from the Department of Environment and Natural Resources to the City Government. In turn, the Palawan Council of Sustainable Development claimed regulatory functions over resource management on Palawan, while the City gained jurisdiction over the national park, its infrastructure, and livelihood projects (Memorandum of Agreement (MOA) 1992: 2). The Mayor quickly replaced existing park staff with his clients and renamed the park (formerly St Paul's Park) the Puerto Princesa Subterranean River National Park (Supplemental MOA 1993). Soon afterward, fearing that swidden plots would scar the eco-landscape and turn away 'green' tourists, City staff used their authority to facilitate a ban on the burning of forests for swidden agriculture. Because of the sustained political pressure and often acquiescing to government authority, many indigenous peoples adhered to the ban reluctantly. As a result, many Tagbanua (and Batak – a neighbouring 'hunter-gatherer' group) had not planted enough crops to ensure a sufficient harvest the following season. In contrast, more assertive migrants continued to clear forests for paddy rice (McDermott 2000), effectively reinforcing each group's agricultural approach. Most Tagbanua farmers have since remained wary of clearing large tracts of forest, instead keeping their swiddens either small, or finding ways to underbrush and even intensify. The freedom with which farmers once prepared swidden according to custom and family needs is all but gone.

Community-based conservation, changes in land use classification, and resistance at the national park

While Tagbanua concerns over park management were ignored, a sense of optimism surfaced due to new legal recognition of indigenous rights to land and resources. From 1993 onward, environmental and indigenous rights NGOs explained to the residents of Cabayugan the new opportunity provided by a national Department of Environment and Natural Resources administrative order: 'recognition' of their territory by the state in the form of a Certificate of Ancestral Domain Claim (DENR 1993). NGOs and the Palawan-wide tribal federation (NATRIPAL)[2] drew on USAID funds to support the (eventually successful) Tagbanua bid to acquire an Ancestral Domain Claim next to the national park in 1997. While the apparent legal benefits of the domain claim were numerous, including the right to impede migrant encroachment and access to forest resources, the claim still failed to grant holders the right to secure the assets necessary to buoy subsistence livelihoods. Moreover, after several attempts, the City Mayor finally expanded the size of the park to 22,202 ha so that it could qualify as a UNESCO World Heritage Site (the initial size of 5,753 ha was too small for such a nomination) (IUCN 1993). In doing so, the park came to encompass the Ancestral Domain Claim as a traditional use zone (discussed below). Soon thereafter, the entire domain claim hosted community-based conservation initiatives that progressively reinforced the need for Tagbanua to maintain the traditional character of their livelihoods.

Community-based conservation polarizing access and benefits

After securing the Ancestral Domain Claim for Tagbanua, the City and Department of Environment and Natural Resources staff continued their struggle over the control and management of the expanded park and its new buffer zones. In the end, the City secured full control over the national park under the new Proclamation No. 212, even though the Department of Environment and Natural Resources tried to re-centralize management authority (RoP 1999a). As the City consolidated control, its management efforts also sustained the power of the migrant elite while further marginalizing Tagbanua vis-à-vis local agrarian change. In particular, the success of certain migrants in gaining service sector jobs and enforcement posts at the park, among other spin-offs, reflected how devolved approaches had reinforced each group's role in agriculture.

In 1999, two years after the Cabayugan Ancestral Domain Claim was awarded, NGOs working in Puerto Princesa City drafted a management plan for the national park. Supporting the park's new designation, the plan's objective was to implement livelihood support initiatives in the park's expanded buffer zone. In this zoning network, the core zone corresponded to the original park boundary of 3,901 ha and prohibited all extractive uses. The remaining area (18,300 ha) included the Ancestral Domain Claim that was now redefined as a 'traditional use' zone. Within this, the Tagbanua could only extract resources for subsistence and ceremonial purposes, or undertake 'light' commercial extraction. The irony is that Tagbanua had harvested certain non-timber forest products extensively for commercial purposes in this area for several centuries (McDermott 2000).

While the Department of Environment and Natural Resources recognized that indigenous residents could legally extract non-timber forest products commercially within the Ancestral Domain Claim, the area's management plan and its confinement to a traditional-use buffer zone limited this option. The management of the national park and the Ancestral Domain Claim imposed multiple bureaucratic requirements and fees on indigenous residents' preferential rights to access and use commercial resources inside the claim boundaries. The Cabayugan Catchment Zone was the only portion of the buffer zone that could potentially limit migrant agriculture. However, this zone actually stood to benefit paddy farmers, since it protected water flows for irrigation. Moreover, migrants benefited from the creation of 'multiple use' zones, for which tourism (see Figure 5.4) and other forms of community development were planned (PPSRNP 1999b). By zoning an 18,300 ha 'buffer zone' that engulfed migrant and Tagbanua households, the City sustained the dominant order of livelihood practices, favouring wealthier migrant farmers by supporting paddy rice through zones and projects. Park managers were thus following new policies that slotted each group's livelihood practices into programmes paralleling pre-existing dichotomies of 'modern' and 'traditional' production.

Rethinking and resisting participation in livelihood support programmes

There is clear evidence that pre-conceived constructs of ethnicity and livelihoods still impact upon how benefits are distributed in Cabayugan. Project planners and members have made decisions on who to contact to participate in the programmes and how certain livelihood practices are privileged over others, resulting in discriminatory outcomes that have caused Tagbanua to resist aspects of programme delivery. Such actions by Tagbanua reflected broader, often indirect, levels of resistance against both migrants and devolved

Figure 5.4 The 'jolly side' of tourism and conservation initiatives on Palawan Island.
Photo credit: Olivier Bégin-Caouette

conservation initiatives controlling indigenous livelihoods. To facilitate a new mandate of 'community organizing and information' dissemination, park managers soon introduced livelihood projects that provided alternatives to activities deemed inconsistent with 'ecosystem management' (PPSRNP 1999a: 18). For community organizers to involve Tagbanua in projects required that they be 'organized' and 'mobilized' to undertake traditional and sustainable livelihoods. Participatory planning handbooks suggested that this be achieved by having planners 'integrate with uplanders, mobilizing them to act on problems and issues confronting their group, and assist them in formalizing their organization' (DENR 1994: xiv). Known as People's Organizations, such organizations had to be state-registered and monitored by the park and 'parent' NGOs (those who first helped organize the People's Organizations). In contrast to Tagbanua, community organizers had few difficulties drawing migrant farmers to form associations for project management due to the farmers' political interests and formal education. While the number of People's Organizations involved with the park grew rapidly, many supported migrant livelihoods because of the park's preference for intensive agriculture. As of 2006, only two organizations represented Tagbanua livelihood interests.

The types of organizations and the range of programmes that each People's Organizations group participated in were divided into forest and non-forest based interventions. Along these lines, park-based livelihood projects unilaterally supported migrant paddy rice by maintaining water flows, nutrient inputs, high-yielding seeds, farm implements, and market outlets for rice sales. These projects reinforced the trend among migrants toward agricultural intensification. Only a few programme initiatives advanced rattan harvesting and agroforestry, but only as a way of restructuring (rather than supporting) the livelihoods of indigenous people towards 'sustainability'. The Cabayugan Catchment Conservation and the UNDP-COMPACT programmes (the Community Management of Protected Areas for Conservation), implemented in 2001 and 2004 respectively, encapsulated how livelihood programmes ran along ethnic lines. In the former project, NGO and state assistance was geared toward supporting the intensification of paddy fields or wage labour, while in the latter case, project planners hoped to see swidden become stabilized with traditional harvesting.[3]

Several strands of evidence demonstrate that migrant households were the main beneficiaries of the Cabayugan Catchment Conservation programme. For instance, an Advisory Report indicated that of the 174 participants in this programme, 155 were migrants and only 19 were Tagbanua. While the vast majority of migrants participated in rice production seminars, only six Tagbanua had done so at the time of the report (PPSRNP 2001). Such disparities in participation rates come as no surprise. Tagbanua were not included in the Catchment Management Committee and few, if any, cultivated paddy rice on a large scale. Second, the Cabayugan Underground River Multipurpose Cooperative's support from COMPACT in 2004 invested heavily in high-yielding rice varieties for paddy rice on the assumption that yields would increase 'by over 60% while reducing pollution in the river', further supporting paddy rice intensification (UNDP 2004: 26). By occupying such management positions, migrant farmers and politicians retained authority over local decision-making, regulated access to substantive livelihood programmes, and further supported divisions in agricultural production.

The fact that devolved livelihood projects and benefits flowed along ethnic lines was clear from different migrant and Tagbanua participation levels in local People's Organizations. Migrants primarily joined organizations such as cooperatives, which supported the production and sale of agricultural (rice) surplus at local and city markets. To illustrate, 30 per cent of migrant household heads interviewed were part of the park-supported Farmers' Cooperative, a People's Organization that provided technical assistance, credit and infrastructure support to paddy rice and vegetable farmers (see Table 5.1). If farmers had collateral, such as private title, they received credit from the cooperative as a cash loan of up to 35,000 pesos (US $870) for 'capital build-up'. In most cases, the loans were used to purchase new implements that further mechanized production (including hand tractors, water pumps and threshers). In contrast, indigenous residents lacked private land title or certificates for collateral, and thus found it difficult to obtain loans from the co-op (or any bank) to cover the costs of paddy rice cultivation.

Table 5.1 Involvement by ethnicity in livelihood initiatives and programmes in Cabayugan

Name of organization	Migrants (% of Household heads by ethnicity, n=111; (#) = raw numbers)	Tagbanua (% of Household heads by ethnicity, n=46; (#) = raw numbers)
Agricultural Productivity Committee	0.9 (1)	–
Barangay Council	0.9 (1)	–
Catchment Committee	3.6 (4)	–
Farmers' Cooperative	30 (31)	–
Hagedorn's Brotherhood	0.9 (1)	–
Handicraft Cooperative	1.8 (2)	4.3 (2)
Multipurpose Cooperative	2.7 (3)	–
Banka Cooperative	1.8 (2)	–
Vendors Association	24 (27)	4.3 (2)
Water Consumers Association	3.6 (4)	–
Water System	5.0 (6)	2.1 (1)
Marble Mountain Women's Association	2.7 (3)	–
TICKA	–	65 (30)
Protected Area Management Board	1.8 (2)	–

Source: Wolfram Dressler

Most indigenous residents instead tended small, rain-fed paddy fields (*tubigan*) by hand, ploughed with (borrowed) water buffalo, and few used fertilizers and pesticides. The outcomes offered Tagbanua few opportunities to negotiate agricultural intensification and migrant encroachment on their own terms, placing their swiddens at the mercy of park management.

It was almost exclusively the members of poorer Tagbanua (and migrant) households who comprised the main participants in 'less' productive activities, such as handicraft training and swidden stabilization initiatives under COMPACT. Even among this group, it was usually the poorer migrants who had the opportunity to sell their crafts at inflated prices locally or in Puerto Princesa City (the raw materials for which Tagbanua had collected). The Vendors' Association membership list, for example, revealed that 27 of the 29 members were migrants, indicating that only two Tagbanua had benefited from accessing start-up capital and/or consistently selling goods in the market centre.

Multiple factors account for the low levels of participation by indigenous people in livelihood projects that offered access to and use of productive resources. The discriminatory beliefs held by project coordinators and migrants about the lack of industry and productivity on the part of indigenous farmers ignored the underlying causes, including a lack of resources, limited education and poor health. Many of these opinions became self-perpetuating prophecies. Pejorative comments and attitudes by both parties tended to be ubiquitous, undermining the confidence of Tagbanua in participating in park-supported activities. Moreover, those migrants running projects also controlled and profited from local trade in rice, vegetables, fish and sometimes non-timber forest products. In most cases, migrants dictated the purchasing price of rice, the resale value of goods and the availability of credit. The livelihood support programmes that were originally designed to relieve pressure on forests were thus redirected to those migrants who were already managing livelihood projects *and* controlling the trade of local products.

The only People's Organizations supporting forest-based livelihood activities in Tagbanua communities were local associations, such as TICKA (*Tinig Katutubo sa Cabayugan*) in Cabayugan, which belonged to the province-wide tribal federation NATRIPAL. Both NATRIPAL and other NGOs had organized TICKA to fall in line with the 'traditional' tribal structure of Tagbanua. In Cabayugan, 30 per cent of Tagbanua households interviewed relied on TICKA to coordinate involvement in park-based projects that supported the 'sustainable extraction' of non-timber forest products, such as rattan and honey, since the felling of larger cane and trees was prohibited. Both park and non-governmental initiatives focused on the sustainability of non-timber forest product collection and swidden, that is, the implementation of livelihood projects with low capital requirements and low returns. For instance, the NGO Budyong Rural Development Foundation Inc (BRDFI) and NATRIPAL worked with TICKA to involve Tagbanua in a swidden stabilization project in the domain claim under the UNDP COMPACT initiative. The project had Tagbanua *relearn* 'traditional' and 'sustainable' forms of swidden cultivation. Rather than harvest, pool and share traditional rice yields in a 'communal' manner, as the NGO Budyong expected, the cooperative effort ran afoul with poor yields due to inappropriate site selection. Without rice yields following from progressively maturing varieties in one 'communal' plot, grains could not be pooled in the local *bodega* and borrowed (with interest) during the lean monsoon months as was originally planned.

An interview with Budyong's Executive Director revealed that the project goal was to 're-instil cultural value' into the Tagbanua swidden harvest by having them 'retrieve, store and develop traditional rice varieties' and, as specified in the project proposal, 'allow limited *kaingin* [swidden] rice culture on appropriate sites' in the park's zoning (Executive Director of BRDFI, pers. comm., Palawan Island, March 2004).[4] More ominously, the project also sought to invest in alternative livelihoods so that Tagbanua would fulfil their new agreement with COMPACT: 'convert more than 50% of a forested area used for resin, rattan and honey production located within their [domain claim] into a *strict protected area*' (UNDP 2004: 55, emphasis added). With the domain claim now considered a 'traditional use' *and* 'preservation zone', Tagbanua were told to harvest forest resources 'sustainably' or not at all, locking their livelihoods in place (PPSRNP 2002).

Interviews concerning the views of Tagbanua on the perceived benefits and drawbacks of such 'community-based' initiatives at the park revealed that a number of Tagbanua resisted involving themselves in livelihood projects that offered few, if any, tangible benefits. In particular, an increasing number of Tagbanua who failed to receive project benefits that would have allowed them to negotiate agricultural intensification saw few reasons to participate in livelihood projects. As one male Tagbanua elder stated:

> [The new superintendent] would not consult with TICKA that much. He only met us to tell TICKA that we must give the best supervision to our members. [But he] . . . also encouraged TICKA members to make handicrafts, like *banig*. But he didn't focus on this for long. He trained us, but not for long and no funding came, since there was no buyer at that time.
> (Thomas Madarcos, pers. comm., Martape, Palawan Island, June 2002)

An elderly Tagbanua woman was more explicit, explaining that she did not want to become involved in livelihood projects because:

> All the livelihood projects were focused and benefited the [coastal, migrant] community, and none of the programmes were extended to us here . . . we are now allowed to farm [but] . . . were lectured on precautionary measures to make sure that forest fires do not happen [from swidden burns].
> (Felecine Pedros, pers. comm., Martape, Palawan Island, June 2002)

She continued by noting that 'still we were not allowed to go fish, even with hook and line, in the Underground River. Rangers are on alert . . . [they have] not assisted us with farm seedlings'. She was also disappointed that 'only people outside [the ancestral domain claim] avail of loans, swine dispersal and farm seedlings, equipment and machineries' (ibid.).

A male Tagbanua elder who also refused to be involved in 'community-based' initiatives stated pointedly:

> No one from the [park] made the effort to come here to inform me. They have not balanced their objectives. They have not made the rules fairly as they push conservation over our culture . . . the only way we can access the park is by introducing ourselves to the Governor.
> (Pabio Pamintel, pers. comm., Bentoan, Palawan Island, July 2002)

This elder went on to describe how 'people like me that live far away don't receive any benefits from projects. Only those who have studied get the benefits, but people like me who have not, receive few benefits' (ibid.). A female Tagbanua elder similarly noted how Tagbanua had not benefited from park ventures, and reflected upon Tagbanua anger over this: 'We do not receive anything. Migrants who were educated and can speak English were employed or hired. Indigenous peoples were belittled; that is why we get little chance of being hired. We are tired of it . . .' (Rosita Gregorina, pers. comm., Sabang,

Palawan Island, July 2002). A male Tagbanua elder explained further how, try as they might to implement 'new' agricultural practices, they had been defeated in their attempts: 'NGOs go away, lots of promises . . . but they just control and give no benefits . . . they want our knowledge but give nothing in return . . . I have no more support for them' (Lubic Baltao, pers. comm., Buenavista, Palawan Island, December 2006). He continued:

> . . . and life in the park is so hard. We are denied anything and everything the park has offered us. The project of the farmer's group was defeated because of this . . . the distribution of animals, machinery and equipment like hand tractors and motor pumps was favourably given to those connected with them [project organizers and local politicians]. There was no transparency in the programme. The share was not given to us.
>
> (ibid.)

These open assertions by Tagbanua reflected strong undercurrents of anger and hostility toward both migrants and park managers, who they considered to be holding them in a subordinate position through the poor design of community-based conservation. Such expressions arose as Tagbanua reflected on their marginal position vis-à-vis the conservation movement's support of agricultural intensification among migrants who already controlled both access to productive resources and livelihood projects. Due to the persistence of actions that fostered feelings of marginalization and subordination, Tagbanua came to self-identify with notions of culture and livelihood, rooted in a sense of indigeneity under the rubric of *katutubo* (innateness), as a subtle form of resistance that began to reveal their own 'hidden transcript' (Scott 1990). They contrasted this sense of belonging strongly against the position of migrants as 'outsiders' who controlled agriculture *and* park management. An outspoken Tagbanua elder, for example, clarified how his social position, imparted by *identifying* with 'being *katutubo*', offered a legitimate means to speak against migrants claiming his land. He argued:

> We used to have a system of *api* [to humiliate and instil a feeling of shame]; you are like a slave and people belittle you; no one respects the person when he is humiliated, that is the meaning of *api* . . . the *katutubo* were afraid, they were afraid and they just follow the outsiders/ migrants. But . . . we *katutubo* have the right to stop people from coming in. I can because I am Tagbanua and this is our land and entire region!
>
> (pers. comm., Tagnipa Crossing, Palawan Island, May 2002)

A Tagbanua elder, Damasao Pomgit, also argued forcefully that:

> the people here are related, and of one *naysion* [nation], we have one language. . . . That's why we *katutubo* grouped here as one; there were no parks, our living was only farming . . . we planted, we looked for *yantok*

[rattan] in the forest, honey, *kaingin* [swidden] . . . lots of people came here, they go to us, asking for papers [land title papers]; but what papers are they asking from us? They are still looking for our land, but we do not have any evidence, we have no papers!! But we do not need any!

(pers. comm., Marufinas, Palawan Island, June 2002)

Drawing on the above sentiments, the Tagbanua leader, Manuel Rodriquez, argued that the livelihood support he received was trivial and borderline offensive. Reflecting on his identity as *katutubo*, he stated:

If I do the analysis of these projects, I would say NGOs fight about/ compete over these projects and funds. Here in the community, we would be thankful if something eventually trickles down to us because the NGOs and the DENR, they compete over the funds and the grants. This is clear to me, I understand this well. So they are only using the *katutubo*.

(pers. comm., Sugod Uno, Palawan Island, June 2002)

Many Tagbanua explained why, as *katutubo*, they felt the need to defend their lands and assert their rights against outsiders (*diwan*) and NGO-driven community-based conservation. They indicated that 'being *katutubo*' or articulating *katutubo* was a political construct to resist migrant agricultural practices and conservation programmes that they believed were exacerbating disparities in production and livelihoods. These sentiments show how Tagbanua ethnic identity was being partly rooted in a position formed and reinforced in opposition to wealthier migrants' control over productive resources and trends in community-based conservation that underpin such control. Expressing notions of *katutubo* offered a social and political basis for mediating and resisting migrant control and unequal conservation. As such, the means to express discontent reflected everyday forms of resistance – those of talks, debates and complaints – an approach less frequently described in studies where resistance takes on distinct public forms such a sabotage or arson (see Kull 2002; Turner and Caouette, introduction to this book). 'Hidden transcripts' – mostly offstage critiques of the dominant actors on Palawan – only occasionally became public, reflecting how Tagbanua negotiated the influence of a dominant migrant culture that limited their choices to engage in agricultural activities and conservation practice in ways that reflected their own needs and concerns.

Conclusions

Although devolved conservation practices have set out to reduce poverty and enhance biodiversity conservation, in the case of Palawan Island, the Philippines, it has instead exacerbated competing claims over resource access, polarizing the division of 'insider' and 'outsider' according to specific visions of ethnicity and livelihoods. With the unravelling of successive local and supra-local political and administrative changes, disparities between migrant and indigenous livelihoods have persisted, while dissimilar 'management zones' have continued to define and contain land uses in the national park. Within the Ancestral Domain Claim, Tagbanua participation in livelihood projects that reified 'traditional' practice, particularly swidden agriculture, has limited their access to productive resources with which to negotiate the impacts of agrarian change. Compared to paddy rice farming, in which the use of capital inputs has enhanced production, non-timber forest product and swidden harvesting has generated few opportunities for capital accumulation and many more for amassing debt. Such outcomes have made Tagbanua increasingly vulnerable to unequal commodity relations and skewed conservation priorities. In contrast, migrants continue to receive support for paddy rice cultivation and market sales in the multiple-use areas and influence park management. As such, NGOs and practitioners who implemented community-based conservation by building on specific constructs of ethnicity and agriculture have actually supported and exacerbated the social disparities that arose through agricultural intensification.

Receiving few, if any, substantive livelihood benefits with which to negotiate the negative impacts of the agrarian transition, Tagbanua have begun to resist, in their own way, being involved in community-based conservation. Expressions of anger, frustration and dissatisfaction, for example, have begun to emerge frequently as symbols of local everyday forms of resistance to migrant control over shifts in agriculture and conservation. On a broader scale, the fact that Tagbanua have repeatedly used specific vocabulary (*katutubo*) to express their 'cultural belonging' as a political position in an increasingly heterogeneous landscape indicates that they have tried to resist the marginalizing effects of the processes that drive agrarian change in ways that they have deemed suitable. As Tagbanua reflect on their marginal position, they come to articulate their ethnic identity as a marker of difference in opposition to those who subordinate them. In sum, although devolved conservation practices have set out to reduce poverty and enhance biodiversity conservation, on Palawan Island it has exacerbated competing claims over resource access, polarizing the division of 'insider' and 'outsider' according to ethnicity and livelihoods. The increasing emergence of what were previously hidden transcripts of resistance as politically charged statements are now gradually more evident as Tagbanua rely on the few means available to them to negotiate the agrarian transition and access to livelihoods.

Notes

1   Much of this chapter is based on research I conducted from 2001 to 2008 in central Palawan Island. As part of this field work I undertook 60 key informant interviews and a livelihood questionnaire with 157 individuals. The principal respondents included both migrant and Tagbanua household members in the

forest *sitios* (villages) of Barangay Cabayugan. Both groups continue to actively farm rice and harvest forest resources in areas overlapping Puerto Princesa Subterranean River National Park.

2 NATRIPAL stands for *Nagkakaisang mga Tribu ng Palawan*.

3 The Cabayugan Catchment Conservation programme covered 2,918 ha of the park's buffer zone in a special Cabayugan Catchment Zone designated to provide additional protection to the Cabayugan watershed. Park staff and paddy rice farmers considered this watershed to be the main source for streams that replenished the underground river and irrigated rice paddies (PPSRNP 2001). The primary micro-projects offered by the programme included fruit tree production, high value/tropical fruits production, improved rice production, and water systems for intensified paddy rice cultivation.

4 Budyong's attempt to 'stabilize' Tagbanua swidden is just one of several attempts to do so among shifting cultivators in Palawan Island.

References

Agrawal, A. and Gibson, C. (1999) 'Enchantment and disenchantment: the role of community in natural resource conservation', *World Development*, 27 (4): 629–49.

Bureau of Forest Development (BFD) (1978) 'Memorandum report to the Director of Forestry', 15 March 1978, Manila, Philippines: Bureau of Forest Development.

Clad, J. and Vitug, M. (1988) 'The politics of plunder', *Far Eastern Economic Review*, 24: 48–52.

Department of Environment and Natural Resources (DENR) (1993) 'Departmental Administrative Order No. 02 S, 1993', Manila, Philippines.

—— (1994) 'Upland development program: participatory planning handbook for people-oriented forestry', Manila, Philippines.

—— (1996) *Executive Order no. 263*. Community-based Forestry Management Guidelines. Manila, Republic of the Philippines.

Dressler, W. and Turner, S. (2008) 'The persistence of social differentiation in the Philippine uplands', *Journal of Development Studies*, 44 (10): 1472–95.

Eder, J.F. (1994) 'State-sponsored Participatory Development and Tribal Filipino ethnic Identity', *Social Analysis*, 35: 28–38.

—— (1999) *A Generation Later: household strategies and economic change in the rural Philippines*, Quezon City: Ateneo de Manila University Press.

—— (2006) 'Land use and economic change in the post-frontier upland Philippines', *Land Degradation and Development*, 17: 149–58.

Eder, J. and Fernandez, J. (1996) 'Palawan, a last frontier', in J. Eder and J. Fernandez (eds) *Palawan at the Crossroads*, Quezon City: Ateneo de Manila University Press, 1–23.

Fox, R. (1982) *Tagbanua Religion and Society*, Manila: National Museum.

Ganapin Jr., D. (1992) *Original nomination dossier for St. Paul Subterranean River National Park, Pasay City, Philippines*, UNESCO, National Commission of the Philippines.

Goldman, M. (2003) 'Partitioned nature, privileged knowledge: community-based conservation in Tanzania', *Development and Change*, 34 (5): 833–62.

Haribon Society (1983) *Philippine National Conservation Strategy*, Manila, Philippines: Haribon Society/IUCN/The Philippine Presidential Committee for the Conservation of the Tamaraw.

Hirtz, F. (1998) 'The discourse that silences: beneficiaries' ambivalence towards redistributive land reform in the Philippines', *Development and Change*, 29 (2): 247–75.

Hobsbawn, E. and Ranger, T. (1983) *The Invention of Tradition*, Cambridge: Cambridge University Press.

International Union for Conservation of Nature (IUCN) (1993) *World Heritage Nomination – IUCN technical evaluation 652: St Paul Subterranean National Park (Philippines)*, field visit by Jim Thorsell, Manila, Philippines.

Kellert, S., Mehta, J., Ebbin, S. and Lichtenfeld, L. (2000) 'Community natural resources management: promise, rhetoric and reality', *Society and Natural Resources*, 13: 705–15.

Kerkvliet, B. (1977) *The Huk Rebellion: a study of peasant revolt in the Philippines*, Quezon City: New Day Press.

Kull, C. (2002) 'Madagascar aflame: landscape burning as a peasant protest, resistance, or a resource management tool?', *Political Geography*, 21 (7): 927–53.

Kummer, D. (1992) *Deforestation in the Post-war Philippines*, Chicago: University of Chicago Press.

Lopez, M. (1987) 'The politics of land at risk in a Philippine frontier', in P.D. Little and M. Horowitz (eds) *Lands at Risk in the Third World: local level perspectives*, Boulder: Westview Press, 230–48.

McDermott, M.H. (2000) 'Boundaries and pathways: indigenous identity, ancestral domain and forest use in Palawan, the Philippines', unpublished thesis, University of California, Berkeley.

Madulid, D. (1998) *Floristic and Faunistic Survey and Assessment of St. Paul Subterranean River National Park and Vicinities and Palawan*, Santa Monica, Palawan: European Union and the Government of the Philippines, the Palawan Tropical Forest Protection Plan.

Memorandum of Agreement (MOA) (1992) 'A memorandum of agreement for devolution' (between the DENR and the City Government), Puerto Princesa City, Palawan.

Nash, R. (1982) *Wilderness and the American Mind*, New Haven: Yale University Press.

National Parks Act (1932) 'An act for the establishment of national parks Act No. 3915', Manila, Philippines.

Natural Resources Management Center and Ministry of Natural Resources (NRMC & MNR) (1983) *An analysis of laws and enactments pertaining to national parks: Study on national park legislation*, vol. 1, Quezon City, Philippines: Natural Resources Management Center, Ministry of Natural Resources.

Novellino, D. and Dressler, W. (forthcoming) 'The Role of "Hybrid" NGOs in the Conservation and Development of Palawan Island', *Society and Natural Resources*.

Pinchot, G. (1903) 'The forester and the lumberman', *Forestry and Irrigation*, April: 176–8.

Puerto Princesa Subterranean River National Park (PPSRNP) (1999a) *A Management Plan for Puerto Princesa (St. Paul) Subterranean River National Park*, Drafted by the PTFPP, PCSDS, City Government and European Union Members, Puerto Princesa City, Palawan.

—— (1999b) *Kasunduan para sa pagtatag ng buffer zone* (consultation minutes), 16 September 1999.

—— (2001) *Cabayugan Catchment Committee Advisory Report*, City Government, Puerto Princesa City, Palawan.

—— (2002) *Puerto Princesa Subterranean River National Park Management Strategy*, June 2002, Puerto Princesa City, Palawan: Protected Area Management Board.

Republic of the Philippines (RoP) (1971) 'Proclamation No. 835', Manila, Philippines.

—— (1975) 'Presidential decree No. 705', Manila, Philippines.

—— (1987) *Constitution of the Philippine Republic of 1987*, Congress of the Philippines, Malacanag, Manila, Philippines.

—— (1992) 'Republic Act No. 7586' (National Integrated Protected Areas System Act of 1992), Manila, Philippines.

—— (1997) 'Republic Act No. 8371' (Indigenous Peoples Rights Act 1997), Manila, Philippines.

—— (1999a) 'Presidential proclamation No. 212. An Act Amending Proclamation No. 835, Series 1971', Manila, Philippines.

—— (1999b) 'Draft proclamation No. 212. An amendment of Presidential Proclamation No. 835 dated March 26, 1971', Palawan Council for Sustainable Development, Manila, Philippines.

Rigg, J. (2005) 'Poverty and livelihoods after full-time farming: A South-East Asian view', *Asia Pacific Viewpoint*, 46 (2): 173–84.

Scott, G. (1979) 'Kaingin management in the Republic of the Philippines', *Philippine Geographical Journal*, 23 (2): 58–73.

Scott, J.C. (1990) *Domination and the Arts of Resistance: hidden transcripts*, New Haven and London: Yale University Press.

Scott, W. (1982) *Cracks in the Parchment Curtain*, Quezon City: New Day Publishers.

Sibal, J. (2001) *Local Government Code* (as amended), Quezon City: Central Professional Books.

Slater, R. (2002) 'Between a rock and a hard place: contested livelihoods in Qwaqwa National Park, South Africa', *The Geographical Journal*, 168 (2): 116–29.

Supplemental MOA (author unknown) (1993) 'A supplemental memorandum of agreement' (between the DENR and the City Government), Puerto Princesa City, Palawan.

United Nations Development Programme (UNDP) (2004) *Partnerships for Conservation: lessons from the 'COMPACT' approach for co-managing protected areas and landscapes*, New York: United Nations Development Programme.

Vandergeest, P. (2003) 'Racialization and citizenship in Thai forest politics', *Society and Natural Resources*, 16: 19–37.

Vitug, M. (1993) *The Politics of Logging: power from the forest*, Manila: Philippine Center for Investigative Journalism.

—— (2000) 'Forest policy and national politics', in P. Utting (ed.) *Forest Policy and Politics in the Philippines*, Quezon City: Anteneo De Manila University Press, 11–40.

World Wildlife Fund (WWF) (1991) *Inception Report: integrated protected areas system of the Philippines*, Feasibility studies, Preliminary Design and other Support Components, Washington DC: World Wildlife Fund-US.

Yengoyan, A. (1991) 'Shaping and reshaping the Tasaday: question of cultural identity', *The Journal of Asian Studies*, 50 (3): 565–73.

6   Oil palm and resistance in West Kalimantan, Indonesia

Lesley Potter

Introduction

In this chapter I examine a range of forms and processes of resistance at the local level in West Kalimantan, Indonesia. This resistance aims to challenge aspects of the agrarian transition currently under way in Southeast Asia, notably agricultural intensification and the greater intrusion than ever before of the global market into local agricultural systems. The cases under examination concern the replacement of the traditional swidden-based mixed farming of the indigenous Dayak[1] population with large oil palm plantations, on which the Dayak sometimes become smallholders. One of the plantations and associated communities selected for detailed study is part of Sime Darby Berhad, Malaysia's leading multinational company; others are government parastatal organizations or private corporations. For the Dayak these cases partly fit two of Rigg's (2005: 3) categories of livelihood change: the transition from subsistence to market, and from self-reliance to dependency. Yet because human agency is important, there is considerable variability in the extent to which local farmers become involved with the plantations or become dependent on them as their only source of income. Farmers deploy a range of tactics and forms of resistance when confronted with new challenges and threats that vary according to their own understandings as well as the context of political opportunities. In constructing a repertoire of forms of resistance, collective frames such as ethnicity and identity become key elements. These farmers are not unfamiliar with the market since they and their forebears have grown rubber for several generations, and they are willing to try new cash crops such as pepper or cocoa. However, oil palm plantations are an entirely foreign type of enterprise, which may reduce them to the status of labourers or smallholder out-growers on tiny plots. Their capacity for independent decision-making is then restricted for several years until they have paid off their holdings, during which time their financial returns remain unclear and partly beyond their control.

West Kalimantan is still overwhelmingly rural: the population was only 26 per cent urban at the time of the 2000 census, while employment in agriculture remained at 64 per cent in 2005, showing some decline from a high of

80 per cent in 1980 (Hill 1989: Table 1.5; BPS 2001; *Kalimantan Barat Dalam Angka* 2006). While Dayaks are dominant in most rural areas,[2] 'local Malays' can also be found, especially in the district of Sambas – near the Malaysian border – where they form almost 80 per cent of the population (BPS 2003). Malays are also prominent as civil servants in district administrations and as members of the police and the army. Javanese used to dominate the administration during the Suharto period, but since decentralization more local Malay people have become involved. Transmigrants are an important minority, largely from Java, brought as part of an Indonesian government initiative to move landless people from densely populated areas to specific less populous ones, first as farmers, and then more recently to occupy a central place in the plantation labour force. Madurese (from the island of Madura off eastern Java), Bugis (from Sulawesi), and Bataks (from North Sumatra) are other minor groups, while Chinese, once prominent in rural areas of the northwest, are now mainly urban residents.

Ethnicity and identity are important elements affecting forms of resistance to the plantations (see also Dressler, and Turner and Michaud, this volume). The kinds of protests made by transmigrants typically relate to working conditions and smallholdings, and are different in nature from those of local people, who have usually lost land to the plantations and may also fear the loss of valuable aspects of their culture, especially those elements bound up in swidden-based rice production. Although both groups have displayed resistance, this does not mean that they have entirely negative feelings towards oil palm, which, under the right conditions, can deliver improved incomes. Yet at the same time, the attitudes of estate management toward villagers, labourers and smallholders have tended to be arrogant and overbearing, generating protest and resistance.

The fieldwork for this research was concentrated in the Sanggau district, particularly the Parindu subdistrict which at the time had the most extensive area of oil palm in the province (Potter and Lee 1998; Potter and Badcock 2007).[3] In February 2007, I was able to return briefly to study villages where I had worked in 2002. A number of other researchers have also worked in this area, thus providing a continuity of information from the very early oil palm plantings to the present.[4] The most recent studies conducted in Parindu have been organized by the Forest Peoples Programme (2005), Colchester *et al.* (2006), and Colchester and Jiwan (2006). To fill out the picture beyond Parindu, I have made extensive use of the *Kalimantan Review*, a journal published from 1992 by the Institute of Dayakology (ID), Pontianak.[5] The ID is largely a research and publishing group, while other important associated non-governmental organizations (NGOs) deal with legal matters and community mapping. The philosophy of the *Kalimantan Review* (*KR*)[6] is pro-Dayak, anti-development, and anti-oil palm, such that over the years the authors have presented many examples of resistance to the plantation by Dayak villagers, and of plantation management behaviour deemed unacceptable.

Rural resistance: questions raised by the literature

Yasmi *et al.* (2006), from an analysis of 118 case studies (mainly of forestry conflicts), have recognized eight stages of conflict escalation, though many conflicts would experience only three or four of these:

1 feeling anxiety
2 debate and critique
3 lobby and persuasion
4 protest and campaigning
5 access restriction
6 taking to court
7 intimidation and physical exchange
8 nationalization and internationalization.

(Yasmi *et al.* 2006: 542)

As will be clear in the detailed case studies that follow, resistance to oil palm tends to follow similar paths to those mentioned above.

Similarly, Foucault's take on resistance seems apposite to the situation discussed in this paper: 'Where there is power, there is resistance . . . there is a plurality of resistances, each of them a special case . . . by definition, they can only exist in the strategic field of power relations' (2005: 87–8). There is no doubt that in the various cases of 'the Plantation versus the People', naked power relations come into play. Not only is the plantation mode of agri-culture representative of the forces of capitalist globalization, its establishment in West Kalimantan has been successful mainly because it has been supported by the government at all levels, backed by the police and the army. This was especially true during the Suharto period (1965–98), but has continued into the current era of decentralization.

The Dayak and Malay farmers, and the Dayak and transmigrant oil palm smallholders who confront these hegemonic forces, attempt various kinds of resistance: while their protests have been mainly confined to their own communities, civil society organizations have sought to provide them with a wider audience (especially in recent times), hence bridging a variety of scales. Their resistance techniques include those described by Scott (1990) as 'hidden transcripts' and 'infrapolitics', which may only be detectable through detailed local fieldwork. More open shows of defiance have taken the form of demon-strations, road closures, destruction of planted oil palm, camp burning and seizures of machinery; while the most violent forms of resistance reflect extreme frustration as reasonable efforts at compromise and dialogue – some attempted over several years – have failed.

Chin and Mittelman (1997) suggest three possible frameworks for studying resistance to globalization and neoliberalism, as outlined in the introduction chapter of this book: Gramsci's idea of counter-hegemony, Polanyi's counter-movements and, as noted above, Scott's infrapolitics. In West Kalimantan the hegemonic grouping of plantation, government, police and army bring Gramsci's ideas into prominence. The Kalimantan experience in some respects resembles Escobar's (2004) description of Colombia's Pacific Coast, where local people have been violently displaced by oil palm companies capitalizing on the expanding EU and US markets for biofuels. To date, there has not been the same level of violence in land expropriation in Indonesia, nor has collective resistance been as organized as in Gramsci's 'wars of movement' or 'wars of position'. The situation in the Philippines, where peasants have fought the plantation through recruitment to the New Peoples' Army, as described by Hawes (1990), also appears more extreme than the Indonesian position.

The kind of 'counter-movement', in Polanyi's terms, represented by groups such as Mexico's Zapatistas, is also not immediately relevant to the Indonesian scene, though a national movement of indigenous people (AMAN, Alliance of Indigenous Peoples of the Archipelago) now exists with strong international links, and a nationwide movement of oil palm farmers is being considered. The Roundtable on Sustainable Palm Oil (RSPO), a voluntary international organization, began as an informal effort at cooperation in 2002 between the Worldwide Fund for Nature (WWF) and palm oil producers, traders and distributors, looking for ways of certifying oil palm products as 'sustainable' to make them acceptable to the European market.[7] RSPO has put pressure particularly on Malaysian and Indonesian companies (producers of much of the world's palm oil) to adopt improved practices. While none of these counter-movements are as yet well developed (and in the case of the RSPO, there is already evidence of a 'backlash' by company interests[8]) they do indicate that resistance is becoming more organized.

The question of whether resistance must be visible and easily recognized as such has been a contentious topic in the literature (Hollander and Einwohner 2004). Scott's well-known works on more hidden forms of resistance and everyday politics (1985, 1990) have been criticized by some authors, but have received support from others, such as Kerkvliet (2005, 2006). Kerkvliet documented the 'unorganized and silent' undermining of collective farming by Vietnamese villagers until officials finally endorsed modifications to the system (Kerkvliet 2006: 261; see also Tran's chapter in this book). Cheru (1997) described similar behaviour on the part of Ethiopian peasants who, by means of prolonged quiet resistance, were able to bring about the collapse of an unpopular government. While oil palm smallholders in West Kalimantan have used everyday politics (as well as more overt methods) to demonstrate their resistance to oil palm plantations, the scale at which they have operated has been smaller (confined to the individual village) and their overall aims more locally directed than in the examples quoted from Kerkvliet and Cheru. While they have achieved some successes, I do not believe that these can be generalized across the entire industry.

The political background

The time frame of this study extends from 1972, the beginning of the modern 'development' era in West Kalimantan, to 2008. It includes three periods in Indonesia's recent political history. For the first 26 years covered here, the country was still under the yoke of the centralized and authoritarian Suharto regime, which lasted from 1965 to 1998. After the fall of Suharto, which was brought about partly by the onset of the Asian financial crisis in 1997, there followed a short transition period of 'reformation' and increasing democracy from 1998 to 2000. The decentralization of governance to the district level began in 2001. This major change produced new subdivisions, new roles for local leaders, and more immediate forms of agricultural regulation. Unfortunately, the need for each district to then attempt to raise its own revenue has tended to reinforce the attraction of investment from large corporations, and to support plantation interests at the expense of local farmers.

Between 1984 – the first year for which we have figures for planted oil palm – and 2005, the area under oil palm production in West Kalimantan increased exponentially, from 5,000 hectares (ha) to 382,000 ha. The most rapid rates of overall growth were between 1991 and 1994 and between 1997 and 1998 (Direktorat Jenderal Perkebunan 1991–2005; Kalimantan Barat Dalam Angka 1984–1990).[9] Although government estates were the first to be established, private enterprises are now dominant, including a number owned by Malaysian investors. Most have some arrangements for accommodating smallholders, who were often transmigrants during the Suharto era.[10] During the mid-1990s more than 60 per cent of the land planted in oil palm in West Kalimantan was occupied by smallholders; since decentralization this has declined to below 50 per cent. New estates and extensions of older properties now attempt to limit their exposure to such arrangements, as smallholders generally return lower yields and are more difficult for estate authorities to control. The total land occupied by oil palm continues to grow – although the momentum has slowed somewhat – despite government interest in new plantings in the Malaysian borderlands and the push for expanding biodiesel. The activities of NGOs are considered partly to blame for this loss in expansionary pace, as they continue to encourage communities to reject the crop (*Pontianak Post* 13 April 2007, 24 April 2007, 11 June 2007).

Resistance to the relentless spread of oil palm plantations has been strong among many local people, who have struggled to retain aspects of their traditional lifestyle, while the levels and types of resistance have grown. This is partly reflective of the newer political freedoms post-Suharto, but also the pace of change in the countryside: while the industry matures in some areas and the trees become over-aged, in more remote districts plantations are still new. In the latter, the concerns of farmers connected with earlier schemes still resonate and are being reinvented with a new group of actors. Indeed, there are specific concerns that arise in the early years of an estate, from the initial negotiations over land, to the need for employment during the planting-up period,[11] the arrangements for release of smallholdings, and credit and payment for fruit harvested. In other locales, trees on the earliest holdings have now become senescent[12] and replanting is a noteworthy problem, especially for smallholders with no alternative income. Some farmers have campaigned against replanting, hoping to have their lands restored, but this outcome is unlikely.

Bringing in other actors, NGOs – local, national and sometimes international – are more visible and active now than 20 years ago. In the particular context of Indonesia, 'resistance' is a highly politicized concept and may be encouraged or dramatized by NGOs or the media, while media exposure is itself a form of resistance that may induce changes in company behaviour. Despite West Kalimantan's reputation for violence,[13] Dayak resistance has taken both covert and overt forms. Those covert forms identified by Scott (1985, 1990) seem to have always been present below the surface, while the overt forms have grabbed the headlines and, increasingly, international attention.

West Kalimantan: Dayak agriculture, agrarian transitions, and oil palm

The large province of West Kalimantan, long considered an economic backwater, became the target of central government attempts at 'development' in the 1970s, partly through the construction of an improved road network. Major roads included the important cross-border link to Sarawak and an east–west road along the Kapuas River to Sanggau and Sintang, as shown in Figure 6.1.

By 1972, following the central government's distribution of large timber concessions to private companies across the province, the value of timber exports exceeded that of rubber for the first time (Ward and Ward 1974). Just 20 per cent of the population lived in urban areas, consisting mainly of ethnic minorities such as Chinese and Malay, while industrial activity was limited to the processing of forest and agricultural products. Perhaps West Kalimantan was a province needing an agrarian transition, but the kinds of structural changes envisioned by the government and multinational capital would not be easily accommodated. Emphasizing the province's relatively narrow resource base, especially its poor soils, Ward and Ward (1974: 53) provide a generalized description of Dayak agriculture: 'Land is used under traditional forms of tenure, labour is mobilized on a kinship basis, trade and exchange are often non-monetary, and the social system is resistant to many aspects of technical and economic innovation.' The authors warned that development projects such as transmigration might create tensions between migrants and locals. Despite these warnings, the central government used a heavy-handed approach in attempting to 'civilize' the Dayaks by destroying longhouses[14] and introducing Javanese transmigrants to wean local farmers from shifting cultivation to wet rice production (Jenkins 1978).

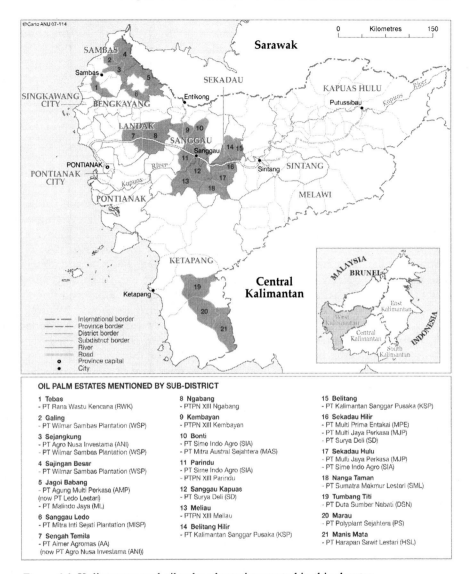

Figure 6.1 Kalimantan and oil palm plantations noted in this chapter.

Map credit: Cartography Unit, Research School of Pacific and Asian Studies, ANU.

While Jenkins is critical of shifting cultivation, suggesting that the Dayaks had brought themselves ecologically to 'the end of the road' (Jenkins 1978: 25), Dayaks themselves insisted that theirs was a circular, rather than a pioneering system (Djuweng 1992). They also emphasized the cultural importance of the swidden for Dayak identity (Tim Adat Talino 1997; Petebang and Bider 2001).

Swidden fallows were perceived by Javanese government officials as 'sleeping land' (*lahan tidur*) or were included in statistics on 'critical land' if *Imperata* grass[15] or erosion were visible. It was precisely the swidden fallows that were targeted by Governor Kadarusno when, in 1975, he suggested the introduction of oil palm plantations in West Kalimantan 'to utilize the critical land' (Perusahaan Negara Perkebunan VII (PNP VII) 1984: 15). The government plantation company PNP VII[16] of North Sumatra then organized a survey in 1978 and the decision was made to set up estates in Sanggau district and at Ngabang, closer to Pontianak (PNP VII 1984: 15; Dominikus *et al.* 2005: 12).

An understanding of the Dayak agricultural system is necessary to fully comprehend the basis for many of the protests against the intrusion of oil palm. Traditional Dayak agriculture has included both dry and wet shifting cultivation of rice,[17] tapping of 'jungle rubber' (in which traditional rubber species are mixed with other trees, especially fruit trees), and harvesting of fruits and nuts from communal fruit groves or *tembawang*.[18] Padoch and Peters (1993) and Momberg (1994), who worked in the Sanggau district, emphasize the high biodiversity of *tembawang*, while Padoch and Peters also note the relatively high population density which can be supported by this agricultural system. Some villages still have areas of *adat* (traditional) forest, from which timber and rattan can be extracted for house building, and wild vegetables or fungi may be gathered. Strict sanctions exist under *adat* law on the unauthorized felling of particular trees, especially honey trees (*Koompassia excelsa*), and burial grounds must not be touched. Those transgressing *adat* law face monetary fines, as well as fines paid in specific amounts of meat, rice wine (*tuak*) and ceramic cups. For Dayak villagers, all parts of their village environment are valuable. If they are asked to give up particular pieces of land to accommodate oil palm, they will more readily cut down old rubber groves (which are family owned) or offer fallow land infested with *Imperata* grass. Clearing of *tembawang* is not generally permitted by *adat* chiefs, nor is it desired.

Early resistance: government plantation company PNP VII in Parindu, Meliau, and Ngabang

The PNP VII Sanggau Project was initiated in 1979 in three locations in the vicinity of Meliau on the Kapuas River. It was followed in 1981 by the Ngabang Nucleus Estate and Smallholder Project (NES), in what is now Landak district, and in 1982 by the World Bank-financed Parindu NES – again near Sanggau – on land partly resumed from a former Dutch rubber estate and partly taken from local people. A further government estate was added in 1985 at Kembayan (see Figures 6.1 and 6.2).[19]

In these initial ventures care was taken to woo local leaders. Pak Donatus Djaman, an educated Dayak who was subdistrict head (*camat*) in Meliau, was sent by the provincial governor to North Sumatra to observe the workings of the oil palm plantations there. On his return he was asked to identify village leaders to take a similar tour. The leaders were impressed by the living conditions of middle management on the estates in North Sumatra and so, upon their return, they agreed to have plantations in their villages. 'The choice seemed to be between *sawit* [oil palm] and development or to remain in poverty with no *sawit*' (Forest Peoples Programme 2005: 7). Later the leaders realized that they had been tricked, that they were not to be treated as 'managers' and that the aim was simply to use villagers as labourers. Many disputes followed over land and compensation. Donatus was sent as *camat* to Parindu 'to calm down the people who had been upset by land acquisition' (ibid.: 8). He argued that the people needed '*plasma*'[20] smallholdings of their own and that there was no room for transmigrants, despite the original plan to bring in 3,000 households.[21] Yet the people at Meliau received no smallholder plots and had to fight years later to obtain some land on the estate, while those at Kembayan experienced similar conflicts (see Table 6.1). Donatus believed that it was only when oil palm and transmigrants began taking over land that the Dayaks put a monetary value on their holdings. Many wanted to sell their land and not join the project, or set up their own oil palm estates, which was not permitted (Forest Peoples Programme 2005). However, from the description issued by the company it appears that those who did not accept the plantation were allowed to opt out, creating 'many enclaves in the midst of the estate' (PNP VII 1984: 17).

Michael Dove, working in the area in 1982, also argued that large numbers of transmigrants could not be supported if the swidden system was to continue, as the fallow lands were being used for oil palm and land shortages would soon be apparent (Dove 1985). Though most villagers were able to combine swidden farming and plantation work,[22] they felt it unfair that transmigrants received plots without having to give up any land. Local farmers received no compensation for their land, even though this had been promised (Dove 1985, 1986).[23] Dove told the story of the 'tea party' to which plantation managers' wives invited local village wives, only to be shocked when the guests gathered up all the food and immediately left. He commented: 'The Dayak "appropriation" of plantation food must be viewed as a counterpoint to the plantation's unsanctioned appropriation of . . . their land' (Dove 1999: 211). Dove argued that the heart of Dayak resistance to plantation management lay in the formers' conviction that they were equal in status to the Sumatran managers who, they believed, wanted too much power. The managers, who were averse to feedback and especially to direct confrontation, believed the Dayaks to be backward and irrational. With the help of the compliant provincial government, managers insisted on a hierarchical complaints structure and would use force – the army – if necessary (Dove 1999). The establishment of such barriers between management and farmers prompted the development of the typical behaviour identified by Scott (1985) as 'weapons of the weak'. Though farmers originally did not perceive themselves as weak, their inferior position was forced upon them by the combined power of the government, army and plantation companies.

By 1997 the government schemes (now renamed PT Perkebunan Nusantara XIII, or PTPN XIII) were regarded as more favourable to the local people than the privately owned plantations that succeeded them. There was still sufficient land for most farmers to continue making rice swiddens and tapping their rubber groves. They complained, however, that returns from their *plasma* plots had been declining as the trees aged, so they diverted part of the fertilizer supplied by the company to their other crops, such as rice. Instead of an intensively developed oil palm *kapling* (a two-hectare plot of oil palm), they were reverting to a 'typically extensive semi-traditional livelihood system' (Potter and Lee 1998: 25).[24] Farmers at the Ngabang government plantation had similar problems with declining yields; they pointed out that although they received their plots in 1986, credit for buying fertilizer had not been available until 1993. When the fertilizer was finally supplied, it was too late to improve yields, so the farmers simply sold it. When the company realized what was happening supplies stopped (Sution 2000). These farmers were in an inferior position to their counterparts in Parindu subdistrict as they no longer had sufficient land for alternative crops.

The arrival of Malaysian company PT SIA in Parindu

The Malaysian based company PT SIA is part of the giant Sime Darby Berhad, one of Southeast Asia's biggest conglomerates. The estate was established gradually between 1997 and 2000 in Parindu and the neighbouring subdistrict of Bonti (Figure 6.2).[25] Its subdivision of land was 60 per cent for the estate nucleus, with 40 per cent for smallholders. This marked a reversal of what had previously been the 'norm' in West Kalimantan.

Using interviews from residents, Colchester *et al.* (2006) summarized an account of the first meeting between officials of PT SIA and district farmers, facilitated by the local government. In outlining its plans to establish oil palm, the Malaysian company presented a one-sided picture of the supposed advantages to the communities, but did not involve them in discussions. Communities were asked by the district head to accept a '7.5 model', in which each farmer should provide 7.5 ha of land: 5 ha would go to the estate, 2 ha would be returned to the farmer planted in oil palm and 0.5 ha would be used for infrastructure. The farmers countered with a '5 model', in which they would release 5 ha – 2 for the estate, 2 for the farmers and 1 for infrastructure – but this was rejected by both the government officers and the company, which began to implement the '7.5 model' regardless of the farmers' wishes. The communities felt that the company had ignored their customary rights and was simply taking over their land for its own interests. In subsequent meetings including the company, the government and the people, the company stated that problems related to land were the government's responsibility (Colchester *et al.* 2006: 126–7). It is easy to understand the concerns of the people in being asked to supply 7.5 ha of land to this new company. The land arrangements of the government estate (PTPN XIII) at Parindu (rather than

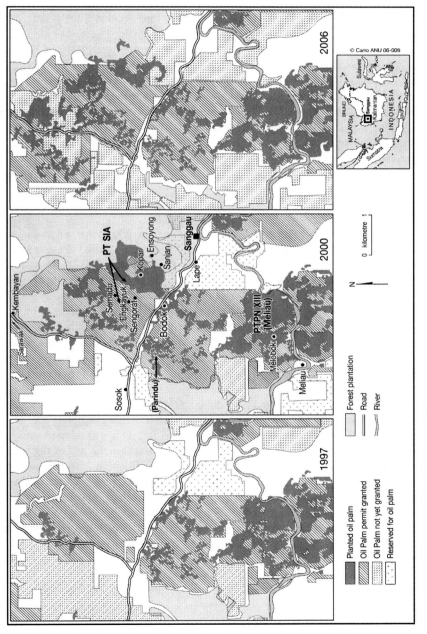

Figure 6.2 Changes in subdistricts Meliau, Parindu, Bonti and Kembayan (Sanggau district) from 1997 to 2000 to 2006.

Map credit: Cartography Unit, Research School of Pacific and Asian Studies, ANU.

this Malaysian conglomerate) were indeed according to a '5 model', with the communities receiving about 3 ha and the company 2 ha.

There was initially much reluctance by the communities to join the scheme, but they were pressured by government officers and some village heads, all rumoured to have received payments from the company. There was also the newness of the plantation system. As the Head of the Sanggau District Legislative Assembly (DPRD) remarked in 2002: 'Most farmers are used to flexible . . . agricultural systems, so those companies that want to develop activities in this area need to be patient and understand that time is needed to change and modify traditional approaches' (pers. comm., 19 February 2002). Referring also to PTPN XIII's plantations in Meliau, where people were campaigning to obtain smallholdings, he noted that 'the whole issue of oil palm and smallholder rights of access to development is a "time bomb" ready to go off in this district' (*ibid.*).

Resistance to PT SIA in 2002: negotiation battles and work practices

In my fieldwork in the Parindu area carried out in 2002, five sub-villages (*dusun*) out of the ten that were targeted by PT SIA were studied (Figure 6.2). Each was at a different position in relation to the company and its demands. While one sub-village (Ensoyong) refused any dealings with the company, and had retained all its land including extensive *tembawang*, considerable areas of oil palm had been planted on lands released by other communities. People worked as day labourers on the estate, but no two-hectare smallholding had as yet been released to farmers, who did not know exactly where their *kapling* would be located.[26] In 2002 rubber prices were very low, so farmers were reasonably willing to convert old rubber land into oil palm and they appreciated the wages paid by PT SIA. However, they continued to grow rice and they especially wanted to preserve their communal *tembawang*. Kopar, the only *dusun* which still had a longhouse, illustrated in Figure 6.3, was luckiest in that half of its land was covered in *Imperata* grass, so it was easy to give it up for oil palm. In exchange, the villagers were able to retain the rest of the land in traditional cultivation, which was still in good condition in 2007, including a communal *adat* forest. Kopar also had a strong *adat* chief, who refused to allow any clearing of *tembawang*. The company built a mill on part of Kopar's land and was able to provide extra employment there, as well as constructing a road that improved village access. By 2007 the people had added clonal rubber, which they had bought from the proceeds of oil palm. As both rubber and oil palm prices were then high, the villagers had increased their incomes and almost paid off their credit. They had moved out of the longhouse and built individual dwellings, but still respected traditional *adat* law. Their main complaints were a continuing lack of electricity and inadequate education facilities for their children (community members, pers. comm., February 2007).

In 2002 the head of Engkayuk sub-village was very enthusiastic in his

Figure 6.3 Longhouse in Dusun Kopar: the last in the district.

Photo credit: Lesley Potter

embrace of oil palm, so he was able to bring all but four families to the plantation. Those four families stubbornly 'enclaved' their land and complained about the head's bonus from the company. They were perceived as backward, troublemakers or simply foolish (Potter and Badcock 2007). Without the oil palm wages, those individuals made a somewhat precarious living, selling rubber and fruit such as durian from the *tembawang* gardens, but they had plans for other crops such as pepper and cocoa. Although she had earlier welcomed the company, one woman in Engkayuk now felt the price had been too high: after the land clearance, rats had decimated their rice crop. This rat problem had become widespread across the district with the advent of oil palm. Yields seemed to be decreasing every year, so that rice was no longer economical to plant, although people continued for cultural reasons. By 2007 the rat problem had abated and the villagers were able to harvest their upland sticky rice (*padi pulut*) for rice wine, but most had to buy at least part of their daily food needs.

Semadu sub-village had set up its own independent oil palm schemes, which pre-dated PT SIA. Two cooperatives were linked to PTPN XIII, which had supplied them with seedlings and later bought their fruit, but the members had been forced to find their own sources of private credit. One cooperative had failed during the financial crisis; the other was continuing, but high input prices meant that insufficient fertilizer was being used, so yields and incomes were low. PT SIA refused to assist these companies unless their members joined like any other farmer. By 2007, Semadu villagers had capitulated and joined the company. They complained that they no longer had much *tembawang* left, while all their old rubber land had been turned over to oil palm. Nevertheless, everybody continued to grow rice and they possessed some new cloned rubber. One marked change that they commented upon was the advent of alcohol drinking and gambling, so that although people had more money, they did not necessarily spend it to meet essential household needs.

Sengorat sub-village was the location of a government-sponsored cloned rubber scheme. Locals had legal ownership of their rubber lands and had actually sold lands to outsiders, unlike other sub-villages. While they had agreed to give land to the company, and in 2002 were even ignoring their mature cloned rubber to concentrate on oil palm, very few could find 7.5 ha for release to PT SIA. One exception was an entrepreneur who had bought land in the village. A former agricultural extension officer, he provided 15 ha, and still had land for cloned rubber (selling seedlings to the villages), fish-ponds and other initiatives.[27] He believed that PT SIA's presence had led to an intensification in farming practices, being more of a catalyst for change in the region than any government agency (Potter and Badcock 2007).

Though some villagers seemed happy enough with the new arrangements, by 2002 the financial crisis had limited their options, so they were taking on oil palm work as a matter of necessity. Theft had become a problem, and before the company organized security, graders and bulldozers were stolen at night. Some labourers stole fertilizers and herbicides for resale elsewhere.[28] Officers employed to check work in the fields had little authority to enforce proper practices and the more distant parts of the estate were not well managed. Workers, supposedly employed between 7 a.m. and 2 p.m., sometimes walked off the job after 9 a.m. Being *absen* like this was a widespread practice, yet nobody had been dismissed. In their work as plantation labourers, local people were displaying some of the typical resistance behaviours identified by Scott (1985) and Peluso (1992), quietly cheating the company with petty larceny and absenteeism, to show their unease with the way in which they were being treated. The Malaysian manager of PT SIA, while quite despondent with local attitudes towards work, noted also that one of the three Dayak subgroups present in the estate's area was more aggressive than the others, being more likely to set up blockades than engage in dialogue.[29]

Farmers worked through a cooperative, which had records of the amounts of land contributed by each household. In 2002, only 30 per cent could provide the full 7.5 ha required by the company, which was refusing to release the first dividend from the smallholder gardens. PT SIA attempted to pay for only 26 per cent of the fruit harvested, which represented the proportion contributed by the farmers. The latter protested and were paid the full amount, but from a company perspective the situation was not sustainable. The manager of PT SIA was threatening to take the matter to court, which was unacceptable to Sanggau officials keen to promote the district's potential for investors. In 2003 the company began to hand over profits to the cooperative, which then became responsible for the management and development of the smallholder gardens.

It was expected, in 2002, that it would take farmers 12 years to pay off the investment fee of Rp26 million (US $2,525 at 2002 exchange rates) per *kapling*, but five years later, with high commodity prices, this was revised downwards to just over eight years (fieldwork observations 2007). Nevertheless, prices of both palm oil and rubber have recently collapsed as a result of the present world economic crisis, leading to further revisions.

The 'tension between advancing modernities and resistant traditions' (Rigg 2001: 45) is still strongly felt in these communities. A modified multi-cropping system is emerging, with oil palm largely replacing jungle rubber, but with rice and certain areas of *tembawang* being allowed to remain, almost for symbolic rather than practical reasons. Cloned rubber, which was not so important in 2002, is now desired, due largely to higher prices and the better yields achievable from cloned stock. People are aware of the social and cultural costs of the plantation, but are no longer resisting the presence of PT SIA.[30] Although there was much to complain about in the company's initial acquisition of village land in Parindu, local attitudes are now more ambivalent, and many see the industry as useful and important for local economies. It is important to stress the role of local agency here and the different responses from particular individuals to the changing possibilities that have emerged, detailed below.

More overt resistance: demonstrations and violent action

The *Kalimantan Review*, introduced earlier, was described in its early days as 'an alternative news source on budding Dayak resistance' (Davidson 2007: 229). During the Suharto period the state-controlled daily available in the Kalimantan region, *Akcaya*, contained little material on Dayaks, while overt resistance to government policies was strongly discouraged and could be dangerous.[31] The *Kalimantan Review* provided focused information, not just on Dayak customs and traditional agriculture, but on the few protests that people were bold enough to make. Early protests were more concerned with the taking of land for transmigrant food crop schemes (see for example Djuweng 1995). By 1997, however, as the plantations exceeded 200,000 ha and the financial crisis began to bite, the level of protest grew and more examples of resistance were published. Even then, village heads were careful with their statements to researchers in the field (Potter and Lee 1998). After the fall of Suharto, the volume of protest escalated, as people were no longer afraid to speak out.[32] Some of these protests referred to long-standing problems that people had already been unhappy about for some years. With the change in political circumstances, covert resistance had become overt.

Table 6.1 lists 20 conflicts between oil palm estates and smallholders, both

Table 6.1 From demonstrations to forceful action: conflicts between oil palm estates and local people 1998–2001

No	Date	Company (PT)	Location (district)	Problem	Action by the people
1	May 1998	Malindo Jaya (ML)	Bengkayang	The company tricked the village head with an inaccurate map and began operations without a permit.	Unanimously rejected: grow pepper, rubber.
2	June 2000	Mitra Inti Sejati Plantation (MISP)	Bengkayang	The company used locals as tools to remove transmigrants because transmigrants were always demanding their rights.	Transmigrants confronted the district legislature in Bengkayang.
3	Sept 1998	Rana Wastu Kencana (RWK)	Sambas	Company took over land including cemeteries and *tembawang* through trickery: obtained a false signature on blank paper.	Held company machines, sought compensation and went to court: lost.
4	May 1999	Aimer Agromas (AA)	Landak	The company cut the peoples' *adat* forest.	The company had to pay an *adat* fine.
5	Sept 2000	PTPN XIII Ngabang	Landak	The income of the local oil palm farmers was below Rp100,000 per month and they could not guarantee their future.	The farmers gave up as they had no power.
6	Oct 1998	Surya Deli (SD)	Sekadau	Slow converting plasma; transmigrants felt deceived.	Demonstration at district legislature.
7	Dec 1998	Multi Prima Entakai (MPE)	Sekadau	Did not convert plasma lands. People demanding at least 3–4ha/family.	Demonstration at district legislature.
8	Feb 2000	MPE	Sekadau	The company promised it would construct a road, but did not. On the contrary it built a factory.	People were angry and destroyed the company's office.
9	Jan 1999	Multi Jaya Perkasa (MJP)	Sekadau	Did not convert plasma lands for local people, only transmigrants. The company deceived them without explanation.	Demonstration both at district legislature and at company's office in Pontianak.
10	June 1999	MJP	Sekadau	The plasma lands still not converted. People felt deceived and apprehensive about their future.	The people burned the company camp and all their heavy machinery.

No.	Date	Company	Regency	Issue	Action/Result
11	Aug 2001	MJP	Sekadau	The company did not fulfil its promises to the people, which made life difficult for them.	They have already demonstrated to local authorities and threaten to take over the company.
12	April 1999	Kalimantan Sanggar Pusaka (KSP)	Sekadau	The company would not divide local people's *kapling* as some had already bought and sold the lands.	Insisted on an independent investigation from local legislature.
13	July 1999	Harapan Sawit Lestari (HSL)	Ketapang	The company violated village land rights.	2,000 ha reoccupied and 400 oil palms cut down.
14	Jan 2000	HSL	Ketapang	The company cleared land under crop, sacred forest, and land about to be opened for swidden.	People demanded justice from the Ketapang District Legislature.
15	May 2000	HSL	Ketapang	The company manipulated data to receive an inflow of foreign investment and sold *kapling* to officials.	Demonstration at the district legislature.
16	Sept 2000	Polyplant Sejahtera	Ketapang	Estate bankrupt, leaving 3,469 transmigrants in a precarious situation. Some were hungry, had no income. They could not sell their oil palm and had no work.	The farmers gave up as they had no power.
17	Sept 2001	Duta Sumber Nabati (DSN)	Ketapang	It was believed that the company did not want to help the people.	Dozens of young people from Dayak Persaguan visited the company offices.
18	July 1999	Mitra Austral Sejahtera (MAS)	Sanggau	The company did not fulfil its promise of scholarships put forth in their propaganda.	Demonstration at the Bupati's office, Sanggau.
19	Dec 1999	MAS	Sanggau	The company deceived the people about its activities, arbitrarily clearing their crops.	Farmers seized the company's tools, despite police intervention.
20	Jan 2001	PTPN XIII Kembayan	Sanggau	The division of the plasma lands did not accord with the agreement when the lands were surrendered. The company was accused of falsifying the data. Peoples' fruits were not accepted by the mill and they lost money.	The people closed the lands and blocked the road.

Source: Adapted and translated from *Kalimantan Review* (2001: 14).

Dayaks and transmigrants, together with the actions taken, as collected by the *Kalimantan Review* between 1998 and 2001 (Anon 2001: 14). The cases shown here are ordered by region instead of chronologically, clearly demonstrating that types of overt resistance may be specific to particular regions, together with the development of problems that affect social relationships on particular plantations (see Figure 6.1 for these locations).

If Sambas, Bengkayang and Landak are considered as one region (Table 6.1 nos. 1–5), the problems that concern local people with the behaviour of new estates are clearly apparent as: obtaining land through trickery (1, 3), or simply cutting the forest without permission (4). The methods of resistance vary all the way from enforcing an *adat* fine to seizing machines and taking the estate to court. Once the estate has been in place for some time, the problems are more complex: 'horizontal' battles between locals and transmigrants (2) or smallholder difficulties of low yields and income, probably resulting from years of inadequate fertilizer (5). The plantation in example 2 (PT MISP) is located in the Sanggau Ledo area, site of the Dayak–Madurese killings in 1997. That particular estate had been in conflict with local Dayaks since 1988, a conflict that escalated in 2000 with the destruction of its camp and the seizure of heavy equipment (Janthing and Pangau 2007).

In Sekadau (Table 6.1 nos. 6, 7, 9, 10, 12), where transmigrants as well as local smallholders are common, questions about the release of *plasma* lands come to the fore. The people are simply unable to gain possession of the small plots promised them; they feel deceived. There is also a clear example of escalating conflict on one estate (MJP), from demonstrations to burning equipment to threats to take over the company (9, 10, 11).

Ketapang (Table 6.1 nos. 13–17) is a very large southern district, parts of which are quite remote. The failure of an estate in such a location can be disastrous for its transmigrants (16). The neighbouring estate (HSL) has caused frequent problems, especially of a cultural nature, which can equally produce a violent reaction or a demonstration (13, 14, 15).

In Sanggau (Table 10.1 nos. 18–20) the main problem, as in Sekadau, appears to be estates breaking promises or deceiving people. In such cases, seizing tools or blocking roads is a better way of attracting attention than mere demonstrations.

The involvement of NGOs in resistance to the plantation: failure and success

The examples of resistance described in Table 6.1 were undertaken by villagers themselves, unassisted by outside organizations except in the reporting of demonstrations and other activities after the initial resistance occurred. Interestingly, my analysis found that the attempted involvement of NGOs in the process of conflict resolution may actually produce negative outcomes, as reported below, especially when the village concerned has *not* requested any outside input. In other instances, the participation of NGOs can be more favourable, for example, in the case when continuing pressure from NGOs eventually resulted in a village head being released from prison, after heavy-handedness on the part of the police. Success also seems to have been achieved where NGOs act behind the scenes, providing information which enables villagers to decide to resist the plantation in ways they themselves determine.

PT Harapan Sawit Lestari (HSL)

This plantation began operations in 1993 in the Manis Mata subdistrict in the far southwest corner of the province, affecting 15 communities. People were forced to hand over their land by the local authorities and village heads, with the local police or military called in to pressure those who refused to comply, labelling them 'communists' or 'anti-government' (WALHI/DTE 2000). They were told that 'if we want to become city people and modernised, we have to plant oil palm' (Ranik 2001: 15). An investigation team from WALHI (Friends of the Earth Indonesia) was told that areas of forest were deliberately burned by the company, after which people were pressured to give up land. Lands and crops guarded by day would be cleared at night. Only a proportion of villagers actually obtained two-hectare oil palm plots, while other plots were allocated to outsiders, including officials such as the police chief. Once the national political regime changed in 1998, people began to express their resentment over their treatment, taking direct action for the first time (Table 6.1 nos. 13, 14, 15).

In November 2002, 100 ha of land in Terusan village was cleared and a burial ground disturbed. The community, who had not agreed to admit the company, decided that it should pay an *adat* fine. Instead of complying, PT HSL called upon the Ketapang district authorities to intervene. The district head (*Bupati*) called a meeting attended by the DPRD, the company and selected Pontianak-based NGOs. The village did not attend since they had not asked for third-party mediation. The meeting became heated and NGOs were accused of being 'anti-development and even terrorists who are stirring up the local people and refusing to recognise the authority of the state' (DTE 2002: 1). Part of the dispute centred on village boundaries: Terusan had constructed a village map with NGO assistance, but the *Bupati*, taking the side of the company, argued that only the government had the right to make maps. He described the NGO's mapping activities as 'invalid, illegal and seditious' (DTE 2002:1). He threatened to send the army into Terusan and to take court action against the Institute of Dayakology.

PT Ledo Lestari vs Semunying village

Semunying village is near the Kalimantan/Malaysia border in Bengkayang district. Villagers there had a negative experience in 2002 when the plantation company PT Agung Multi Perkasa removed timber from the village forest and sold it in Malaysia. The company then had its permit cancelled. That estate was replaced in 2004 by PT Ledo Lestari (LL), which first built a road, destroying rubber gardens and then, in October 2005, cut 4,000 ha of Semunying's traditional forest. After complaints to the company proved useless, locals approached the acting *Bupati* who suggested that they 'enclave' their forest by pegging it out and informing the company. However, that technique failed and the clearing continued, upon which village leaders seized an excavator and chainsaws. So that they would not be considered 'anarchists' by this action, they carried the Indonesian flag as a symbol that they still loved Indonesia. The company immediately called the police, who intimidated village members and, following more exchanges in January 2006, the village head and the secretary of the village council were put in jail. After intense negotiations between the police on the one hand, and the village assisted by NGOs on the other, they were released 20 days later. This was followed by further NGO pressure in recognition of the environmentally rich nature of the area, after which the estate gradually shut down its activities. In November 2006 the villagers were planting rubber on their former forest land that had been burned by PT LL and vowed never to plant oil palm (Aloy 2006; Gindra 2006; Gunui 2006; Wakker 2006; Lorent.wordpress.com 21 May 2007).

PT Sumatra Makmur Lestari (PT SML) and PT SIA in Sekadau

PT SML, originally a plantation from Riau, Sumatra is an offshoot of PT SIA. Both companies recently obtained permits to establish themselves in the southern part of Sekadau district, with SML concentrating on the subdistrict of Nanga Taman (Kanwil BPN 2006). PT SML used the local *camat* to 'socialize' the idea of oil palm from village to village, accompanied by promises of road building. One villager commented: 'We didn't know what oil palm was, but we weren't able to reject it, as they were the government' (Gunui 2006: 33). In 2005 PT SML began by offering a '9:1 model' – 9 ha for the plantation and 1 ha for the smallholder. That changed in 2006 to 8:2, but these terms were still very difficult for locals to meet. A team from *Kalimantan Review* learned that officials had been given a bonus payment calculated for each hectare of village land delivered. The officials receiving these bonuses extended from the *camat* down to each *dusun* head and *adat* chief, with an additional large 'sweetener' if 50,000 ha could be acquired. It was suggested that 8 out of 13 villages had already agreed to give up between 50 and 100 per cent of their land. The company began clearing rubber, *tembawang* and fallow lands in one village, leaving people scarcely any land around their houses and in a few cases removing the houses as well (Gunui 2006: 33).

As a counter to these activities, an internationally funded NGO visited the 13 villages and shared information about the threat of oil palm, enabling villagers to reject the company's propaganda. As a result, all 13 communities decided to oppose PT SML, blockading a road where the heavy machinery was to pass, and eventually forcing the company to withdraw and close its offices in the district. This action was funded by the Borneo Orangutan Society (Australia), Humane Society International (Australia) and Rettet den Regenwald (Germany), indicating that a process of internationalization of resistance is beginning to have an impact at the local level (Rainforest Information Centre 2007).[33]

The AMA, a local NGO turned national

The *Aliansi Masyarakat Adat* (Alliance of Indigenous People) was founded in Pontianak in 1998, two months after Suharto stepped down from power. Its purpose was to campaign against the large-scale conversion of community land to oil palm, as well as industrial tree plantations, transmigrant settlements and mining, and to impress the government with the quality of traditional Dayak land management (Royo 2000). Through networking with other regional and Jakarta NGOs, AMA became a national organization, AMAN (*Aliansi Masyarakat Adat Nusantara*). The first meeting of indigenous people from all parts of Indonesia was organized in Jakarta in 1999, with its now famous declaration: 'If the state will not acknowledge us, then we will not acknowledge the state' ('*Kalau negara tidak mengakui kami, kamipun tidak akan mengakui negara*'). Although this sounded radical, by the time of its second meeting in 2003, AMAN had specified that it was really interested in developing a more participatory civil society within Indonesia and did not seek to undermine the state as such (Acciaioli 2007: 304–5). Since the national organization included such a range of groups, it was not specifically concerned with oil palm, but with indigenous rights in general. It has continued with a strong focus on land, challenging the sovereignty of the state and asserting the competing sovereignty of customary societies, though district administrations have tended to reject such claims (Acciaioli 2007). Back in West Kalimantan, the local branch of AMA has continued an anti-oil palm campaign, similar to that of the Institute of Dayakology.

Controlling the companies through the market: the Roundtable on Sustainable Palm Oil (RSPO)

As noted earlier, the RSPO is a voluntary organization with support from WWF and mainly European business interests. It targets large companies, primarily in Malaysia and Indonesia, together with traders, processors, distributors and financiers who are part of the palm oil marketing chain. Organizations such as Down to Earth (DTE) have dismissed sustainable palm oil as 'mission impossible', and the equating of good management with sustainability as 'greenwash' (DTE 2004: 1). However, if pressure can be put on companies to change their behaviour or risk losing markets, then there may be positive outcomes. European consumers prefer products certified as coming from sustainable sources, but in this case, the industry's environmental and social record has already been strongly criticized by NGOs. Principles and criteria for the operation of large estates have been drawn up and ratified after a series of RSPO meetings. They restrict plantations from forest clearing, especially of High Conservation Value forests, while burning is not permitted. Estates are expected to retain or restore biodiversity on and around the property: they must control pesticide use and factory effluents; minimize soil degradation; and maintain the quantity and quality of surface and ground water. There must be an assessment of social impacts on local communities and proper systems for dealing with grievances and paying compensation, while employees must receive acceptable pay and conditions.

In June 2007, a special set of draft guidelines was drawn up to be applied to smallholders seeking certification of their holdings and produce. In the case of smallholders tied to estates, mills and plantations are given three years to bring their smallholders up to the same standards as the core estates and much of the guideline details are in fact directed at estate management. The first two principles – if adhered to – would remove many of the current difficulties surrounding relationships between smallholders and the plantation. They are:

1   Commitment to transparency.
2   Compliance with applicable laws and regulations (specifically dealing with the right of the company to only use land which is 'not legitimately contested by local communities with demonstrable rights'). Active participation by smallholders in present and future planning is emphasized throughout the guidelines.

(RSPO 2007)

While few Indonesian estates have so far signed up to the RSPO, some important properties have become members. Sime Darby has joined, and hence PT SIA and its Indonesian subsidiaries, while in Ketapang, the Commonwealth Development Corporation which owned PT HSL has recently sold to agro-industry transnational Cargill, also an RSPO member. However, membership does not guarantee that a company will behave responsibly and respect guidelines. A recent study of the companies of the Wilmar group (an RSPO member) in Sambas district uncovered several violations, including deliberately using fire for land clearing, failing to properly consult local communities, and not adhering to correct land acquisition procedures (Milieudefensie and Kontak Rakyat Borneo 2007). Indeed, the major limitations of the RSPO are its voluntary status and the fact that Asian markets for palm oil, such as China and India, do not insist that the product they buy is grown sustainably.

'Why does farmer opposition in West Kalimantan always fail?' is the title of a critical article in the *Kalimantan Review* (Purwana 2006: 17). The author, Bambang H. Suta Purwana,[34] quoting a recently completed thesis at the University of Indonesia on 'Resistance of Farmers Towards Oil Palm', writes of the need for more coordinated resistance. He highlights the close relationship between the plantation and local government, including the security apparatus of the state. Farmer resistance so far has been extremely local and limited to the level of the village. There is a need to develop an organization that is independent and ideological, with strong leadership. He draws on the example of the successful Zapatista revolt in Mexico as a possible model, concluding that in an era of economic liberalism there is no hope that the state will protect the farmer from exploitation by the market: it is the expectation that some umbrella of protection will be provided through the strength of civil society.

In compiling the data on which the RSPO smallholder guidelines were based, Marcus Colchester and his colleagues visited Parindu (Colchester *et al.* 2006; Colchester and Jiwan 2006). One result of their activities was the formation of a new NGO, *Serikat Petani Kelapa Sawit* (Organization of Oil Palm Farmers), the aim of which is specifically to unite oil palm smallholders into a stronger organization that will be able to fight for their rights. This body may provide the leadership that Bambang Purwana is seeking. There are also suggestions for widening its scope by setting up branches in Jambi and other provinces of Sumatra.

Conclusions

In this paper I have examined the question of resistance to the agrarian transition in West Kalimantan, Indonesia, specifically the reaction of the indigenous Dayak population to the replacement of traditional agriculture by oil palm estates. Field studies and examples collected from the pro-Dayak journal *Kalimantan Review* have been used to trace the growth of oil palm plantations from the 1970s to the present and to document the forms of resistance that have emerged in response to various aspects of this transition. It has been argued that the unequal power relations between plantation management and peasants or smallholders (relations intensified by the support offered to plantations by governments at all levels) have consistently been resisted. Such resistance has generally been at the level of Scott's infrapolitics or 'weapons of the weak', especially during the Suharto period, which has continued as a kind of undercurrent to other forms that have adapted to the greater political space for more open and defiant actions in more recent times. This observation is consistent with the arguments put forth by contemporary writers on resistance, who see such everyday acts as often integral and related to – rather than opposite to – more public displays of protest (see discussion in Chapter 2 of this book). Individuals have exercised agency and have either rejected plantations or sought to modify their impact, specifically by continuing various practices associated with traditional agriculture. Some have benefited financially, while recognizing the social disruption which oil palm has brought to the villages.

More overt types of conflict have surfaced with greater frequency since the fall of Suharto, but these have also coincided with the continuous expansion of oil palm in parts, but not all, of the province. The subdistricts identified for closer analysis, either through detailed fieldwork or secondary data, and represented in Figure 6.1, are those in which the impact of plantations have been the strongest. They do not represent the entire province, nor are they likely to do so. In their actions of protest and resistance, Dayaks have been especially keen to retain their cultural practices, which they perceive as essential to their identity and legitimacy as owners of the land. They see this as empowering, both in their relationships with plantation management and in their disputes with transmigrants and others. Local NGOs have worked to assist this empowerment, which has led to the rejection of plantation-style agriculture by particular villages. Strong local leaders have also been instrumental in this process. Other NGOs have been busy publicizing farmers' problems, although actions initiated by villagers have until recently had largely disappointing results in redressing grievances; however, the role of civil society has increased with greater internationalization of indigenous struggles. The advent of the AMA, followed by the RSPO – despite its weaknesses – provides some basis for hope. While there is still a long way to go in the improvement of plantation/farmer relationships, one can detect a desire for change that hopefully will have a lasting effect.

Notes

1 'Dayak' is the generic term given to indigenous groups in Kalimantan, Indonesian Borneo. Many different sub-groups of Dayaks exist in West Kalimantan, but the basic elements of culture and traditional livelihoods are similar.

2 In 2003 they formed less than 5 per cent of the inhabitants of Pontianak, West Kalimantan's main city (BPS 2003).

3 For the field studies of oil palm smallholders on which this paper is based, I was fortunate to have two excellent research assistants, Justin Lee (1997) and Simon Badcock (2002).

4 For his detailed reports of the early period, I am indebted to Michael Dove (1985, 1999).

5 The ID is one of a suite of NGOs begun in association with Pancur Kasih, an organization linked to the Catholic Church and devoted to the improvement of Dayak education and economy. Pancur Kasih runs a school and a highly successful credit union. Pancur Kasih celebrated 25 years of existence in December 2006, a date that coincided with the fifteenth anniversary of the ID. Important guests at the celebrations in Pontianak were the Head of the UN Permanent Forum on Indigenous Peoples and Abdurrahman Wahid, former president of Indonesia during the *Reformasi* period (Musa 2007).

6 Published monthly, mainly in Indonesian (and occasionally in English) and widely distributed locally; it is now available online at http://kalimantanreview.com.

7 The organization held its first meeting in Kuala Lumpur in 2003 and was formally established in April 2004.

8 *Down to Earth* 72, March 2007a and b. See also the discussion later in this chapter on the Wilmar Group of plantations.

9 Data from the central agency were mainly used here, together with provincial

statistics before 1991. After decentralization in 2001, the central and provincial data tended to diverge, but I retained the central data for the sake of continuity.

10 The transmigration programme was no longer acceptable to locals after decentralization, though it still continued in a minor way. There have been suggestions that it might be revived in President Yudhoyono's plan to extend oil palm planting along the Kalimantan–East Malaysia border, a plan which has been heavily criticized by activists and environmentalists but is likely to continue in modified form (Wakker 2006).

11 It normally takes four years before oil palms bear fruit, with full productivity not reached for another two years.

12 Trees are supposed to continue bearing fruit for 20 to 25 years, but yields may decline prematurely, especially if inadequate fertilizer was used. See discussion in Potter and Lee (1998: 23).

13 The violence seems to have begun in the 1960s through Sukarno's confrontation with Malaysia, followed by the anti-Chinese and anti-Communist purges of 1965. Intermittent Dayak/Madurese skirmishes over resources then occurred on several occasions, largely confined to the Sambas–Bengkayang–Pontianak region in the west, culminating in the serious ethnic troubles of 1997, which led to many deaths on both sides and the permanent removal of Madurese from much of the area (Peluso and Harwell 2001; Davidson 2002, 2007).

14 Out of an estimated 126 longhouses in the Sanggau area, only eight remained in 1978 (Jenkins 1978: 23). Today there is just one, but it is no longer occupied.

15 A perennial rhizomatous grass native to east and southeast Asia, India, Micronesia and Australia.

16 PNP or *Perusahaan Negara Perseroan* was the earlier acronym for a government-run plantation. It was later changed to PTPN (*Perseroan Terbatas Perusahaan Negara*) (Government Limited Liability Plantation).

17 A wet swidden is known as *padi paya*. It involves sowing the rice in a swampy area after burning the grass or swamp forest. While some drainage may be attempted, there is not the careful water control associated with true wet rice or *padi sawah*, though the first may evolve into the second (Padoch, Harwell, and Susanto 1998).

18 *Tembawang* are diverse combinations of fruit and timber trees, usually including the *illipe* nut-bearing *Shorea* species *tengkawang*. The most famous represent former longhouse sites, which are often very old. Those gardens are generally entirely communal; family *tembawang* also exist with more limited shared rights, generally evolving from old rubber holdings.

19 Figure 6.2 shows the changes in subdistricts Meliau, Parindu, Bonti and Kembayan (Sanggau district) in 1997, 2000 and 2006. Place names are written only on the 2000 map.

20 Under the plantation and smallholder system (PIR, *Perkebunan Inti Rakyat*), the plantation core, or *inti* was surrounded by 2 ha plots, known as *plasma*, managed by smallholders.

21 Eventually 350 households were admitted from a failed food crops scheme.

22 It was customary for plantations to employ smallholders as labourers for the first few years until their holdings became productive, after which they would have to pay back the cost of land preparation and credit for fertilizer and other inputs.

23 Compensation payment for land was apparently paid in Meliau, though much of it disappeared into the pockets of officials and others and did not reach the people. After that experience, payment of compensation seems to have been discontinued.

24 There are resemblances here to the African experience described by Cheru (1997), in which peasants switched from export to subsistence crops, albeit without the complete withdrawal from the market that she identifies.

25 PT SIA does not appear on the 1997 section of Figure 6.2; nor does PT MAS,

another Malaysian-owned estate immediately to the north of PT SIA, which is named in Figure 6.1.

26 The land was released the following year.

27 By 2007, that individual, a Malay from Ngabang, had expanded his oil palm to 18 hectares, had 9 hectares of *gaharu* (a valuable perfumed wood), plus cocoa and oranges, and also multiple fishponds (fieldwork observations 2007).

28 During fieldwork in 2002, a small shop was visited where imported fertilizers marked 'not for resale' were being sold in a rubber-growing village.

29 It is unclear what kind of evidence was used by the Malaysian manager to make this judgement. All of the Dayaks in the Parindu area are from several subgroups of 'Bidayuh', the same identification used in neighbouring Malaysian Sarawak.

30 There is a consensus in Sanggau that PT SIA has treated its smallholders quite well, in contrast to other estates in the district (Piers Gillespie, pers. comm., 27 November 2008).

31 Pak Donatus, a Dayak subdistrict head reporting the tensions around loss of land to oil palm estates and transmigrants in the early 1980s, noted that a colleague was imprisoned as a result of his criticism (Forest Peoples Programme 2005).

32 A nationwide study on forest conflicts reported in the Indonesian media between 1997 and 2003 found that conflict built up to the year 2000 and after this time conflict decreased; whereas in East Kalimantan (the leader in numbers of conflicts among 11 provinces listed) the peak year for reported conflict was 2002 (Wulan *et al.* 2004). Unfortunately data for West Kalimantan were not presented in this study.

33 *Down to Earth* 72 (March 2007) has a similar story in which villagers succeeded in fining a company for bulldozing graves without permission, using the local NGO PENA, together with WALHI, to publicize the story in the national media. PENA also provided the villagers with information on the negative impact of oil palm, which led them to blockade the company's seed nursery.

34 The writer is a member of the research staff of the Office for Historical and Traditional Knowledge in Pontianak.

References

Acciaioli, G. (2007) 'From customary law to indigenous sovereignty: reconceptualizing masyarakat adat in contemporary Indonesia', in D. Henley and J. Davidson (eds) *The Revival of Tradition in Indonesian Politics*, London and New York: Routledge, 295–318.

Aloy, S. (2006) 'Kisah sedih warga Semunying Jaya' ('Sad story of the people of Semunying Jaya'), *Kalimantan Review*, 127 (March): 39–42; 128 (April): 39–40.

Anon (2001) 'Dari demo sampai tindak kekerasan: konflik perkebunan sawit vs MA Kalbar 1997–2001' ('From demonstrations to forceful action: conflicts of oil palm estates vs traditional people in West Kalimantan 1997–2001'), *Kalimantan Review*, 74 (October–November): 14.

Badan Pusat Statistik (BPS) (2001) *Penduduk Kalimantan Barat* (Population of Kalimantan Barat) *Hasil Sensus Penduduk 2000* (Results of the 2000 Population Census), Jakarta: BPS.

—— (2003) 'Data suku bangsa Kalimantan Barat per kabupaten/kota' (Ethnic data for West Kalimantan by district/town), *Kalimantan Review*, Edisi Khusus No III (Special Issue).

Cheru, F. (1997) 'The silent revolution and the weapons of the weak: transformation and innovation from below', in S. Gill and J.H. Mittelman (eds) *Innovation and*

Transformation in International Studies, Cambridge: Cambridge University Press, 153–69.

Chin, C.B.N. and Mittelman, J.H. (1997) 'Conceptualising resistance to globalisation', *New Political Economy*, 2 (1): 25–37.

Colchester, M. and Jiwan, N. (2006) *Ghosts on Our Own Land: Indonesian oil palm smallholders and the roundtable on sustainable palm oil*, Moreton-in-Marsh, England: Forest Peoples Programme; Bogor, Indonesia: Perkumpulan Sawit Watch.

Colchester, M., Jiwan, N., Andiko, Sirait, M., Firdaus, A.Y., Surambo, A. and Pane, H. (2006) *Promised Land: palm oil and land acquisition in Indonesia: implications for local communities and indigenous peoples*, Moreton-in-Marsh, England: Forest Peoples Programme; Bogor, Indonesia: Perkumpulan Sawit Watch.

Davidson, J.S. (2002) 'Violence and politics in West Kalimantan, Indonesia', unpublished thesis, University of Washington.

—— (2007) 'Culture and rights in ethnic violence', in D. Henley and J.S. Davidson (eds) *The Revival of Tradition in Indonesian Politics*, London and New York: Routledge, 224–46.

Direktorat Jenderal Perkebunan 1991–2005 'Statistik Perkebunan Indonesia: Kelapa Sawit' ('Indonesian estate crop statistics: oil palm'), Jakarta.

Djuweng, S. (1992) 'The conflicts between the Dayak's customary land rights and the development policy in West Kalimantan: the case of Ngabang, Nobal and Tumbang Titi', paper presented at 8th INGI conference, Odanawa, Japan, February 1992.

—— (1995) 'RUU transmigrasi dilihat dari perspektif hak-hak masyarakat adat di wilayah tujuan' ('The transmigration bill seen from the perspective of traditional people in the destination area'), *Kalimantan Review*, 10: 39–50.

Dominikus, U., T. Kusmiran, Uju (no initial) (2005) 'Sawit! Penjajahan gaya baru' ('Oil palm! A new form of colonial domination') *Kalimantan Review* 116, April: 9–13.

Dove, M.R. (1985) 'Plantation development in West Kalimantan I: extant population/ labour imbalances', *Borneo Research Bulletin*, 17 (2): 95–105.

—— (1986) 'Plantation development in West Kalimantan II: The perceptions of the indigenous population', *Borneo Research Bulletin*, 18 (1): 3–27.

—— (1999) 'Representations of the "Other" by others: the ethnographic challenge posed by planters' views of peasants in Indonesia', in T. Murray Li (ed.) *Transforming the Indonesian Uplands: marginality, power and production*, Singapore: Harwood Academic Publishers, 203–26.

Down To Earth (DTE) (2002) 'Conflicts between community and British-owned plantation company in Kalimantan', no. 55. Online. Available HTTP: <http://dte.gn.apc.org/55OP.htm> (accessed 19 February 2009).

—— (2004) 'Sustainable palm oil: mission impossible?', no. 63. Online. Available HTTP: <http://dte.gn.apc.org/63OP1.HTM> (accessed 19 February 2009).

—— (2007a) 'Dayak villagers succeed in fining oil palm company', no. 72. Online. Available HTTP: <http://dte.gn.apc.org/72op6.htm> (accessed 19 February 2009).

—— (2007b) 'Smallholders and the RSPO', no. 72. Online. Available HTTP: <http://dte.gn.apc.org/72op3.htm> (accessed 19 February 2009).

Escobar, A. (2004) 'Beyond the Third World: imperial globality, global coloniality and anti-globalisation social movements', *Third World Quarterly*, 25 (1): 207–30.

Forest Peoples Programme (2005) 'Dayak leaders' memories and dreams: report on a survey of oil palm plantations and indigenous peoples in West Kalimantan July 2005', Moreton-in-Marsh, England: Forest Peoples Programme. Online. Available HTTP: <http://www.forestpeoples.org/documents/prv_sector/oil_palm/dayak_surv_oil_palm_jul05_eng.pdf > (accessed 19 February 2009).

Foucault, M. (2005) 'Method' in *The Will to Knowledge: the history of sexuality*, vol. 1, London: Penguin; reprinted in L. Amoore (ed.) *The Global Resistance Reader*, London: Routledge, 86–91.

Gindra (no initial) (2006) 'Masyarakat Semunying Inginkan Karet' ('People of Semunying like [to grow] Rubber'), *Kalimantan Review*, 135 (November): 42.

Gunui (no initial) (2006) 'PT SML meluluhlantakkan tanah adat Namga Taman' ('PT SML shatters the adat land of Nanga Taman'), *Kalimantan Review*, 131 (July): 33.

Hawes, G. (1990) 'Theories of peasant revolution: a critique and contribution from the Philippines', *World Politics*, XLII (2): 261–98.

Hill, H. (1989) *Unity and Diversity: regional economic development in Indonesia since 1970*, Singapore: Oxford University Press.

Hollander, J.A. and Einwohner, R.L. (2004) 'Conceptualizing resistance', *Sociological Forum*, 19 (4): 533–53.

Janthing and Pangau (no initials) (2007) 'Fenomena sawit dan kabut asap di Kaliman-tan Barat' ('The phenomena of oil palm and smoke haze in West Kalimantan') *Kalimantan Review* 25 May. Online. Available HTTP: <http://kalimantanreview.com/online/2007/004.php > (accessed 19 February 2009).

Jenkins, D. (1978) 'The Dyaks: goodbye to all that', *Far Eastern Economic Review*, June 30: 22–7.

Kalimantan Barat Dalam Angka ('West Kalimantan in Figures') (1984–1990, 2006) BPS Pontianak (Statistics Bureau, Pontianak).

Kanwil BPN (Kantor Wilayah, Badan Pertanahan Nasional) (Regional Branch, National Lands Office) (2006) *Peta Penyebaran Kegiatan Pembangunan Perkebunan Transmigrasi dan Hutan Tanaman Industri, Kabupaten Sekadau Provinsi Kalimantan Barat* ('Map of the spread of development of estate crops, transmigration and industrial forest estates, Sekadau District, West Kalimantan') 1:250,000.

Kerkvliet, B. (2005) *The Power of Everyday Politics: how Vietnamese peasants trans-formed national policy*, Ithaca, NY: Cornell University Press.

—— (2006) 'Agricultural land in Vietnam: markets tempered by family, community and socialist practices', *Journal of Agrarian Change*, 6 (3): 285–305.

Lorent.wordpress.com (2007) 'Minyak sawit nan licin: Tangis sedih di rimbun sawit ('Slippery palm oil: sad weeping of the leafy palm branch'), 21 May 2007. Online. Available HTTP: <http://lorent.wordpress.com> (accessed 19 February 2009).

Milieudefensie, L.G. and Kontak Rakyat Borneo (2007) *Policy, Practice, Pride and Prejudice: review of legal, environmental and social practices of oil palm plantation companies of the Wilmar Group in Sambas District, West Kalimantan (Indonesia)*, Amsterdam: Milieudefensie (Friends of the Earth, Netherlands).

Momberg, F. (1994) 'Managing complex agroforestry systems', paper presented at Borneo Research Council Third Biennial International Conference, Pontianak, West Kalimantan, 10–14 July 1994.

Musa, T.K. (2007) 'Refleksi gerakan social di Kalimantan Barat' ('Reflections on social movements in West Kalimantan'), *Kalimantan Review*, 138 (February): 9–13.

Padoch, C. and Peters, C. (1993) 'Managed forest gardens in West Kalimantan, Indonesia', in C.S. Potter, J. Cohen and D. Janczewski (eds) *Perspectives on*

Biodiversity: case studies of genetic resource conservation and development, Washington DC: American Association for the Advancement of Science, 167–76.

Padoch, C., Harwell, E. and Susanto, A. (1998) 'Swidden, sawah and in-between: agricultural transformation in Borneo', *Human Ecology*, 26: 3–20.

Peluso, N.L. (1992) *Rich Forests, Poor People: resource control and resistance in Java*, Berkeley and Los Angeles: University of California Press.

Peluso, N.L. and Harwell, E. (2001) 'Territory, custom and the cultural politics of ethnic war in West Kalimantan, Indonesia', in N.L. Peluso and M. Watts (eds) *Violent Environments*, Ithaca and London: Cornell University Press, 83–116.

Perusahaan Negara Perkebunan VII (PNP VII) (1984) *Pertama di Kalimantan Barat: pabrik kelapa sawit* ('First in West Kalimantan: Gunung Meliau Palm Oil Mill'). 'Proyek Pengembangunan Kelapa Sawit di Kalimantan Barat' ('Oil Palm Plantation Development in West Kalimantan').

Petebang, E. and Bider, B. (2001) 'Ladang hilang, Dayak pun hilang: masih pantaskah disebut Dayak?' ('The swidden disappears, so the Dayak disappears: can they reasonably still be called Dayaks?'), *Kalimantan Review*, 67 (March–April): 26–7.

Pontianak Post (13 April 2007) 'Bachtiar: Penolakan sawit tanggung jawab provokator' ('Bachtiar: Provocateurs are responsible for the rejection of oil palm').

—— (24 April 2007) 'Stop konsensi baru' ('Stop new concessions').

—— (11 June 2007a) 'Cabut dan alihkan izin perusahaan tak aktif: Investasi sawit Kalbar stagnan' ('Cancel and transfer the permits of companies no longer active. Investment in oil palm is stagnant in West Kalimantan').

—— (11 June 2007b) 'Perbaiki kinerja pembangunan' ('Improve the synergy of development'). All the above online. Available HTTP: <http://www.pontianakpost.com> (accessed 19 February 2009).

Potter, L. and Badcock, S. (2007) 'Can Indonesia's complex agroforests survive globalisation and decentralisation? Sanggau District, West Kalimantan', in J. Connell and E. Waddell (eds) *Environment, Development and Change in Rural Asia-Pacific: between local and global*, London and New York: Routledge, 167–85.

Potter, L. and Lee, J. (1998) *Tree Planting in Indonesia: trends, impacts and directions*, Occasional Paper No 18, CIFOR, Bogor, Indonesia: Center for International Forestry Research.

Prijono, M.A. (2003) 'Gubernur melarang publikasi data etnis Kalimantan Barat' ('The Governor forbids the publication of [population] data by ethnicity for West Kalimantan'), *Kalimantan Review*, Edisi Khursus (Special Issue) No III: 9–10.

Purwana, B.H.S. (2006) 'Mengapa perlawanan petani di Kalbar selalu gagal?' ('Why does farmer opposition in West Kalimantan always fail?'), *Kalimantan Review*, 132 (August): 17.

Rainforest Information Centre (2007) *Small Grants Fund, 2006–2007 Financial Year, Indonesia*, Lismore, Australia: Rainforest Information Centre, Online. Available HTTP: <http://www.rainforestinfo.org.au/projects/grants.htm> (accessed 19 February 2009).

Ranik, E.S. (2001) 'Land for the price of a sack of rice', *Kalimantan Review* (English Edition), V (August): 15.

Rigg, J. (2001) *More Than the Soil: rural change in Southeast Asia*, London: Prentice Hall.

—— (2005) *Living with Transition in Laos: market integration in Southeast Asia*, London and New York: Routledge.

RSPO (Roundtable on Sustainable Palm Oil) (2007) *RSPO Principles and Criteria for Sustainable Palm Oil Production: consultation draft guidance on smallholders*, prepared for comments from the Task Force on Smallholders by M. Colchester (ed.), 15 June 2007, Moreton-in-Marsh, England: Forest Peoples Programme, Online. Available HTTP: <http://www.rspo.org/resource_centre/Consolidated_Consultation_Draft.pdf > (accessed 19 February 2009).

Royo, A.G. (2000) 'The power of networking: building force to navigate cross-scale turbulence where solo efforts fail', in J.B. Alcorn and A.G. Royo (eds) *Indigenous Social Movements and Ecological Resilience: lessons from the Dayak of Indonesia*, Washington DC: Peoples, Forest and Reefs (PeFoR) Program Discussion Paper Series, Biodiversity Support Program, 73–83.

Scott, J.C. (1985) *Weapons of the Weak: everyday forms of peasant resistance*, New Haven: Yale University Press.

—— (1990) *Domination and the Arts of Resistance: hidden transcripts*, New Haven and London: Yale University Press.

Sution, T.T. (2000) 'Nasib Petani Bak Telur di Ujung Tanduk' ('The precarious fate of the oil palm farmers'), *Kalimantan Review*, 62 (October–November): 16.

Tim Adat Talino (The Adat Talino team) (1997) 'Berladang, itulah hidup kami' ('To make swiddens is our life'), *Kalimantan Review*, 27: 5–9.

Uyub, D. (2006) 'Warga Semunying Jaya kembali diintimidasi: Mereka diintimidasi oknum petinggi Polres dan TNI Bengkayang' ('People of Semunying Jaya return intimidated: they were intimidated by high officials of the police and the army in Bengkayang'), *Kalimantan Review*, 131 (July): 38.

Wakker, E. (2006) *The Kalimantan Border Oil Palm Mega-project*, commissioned by Milieudefensie – Friends of the Earth Netherlands and the Swedish Society for Nature Conservation, Amsterdam: AID Environment.

WALHI Kalbar and Down to Earth (DTE) (2000) *Manis Mata Dispute: the dispute between the indigenous community and PT Harapan Sawit Lestari oil palm plantation, Manis Mata Ketapang District – West Kalimantan*, Jakarta: National Executive Walhi.

Ward, M.W. and Ward, R.G. (1974) 'An economic survey of West Kalimantan', *Bulletin of Indonesian Economic Studies*, X (3): 26–53.

Wulan, Y.C., Yasmi, Y., Purba, C. and Wollenberg, E. (2004) *Analisa Konflik Sektor Kehutanan di Indonesia 1997–2003* ('Analysis of forestry conflicts in Indonesia 1997–2003'), Bogor, Indonesia: Center for International Forestry Research.

Yasmi, Y., Schanz, H. and Salim, A. (2006) 'Manifestation of conflict escalation in natural resource management', *Environmental Science and Policy*, 9: 538–46.

7 Development and its discontents: The case of the Pak Mun Dam in northeastern Thailand

Erik Martinez Kuhonta [1]

'It isn't fun to be in Bangkok. If the dam hadn't been built across our river, our shadows would never have fallen on the gates of Government House.'
– Sompong Viengchan, a leader of the Pak Mun Dam group
(*Bangkok Post* 13 August 2000)

In the standard analysis of Thai political economy, the late 1980s and early 1990s are regarded as the height of Thailand's modern economic boom. From 1988 to 1990, Thailand registered double-digit growth rates – 13.3, 12.4 and 10 per cent respectively – ranking it among the world's most dynamic economies. This period, however, was not just a time of economic expansion, but also a time of increasing resistance to that expansion. While Thailand's middle class began to see solid gains in their incomes thanks to the economic boom, marginalized peasants in the north and northeast of the country were engaged in a protracted struggle against the Thai developmental model.

This developmental model has centred on export-oriented industrialization and agribusiness, the latter being central to the Thai agrarian transition. The exploitation of natural resources has been a crucial element of this model because such resources are necessary to feed the engines of industry and agribusiness. From dams to wastewater plants to eucalyptus plantations, economic growth has required the appropriation of land, forests, minerals and water. As large development projects, whether built by the state or the private sector, have seized control of these natural resources on which peasants depend for their livelihood, a fierce struggle has ensued.[2]

Geographer Philip Hirsch (1990) has characterized Thailand's pattern of development as 'incorporative', whereby peripheral people and resources are pulled into the path of economic growth; however, 'incorporative' fails to capture the more political dimensions of this form of development. What has been occurring in Thailand is more than the incorporation of the periphery into a developmental model, but the very displacement of the periphery in favour of the instruments of modernity. This is the perennial struggle of development, whether experienced by an early modernizer such as eighteenth-century England or the late modernizers of the Third World. In the past two decades, this tension has boiled over in Thailand precisely because of the country's economic take-off.

Not only has development in Thailand steamrolled over the peasantry, but it has also cobbled together a formidable modernizing alliance: state, domestic capital, and international financial institutions. This represents an important turning point in Thailand mainly because state and capital were never so closely aligned. In fact, until the mid-1970s, capital was a relatively weak force in society, largely forced to follow the dictates of the 'bureaucratic polity'.[3] However, as an incipient bourgeoisie began to emerge in the 1970s, it eventually took over the levers of political power once Thailand moved towards a more democratic form of government.

The alliance between state and capital has not been just a case of business-people taking over public office. This alliance has also been a consequence of the state's ideological commitment to industrial development and its belief that the agrarian sector should be eclipsed in favour of industry. Furthermore, state officials have often colluded with capital to enable massive resource exploitation because they have gained kickbacks by providing permits for resource extraction. The consequence of this formidable alliance has been devastating for the peasantry. Squeezed by both political coercion and capital, peasants have been forced to fight a rearguard battle armed only with the power of mobilization.[4]

The scope of conflict between peasants and the state has ranged widely over the whole national terrain and across virtually every natural resource sector. Dam-building has displaced tens of thousands of peasants throughout Thailand, but has been most contentious in the northeast. Struggles over land encroachment and salt mining have also been acute in the northeast. Battles over logging have been concentrated in the north. Threats to mangrove forests have involved parts of the southern coast. Natural gas pipelines connecting Burma to eastern Thailand and Malaysia to southern Thailand have incited civil society to action, while wastewater plants have rallied community residents in the outskirts of Bangkok. In these struggles the number of demonstrations against the state has grown exponentially. In 1978, there were 42 demonstrations, in 1990 there were 170, and by 1994 protests had skyrocketed to 988 (Praphat 1998).

It is important to point out that resistance to state development in Thailand has historically come from two different streams of the peasantry (Baker 2000). On the one hand are small-scale, commercial farmers whose main concern is maintaining a viable income in relation to the price of their products and the cost of farm inputs. On the other hand are subsistence peasants whose livelihoods have been displaced by large projects, such as dams, wastewater plants, or other forms of land eviction. This latter group, whose concern is less about income than about food security, is the focus of this chapter. While both groups have been affected by agrarian transformations, it is the latter that has suffered more drastic changes and whose plight has caught the attention of the national media. In James Scott's words, it is these subsistence peasants who are closer to 'the subsistence crisis level . . . a threshold below which the qualitative deterioration in subsistence, security, status, and family social cohesion is massive and painful' (1976: 17).

This chapter will analyse the Pak Mun hydropower dam as an illustrative case of developmental malaise, peasant resistance and agrarian change in Thailand. The dam is a classic example of Thailand's developmental pathology: a rush to extract resources for industrial growth, failure to submit the project to public scrutiny, destruction of local communities and their livelihoods, and repression of those who would challenge a state project. Built at the head of the Mun River – the largest tributary of the Mekong River – in the northeastern province of Ubon Ratchatani, the Pak Mun Dam has been at the centre of debate over development policy since the late 1980s. The main rationale for the dam's construction in 1991 was to increase power generation for electrification in the northeast, although additional benefits were envisaged for irrigation and tourism. The economic boom of the late 1980s led to a shortage of energy, which the Pak Mun Dam was meant to address. The dam's impact, however, has been largely counterproductive, neither supplying the requisite energy levels nor improving the livelihoods of villagers. Rather, it has depressed the income of approximately 20,000 villagers in the province of Ubon Ratchatani. Fisherfolk have witnessed a substantial decline in the stock of fish; villages have been uprooted by flooding caused by the re-routing of water flows; and families have been split apart by the need to find employment in the urban economy.

For almost two decades the villagers affected by the Pak Mun Dam have ardently challenged the government's policies, rallying in the province and with greater fanfare in Bangkok. Their protests have been supported by non-governmental organizations (NGOs), academics and select members of the media and the middle class. The role of political parties, however, has been negligible. Except for the governments of two former prime ministers, Chavalit Yongchaiyudh (1996–7) and Thaksin Shinawatra (2001–6), most politicians have shown little interest in solving the crisis over the Pak Mun Dam. Civil society actors have thus taken on the mantle as spokespersons for the poor. The central coordinating group for the villagers of the Pak Mun Dam, and for a host of other concerns of the urban and rural poor, is the Assembly of the Poor (AOP, *Samacha Khon Jon*), an organization that in other countries might conceivably have formed the basis for a left-of-centre political party.[5]

Caught between the rudimentary institutions of a transitional democracy and a form of livelihood that is at odds with the modernizing impulse of Bangkok technocrats, the villagers of the Mun River have failed so far to achieve their ultimate goal – the decommissioning of the dam – although they have gained some concessions from the government. Their struggle, however, has helped highlight other developmental dilemmas throughout Thailand's vast periphery, where numerous local communities battle against state-sponsored projects. Thus, while discontent continues to simmer along the banks of the Mun River, the crisis of Pak Mun has taken on wider meaning, standing as the symbol of local communities' struggles.

Before looking in-depth at the case of the Pak Mun Dam, I want to place this in a broader context by discussing the role of civil society in this struggle over development. Despite the dominance of state and capital, a tenacious resistance movement has emerged, sustained by NGOs, academics, and peasant organizations. These actors may not have levelled the playing field, nor have they won most battles, but they have experienced some limited success over the past two decades. More importantly, they have shown that open resistance to the state has not been futile. While scholars such as James Scott (1985) have made a compelling case for the value of 'everyday forms of resistance', resistance in Thailand has largely remained on the terrain of an open 'battlefield' and therefore needs to be assessed on such terms.

Civil society, resistance, and development

The more vibrant civil society in Thailand can be traced to the 1970s, during a period of democratization and social reforms. It was at this time that the NGO movement was born through the initiatives of Puey Ungpakorn, Rector of Thammasat University and Head of the Bank of Thailand. In 1969, Puey founded the Thailand Reconstruction Movement and in 1970, the Thammasat Graduate Volunteer Center. The goal of these initiatives was to send university students to the countryside to engage in volunteer development work. In 1974 another important initiative involving universities came about through the Mae Klong Integrated Rural Development project. The idea of this project was to catalyze action-oriented research within major universities.

The mid-1970s was one of the most turbulent periods in modern Thai history, with the rise and fall of a democratic regime between 1973 and 1976.[6] During this period, farmers and workers mobilized to advance an agenda of social reform. The Peasants' Federation of Thailand was the most active association, representing the farmers of the north and northeast; however, by the time the military struck back with a devastating coup in October 1976, the Peasants' Federation had been severely weakened through assassinations and intimidation. Students and activists who had championed the rights of farmers and workers fled to the jungles in the northeast and took up arms with the Communist Party of Thailand.

In the early 1980s, pragmatic generals in the military began a process of political amnesty, calling upon students to return to the cities. As students gave up their ties with the Communist Party, some enrolled in graduate school to eventually become prominent academics, while others went into NGO development work, and a few eventually gained public office.[7] By the mid-1980s, about 50 new NGOs had sprouted in Thailand.

The renaissance of the NGO movement in the early 1980s saw a focus on the basic livelihood problems of peasants. The strategy of NGOs was to concentrate on self-reliance and people's participation. The kinds of activities that these NGOs championed included integrated farming, savings groups, rice banks, buffalo banks, fertilizer banks, community revolving funds for village stores, and handicraft groups. The thrust of these activities was to stimulate and encourage local activities, indigenous knowledge and, in general, a return to the village community as the fundamental unit for human development. While the focus on livelihood problems remains a staple of current NGO work, the NGO movement eventually shifted towards more direct confrontation with the state over peasant interests rather than a simple 'horizontal' developmental effort.[8] This shift became pronounced in the mid-1980s, particularly in the battle over the Nam Choan Dam.

The Nam Choan Dam was a project in the Thung Yai Naresuan Wildlife Sanctuary in Kanchanaburi Province in western Thailand. The dam was opposed by a broad coalition of middle-class forces, students, academics, NGOs, religious leaders, and some notable political elites, including former Prime Minister Kukrit Pramoj (1975–6) and the ascetic Governor of Bangkok, Chamlong Srimuang (So and Lee 1999). Critics of the dam argued that it would flood and destroy the nature reserve. Under intense pressure, the government of Prem Tinsulanonda cancelled the project in 1988. The movement against the Nam Choan Dam succeeded because of the breadth of the anti-dam coalition, as well as the variety of tactics employed. One notable tactic was the effective manipulation of traditional rites and beliefs (Dome 2007). Anti-dam activists erected a shrine to the spirit of King Naresuan within the wildlife reserve in order to call forth the spirit of the king to protect the wildlife reserve zone.

Since the battle against the Nam Choan Dam, numerous other struggles have been waged between local communities and major development projects. A brief listing of the more prominent struggles would include: the case of tantalum mining in Phuket in 1986; the 1991–2 *Khor Jor Kor* Scheme to evict forest dwellers in the northeast in order to plant eucalyptus trees as a source for the lucrative pulp and paper industry; the polluting in 1993 of the Nam Pong River by a pulp and paper plant in the northeastern province of Khon Kaen; industrial poisoning in the northern province of Lamphun in 1994; the construction of the Yadana gas pipeline from Burma through rainforests in western Thailand; the proposed construction of the Prachuab Khiri Khan power plant in the south; and the Asian Development Bank-funded waste-water treatment plant in Samut Songkram, on the outskirts of Bangkok.

The number of NGOs and people's organizations that has proliferated in the midst of all these struggles is enormous. Indeed, perhaps second only to the Philippines, Thailand now has one of the most vibrant civil societies in Southeast Asia. Some of the most important groups include the NGO Coordinating Committee on Rural Development (NGO-COD, established 1985) which is a major umbrella organization for NGOs, the Foundation for Ecological Recovery (1986), the Assembly of Small-Scale Farmers of the Northeast (1992), the Northern Farmers Development Network (North-Net,

1994) and the Isan Farmers Assembly (1998). By one estimate, the number of primarily developmental NGOs is now at least 350 (*Thai Development Newsletter* 1995a: 114). This phenomenal growth in the number of development NGOs and people's organizations is a direct result of Thailand's rush to industrialize and peasants' efforts to engage such challenges.

Just as the nature of NGO work has shifted from horizontal community work towards direct resistance to development projects, the scope of NGO activism has also shifted from the local to the national level. In an effort to broaden its influence beyond local communities and onto the national agenda, in 1991, the NGO Coordinating Committee on Development put forth the People's Development Plan (see *Thai Development Newsletter* 1995b: 120–1). This was an attempt by the NGO community to articulate a national agenda that pulled together the variegated concerns of the rural sector. The People's Development Plan was presented at a seminar on 'The Seventh [Economic] Plan' in May 1991 at Chulalongkorn University. The People's Plan set out a clear agenda for development, emphasizing a bottom-up process as well as the integral relationship between the environment and poor people's livelihoods.

The founding of the Assembly of the Poor (AOP) on 10 December 1995 at Thammasat University marked a heightening of the struggle and the organizational capacity of peasants and the NGO community. At the heart of the AOP is the fight over the Pak Mun Dam. Nevertheless, the AOP actually represents 121 villagers' groups centred around seven distinct issues, each with their own local constituency: forest and land; dams; state projects; slum communities; work-related illness; alternative agriculture; and small-scale fishing. Most of the peasants represented by the AOP have seen their livelihood security threatened by development projects. Their goal is to reclaim the natural resources that are the fundamental basis of their livelihoods.

At the inaugural meeting, the AOP adopted the Mun River Statement which demanded state recognition of community rights, political reform, public participation in natural resource management, and people-centred development policy. The AOP also attempted to deliver its statement to the prime minister during the ASEAN Summit, but was blocked from doing so, although the fracas that ensued at the height of the Summit ensured that its demands were publicized by the national media. In February 1996, the AOP again took advantage of an international meeting in Bangkok by rallying during the Asia–Europe Meeting (ASEM).

The AOP is supported by a network of NGO advisers, academics and students, who provide strategic and intellectual focus for the large group, but who also make sure that leadership remains in the hands of the local communities. The secretariat is housed with an NGO called Friends of the People. The structure of the AOP is relatively decentralized, in part to maintain its local roots, but also to avoid repression and intimidation against its designated leaders. Within the AOP there is no one leader, although there are a number of leaders who represent the assembly as a whole. The AOP's strength stems from its ability to bring together several groups with outstanding grievances. But this also means that there has to be coordination among these groups for the movement to work effectively. Each group with a grievance is represented by a *pho khrua yai*, or a male group leader.[9] The *pho krua yai* coordinates between the villagers and the general assembly and represents villagers when negotiating directly with government officials. A *mae krua yai*, or female group leader, is in charge of logistics during demonstrations.[10]

The AOP's strategy relies on sustained non-violent action, and both peasants and the NGOs involved are committed to resistance based on non-violence. Key advisers of the AOP stress the long-term staying power of this poor people's movement as well as its autonomy from conventional political forces. Rejecting the need for political institutions, Wanida Tantiwitthayaphitak, one of the most prominent advisers, articulates a common refrain among NGO activists: 'It's not worthwhile to set up a political party ... More time should be dedicated to strengthening the people's movement. Representative democracy is now a failure.' (*Thai Development Newsletter* 1999a: 51). Another adviser, Lao-thi Nilnuan, also emphasizes the importance of the movement as an overarching force rather than simply a temporary bill of grievances. He comments: 'Demanding for compensation claims or immediate solutions shouldn't be the AOP's objectives. Its direction must be sustainable and aim at strengthening its self-reliant movement' (*Thai Development Newsletter* 1999b: 51).

To generate broader support and publicize its agenda, the AOP has made strategic alliances with other social movements at the international level (*Thai Development Newsletter* 1995a). It has joined the *Via Campesina* (a World Peasant Movement) (see also Vu Tuong's chapter) and was elected as the International Coordinating Committee for Southeast Asia and East Asia. The Asian Cultural Forum on Development has also pledged to strengthen the AOP's regional and international coordination. Rallies against the Pak Mun Dam, the core concern of the AOP, have been staged outside Thailand, including in front of the Thai Embassy in Washington DC, United States. Other international NGOs concerned with dams, such as International Rivers, have also taken up the cause of the Pak Mun Dam.

The importance of the AOP, then, is that it has aggregated the grievances of the rural (and to a lesser extent, urban) marginalized peoples in a broad overarching movement. Although the AOP may lack the resources that state and capital possess, it is an extremely well-organized association, strategically savvy, and committed to long-term resistance. As we will see next, in the battle over the Pak Mun Dam, the AOP has played a central role in mobilizing peasants and in bringing the world's attention to this particular struggle. Since the turbulent mid-1970s there has been no poor people's organization in Thailand with a similar scope.

The case of the Pak Mun Dam

The Pak Mun Dam (location shown in Figure 7.1) was first conceived by the Electricity Generating Authority of Thailand (EGAT) in 1970 as a hydroelectric project. Its chief purpose was to address the increasing peak demand for electricity in the northeast during the economic boom, especially during the dry months (January to May). In 1989, the cabinet of Prime Minister Chatichai Choonhavan approved the construction of the dam and in May 1991 EGAT began construction, with the initial construction costs estimated at 3.8 billion baht (US $155.2 million). The project was completed in June 1994 with a total construction cost of 6.5 billion baht (US $260 million), an increase of 91 per cent in nominal terms. Compensation and resettlement costs totalled 1.1 billion baht (US $44.24 million). As part of these costs, compensation for fisheries amounted to 395.6 million baht (US $15.8 million) by April 1999 (Sakchai *et al.* 2000). The project received US $24 million from the World Bank as part of a loan for Thailand's power development programme. This loan constitutes 13 per cent of the total cost.

The dam is located 5.5 kilometres upstream from the Mekong River. It operates as a run-of-the-river hydropower plant, meaning that it does not function with an enclosed reservoir. The storage capacity of the dam is therefore based on the water levels of the river. During the dry season, the water level of the dam generally does not rise 106 metres above mean sea level (MSL), while during the wet season, the water rises to a level of 108 metres above MSL (Sakchai *et al.* 2000).

The socio-economic costs of the dam for local rural communities have been extensive. The dynamiting of the river, and the subsequent flooding of the riverbanks, has led to a loss of livelihood for many villagers through the reduction in fish stocks and the loss of fertile land. The dam's impact on the river has sharply reduced the ability of fisherfolk to catch fish, while the loss of land, such as swamps, wetland forests, cultivation strips and paddy fields, has prevented peasants from raising a few crops or harvesting herbs and mushrooms. These all constitute basic needs for peasants who live by the Mun River (Thailand Development Research Institute (TDRI) 2000: 11). Thus the socio-economic and environmental impacts of increased energy needs have resulted in significant impacts on local rural villagers.

The construction of the dam affected 238 households at the actual dam site. Additionally, after impoundment of the reservoir, 705 households were relocated because their land was inundated or surrounded by water. The actual total number of households displaced by the Pak Mun Dam was 1,700. By April 1999, 6,202 households were awarded some degree of compensation for loss of livelihood due to the impact on fisheries (Chayan 2000: 2). In total, the dam has affected more than 20,000 villagers around the Mun River.

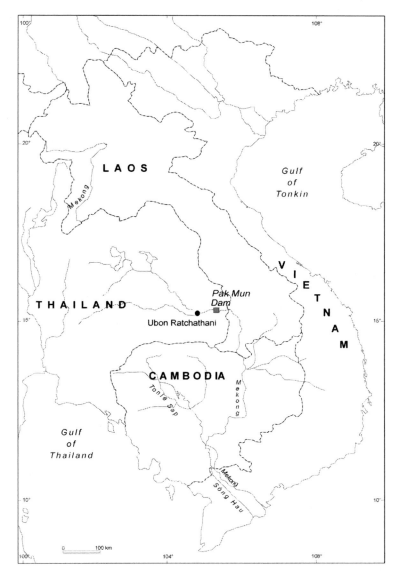

Figure 7.1 Pak Mun Dam location, Thailand.

Map credit: Jean Michaud

The process of decision-making: planning the dam

The origins of the controversy over the dam can be traced to its planning phase. During the initial planning of the dam, EGAT made some effort to mitigate its anticipated, deleterious effects. In 1982, two separate reports were commissioned by EGAT: an environmental and ecological investigation (EEI) and a resettlement planning (RP) investigation. Based on these reports, EGAT decided to move the planned construction of the dam away from the original site at the Kaeng Tana Rapids to Ban Hua Heo. This was done to avoid compensation to 3,970 households that would have been affected. In order to reduce the dam's impact on village households, in 1985 EGAT lowered the reservoir of the dam from 113 metres above MSL to 108 metres above MSL. This then ensured that only 248 households would be displaced, down from an earlier figure of almost 4,000. Two other important modifications were also made: the dam was moved 1.5 kilometres upstream to avoid the submergence of the Kaeng Tana Rapids; and EGAT also lowered the reservoir to 106 metres above MSL during the dry season (January to May) to uncover the upstream Kaeng Saphue rapids. Hence, it could be argued that EGAT made notable efforts to address environmental and social concerns at the initial stage of the planning of the dam (Sakchai *et al.* 2000: xi).

However, once EGAT decided to build at the *new* site at Ban Hua Heo, it did not commission another environmental impact or resettlement study (Chayan 2000: 4). During and after the construction, three studies on the environmental and resettlement impacts were undertaken, but none was disseminated widely to the public. Furthermore, the first EEI and RP studies of the original site were not made accessible to the public nor to the villagers (Chayan 2000). EGAT's planning style reflected a top-down process that was sorely lacking in transparency (Chanida, pers. comm., August 2000).[11]

EGAT's strategy to ensure that the dam would be completed was based on gaining the loyalty of the subdistrict leaders (*kamnan*) and the village headmen (*puu yai baan*) (Khun Bundeum, pers. comm., March 2001). EGAT courted the local officials by personally visiting them and providing them with food and drinks. It gave them promotional posters and banners to place at the front of their homes, and it assured them that they would personally gain greater employment opportunities. EGAT also selectively gave more information to local leaders than to the villagers and often neglected to mention the harmful consequences that would ensue from the construction of the dam (Chayan 2000).

Moreover, EGAT actively employed a 'divide and conquer' strategy among villagers. It persistently lobbied villagers to support the dam by enticing them with money and by supplying blatant disinformation on the effects of the dam. Many of those who initially supported the construction of the dam believed that it would bring electricity and a better income. When villagers realized that this was not happening, that much of the river ecology was being destroyed, and that they were not even being paid as promised, many switched sides, joining those who had opposed the dam from its inception (Khun La, pers. comm., March 2001).[12] Commenting on how the dam has split villages and families, Khun La, an adviser to the AOP, noted that 'villagers within families are now fighting amongst each other about the relative benefits of the dam. In the past, there was more cooperation and communal support. There was little need for law or the police. Now anything small that happens has to be mediated by the police' (ibid.).

EGAT's use of its financial and institutional influence, coupled with its hierarchical and tightly circumscribed administrative planning, thus led to major long-term problems. First, no baseline study of fisheries was undertaken because EGAT did not assume that the dam would have a negative impact on fisheries. Without a baseline from which to assess the difference in the level of fish after the construction of the dam, EGAT officials were naturally more sceptical of the villagers' claims. Second, because this was the first run-of-the-river dam being built in Thailand, the effects of flooding and resettlement were not thought to be very grave. Finally, in its preliminary studies, EGAT assumed that the villagers were primarily rice farmers – rather than fisherfolk – and therefore failed to address the integral relationship between villagers and the river. Had there been greater openness and consultation with villagers and environmental agencies at the earlier planning stages, it is possible that some problems could have been foreseen. In particular, the oversight of the impact on fisheries looms as a major error given the magnitude of the eventual losses.

Resistance to Pak Mun Dam

Much of the battle against the dam and acts of resistance played out initially through demands for compensation. This was, however, a particularly taxing process for villagers, as they found themselves severely disadvantaged by a lack of formal, political representation. Several problems should be highlighted. First, the committees established to address compensation packages were composed of local elites (*kamnan* and *puu yai baan*) and bureaucrats, who made it difficult for the villagers to gain a fair hearing. Second, compensation packages were often inconsistent and difficult to implement. Third, as discussed above, EGAT had made no baseline study of fisheries and was therefore unsure whether to accept the figures given by the villagers estimating the loss of fish. Finally, the lack of an actual economic valuation of villagers' social systems and cultural values made it impossible to gain compensation for the dam's impact on community life.[13]

Compensation can be categorized into three types according to how villagers were affected by the dam: (1) those affected directly by the dam construction; (2) those impacted by inundation and resettlement; and (3) those affected by the loss of fishing during construction.[14] For each form of compensation, villagers had to bargain arduously with EGAT. For many, it took years of negotiations to reach a fair compensation, if one was ever achieved.

With regards to the first type of compensation – to take one example – a group of villagers from Ban Hua Heo directly affected by dam construction were promised new housing, land for agriculture, and money (135,000 baht per household). Several problems, however, ensued in the actual implementation of the compensation package. For some villagers, EGAT was unable to find agricultural land. For others, the land was not appropriate for agriculture. Other problems in the resettlement of villagers included the fact that drinking water was not accessible and that the houses constructed by EGAT were too small.[15]

Another group of villagers from Ban Hua Heo were simply provided with 135,000 baht to relocate. They discovered that this was not enough to buy titled land in their new area. Therefore, they decided to move to the state forest reserve, where many of the villagers had lived before it had been claimed by the state. This move was declared illegal by the state and led to further confrontation between villagers and local authorities. EGAT then offered these villagers land to resettle, but this was rejected on the grounds that there was not enough land for farming (Chayan 2000).

For the villagers whose land was inundated – those in the second category of compensation above – it is instructive to see how committees to assess compensation actually formed. Two committees were established on 15 May 1992 that assessed the rate of compensation for assets lost by inundation. The governor of the province of Ubon Ratchatani was the head of both committees. Out of these two committees, seven subcommittees were formed, of which none included villagers. On 15 December 1993, another committee was created with two subcommittees. In the first subcommittee, the district officer (*nay ampoe*) was the chair, while the subdistrict head (*kamnan*) was the representative of the villagers. In the second subcommittee, one representative from each of the three districts was appointed as a committee member. None of the representatives on these subcommittees that were supposed to be on the side of the villagers were considered to be genuine representatives by the villagers themselves. In fact, all of them were believed to be EGAT supporters (Chayan 2000: 7).

The issue of land is particularly problematic because it reflects the compounding of several unsolved problems confronted by the rural poor in the face of agrarian change and state development. Villagers around the Mun River do not have titles to land that they have inhabited for generations. This makes it more difficult for them to claim their rights against the state. When they are displaced, often they find that they cannot farm on land that has been allotted to them, partly because much of the land in the northeast is not fertile and partly because most of the villagers who have been displaced are more inclined towards fishing and foraging in the forests than farming. When villagers then decide to find their own plot of land in the national forest, where they are more likely to be able to make a living, they run up against the iron hand of the state that has claimed authority over all public land. Many of these villagers – now labelled as encroachers – are sued by the state for trespassing (Khun La, pers. comm., March 2001).

Finally, the third form of compensation for the loss of fisheries was the most contentious, since it was this particular problem that had been neglected by EGAT in its earlier estimations. The first plan drawn up by EGAT sought to compensate villagers for the loss of fisheries during the three years of construction. This plan would then allocate funds based on a villager's proximity to the dam. Villagers designated in zone 1 (closest to the dam) would receive 90,000 baht (US $3,600) while those in zone 5 (furthest from the dam) would receive 15 baht. This scheme was clearly unsatisfactory to the villagers and led to a one-month protest at the Provincial Hall. After about two years of negotiations, EGAT proposed in 1995 that each household would receive 30,000 baht (US $1,200) for compensation over three years of construction and an additional 60,000 baht (US $2,400) to assist in developing new occupations. Although this compensation was implemented, by this time many villagers, now exasperated by the government's seesawing, were calling on the state to provide compensation for the *permanent* loss of fisheries and for the complete decommissioning of the dam.[16]

In an act of open resistance, in March 1996, the AOP held its first major rally over 26 days at Government House (the complex of offices of the prime minister). About 10,000 villagers joined the month-long protest. Although Prime Minister Banharn Silpa-archa initially equivocated about meeting the protesters, he eventually decided to do so. The cabinet also made several important concessions. It agreed to grant land rights documents to all who could prove claims to land. Those who could not prove ownership of land would receive *Sor Por Kor* deeds or be allowed to lease lands at low prices.[17] Other concessions that overlapped with the grievances of the Pak Mun Dam villagers included compensation for those displaced by the Sirindhorn Dam and the suspension of future dam projects. The concessions made by Banharn's cabinet were significant, but they did not last after Banharn's government collapsed in November 1996 amid factional rivalries and allegations of corruption.

In 1997, a 99-day protest in Bangkok put more pressure on the new government of Chavalit Yongchaiyudh (Praphat 1998). In part because Chavalit was a native of the northeast, he appeared much more willing to address the grievances of the villagers. Sidestepping cabinet ministers who evinced little interest in the problems of the poor, Chavalit assigned a group of young, reform-minded, deputy ministers, including Chaturon Chaisaeng and Adisorn Piangket, to negotiate with the villagers. These young ministers made a genuine effort to give the villagers a fair hearing. At one of the meetings in March, the discussion centred around the need to clearly assess the impact of the dam on peasant livelihoods. EGAT and the Fisheries Department claimed that the quantity of fish and the income from fishing had remained stable or even increased since the dam's construction. The NGO representatives for the AOP responded that their interviews with fishermen indicated that the opposite had occurred. While the NGO representatives admitted that it would be difficult to prove conclusively whether there were more or less fish after the construction of the dam, since no scientific studies had been conducted before the construction, they argued that fisherfolk's own testimony should be considered as expert information

(Missingham 2003). At one point, an official from the Irrigation Department became irate, complaining that

> every time the state builds something people always complain to the government, or EGAT, or us. First, we should consider whether this group of people have a right to petition or not. If you accept that they do, then second, is their petition plausible?
>
> (ibid.: 167)

To this Deputy Minister for Science Adison replied:

> Here in Thailand everyone has the right to petition. It's part of our democratic system. You probably shouldn't ask such questions. People have a right to petition directly to the government, because I'm well aware that district officials cover things up, or even EGAT covers things up.
>
> (ibid.: 167)

On 11 April 1997, Chavalit's cabinet agreed to a major resolution that was co-signed by Deputy Finance Minister Chaturon and the AOP adviser Wanida Tanthiwitthayaphitak. This resolution included measures to protect villagers' lands, compensation for villagers affected by dams and reforestation programmes, and a pledge to listen to local opinion before initiating construction on other projected dams. At the negotiation table, Chavalit was clear about his intentions: 'I bring a sincere heart to this negotiation with the people. I will do anything I can for the benefit of the people' (*Bangkok Post* 4 May 1997). In May, the villagers returned to their province believing that this agreement would finally stick.

Yet with the financial crisis then burning down Thailand's economy, and Chavalit's incapacity to douse its flames, Chuan Leekpai's Democrat Party took charge in November 1997 and summarily revoked the resolutions of the previous cabinet.[18] Faced with a difficult political situation, the AOP pursued a *dao krachai* (scattered star) resistance strategy of establishing protest villages in areas where the AOP had bases, including at the Pak Mun Dam site itself. This strategy, however, failed to yield any response from the politicians and in March 2000 the siege of Bangkok's government resumed. More than 3,000 villagers set up permanent camps outside Government House. Pressured to respond to the renewed mobilization, the Chuan government formed a ten-member committee (five of whom had been nominated by the AOP) to address the AOP's sixteen demands. On 6 July 2000, the committee recommended to the Ministry of Interior the opening of the sluice gates; however, Chuan ignored the recommendations. Ten days later, out of rising desperation, 225 protesters scaled the walls of Government House but were eventually beaten back by riot police.[19]

During this period, the AOP turned towards high-profile theatrics in order to garner the attention of the national media to its resistance measures, and thereby broaden its appeal. Wanida, the main AOP adviser, observed: 'When we are to mount a demonstration, we need to gauge if the media will be interested to cover our activities' (Rungrawee 2004: 549). At times, the AOP would raise the stakes through acts such as the scaling of Government House or occupation of the Pak Mun Dam itself. These acts were done with the knowledge that confrontation would generate more media exposure. The AOP also undertook dramatic political events that were tailor-made for photojournalism (see Figure 7.2). In one instance, an activist from the Student Federation of Thailand suspended himself from the dam under which was a huge banner stating in English 'No Dams'. This event was featured on the front page of *The Nation* on 1 June 2000.

An even more creative effort to gain the media spotlight, conducted this time by the villagers near the Rasi Salai Dam, also on the Mun River, was the enactment of a morning ritual to worship the goddess of the river, *phra mae*

Figure 7.2 Assembly of the Poor protests for the media at the Pak Mun Dam.

Photo credit: Assembly of the Poor, Thailand.

khongkha. In this ritual, villagers waded into the river and prayed to the goddess every morning. What was remarkable about this act was that this ritual, although related to Isan (northeastern) culture, was in effect manufactured as a tool for social resistance. 'A village leader gave me a call to consult about what they should do, as his fellow villagers were intensely demoralized,' recalled Chainarong Setthachuea, an adviser to the AOP and head of the South East Asian River Network. He continued:

> Then, I asked him if there was any activity they could create based on their own traditional beliefs. He said villagers believed that every river had a *phra mae khongkha* who guards the river. At that time, I happened to see a photograph of a ritual called *sattayakhroa* [performed at the Narmada River Valley in India] on a website. So, we borrowed the form of this ritual from the *sattayakhroa*; however, its content was essentially based on the villagers' own tradition.
>
> (recalled in Rungrawee 2004: 555)

This ritual, serving both as an act of collective solidarity and as a vivid picture of dissent, ended up on the front page of the *Khao Sod* newspaper on 24 May 2000.

One analyst of the AOP has noted that its tactics have often veered towards confrontation that could lead to violence (Rungrawee 2004). Although the movement remains non-violent, it has to some extent benefited from rising tensions because the media is more likely to cover an event when the likelihood of a physical clash is imminent. Veteran Thai analyst, Chris Baker (2000: 18), has argued that the AOP's mobilization has involved a process of 'invasion, siege, and peace treaty'. The AOP has repeatedly trooped down from the northeastern plains and surrounded Bangkok's Government House. Under the Chavalit government, the 'invasion' and 'siege' did lead to a 'peace treaty' with significant concessions, but Baker notes that 'in this public drama, the role of violence was inverted. Injuries received counted as victories, injuries inflicted as defeats' (Baker 2000: 22–3). For the AOP, the compiling of the sufferings they received during their protests, including physical injuries from scuffles, deaths attributed to stress, suicide and miscarriages, were further proof of the righteousness of their struggle.[20]

The scaling of Government House and the subsequent beating and arrest of the protesters was widely covered in the media and raised the stakes of the struggle. The government was under increasing pressure to respond in some way, and accepted the call to organize a televised debate with the AOP. The terms of this debate were extremely important if it were to yield any positive results for the AOP and, after much negotiation, the AOP agreed to a debate at Thammasat University in August 2000 in which Banthorn Ondam, a leading adviser to the AOP and former university lecturer, would moderate. While the debate did not resolve any major issues, it was significant in that the government had for the first time granted the villagers a televised public platform on which to air their views.[21] Wattana Nakpradit, an adviser to the AOP and a member of the NGO Friends of the People, observed that 'a public conference is critical. If the public understands [the problems of the poor], it will strengthen [their cause]' (Wattana, pers. comm., June 2000).

Despite the AOP's inventive tactics and increasing national exposure, the Chuan government refused to budge. Compared to his predecessors, Chuan's reaction was much harsher and more dismissive. Reflecting his legal background, Chuan repeatedly argued that the protesters must follow the law and could not expect the government to cave in to their demands simply because of their mobilizing and resistance tactics. He refused to meet the protesters, accusing them of being manipulated by a 'third hand' (generally meant to mean foreign NGOs). Instead, he focused his attention on rescuing banks and financial companies drowning in debt in the wake of the financial crisis. One AOP leader summarized the different prime ministers thus:

> Chuan just did not want to talk to us. He was just too conservative. Banharn was a little better. At least he accepted we have a case in principle. But nothing came of it. In the end, he's just a wealthy businessman. Chavalit has done more. He has gotten down to details.
>
> (*The Nation* 23 April 1997)

Thaksin Shinawatra's resounding victory in the January 2001 polls was greeted by many political analysts and AOP advisers as a positive development for the Pak Mun villagers (*Bangkok Post* 4 April 2001). Elected on a populist platform, Thaksin pledged to have the sluice gates opened on a trial basis for four months during the rainy season (July to October) to see whether there would be a significant increase in the stock of fish. In direct contrast to the plodding, legalistic style of Chuan, Thaksin made good work of his campaign slogan of '*khit mai, tham mai*' ('think new, act new'). He appeared extremely responsive to the demands of the AOP, and personally met with the protesters camped outside Government House on 10 February 2001, one day after officially becoming prime minister. After meeting with the prime minister, the protesters decided to return to Ubon Ratchatani, hopeful that there would be meaningful change.

In October 2002, protests resumed after the four-month trial period came to an end, and after the cabinet voted on 1 October to maintain the four-month opening of the gates, rather than a year-round opening. While the opening of the gates for four months did lead to the return of 184 species of fish and to the rise of the average yearly household income from 3,045 baht to 10,025 baht this was still significantly less than what the fisherfolk had earned prior to the construction of the dam, estimated to be a yearly income of 25,742 baht (Ubon Ratchatani University 2002). Villagers have consistently claimed that the four-month period was insufficient to allow the fish stocks to be replenished.

Tensions came to a head in December 2002 as the protest camp outside

Government House in Bangkok was vandalized in the early morning of 5 December and the protest site by the Pak Mun Dam (shown in Figure 7.3) was burned down ten days later (*Bangkok Post* 16 December 2002). Once again, Thaksin met with the villagers, offering them over 7,000 baht worth of food as well as personally providing ice cream, and promising that the government would review the cabinet decision made in October (*Bangkok Post* 9 December 2002).

On 20 December 2002, Thaksin convened a televised conference at Government House, in which all sides of the debate were allowed to air their views. EGAT first provided its argument, followed by presentations from various research groups, and then by the Pak Mun villagers. Although Thaksin refused to allow NGO representatives to attend the meeting, this was an important opportunity for the villagers to gain some degree of legitimacy and a second chance to express their views on national television.[22]

The pivotal moment in this conference was the report of the Ubon Ratchatani University research team. This research team had been commissioned by the government and for the first time officially recommended to the government that the gates be opened permanently.[23] Until then, the report from this research group had limited itself to the more modest task of assessing the costs and benefits of four possible scenarios. The shift in the opinion of the rector of Ubon Ratchatani University was just as critical. Prakob Virojanakuj had earlier agreed with the cabinet decision to keep the gates open for four months, but at the conference surprised many by unequivocally supporting the villagers:

> The university is in favor of helping the people to solve their problems once and for all by opening the dam sluice gates year-round. This is because EGAT can solve the technical problems, but the villagers cannot change their way of life. Their only mistake was that they were born poor and lacking opportunities. Every party will win (if the dam gates are opened). EGAT wins by helping the government solve the longstanding Pak Mun problem. What the villagers will get, however, is only what they have lost. Nothing more.
>
> (*Bangkok Post* 21 December 2002)

Following the conference, Thaksin decided to travel and see the dam firsthand. He chose to take a helicopter trip with two villagers as well as a boat ride on the river. After the trip, Thaksin still refused to commit himself one way or the other, arguing that he had to make a decision that was in the best interests of the country even if it disappointed minority interests (*The Nation* 25 December 2002).[24] Finally, on 15 January 2003, Thaksin decided not to repeal the cabinet decision of 1 October 2002 and thus to allow the gates to be open for only four months of the year. He concluded that the majority of people in Ubon were in favour of the dam and that the government-commissioned study by Ubon Ratchatani University was incomplete.[25] The

Figure 7.3 Protest site at the Pak Mun Dam.

Photo credit: Tim Forsyth

compromise that remains in place as of 2008 is to keep the sluice gates open for four months of the year.[26]

Conclusions

A central question that needs to be asked in conclusion is whether open resistance to state projects has netted any political gains for the peasantry – those often the most directly affected by key features of the agrarian transition. The question can be answered in two ways. First, if one assesses the actual outcome of demonstrations and negotiations, the solution has not been optimal for the poor. Although the sluice gates are open for four months of the year, fisherfolk have consistently argued that this is not enough to bring back the earlier supply of fish, and local livelihoods have not improved. Yet one cannot also conclude that this situation means that resistance has been of no value. While not optimal for the poor, the current solution is a compromise that has forced the state to backtrack to some extent.

The second way to answer this question is to assess whether a different form of peasant resistance, such as the everyday forms discussed in other chapters of this book, including pilfering, foot-dragging and petty arson, might have yielded different – perhaps better – results. With an absence of comparative cases, one can simply think in counterfactual terms. Is there something about small-scale acts of resistance that might have enabled a different outcome? In many cases, where small-scale acts of resistance have led to significant political change, this has come when individuals or groups could take away something from their adversary, whether the landlord or the state. In Vietnam, for example, Benedict Kerkvliet (2005) has shown how peasants' refusal to work within agricultural cooperatives gradually undermined the government's collective economic system (also see Tran Thi Thu Trang's chapter in this volume).

However, in a situation where the struggle is over the appropriation of resources, it is difficult to see how one can avoid open confrontation. As state or capital actively take over natural resources, peasants' options are very limited. Precisely because their livelihoods are based on subsistence through natural resources, it is essential that they fight back to retake control of their basic needs. For peasants engaged in commercial agriculture the situation is somewhat different. The state wants agricultural products to enter the market, and if state behaviour tends to be excessively repressive, farmers can 'defect' from the state. However, for peasants whose lives depend on natural resources and who are not involved in commercial agriculture, the only real option appears to be open resistance.

Open and organized resistance, then, may not have achieved the ultimate goal sought by the Pak Mun villagers – decommissioning the dam – but it has clearly achieved some limited success. Although Scott (1985) has argued that, given the odds against which the subaltern class struggles, there is something to be celebrated in their everyday acts of resistance, what this case study has shown is that there is still something to be gained from open confrontation that most likely would not have been achieved through the use of 'weapons of the weak.' Rather than submitting that open rebellion may be futile, we should acknowledge that piecemeal gains can be made through sustained civil action in certain contexts. In the end, the struggle over the Pak Mun Dam may not be a case of the glass being half full, but it is also not quite half empty.

Notes

1 I thank Pannate Rangsinturat and Cleofe M. Kuhonta for valuable research assistance; Patcharin Lapanun and her anthropology team at Khon Kaen University for facilitating my trips to the Pak Mun Dam; Michael Montesano for inviting me to present an earlier version of this paper at the National University of Singapore; Princeton University for funding support; and Sarah Turner and Dominique Caouette for comments that have helped in revising this paper. Note that Thai names are referred to in the in-text citations and in the references by their first name.
2 For a sampling of general texts on the political economy of resource conflict in Thailand and Southeast Asia, see: Hirsch and Warren (1998); Parnwell and Bryant (1996); Rigg (1995); Lim and Valencia (1990); Hirsch and Lohmann (1989).
3 The concept of the bureaucratic polity comes from Riggs' classic study (1966).
4 Pasuk advances this argument in a brilliant essay (1999).
5 NGOs in Thailand generally spurn the idea of forming a political party or of allying with one particular party. This is due to the volatility of the party system

and a certain amount of distrust of politicians (interviews with NGO members, Bangkok, December 2000).
6 An excellent analysis of this period is provided by Girling (1981).
7 Chaturon Chaisaeng, the deputy finance minister who negotiated with the AOP under the Chavalit government, and who has been sympathetic to the cause of the Pak Mun Dam, was a student activist in the turbulent 1970s (see *Asiaweek* 5 November 1999).
8 For a concise analysis of the tensions in the NGO movement – whether to focus on community development or a broader national policy – see Sanitsuda (1994).
9 The literal translation is 'male head cook'.
10 In my trips to the Pak Mun Dam village site in 2001, I observed impressive coordination among the villagers and NGOs. In the mornings, NGO activists registered villagers' complaints and names to create a systematic record that would then be presented to the government.
11 Chanida (August 2000) of Focus on Global South comments that 'villagers are up against an arrogant state agency. EGAT is traditionally very secretive about its electricity figures'.
12 In my trips to the villages around the Mun River, villagers pointed out how their communities had become politically and geographically riven. Some groups of villagers who sided with EGAT stayed close to the river, while others who opposed the dam were displaced further away from the river.
13 Important lessons have been learned from the Pak Mun Dam. Suthawan Sathirathai led a research team that combined institutional questions with economic valuation in assessing the social and economic impact of the proposed Kaeng Sua Ten Dam in the province of Phrae, northern Thailand. Suthawan provided an economic value not just for the loss of forest that would ensue from the construction of the dam, but also from the loss of non-timber forest products, such as bamboo shoots, mushrooms, ants' eggs, labour skills, eco-tourism and spiritual and cultural activities. This policy report was submitted to the Department of Irrigation (interview with the author in Bangkok in October 2000).
14 The third category overlaps with the first two, since most villagers are fisherfolk.
15 This was noted by villagers interviewed by the author at the Pak Mun Dam, March 2001. One resettlement site with EGAT-constructed houses was virtually empty because villagers had chosen not to move into the new houses.
16 Criticism in the media that villagers were just interested in financial compensation also led to a shift in the nature of the demands. Instead of pushing for financial adjustments to the compensation packages, villagers made claims for total compensation for loss of livelihood. The dam's impact, they argued, had not just depressed their income, but had had systemic effects on the social and economic structure of the community.
17 *Sor Por Kor* is a land title as well as a land reform programme. Land under the *Sor Por Kor* programme was supposed to be given to poor people, but it was mired by accusations in the 1990s that relatives of government officials of the Democrat Party were being given *Sor Por Kor* land titles.
18 Chuan Leekpai was prime minister of Thailand from September 1992 to May 1995 and again from November 1997 to February 2001.
19 Interview by the author with two villagers, Khun Kamta and Khun Saengchai, from the district of Khong Jiam in the province of Ubon Ratchatani at the protest site in Bangkok, July 2000.
20 One of the scuffles was with Samak Sundaravej, a cabinet minister in the 1990s, and prime minister following the December 2007 elections.
21 The excitement at this debate was palpable. The government had bussed in many rural people who protested on the grounds of Thammasat University in favour of the dam. Some of them appeared to be itching for a fight, but the police kept

things relatively calm between both groups (fieldwork observations in Bangkok, August 2000; see also *Matichon* 19 August 2000).
22 Thaksin accused NGOs of inciting protesters and of being funded by foreign organizations (see *Bangkok Post* 17, 18 and 19 December 2002). For an extensive report on the relationship between government and NGOs, see *Bangkok Post* (5 January 2003).
23 This report had already been made public in September 2002.
24 Journalists and activists noted that Thaksin continued to delay his decision even when there was clear evidence of the high costs and low benefits of the dam. See *The Nation* 14 December 2002.
25 Thaksin argued that a survey run by the National Statistical Office showed that 41 per cent of the people living by the Mun River wanted the government to open the sluice gates for four months only (see *Bangkok Post* 8 January 2003; *Inter Press Service* 16 January 2003).
26 Surayud Chulanont, prime minister of Thailand during the 2006–07 military regime, also visited the Pak Mun Dam site but did not change government policy.

References

Asiaweek (1999) 'People power', 5 November.
Baker, C. (2000) 'Thailand's Assembly of the Poor: background, drama, reaction', *South East Asia Research*, 8 (1): 5–29.
Bangkok Post (1997) (title unknown), 4 May.
—— (2000) 'Catalog [sic] of woes goes on', 13 August.
—— (2001) 'Villagers set to end marathon protest', 4 April.
—— (2002a) 'Activists accused of setting fire', 17 December.
—— (2002b) 'Protesters see PM on his turf', 18 December.
—— (2002c) 'Little hope talks will bear fruit', 19 December.
—— (2002d) 'Tension on both sides for 4-hour cabinet-room talks', 21 December.
—— (2003a) 'Enemies of the state?', 5 January.
—— (2003) 'Villagers call Thaksin liar, urge decision', 8 January.
Chanida Chanyapate Bamford (Focus on the Global South) (2000) Interview with author, Bangkok, August.
Chayan Vaddhanaphuti (2000) 'Pak Mun case study: social aspects', Report submitted to the World Commission on Dams, January.
Dome Kripakorn (2007) 'Social movement and the natural resources management: a study of the anti-Nam Choan Dam Movement', *Silpakorn University International Journal*, 7: 112–42.
Girling, J.L.S. (1981) *Thailand: society and politics*, Ithaca: Cornell University Press.
Hirsch, P. (1990) *Development Dilemmas in Rural Thailand*, Singapore: Oxford University Press.
Hirsch, P. and Lohmann, L. (1989) 'Contemporary politics of environment in Thailand', *Asian Survey*, 29, 4: 439–51.
Hirsch, P. and Warren, C. (eds) (1998) *The Politics of Environment in Southeast Asia*, London: Routledge.
Inter Press Service (16 January 2003) 'Thailand: protests widen over dam project'.
Kerkvliet, B. (2005) *The Power of Everyday Politics: how Vietnamese peasants transformed national policy*, Ithaca, NY: Cornell University Press.
[Khun] Bundeum (Villager from Khong Jiam Province) (2001) Interview with author, Pak Mun Dam, March.

[Khun] La (Adviser to AOP) (2001) Interview with author, Pak Mun Dam, March.

Lim Teck Ghee and Valencia, M. (1990) *Conflict over Natural Resources in Southeast Asia and the Pacific*, Singapore: Oxford University Press.

Matichon (2000) 'Government uses destructive strategy and poor people are upset', 19 August.

Missingham, B.D. (2003) *The Assembly of the Poor in Thailand: from local struggles to national protest movement*, Chiang Mai: Silkworm Books.

Parnwell, M. and Bryant, R. (eds) (1996) *Environmental Politics in Southeast Asia*, London: Routledge.

Pasuk Phongpaichit (1999) 'Civilizing the Thai state: state, civil society, and politics in Thailand', Wim Wertheim Lecture, Amsterdam.

Praphat Pintoptaeng (1998) *Kanmuang bon thong thanon: 99 wan prawatisat kan doen khabuan chumnum nai sanghkom thai* (*Politics on the Street: 99 days of the Assembly of the Poor*), Bangkok: Center for Research and Production of Textbooks, Krik University.

Rigg, J. (1995) *Counting the Costs: economic growth and environmental change in Thailand*, Singapore: Institute of Southeast Asian Studies.

Riggs, F. (1966) *Thailand: the modernization of a bureaucratic polity*, Honolulu: University of Hawai'i Press.

Rungrawee Chalermsripinyorat (2004) 'Politics of representation: a case study of Thailand's Assembly of the Poor', *Critical Asian Studies*, 36 (4): 541–66.

Sakchai Amornsakchai, Philippe Annez, Suphat Vongvisessomjai, Sansanee Choowaew, Thailand Development Research Institute, Prasit Kunurat, Jaruwan Nippanon, Roel Schouten, Pradit Sripapatrprasite, Chayan Vaddhanaphuti, Chavalit Vidthayanon, Wanpen Wirojanagud and Ek Watana (2000) 'Pak Mun Dam, Mekong River Basin, Thailand', a WCD Case Study prepared as an input to the World Commission on Dams, Cape Town, November.

Sanitsuda Ekachai (1994) 'Grassroots activists in a quandary', *Bangkok Post*, 11 July.

Scott, J.C. (1976) *The Moral Economy of the Peasant: rebellion and subsistence in Southeast Asia*, New Haven: Yale University Press.

—— (1985) *Weapons of the Weak: everyday forms of peasant resistance*, New Haven: Yale University Press.

So, Alvin Y. and Yok-shiu F. Lee. (1999) 'Environmental movements in Thailand', in Yok-shiu F. Lee and Alvin Y. So, (eds) *Asia's Environmental Movements: comparative perspectives*, Armonk: M.E. Sharpe, 120–42.

Suthawan Sathirathai (Economist at the Institute of Social and Economic Policy) (2000) Interview with author in Bangkok, October.

Thai Development Newsletter (1995a) 'NGOs in an industrializing society: past experience and future directions', 27–28: 114–8.

—— (1995b) 'People's Development Plan', 27–28: 120–1.

—— (1999a) 'The AOP's movement is non-violent', 37: 50–1.

—— (1999b). 'AOP is here to stay', 37: 51–2.

Thailand Development Research Institute (TDRI) (2000) 'Pak Mun Dam case study: synthesis report', report submitted to the World Commission on Dams, February.

The Nation (1998) 'Academic-NGO alliance: the third force', 31 August.

—— (2002a) (title not known), 23 April.

—— (2002b) 'PM Thaksin needs a cool head on Pak Mun', 14 December.

—— (2002c) 'Thaksin's Pak Mun trip leaves Kingdom in suspense', 25 December.

Ubon Ratchatani University (2002) 'Project to study approaches to the restoration of the ecology, livelihood, and communities receiving impact from the construction of the Pak Mun Dam', September (in Thai).

Wattana Nakpradit (Friends of the People, and adviser to the AOP) (2000) Interview with author, Bangkok, June.

8 State–society relations and the diversity of peasant resistance in Việt Nam

Trần Thị Thu Trang[1]

Introduction

The Vietnamese peasantry made its mark in history by successfully resisting the exploitation of colonialism and imperialism in 1954 in the north of the country and later in 1975 in the south. The tenacious resolve of this otherwise destitute social group to overthrow its oppressors has attracted much attention from scholars studying the politics and movements of resistance emerging in the so-called 'developing world'. After independence in 1954, however, Vietnamese peasants in the north engaged in different forms of resistance under the newly independent state. These included everyday forms of resistance during the central planning and collectivization period from the early 1960s to the early 1980s, and more open and collective protests since the economic reforms initiated in the 1980s. Despite the seriousness of rural poverty and a long history of struggle, these instances of resistance remain localized and small-scale, rarely spreading beyond district or provincial boundaries, and even more rarely targeting the central government. This rather stable political environment is surprising considering several upheavals in neighbouring countries such as those in Thailand, the Philippines and Burma over the last 50 years (Vasavakul 1995), as well as the political crises in former socialist countries in the 1980s and 1990s.

This chapter, building upon field research findings in a Mường rural community in Hòa Bình province, Việt Nam, conducted from 2001 to 2004, as well as relevant literature, investigates changes in rural resistance by looking at why and how resistance takes place and against whom.[2] In other words, it studies the *causes*, *forms* and *targets* of peasant resistance, and why these have changed over the last 50 years. In order to answer these questions, I adopt a conceptual framework that provides a coherent and flexible understanding of resistance while emphasizing the particular interaction between structure and agency in specific contexts. I then utilize this to analyse peasant resistance in Việt Nam covering the periods of collectivization from the 1960s to 1980s, and of reform from the early 1980s onwards. The chapter underlines that the interactions between structure and agency influence how peasants perceive the causes of their difficulties, and whether or not they decide to engage in resistance, in what form, and against whom. This explains why the causes, forms and targets of peasant resistance are not static but vary across time and space.

Contextualizing Việt Nam's peasant resistance

As discussed in this book's introduction by Turner and Caouette, previous approaches to resistance have tended to form dichotomies which continue to dominate the literature and are, for many researchers, difficult to reconcile. Frequently authors feel the need to 'take sides', pitting one theory against the other. Yet the richness of Việt Nam's history of resistance renders such choices limiting, supporting the need for a revised framework as argued for here, and in this book as a whole. In Việt Nam, different forms of resistance have existed during different historical periods, as well as simultaneously in separate locations. For instance, while organized warfare was the dominant strategy of the Việt Minh[3] under colonial oppression, everyday forms of resistance became widespread during the collectivization period. In turn, since the economic reforms that began in the 1980s, protests have increasingly become more open and collective in some places, while everyday forms of resistance continue to dominate in other locales. The level of success of these different forms of resistance also varies across political and economic contexts while, in addition, it is also not uncommon to find combinations of resistance measures adopted by individual agents.

As such, when wanting to understand resistance in the Vietnamese context, an innovative and flexible framework is important. Here I draw on the work by Mittelman and Chin (2000) that distinguishes different aspects of resistance, namely forms, agents, sites and strategies of resistance, without taking sides in the aforementioned debate. This framework is similar to the methodology suggested by Ben White (1989), which I have supported elsewhere (Trần Thị Thu Trang 2004a) in relation to agrarian differentiation. Building upon these works, I adopt some of Mittelman and Chin's (2000) descriptions of the *forms* and *agents* of resistance; however, I add two other important aspects of resistance, namely the *causes* and *targets*, encompassing parts of what Mittelman and Chin describe as *strategies* of resistance. Most importantly, I emphasize how these aspects of resistance relate to one another and are the results of the interactions between structure and agency across specific times and space.

Agents are at the centre of the resistance process. They decide whether or not to engage in resistance, in what form, and against whom. Agents of resistance are not limited to certain classes such as industrial versus agricultural workers, or middle-class versus landless peasants, but come from diverse backgrounds. While the primary focus of this chapter is peasant resistance, this does not imply that peasants form a homogenous group, as their different and multiple identities frequently form the basis of very different resistance measures. The resistance process starts with the agents' perception of the causes of their difficulties, such as poverty, economic depression, discrimination, oppression and so on. In the case of contemporary Việt Nam such causes include, but are not limited to, the overall processes of agricultural commoditization and globalization as well as concrete policies and programmes by the central and local governments. State strategies and local authorities influence how resources are allocated, whether through distributive policies or market mechanisms. These, in turn, can create opportunities for corruption and exploitation by public or private actors. However, such actions only become the causes of resistance if they are actually perceived by peasants as problems and then acted upon. This explains why under similarly difficult circumstances some groups might engage in resistance measures and others not. Those resisting might perceive that their difficulties are unjustly caused by other social actors and that changes are needed to improve their situation. Alternatively, those who remain inactive might perceive that exploitation or difficulties are inevitable, that they are even natural and necessary (for instance, giving larger shares of production outputs to landlords can be seen as necessary to sustain the latter's protection and support in cases of social crises or calamities).

Differences in peasant perceptions are the result of the interaction between structure and agency.[4] Elites might, in an effort to maintain or restore their legitimacy, try to convince peasants that the latter's difficulties result from a specific set of circumstances and are not the intentional result of state policies or other power structures. Other groups, in order to rally popular support to their opposition agenda, might explicitly hold elites responsible for such difficulties. When peasants perceive that their problems are unjustly caused by other actors they are most likely to resist. However, the strategies or forms of resistance that agents actually choose vary greatly, ranging from everyday acts to organized movements (Mittelman and Chin 2000). Choosing a form or strategy of resistance that they believe most appropriate and effective, they consider both structural obstacles and their available resources. Under an authoritarian state, for example, large-scale and open resistance might be too costly. Alternatively, under a democratic political system, strikes and large protests might bring some positive results, as Erik Martinez Kuhonta's chapter demonstrates in the case of Thailand. The personality of agents also influences the type of action that they are likely to engage in, whether violent or peaceful, legal or illegal acts.

Finally, as the perceived causes of difficulties may vary, so too does the identity of the culprits. Even when peasants agree on the causes of their difficulties, they might blame different social actors. For instance, in Việt Nam some peasants might attribute the cause of their difficulties to the incompetence and corrupt behaviour of local cadres while others may blame the state's overall economic policies. The state, in turn, might blame external factors for economic difficulties to divert peasant anger.

In the next section I use this resistance framework – built on the context-specific interactions between structure and agency – to answer three questions regarding two distinct periods of collectivization and economic reform over the last five decades in Việt Nam: why does resistance occur; in what particular forms; and against whom? While I address several representative forms and processes of resistance in this chapter, this does not, however, imply that other forms and processes do not exist. Rather, the purpose is to illustrate how the interactions between structure and agency influence changes in different aspects of resistance through time.

Peasant resistance in Việt Nam during the collectivization period: 1960s to 1980s

Everyday forms of resistance

The collectivization period in Việt Nam was characterized by a centrally planned economy, which implied control and direct management by the state of both production and circulation processes. In the countryside, such control was manifested through the cooperative system, in which peasants were confined to the sphere of production while state agencies were responsible for the exchange and distribution of agricultural inputs, outputs and consumer goods. 'During the 1960s–1970s, the government's desired minimal level of staple foods (*lương thực*), measured in "paddy equivalents," was twenty kilograms per person per month' (Kerkvliet 2005: 83).

In order to achieve this objective, the government implemented policies that collectivized the means of production and labour under a cooperative system. It also invested significantly in the agricultural sector, notably irrigation, agricultural mechanization and new high-yielding varieties. The budget allocated to agriculture for the first half of the 1960s was five times higher than that of the 1958–60 period. These policies, as well as early peasant enthusiasm towards the new regime, resulted in the growth of grain production (Bhaduri 1982; Hà Vinh 1997). During the first half of the 1960s, the productivity of land and workers almost doubled, reaching the target of 20 kilograms per person per month in the early 1960s (Ngô Vĩnh Long 1993: 166; Kerkvliet 2005: 83). Such achievements helped consolidate peasant trust in the communist government's capacity and right to rule.

However, this availability of rice steadily declined to 17 kilograms in the early 1970s and further to '15.4, 12.0, 11.6, 11.9, and 10.4 kilograms a month in 1976, 1977, 1978, 1979, and 1980 respectively' (Ngô Vĩnh Long 1993: 173; see also Kerkvliet 2005: 83). In some localities, hunger crises were also reported and individuals required significant assistance from the state (Trần Thị Thu Trang 2004a). As a result, Việt Nam had to import 1.2 million tonnes of food in 1976; an amount that increased to 2.2 million tonnes in 1979 (Hà Vinh 1997: 119). The above difficulties led to widespread peasant discontent and resistance. However, such resistance mostly took *everyday forms* without questioning the legitimacy of the state.

In his persuasive and influential book, *The Power of Everyday Politics:*

How Vietnamese Peasants Transformed National Policy, Ben Kerkvliet (2005) gives a rich account of everyday forms of peasant resistance and how these successfully forced the government to engage in reforms. Peasant discontent towards the cooperative led them to try to 'minimize the cooperative's claim on their labor and to maximize their household-based production' (Kerkvliet 2005: 2). Their struggles to survive within the cooperative system were part of what Kerkvliet (2005: 22) calls 'everyday politics', including, for instance, avoiding tedious tasks while still accumulating work points,[5] stealing collective produce and equipment, securing more lucrative tasks, and devoting time and energy to private plots (Trần Thị Thu Trang 2004a; Kerkvliet 2005; McElwee 2007). These tactics were often carried out in secret at the individual level and were rarely confrontational. They occurred, however, in many localities at the same time and thus contributed to the ongoing difficulties the cooperatives faced in meeting the required levels of production. Such everyday politics led to a range of concessions by local cadres. In the 1960s, for instance, the leaders of Hải Phòng and Vĩnh Phúc provinces contracted out all or part of the production tasks to peasant families (Kerkvliet 2005). Although the central authority at first resented and forbade such deviations from the cooperative model, the perseverance of everyday politics eventually forced policy changes in later decades including the nationwide legalization of the production contract – already illegally practised in many localities – via the Party's Central Committee Decree 100/CT/TW issued in 1981 (Ban Bí Thư Trung Ương Đảng 1983; see also Kerkvliet 1993: 18–19, 2005: 190; Ngô Vĩnh Long 1993: 175; Kleinen 1999: 138) and the *Đổi mới* (economic reform), discussed later on in this chapter.

Legitimacy and the war context

According to Kerkvliet (2005), everyday politics and forms of resistance were chosen by many Vietnamese peasants because they were considered more effective than open protests, especially under the prevailing political environment during collectivization. That political environment provided little space for discussion and protestation, and often severely pressured and punished those who dared to challenge it. This was further intensified by the war context in which ideological divergence was not well tolerated (Lương Văn Hy 2003; Kerkvliet 2005). (Allina-Pisano 2008 has similar observations for Russia and Ukraine.)

While political oppression by the state presents structural obstacles to peasants' open contestation, the repressive nature of a political regime alone cannot prevent resistance per se. As demonstrated by the Vietnamese revolution, peasants of different social and economic backgrounds had openly confronted ruling classes despite much repression and hardship. The choice of the *everyday forms* in the collectivization period could not therefore be fully explained by such structural obstacles, but rather by peasant perceptions of the difficulties. For many peasants, the economic hardships during collectivization resulted from the poorly designed organization of production and distribution within the cooperative system. According to Kerkvliet (2005), cooperatives in this period lacked effective monitoring, transparency, and trust among cooperative members, which were crucial for the organization to succeed. For instance, the cooperative lacked monitoring mechanisms to effectively reward zeal and punish freeloaders, hence discouraging efforts to contribute positively. In addition, peasants were frustrated by the lack of transparency in decision-making processes; local cadres often appropriated public resources and imposed decisions on peasants with little opportunity for consultation and participation. Finally, when cooperative members came from different villages, sometimes previously hostile to each other, trust was difficult to establish.

Peasants perceived these problems as being rooted in local politics and governance, influencing why they targeted specific policies and the processes of their implementation. At the same time, peasants did not target the regime itself because they believed in the government's legitimate right to rule and its good intentions towards the peasant population. Local cadres in a Mường village in Hòa Bình province – where I have undertaken extensive fieldwork – stated that during collectivization peasants trusted the Party and the state (Trần Thị Thu Trang 2004b). In fact, this trust was built through a number of the government's concrete economic and social policies. This included the implementation of land reform in the first half of the 1950s, which distributed agricultural land and other means of production more equally within the peasantry. This reform granted or increased formal ownership of land and other productive resources to small farmers, ending many exploitative relations of production (Trần Phương 1960; Kerkvliet 2005). In the eyes of the majority of peasants, such land reform concretized the government's support for the rural poor and consolidated its right to rule (Bhaduri 1982; Lương Văn Hy 1992; Kleinen 1999). Under collectivization, the cooperative also implemented mechanisms 'that minimized inequalities and assisted those who were ill, weak, or too young or old to work' (Kerkvliet 2005: 84). This led to an improved equality in wealth distribution, noted in a reduction of the Gini coefficient value. According to Đào Thế Tuấn (1995: 157), the Gini coefficient by income of the Red River Delta was 0.35 in 1954, but decreased dramatically to 0.07 in 1957. Nevertheless, this index increased to 0.15 in 1965, 0.25 in 1978, and maintained this level until the end of collectivization in 1990 (see also Lương Văn Hy and Unger 1998: 64).

In addition to those economic policies, the government also ensured accessibility to basic social services for the whole population. The government considered 'formal education and health services as rights of citizenship' (London 2004: 128). It systematically built primary schools and healthcare centres at the commune level to make these services free and accessible to all. As Kerkvliet notes with regards to education:

> Whereas only two or three hundred Vietnamese – nearly all of them male –
> out of every ten thousand had gone to school during the 1930s and

1940s, the proportion in the north climbed to nearly eight hundred of every ten thousand by 1956, doubled to seventeen hundred by 1960, and reached nearly twenty-five hundred by 1970. And 47 percent of those schooled were women.

(Kerkvliet 2005: 81)

Similarly, regarding health,

the number of health clinics and local hospitals increased from about 750 throughout north Vietnam in the early 1940s (about six beds for every ten thousand people) to 4,800 in 1960, and exceeded 7,500 by 1970 (thirty-three beds per ten thousand).

(ibid.)

Even when peasant discontent and resistance were at their peak by the end of the 1970s, the government's commitment to social development remained. 'Between 1975 and 1980, gross enrollments in primary, lower secondary and upper secondary education increased by 19, 25, and 28 per cent respectively' (London 2004: 129). The coexistence of poor economic performance but impressive improvements in equality and the provision of free social services resulted in the nuanced forms of discontent that occurred during the collectivization period. In addition, while the war against the United States drained resources from the peasantry, it was also used to divert anger away from the state.

As soon as the war was over, the ineffectiveness of the cooperative system was exposed in full, leading to intensified peasant resistance. Instead of holding on to the old economic policies and repressing dissident peasants, the government opted for reform. While this decision was also influenced by the international context, it did demonstrate the flexibility of the Vietnamese government in dealing with peasant discontent and resistance in this period.

Reform and globalization: 1980s onwards

More open protests

In response to local peasant resistance, as well as changes in the international context such as reforms in China and the Soviet Union, the Vietnamese government implemented *đổi mới* (economic reform) policies at the Sixth National Congress in December 1986, marking the transition from a central planned to a market economy. *Đổi mới* emphasized market demand as producing the signals and incentives for economic production and the allocation of resources. It stressed the important role of non-state sectors in economic development, which had been neglected or restrained until then, and introduced various institutional changes regarding the ownership and management of resources (Kerkvliet 1993; Porter 1993; Turley 1993; McNicoll and Durst 1995).

In 1988, the government implemented Resolution 10, which introduced household contracts (*khoán hộ,* also called *khoán gọn, khoán 10,* or Contract 10). Following this Resolution, cooperatives were to distribute paddy land to households for a period of 10 to 15 years, while retaining the right to adjust landholdings following changes in household demographic composition. Other agricultural lands and productive resources were also distributed equally to all peasants, based on the number of household labourers, with some variations in implementation between localities. Households were henceforth free to decide on the organization of their agricultural production (Kleinen 1999).

As a result of such reform policies, the gross domestic product (GDP) growth rate increased from 2.8 per cent in 1986 to 5 per cent in 1990, and peaked at 9.5 per cent in 1995. In the agricultural sector, including forestry and fishery, the growth rate was negative in 1987 but increased to 3 per cent the following year and peaked at 7 per cent in 1989 (General Statistical Office 2000: 7; General Statistical Office website 2008). Việt Nam moved from 'importing about half a million tons of food annually in 1986–88, [to becoming] the third-largest exporter of rice by 1989' (Dodsworth *et al.* 1996: 4). In 1997, Việt Nam became the world's second largest exporter of rice, just behind Thailand (Minot and Goletti 2000). The revenues from overall agricultural exports also increased significantly, 'from US $1 billion in 1990 to US $4.3 billion in 2000' (Socialist Republic of Việt Nam 2002: 5).

The reforms also succeeded in improving the living standards of the majority of the Vietnamese population (Kerkvliet 1993; Ngô Vĩnh Long 1993; Abrami 1995; Đào Thế Tuấn 1995; Lagrée 1995; Fforde and de Vylder 1996; Kleinen 1999). The percentage of the population living under the *total poverty line*[6] decreased from 75 per cent in 1988 to 55, 37 and 29 per cent in 1993, 1998 and 2002 respectively. The percentage of the population living under the *food poverty line*[7] also decreased from 25 per cent in 1993, to 13 and 10 per cent in 1998 and 2002 respectively (Bùi Thái Quyên *et al.* 2001; Haughton 2001; Tổng cục thống kê 2004; Võ Trí Thanh and Phạm Hoàng Hà 2004).

Access to safe water and other basic infrastructure was also improved. In 2004, 90 per cent of communes throughout the country had access to electricity, broadcasting stations, post offices and cultural centres, while 65 per cent of communes had clean water (Socialist Republic of Việt Nam 2005: 60; see also Socialist Republic of Việt Nam 2002: 14–15). In addition, overall life expectancy increased from 65 years in 1993 to 71.3 years in 2004 (Bloom 1998: 3; Socialist Republic of Việt Nam 2005: 8). As such, Việt Nam's Human Development Index (HDI) increased from 0.617 in 1990 to 0.709 in 2006, thus raising the country's HDI ranking from 120/174 in 1992 to 109/177 in 2006 (United Nations Development Programme 1990, 1995, 2006).

While most peasants welcomed the decollectivization process and were satisfied with the initial improvements in their livelihoods, peasant resistance has increasingly become more open and confrontational since the mid-1990s. Among the most well-known events was the unrest in Thái Bình in 1997 and in the Central Highlands in 2001 and 2004, along with numerous other smaller incidents involving peasants in different localities (Human Rights Watch 1997; Kleinen 1999; Raymond 2003; McElwee 2007).

The Thái Bình event can be considered to be the first and most serious rural unrest under the communist government for several reasons. First, it occurred in a province which had strongly supported the Communist Party throughout the wars. Second, the unrest mobilized a large number of supporters, up to 10,000 at one point, from almost 40 rural communes. Third, it used both illegal and legal methods to protest against local cadres. Finally, with the destruction of a Hồ Chí Minh bust, the unrest signalled a strong attack on the key symbol of the Vietnamese state and its legitimacy (Lương Văn Hy 2005).

Unlike the collectivization period, in which contestation was largely hidden and occurred mostly at the individual level, these recent events are more open and confrontational (Lương Văn Hy 2005). Some have involved violent acts such as assaulting officials – even holding them hostage – or destroying public property (Kerkvliet 2003; Raymond 2003; McElwee 2007). Some farmers have framed their vocal anger within legal boundaries, using 'state laws and policies, alongside traditional values, . . . to endorse and strengthen public resistance' (Nguyễn Văn Sửu 2007: 318; see also Lương Văn Hy 2005). In other cases, protesters have combined both violent confrontation and peaceful demonstration to exert pressure on authorities (Nguyễn Văn Sửu 2007).

Such changes in the forms of resistance in Việt Nam since the reforms are quite similar to what Li and O'Brien (1996) and O'Brien (1996) observe in their studies of peasant resistance in China. They also find two main forms of resistance, namely 'recalcitrants' and 'policy-based resisters' or 'rightful resistance'. The former 'boldly defy orders as well as policies and laws and frequently challenge village leaders who confront them. They show little deference to township officials and may even threaten to use violence against village cadres who offend them' (Li and O'Brien 1996: 35). Policy-based resistance in turn is

> a form of popular contention that (1) operates near the boundary of an authorized channel, (2) employs the rhetoric and commitments of the powerful to curb political or economic power, and (3) hinges on locating and exploiting divisions among the powerful. In particular, rightful resistance entails the innovative use of laws, policies, and other officially promoted values to defy 'disloyal' political and economic elites; it is a kind of partially sanctioned resistance that uses influential advocates and recognized principles to apply pressure on those in power who have failed to live up to some professed ideal or who have not implemented some beneficial measure.
>
> (O'Brien 1996: 33)

According to O'Brien (1996), recalcitrant peasants have little chance of success as their confrontational and violent methods can be easily charged as illegal and therefore oppressed by authorities. On the other hand, policy-based resistance, similar to Gramsci's 'war of position', is more successful because protesters accept and use the same dominant discourse to denounce and charge individuals whose acts fall outside that framework (O'Brien 1996). Authorities also fear these policy-based protesters the most for their understanding of state laws and policies as well as their argumentative articulation. Such a line of reasoning is supported by my own fieldwork. In Hòa Bình province I found that local authorities often carefully examined the writing style and calligraphy of anonymous complaints in trying to identify the protesters. They often disregarded those written by *không biết gì* (ignorant) peasants while paying far greater attention to those written by knowledgeable peasants, who are often familiar with government policies and know the legal boundaries of their actions.

Political reform, peasant perceptions and liberalization policies

The observable changes from everyday forms of resistance during the collectivization period to more open and sometimes violent protests since the reforms have generated some important questions: why have peasant protests become more intensive despite impressive economic growth and improved living standards; and why do such protests still remain localized and rarely target the state? The answers to these questions can be found by analysing the interaction between structure and agency since the reforms in Việt Nam, which explains why peasants resist, in what form and against whom. Indeed, one of the reasons that could explain the emergence of open protests in the reform era is the softening of the political system. While the level of organization and intensification of the Thái Bình unrest in 1997 might have taken authorities by surprise, the central government reacted quite quickly to address peasant complaints. This included the dismissal of the Thái Bình Party Secretary and the launching in the following year of Decree 29 to promote local democracy (Lương Văn Hy 2005). The Decree stressed the importance of local people being informed and participating in decision-making. It specified different levels of peasant participation, ranging from being informed or consulted to discussing and deciding, as well as supervising and controlling.[8]

Apart from this political reform, the government also wanted to demonstrate its determination to fight corruption. In 2002 Nông Đức Mạnh, the Party Secretary General, requested all governing bodies to take this issue seriously (Abrami 2003). The government also encouraged individuals and the media to participate in this struggle by denouncing *tiêu cực* (wrongdoings) in their localities. However, while the above political changes give more space to public grievances, the government seems to maintain a hard line towards protests directed at the state. The arrests over the years of several human rights activists demonstrate such determination (BBC News 2007). In this context, many agents of resistance prefer to stay within permissible boundaries, focusing on socio-economic issues, targeting local cadres within their jurisdiction, and avoiding demanding political changes such as a multi-party democracy which would directly target the state.[9]

Yet the main reasons for more open but localized acts of resistance in the reform period are found in the way peasants experience inequalities and perceive the causes of such inequalities. While economic and human developments have been impressive, they have not benefited all Vietnamese equally throughout the country. The Gini coefficient for expenditure increased from 0.34 in 1993 to 0.37 in 2002 (Socialist Republic of Việt Nam 2005: 21). Axes of inequality have been found in all economic, social and political aspects, between urban and rural areas, deltas and uplands, men and women, and Kinh (lowland Vietnamese), Chinese and ethnic minorities (for more on this final category see Turner and Michaud's chapter in this volume). According to the 2002 Việt Nam Living Standards Survey (VLSS: General Statistics Office of Vietnam 2002), the percentage of the population living under the poverty line in urban areas was 6.6 compared to 35.6 in rural areas, and 22.4 in the Red River Delta compared to 68 in the Northwest mountainous regions (VLSS 2002: 24). Expenditure for education per student in the urban centres was three times higher than in rural areas (VLSS 2002: 17). Additionally, 10.6 per cent of sick people in rural areas relied on ill-equipped commune health centres, compared to only 1.9 per cent in cities (VLSS 2002: 18).

According to the same survey, disparities between the richest and the poorest income quintiles are significant. The average monthly income per capita of the former is eight times higher than the latter (VLSS 2002: 21). The former group spends about 4.5 times more than the latter, including 7.5 times more on non-food items, 4 times more on healthcare, 6 times more on education, and – a dramatic – 95 times more on entertainment (VLSS 2002: 22). Differences are also found between women and men. While the gender gap in education is small, women are more likely to find jobs in the agricultural, garment and informal sectors where returns are low. In addition, their participation in local politics is limited, having only nominal power through the Women's Union (Taylor 2004a: 4–5).

Such inequalities have led, albeit not everywhere, to the re-emergence of class structures and related exploitation, against which the Vietnamese state had bitterly fought. Akram-Lodhi (2005) finds that in the Mekong delta, where the market economy is the most advanced, agricultural land has been increasingly concentrated as poor peasants have had to sell their land to richer farmers, mostly due to debts, production failures and adversity, notably illness. As a result, the proportion of landless peasants in the Mekong Delta has increased significantly (Akram-Lodhi 2005; see also Lường Văn Hy 2003; McElwee 2007; Taylor 2004b). Thus, while statistics still reflect impressive growth in the agricultural sector, this hardly benefits those landless and poor peasants.

Land concentration and peasant differentiation are also observed in other parts of the country, notably in the Central Highlands, where ethnic minorities have lost their land to state farms and Kinh migrants for the cultivation of new cash crops such as coffee (Nguyễn Văn Sửu 2004). Henin (2002) also observes proletarianization and land concentration in both cash-crop and rice farms in the northern uplands, resulting from reform and commercialization of the agricultural sector there.

While the above provide many grounds for peasant resistance, it is surprising that these resistance acts rarely spread beyond a given locality. One of the reasons that could explain this phenomenon has been peasant perception of the causes of their difficulties. Through field research in Hòa Bình province, I observed that most peasants attributed their lack of access to key resources such as land, credit or information, to corruption at the local level. In turn, peasants have so far still perceived such corruption as being rooted in local politics and governance. They often attribute corruption to the personality of local cadres, holding the latter as the main culprits for their difficulties (a similar observation was made by Akram-Lodhi in an interview conducted by BBC Vietnamese.com 2007; see also McElwee 2007: 96). Such perceptions are not unfounded as the number of corruption cases by local cadres is significant. As noted by Nguyễn Văn Sửu:

> In Ha Bac province, during the 1988 distribution of agricultural land use rights, the provincial party committee revealed 10,000 violations, mainly in the form of unauthorised allocation and illegal sale of use rights on the redesignated agricultural land, one of the key sources of communal land after 1993. In 1989, the Ha Bac Department of Agriculture investigated a number of communes in two districts and discovered a further 1,174 cases of land law violations, including 848 cases of illegal encroachment, 183 cases of unauthorised allocation of use rights, and 143 cases of illegal sale of use rights. From 1989 to mid-October 1993, cadastral inspectors continued to discover 4,443 cases of violation of state land laws in an area with 113 ha of land.
>
> (Nguyễn Văn Sửu 2007: 329–30)

Similarly, in Thái Bình province, 'from 1994–1997, authorities in 260 of 280 communes, precincts, and district capital towns in total had illegally sold use rights of 288.2 ha of communal land to 17,650 households to collect 140 billion dong (VND)' (ibid.: 329).

Such localization and individualization of difficulties therefore does not lead peasants to protest against authorities beyond their immediate jurisdiction, or to mobilize supporters across localities and socio-economic backgrounds. Nevertheless, while peasants have so far perceived their problems as linked to specific individuals and specific localities, this perception might change if corruption and difficulties persist or intensify. Peasants might start questioning the linkages between these more localized problems with broader political, economic and social policies resulting from the state's changing development strategy. While *Đổi mới* and the associated reforms were a response to the crisis of collectivization, the economic growth achieved has opened the way for further radical changes that are more in line with neoliberal policies, often with negative impacts upon the majority of peasants (Taylor 2007).

This includes, for instance, the 1993 Land Law that allowed for the commoditization of land despite the fact that land is one of the most important means of production for peasants, guaranteeing at least their subsistence. Under such a policy, land concentration and appropriation by rich peasants, cadres or the state for industrial and commercial purposes (including tourism and entertainment) are tolerated and even encouraged at the expense of poor peasants. In addition, the state has promoted an export economy integrated into the global market while, at the same time, reducing agricultural subsidies. Although these policies might have brought economic growth, they have had considerably uneven impacts on the rural economy and the poor, and could eventually trigger stronger peasant resistance.

Similarly, integration into the global economy presents noteworthy risks for a country such as Việt Nam, and its peasantry in particular. Powerful countries often manipulate international trade rules to impose different barriers and taxes to protect their own producers. One of the latest and most detrimental cases so far concerns the dispute over Vietnamese catfish exported to the United States. This resulted in the American imposition of tariffs ranging from 37 to 64 per cent (*New York Times* 22 July 2003) that directly affected half-a-million Vietnamese catfish producers.

Furthermore, as Việt Nam has been isolated from international trade for several decades, the country has rather inefficient market institutions in relation to domestic production planning (Goletti and Rich 1998; Hill 2000). The government has been incapable of enforcing production zoning and quotas, leaving peasants to freely produce whatever they deemed profitable. Peasants, due to their lack of investment and market information, tend to embark on activities that momentarily have high market returns, and then pull out when markets fluctuate or collapse. Coffee is one of the clearest examples of this lack of production control, leading to market saturation and the collapse of prices that affected even the international market. In the early 1990s, the Vietnamese government and international development agencies strongly promoted coffee as a poverty reduction crop and as an important export commodity. However, the government had not paid sufficient attention to the risk of market saturation and remained unable to limit the cultivated acreage or enforce production quotas. As a result, peasants, wherever possible, embraced coffee production in response to the high prices of the mid-1990s. The sown area increased rapidly from 66,000 hectares in 1986 to 190,000 in 1995, and 500,000 hectares in 2001 (Goletti and Rich 1998: 27; see also BBC News 2003b; InternationalReports.Net 2003). This resulted in a record high output of 900,000 metric tonnes of coffee in 2001, mostly of robusta type (a lower quality bean), making Việt Nam the world's second largest exporter of coffee, after Brazil (BBC News 2003b). Production exceeded demand by 8 per cent on the international market in 2001, leading to a collapse in prices to a 30-year low (ASRIA 2002; BBC News 2003b). 'The World Bank data shows that coffee prices in real terms are less than one-third of their 1960 level, making returns for the world's estimated 20 million farmers less than the cost of production' (BBC News 2003b: online). This price collapse forced many Vietnamese coffee growers to abandon their crops and move to other activities. However, the recurrent destruction of agricultural crops due to market fluctuations does not only imply losses in profits and investments for peasants but also the erosion of their morale and trust in the prospective of market integration policies. Peasants whom I interviewed in a village in Hòa Bình province, for instance, expressed their despair over the hardship of agricultural production under the current context of globalization, not knowing how to overcome this impasse. Yet, they still perceived such difficulties as a result of individual failure and not due to structural obstacles induced by state neoliberal policies (Trần Thị Thu Trang 2004a). As such, this has not – yet – led to resistance targeted at the state.

Initial integration into the global market has thus resulted in vulnerability for both rich and poor peasants (Lương Văn Hy 2003; Trần Thị Thu Trang 2004a; Taylor 2007). The recent accession to the World Trade Organization worsens the situation. This time, the Vietnamese government itself has lowered import tariffs on several agricultural products, reducing the competitiveness of Vietnamese producers in their own market (Giang Long 2007; McElwee 2007; Quang Thuần and Quang Duẩn 2007).

The state has also privatized most of its social services, seriously affecting poorer groups. Lương Văn Hy details how 'despite its official commitment to socialism, the Vietnamese state financed only 51 percent of the total educational expenditures and 16 percent of total health care expenditures in 1992–3, and 48 percent of the former and 21 percent of the latter in 1997–8' (2005: 127). The government has transferred the remaining cost to service users under the programme and slogan *xã hội hóa* (socialization). This socialization, considered by many to be equivalent to privatization, has led to a significant decline in student enrolment and added numerous burdens for the rural poor (London 2004; Taylor 2007). At the same time, decentralization policies have allowed local cadres to mobilize resources from the population through the creation of numerous levies and dues, further draining peasant income. According to a recent survey conducted by the Ministry of Agriculture and Rural Development, peasants have to pay up to 122 different funds and fees per year, of which those paid to the commune account for 28 types and already represent 5 per cent of the average income earned by peasants (Đức Kế and Phong Cầm 2007).

The above shows how liberalization policies have negatively affected the peasant economy, especially the poor. So far, peasants have not linked their difficulties with these policies or identified them as a shift in government strategies that departs from a rural development model committed to protect the interest of peasants against other and more powerful economic sectors (Raymond 2003; Rato 2004; McElwee 2007). While such a shift has not yet led to peasant resistance, it has nevertheless sparked tensions between socialist and neoliberal advocates at the national level. In this regard, Lương Văn Hy notes that:

> In the November 1998 debates in the Vietnamese National Assembly on land law amendments, the northern and central representatives voted against the liberalization of the land market in the lowlands – more specifically, against removal of the three-hectare-per-household restriction and lengthening usufruct rights to more than 20 years. In contrast, southern representatives and the southern press strongly favored land-market liberalization that would increase the inequality in landholdings for the sake of productive efficiency.
>
> (Lương Văn Hy 2005: 137)

At the local level, tensions have also risen between peasants who have benefited from egalitarian policies in the past and authorities who try to implement policies along newer neoliberal prescriptions. In some places, those tensions have caused local authorities to adapt central policies. In a village in Hòa Bình province, for instance, peasants successfully compelled local authorities in 1995 to redistribute land more equally, despite the central government provision for unequal distribution based on efficiency of production (Trần Thị Thu Trang 2004a).

On the other hand, while the state initiated several political reforms in the mid-1990s, notably the processes of decentralization and 'statization', the shifting of power from the Communist Party to the state, these efforts remain rather ineffective, particularly at the local level. For instance, decentralization has granted local executive branches, often constituting a small group of cadres, the power to mobilize resources (notably from the local population), manage local budgets and staffing, and allocate key resources such as land, buffaloes and credit (Nguyễn Trung Tiệp 1998; Trần Thị Thu Trang 2004b). Local authorities have thus become 'one-stop-shops' for almost all aspects of peasant everyday life. Such a concentration of power at the local level is further intensified by the statization process (Đặng Phong and Beresford 1998). At the national level, statization contributes to the democratization process by giving the National Assembly more space to carry out its mandate, such as debating and scrutinizing government activities, as well as appointing or dismissing government officials (Đặng Phong and Beresford 1998; McCarty 2001; UNDP Việt Nam 2001; Koh 2004). The statization process, however, has not had the same impact at the local level. During my own fieldwork I found that while the Party Chapter in a Mường community in the north of the country had lost much control over economic affairs and its ability to expose and redress misconducts and corruption, the People's Council[10] had not been able to take over this check and balance function. As a result, the People's Committee often freely governed without much scrutiny from any other institution (see similar observations for China in White 1987, and for Russia and Ukraine in Allina-Pisano 2008). With ineffective check and balance mechanisms at the local level, these political reforms unfortunately created new opportunities for corruption, allowing cadres to appropriate resources with little risk of being exposed and sanctioned while failing to provide peasants with the necessary means to voice their discontent and challenge injustice at the local level (Trần Thị Thu Trang 2004b).

So far, peasants have not perceived their difficulties as a result of the government's overall neoliberal policies; however, they might do so if such policies continue to threaten their livelihoods. This could lead to more large-scale radical resistance, which might be also articulated alongside the political demands of other groups. According to the *Wall Street Journal* (15 August 2007), an indication of this trend has already been found in a petition circulated in July 2007. Peasants from different southern provinces gathered in Hồ Chí Minh City to protest over land issues. For the first time they were joined by a religious group led by Thích Quảng Độ, an eminent monk and political activist, who called for peasants to unite forces with political dissidents. Thích Quảng Độ's actions have been criticized by the government and the media, but this new development might bring the state to reflect on its development strategies.

Conclusions

In this chapter I proposed a conceptual framework for the analysis of peasant resistance in Việt Nam that emphasized the interaction between structure and agency. By examining the perceived causes of difficulties, and the forms and targets of resistance, it was found that such interactions vary considerably according to context, through both time and space, revealing the diversity of resistance processes. Peasants adjust their forms and methods of collective action according to the context of political opportunities and their understandings of what might be effective resistance.

During collectivization in Việt Nam from the 1960s to 1980s, the main forms of peasant resistance were articulated through everyday acts. Peasants chose this form as the most appropriate in the repressive political environment of that time. Most importantly, however, that choice reflected peasant perceptions of the causes of their economic difficulties, believed to be rooted in the inefficient design and implementation of economic policies. Peasants did not engage in more open protests against the government because they trusted its benevolent intentions towards rural development.

The economic reforms that began in the 1980s initially brought economic improvements, but liberalization policies then created havoc in rural areas and many peasants have suffered significantly since. Peasant discontent has resulted in more open protests due to changes in the political environment that have permitted fights against corruption and the promotion of local democracy. Such open resistance has, however, remained localized and has rarely targeted the central state for two reasons. First, the central government has tolerated resistance at the local level, but has shown much less leniency towards protests directed at itself or the very legitimacy of its rule. Most importantly, however, peasants have continued attributing their difficulties in this period to the corruption of local cadres, and not to national liberalization policies. But they may start questioning this new development model if their difficulties persist and worsen, potentially resulting in a revision of forms of resistance, be they everyday forms or more overt, finding different targets for these struggles, and in a very different political climate.

Notes

1 I am grateful to Sarah Turner and Dominique Caouette for their comments and meticulous editing of this chapter.
2 The Mường is the third largest ethnic minority group in Việt Nam. They are closely related to the Kinh (lowland Vietnamese).
3 League for the Independence of Việt Nam.
4 Structure refers to, among other things, social class, ethnicity, customs, but also the various discourses used by elites and other groups to influence peasant perceptions. Agency, in turn, is constituted by peasants' endowments, notably their experience, level of education, knowledge, networks, and so on, that determine their capacity to analyse and act on their own problems.
5 Points received in payments for various units of work which were converted into staple foods at the end of a season.
6 The *total poverty line* 'measures the cost of buying enough food to provide 2,100 calories and also makes a provision for non-food items' (Haughton 2001: 13).
7 The *food poverty line* 'measures the expenditure level that would be required to ensure that a family can buy enough food to provide each member with 2,100 calories per day' (Haughton 2001: 13).
8 Zingerli (2004) and Trần Thị Thu Trang (2004b), however, find little change in local practices despite the implementation of Decree 29 on local democracy.
9 Li and O'Brien (1996: 54) have similar observations in relation to China.
10 Local authorities are comprised of three governing bodies: the Party Chapter (Communist Party), the People's Committee (executive), and the People's Council (legislative).

References

Abrami, R.M. (1995) 'Gourou's symbiotic villages revisited: inter-village relations, socioeconomic differentiation, and the place of the past in northern Vietnam', Working Paper No. 5, Berkeley: University of California Press.
—— (2003) 'A survey of Asia in 2002: Vietnam in 2002: on the road to recovery', *Asian Survey*, 43 (1): 91–100.
Akram-Lodhi, H. (2005) 'Vietnam's agriculture: processes of rich peasant accumulation and mechanisms of social differentiation', *Journal of Agrarian Change*, 5 (1): 73–116.
Allina-Pisano, J. (2008) *The Post-Soviet Potemkin Village: Politics and Property Rights in the black earth.* New York, NY: Cambridge University Press.

ASRIA (Association for Sustainable and Responsible Investment in Asia) (2002) 'Vietnam coffee growers find hope in OXFAM Fair Trade Campaign', 30 October. Online. Available HTTP: <http://www.asria.org/news/press/1037760602> (accessed 20 February 2009).

Ban Bí Thư Trung Ương Đảng (1983) *Chi thị 100-CT/TW của Ban Bí Thư: Cải tiến công tác khoán, mở rộng 'khoán sản phẩm đến nhóm lao động và người lao động' trong hợp tác xã nông nghiệp* (Directive 100-CT/TW issued by the Secretariat of the Communist Party of Vietnam: 'Expanding the product on to the group work and workers in agricultural cooperatives'.), Hanoi: Truth Publishing House.

BBC News (2003a) 'Nam Cam sentenced to death', 5 June. Online. Available HTTP: <http://news.bbc.co.uk/2/hi/asia-pacific/2964544.stm> (accessed 20 February 2009).

—— (2003b) 'Vietnam plans chop for coffee crop', 22 May. Online. Available HTTP: <http://news.bbc.co.uk/2/hi/business/3049565.stm> (accessed 20 February 2009).

—— (2007) 'Vietnam dissident lawyers jailed', 11 May. Online. Available HTTP: <http://news.bbc.co.uk/2/hi/asia-pacific/6645463.stm> (accessed 20 February 2009).

BBC Vietnamese.com (2007) 'Giai pháp cho tranh chấp đất đai?' *(Solutions for Land Disputes), 10 July. Online. Available HTTP: <http://www.bbc.co.uk/vietnamese/vietnam/story/2007/07/070710_land_disputes_interview.shtml> (accessed 20 February 2009).*

Bhaduri, A. (1982) 'Agricultural cooperatives and peasant participation in the Socialist Republic of Vietnam', in A. Bhaduri and A. Rahman (eds) *Studies in Rural Participation*, Geneva: International Labour Organisation, 34–57.

Bloom, G. (1998) 'Primary health care meets the market: lessons from China and Vietnam', International Development Studies Working Paper 53. Brighton: Institute of Development Studies, University of Sussex.

Bùi Thái Quyên, Cao Như Nguyệt, Nguyễn Thị Kim Dung, Trần Bính Phượng with Dominique Haughton and Jonathan Haughton (2001) 'Education and income', in D. Haughton, J. Haughton and Nguyễn Phong (eds) *Living Standards During an Economic Boom: the case of Vietnam*, Hanoi: UNDP and Statistical Publishing House, 79–94.

Đặng Phong and Beresford M. (1998) *Authority Relations and Economic Decision-Making in Vietnam: an historical perspective*, Copenhagen: Nordic Institute of Asian Studies.

Đào Thế Tuấn (1995) 'The peasant household economy and social change', in B.J.T. Kerkvliet and D.J. Porter (eds) *Vietnam's Rural Transformation*, Boulder, CO: Westview Press, 139–63.

Dodsworth, J.R., Spitäller, E., Braulke, M., Keon Hyok Lee, Miranda, K., Mulder, C., Shishido, H., and Srinivasan, K. (1996) 'Vietnam's transition to a market economy', Occasional Paper 135, Washington, DC: International Monetary Fund.

Đức Kế and Phong Cầm (2007) 'Nông dân phải nộp 122 khoản thu' (Peasants have to pay 122 types of fees), *Thanh Nien*, 4 September.

Fforde, A. and de Vylder, S. (1996) *From Plan to Market: the economic transition in Vietnam*, Boulder, CO: Westview Press.

General Statistics Office, Department of Agriculture, Forestry and Fishery (2000) Statistical Data of Vietnam: Agriculture, Forestry and Fishery 1975–2000, Hanoi: Statistical Publishing House.

General Statistics Office of Vietnam (2002) *Vietnam Living Standards Survey*, Hanoi: General Statistics Office of Vietnam.
—— (2008) 'National accounts'. Online. Available HTTP: <http://www.gso.gov.vn/default_en.aspx?tabid=468&idmid=3> (accessed 20 February 2009).
Giang Long (2007) 'Giá heo ngoại rẻ, giới chăn nuôi kêu trời' (Cheap Imported Pork Hurt Domestic Producers), *Người lao động*, 29 August.
Goletti, F. and Rich, K. (1998) 'Policy simulation for agricultural diversification', UNDP VIE/96/008/A/01/99 Strengthening Capacity for the Renewal of Rural Development in Vietnam (Phase 1), Final Report.
Hà Vinh (1997) *Nông Nghiệp Việt Nam Trong Bước Chuyển Sang Kinh Tế Thị Trường* (Vietnamese Agriculture in the Transition to a Market Economy), Hanoi: Social Sciences Publishing House.
Haughton, J. (2001) 'Introduction: extraordinary changes', in D. Haughton, J. Haughton and N. Phong (eds) *Living Standards During an Economic Boom: the case of Vietnam*, Hanoi: UNDP and Statistical Publishing House, 9–32.
Henin, B. (2002) 'Agrarian change in Vietnam's Northern Upland Region', *Journal of Contemporary Asia*, 32 (1): 3–28.
Hill, H. (2000) 'Export success against the odds: a Vietnamese case study', *World Development*, 28 (2): 283–300.
Human Rights Watch (1997) 'Grievances in Rural Vietnam'. Online. Available HTTP: <http://www.igc.org/hrw/reports/1997/vietnm/Vietn97d-01.htm> (accessed 20 February 2009).
InternationalReports.Net (2003) 'Coffee: upmarket or uprooted'. Online. Available HTTP: <http://www.internationalreports.net/asiapacific/vietnam/2003/coffee.html> (accessed 20 February 2009).
Kerkvliet, B.J.T. (1993) 'State-village relations in Vietnam: contested co-operatives and collectivization', Working Paper 85, Monash University.
—— (2003) 'Authorities and the people: an analysis of state-society relations in Vietnam', Lương Văn Hy (ed.) *Postwar Vietnam: dynamics of a transforming society*, Singapore: Institute of Southeast Asian Studies, 27–54.
—— (2005) *The Power of Everyday Politics: how Vietnamese peasants transformed national policy*, Ithaca, NY: Cornell University Press.
Kleinen, J. (1999) *Facing the Future, Reviving the Past: a study of social change in a northern Vietnamese village*, Singapore: Institute of Southeast Asian Studies.
Koh, D. (2004) 'Vietnam's recent political developments', in P. Taylor (ed.) *Social Inequality in Vietnam and the Challenges to Reform*, Singapore: Institute of Southeast Asian Studies, 41–62.
Lagrée, S. (1995) 'Évolution de l'agriculture vietnamienne dans un district du delta du Fleuve Rouge', *Cahiers d'Outre-Mer*, 48 (190): 139–56.
Li, L. and O'Brien, K.J. (1996) 'Villagers and popular resistance in contemporary China', *Modern China*, 22 (1): 28–61.
London, J. (2004) 'Rethinking Vietnam's mass education and health systems', in D. McCargo (ed.) *Rethinking Vietnam*, London and New York: Routledge, 127–42.
Lương Văn Hy (1992) *Revolution in the Village: tradition and transformation in North Vietnam, 1925–1988*, Honolulu: University of Hawai'i Press.
—— (2003) 'Introduction', in V.H. Luong (ed.) *Postwar Vietnam: dynamics of a transforming society*, Singapore: Institute of Southeast Asian Studies.
—— (2005) 'The state, local associations, and alternate civilities in rural northern

Vietnam', in R.P. Weller (ed.) *Civil Life, Globalization, and Political Change in Asia: organizing between family and state*, London and New York: Routledge.

Lương Văn Hy and Unger, J. (1998) 'Wealth, power and poverty in the transition to market economies: the process of socio-economic differentiation in rural China and northern Vietnam', *The China Journal*, Special Issue, Transforming Asian Socialism: China and Vietnam Compared, July, 40: 61–93.

McCarty, A. (2001) 'Governance institutions and incentive structures in Vietnam'. Online. Available HTTP: <http://ideas.repec.org/p/wpa/wuwppe/0110002.html> (accessed 20 February 2009).

McElwee, P. (2007) 'From the moral economy to the world economy: revisiting Vietnamese peasants in a globalizing era', *Journal of Vietnamese Studies*, 2 (2): 57–107.

McNicoll, A. and Durst, P.B. (1995) 'Reform of the forestry sector: towards a market orientation in China, Laos, Mongolia, Myanmar, and Vietnam', FAO/RAPA Publication No. 1995/4, Bangkok, Thailand.

Minot, N. and Goletti, F. (2000) 'Rice market liberalization and poverty in Viet Nam', Research Report 114, Washington: International Food Policy Research Institute.

Mittelman, J.H. and Chin, C.B.N. (2000) 'Conceptualizing resistance to globalization', in J.H. Mittelman, *The Globalization Syndrome: transformation and resistance*, Princeton: Princeton University Press, 165–78.

Ngô Vĩnh Long (1993) 'Reform and rural development in Vietnam: impact on class, sectoral and regional inequalities', in W.S. Turley and M. Selden (eds) *Reinventing Vietnamese Socialism*, Boulder: Westview, 165–207.

Nguyễn Trung Tiệp (1998) 'Government reform for socio-economic development in Vietnam', *Asian Review of Public Administration*, 10 (1–2): 172–82.

Nguyễn Văn Sửu (2004) 'The Politics of Land: Inequality in Land Access and Local Conflicts in the Red River Delta since Decollectivization', in P. Taylor (ed.) *Social Inequality in Vietnam and the Challenges to Reform*, Singapore: Institute of Southeast Asian Studies, 270–96.

—— (2007) 'Contending views and conflicts over land in Vietnam's Red River Delta', *Journal of Southeast Asian Studies*, 38 (2): 309–34.

New York Times (2003) 'Harvesting Poverty: the great catfish war', 22 July. Online. Available HTTP: <http://query.nytimes.com/gst/fullpage.html?res=9B01EED7163 FF931A15754C0A9659C8B63> (accessed 20 February 2009).

O'Brien, K.J. (1996) 'Rightful resistance', *World Politics*, 49 (1): 31–55.

Porter, G. (1993) *Vietnam: the politics of bureaucratic socialism*, Ithaca, NY: Cornell University Press.

Quang Thuần and Quang Duẫan (2007) 'Giảm thuế nhập khẩu thịt heo: Nỗi lo mới của người chăn nuôi' (Tax Reduction to Imported Pork: Concern to Domestic Producers), 14 August, *Thanh Nien*. Online. Available HTTP: <http://www.thanhnien.com.vn/2007/Pages/200733/204966.aspx> (accessed 20 February 2009).

Rato, M. (2004) 'Class, nation, and text: the representation of peasants in Vietnamese literature' in P. Taylor (ed.) *Social Inequality in Vietnam and the Challenges to Reform*, Singapore: Institute of Southeast Asian Studies, 325–50.

Raymond, C. (2003) 'The effect of agricultural privatization on communist political legitimacy in Vietnam', *Journal of Third World Studies*, 20 (1): 157–78.

Socialist Republic of Việt Nam (2002) 'The comprehensive poverty reduction and growth strategy', Document No. 2685/VPCP-QHQT, 21 May, Hanoi.

—— (2005) 'Vietnam achieving the Millennium Development Goals', Document No. 4947/VPCP-QHQT, 1 September, Hanoi.

Taylor, P. (2004a) 'Introduction: social inequality in a socialist state', in P. Taylor (ed.), *Social Inequality in Vietnam and the Challenges to Reform*, Singapore: Institute of Southeast Asian Studies, 1–40.

—— (2004b) 'Redressing Disadvantage or Re-arranging Inequality? Development Interventions and Local Responses in the Mekong Delta', in P. Taylor (ed.), *Social Inequality in Vietnam and the Challenges to Reform*, Singapore: Institute of Southeast Asian Studies, 236–69.

—— (2007) 'Poor policies, wealthy peasants: alternative trajectories of rural development in Vietnam', *Journal of Vietnamese Studies*, 2 (2): 3–56.

Tổng cục thống kê (2004) *Kết quả điều tra mức sống hộ gia đình năm 2002* (Results from the 2002 Household Living Standard Survey), Hanoi: Statistical Publishing House.

Trần Phường (1960) *Một số ý kiến về Chủ nghĩa tử bản ở nông thôn miền bắc ngay sau cải cách ruộng đất* (Some Reflections on Capitalism in Rural Areas of North Vietnam after Land Reform), Hanoi: Truth Publishing House.

Trần Thị Thu Trang (2004a) 'From collectivization to globalization: social differentiation in a Mưòng ethnic community of Vietnam', in P. Taylor (ed.) *Social Inequality in Vietnam and the Challenges to Reform*, Singapore: Institute of Southeast Asian Studies, 123–65.

—— (2004b) 'Local politics and democracy in a Mưòng ethnic community', in B. Kerkvliet and D. Marr (eds) *Beyond Hanoi: local government in Vietnam*, Singapore: Institute of Southeast Asian Studies, 137–66.

Turley, W.S. (1993) 'Introduction', in W.S. Turley and M. Selden (eds) *Reinventing Vietnamese Socialism*, Boulder: Westview, 1–15.

United Nations Development Programme (1990) *Human Development Reports*, New York: UNDP.

—— (1995) *Human Development Reports*, New York: UNDP.

—— (2006) *Human Development Reports*, New York: UNDP.

UNDP Viet Nam (2001) *Modernizing Governance*, Hanoi: UNDP Viet Nam.

Vasavakul, T. (1995) 'The changing models of legitimation', in M. Alagappa (ed.) *Political legitimacy in Southeast Asia: the quest for moral authority*, Stanford, CA: Stanford University Press, 257–89.

Võ Trí Thanh and Phạm Hoàng Hà (2004) 'Vietnam's recent economic reforms and developments: achievements, paradoxes, and challenges', in P. Taylor (ed.) *Social Inequality in Vietnam and the Challenges to Reform*, Singapore: Institute of Southeast Asian Studies, 63–89.

Wall Street Journal (15 August 2007) 'Headache in Hanoi'. Online. Available: <http://online.wsj.com/article/SB118712635750597658.html> (accessed 20 February 2009.

White, B. (1989) 'Problems in the empirical analysis of agrarian differentiation', in G.P. Hart, A. Turton and B. White (eds) *Agrarian Transformations: local processes and the state in Southeast Asia*, Berkeley: University of California Press, 15–30.

White, G. (1987) 'Riding the tiger: Grass-roots rural politics in the wake of the Chinese economic reforms', in A. Saith (ed.) *The Re-emergence of the Chinese Peasantry*, New York: Croom Helm, 250–69.

Zingerli, C. (2004) 'Politics in mountain communes: exploring Vietnamese grassroots democracy', in D. McCargo (ed.) *Rethinking Vietnam*, London and New York: Routledge, 53–66.

9 Indonesia's agrarian movement: Anti-capitalism at a crossroads

Vu Tuong [1]

Introduction

The contemporary agrarian movement in Indonesia began in the last decade of the New Order regime (1966–98). Several land disputes turned into violent clashes when farmers protested against low compensation and the heavy-handed methods used by state agents to expropriate lands for development projects (Aditjondro 1998; Lucas and Warren 2000, 2003; Afiff *et al.* 2005). Contests over rights to natural resources represented part of this wave of conflict, and in many cases, farmers' causes were endorsed by student groups and urban non-governmental organizations (NGOs) (Warren 1998a, 1998b; Afiff and Lowe 2007). Although early protests were suppressed, they set the scene for a vigorous movement to emerge after President Suharto resigned in 1998. Within a few years, the movement succeeded in pressuring the Indonesian parliament to pass a decision on agrarian reform and on the management of natural resources. Farmers' unions have also organized numerous protests against rice imports, trade agreements and international financial organizations.

After a decade of fast growth, the movement is now at a critical stage. Despite numerous protests and greater access to politicians under *Reformasi* (reformation period or post-1998 era), the agrarian movement has not generated sufficient political support among elites for its goal of land redistribution. The parliament's decision on agrarian reform remains to be fleshed out in specific laws and regulations. The government has gradually restored the power of the Indonesian Bureau of Logistics (*Badan Urusan Logistik*: BULOG), partly in response to popular protests, but rice imports keep arriving.[2] In 2003, Indonesia was the world's largest rice importer, much to the indignation of farmers' groups.

Activists from Indonesian urban NGOs and collaborating foreign academics have produced an important array of literature concerning the agrarian movement in Indonesia (see for example Wiradi 2000; Fauzi 2003; Afiff *et al.* 2005; and others cited throughout this chapter). While valuable, these accounts tend to reflect the view of a few groups rather than the entire movement; in particular, the views of more radical groups have been neglected by this literature. Besides the fact that urban NGOs are more accessible than those attempting to become established in rural areas, the greater coverage given to them in academic literature is also somewhat indicative of academics' broader interests in themes of greater significance to a Western audience such as environmental protection, civil society and democratic transition.

The agrarian concerns that lie at the heart of these NGOs' activities are not new phenomena in Indonesia. The first decade after independence (gained in 1949) saw a spontaneous movement by landless farmers to squat on plantation lands. In the 1960s, the Communist Party of Indonesia (*Partai Komunis Indonesia*: PKI) led farmers in a violent campaign to claim lands that legally belonged to them according to the Basic Agrarian Law (*Undang-Undang Pokok Agraria*: UUPA) promulgated in 1960.[3] Simmering conflicts led to massive violence during 1965–6, when a coup brought General Suharto to power. In this event, the military coordinated a campaign that killed or imprisoned hundreds of thousands of farmers belonging to communist groups.

What role does this history play in the current agrarian movement? Does the rise of today's movement owe only to developments in the last decade of the New Order regime, or does its genealogy go back further? This chapter builds on existing accounts but takes a step back to aim at two related goals. First, I hope to provide a more comprehensive overview of the agrarian movement in Indonesia, especially its often overlooked anti-capitalist discourse. Second, based on a critical review of activist and academic literature, I endeavour to offer a different perspective on the origins of the movement. Existing accounts have analysed this movement within the context of an emergent civil society or democratizing trends (Eldridge 1995; Uhlin 1995; Aspinall 2004; Nomura 2007). These accounts have paid insufficient attention to the ideological roots of this movement. As I argue below, there is a close affinity between the discourses of agrarian activists today and those of the broader anti-capitalist movement that dates back to colonial times.

Anti-capitalism is defined here both as a theme in political discourse and as a movement. Originally a counter-hegemonic movement under colonialism, after Indonesian independence it became more mainstream. Anti-capitalism differs from anti-globalization: globalization is of recent use in Indonesia and is not consistently opposed by activists as is capitalism. After three decades of rapid capitalist development under Suharto, anti-capitalism remains surprisingly robust and relevant. I argue that this particular perspective illuminates many aspects of the current movement of agrarian resistance heretofore obscured.

The shape and scale of Indonesia's agrarian movements

Since 1998, Indonesia has seen the birth of hundreds of farmers' unions. The largest national network of farmers' unions is the Indonesian Federation of Farmers' Unions (*Federasi Serikat Petani Indonesia*: FSPI). Acting jointly with these unions are numerous local and national NGOs, perhaps the best known being the Consortium for Agrarian Reform (*Konsorsium Pembaruan Agraria*: KPA) which was founded in the mid-1990s and now has about 200 member organizations. On environmental and natural resource issues, the largest NGO is the Indonesian Forum on Environment (*Wahana Lingkungan Hidup Indonesia*: WALHI), also founded very early, over 25 years ago (Di Gregorio 2006). Farmers have received sustained support from NGOs working on human rights and legal aid, especially during the early and difficult years of the movement in the 1980s, when the political environment was repressive.

Most Indonesian NGOs are urban-based and enjoy extensive transnational links to Western organizations (Eldridge 1995, 2007; Uhlin 1995), including being the recipients of substantial funding from foreign donors. Yet the links go beyond the West. The Secretary General of FSPI, Henry Saragih, is also the Regional Coordinator of *Via Campesina* (International Farmers' Movement), whose International Operative Secretariat is based in Jakarta. Saragih sometimes leads protests around the world against the World Trade Organization (WTO) and was recently named by the British newspaper *The Guardian* (5 January 2008) as one of the 50 people who could change the fate of the planet, together with figures like former US Vice President Al Gore and German Prime Minister Angela Merkel.

Substantively, the agrarian movement in Indonesia involves struggles over three key issues: land rights, natural resources and trade policy. The issue that has generated the most visible resistance in the form of violence, and the most literature, is no doubt land rights. There have been thousands of disputes involving farmers, state agencies, state plantations and private developers throughout Java alone (for cases in West Java, see Afiff *et al.* 2005). In 2007, according to a count by the Indonesian Peasant Union (*Serikat Petani Indonesia*: SPI), there were 76 new or ongoing agrarian conflicts.

Even before the fall of Suharto, farmers had occupied thousands of hectares of plantation lands. In the eight years after 1998, according to the West Javanese branch of the Association of Plantation Corporations, 2,660 hectares (ha), or 12 per cent of total plantation areas, in West Java's Garut district were 'plundered' by farmers (Fauzi 2007). A well-studied case involved Cieceng village in Garut district, where landless farmers occupied and divided among themselves 200 ha of land leased to a state plantation company. This took place after villagers learned from farmers' union leaders that the lease had expired in 1997 (Afiff *et al.* 2005).[4] In response, the state-owned plantation company trucked in hundreds of thugs to try to evict farmers, and the ensuing clash led to many houses and trucks being burned. Nationwide, farmers' movements to seize land have triggered a counter-movement by affected parties: according to the SPI, nearly 200,000 ha were seized from farmers and conflicts led to eight deaths in 2007.

Parallel to farmers' resistance in the shape of organized protests and spontaneous actions are NGOs' attempts to push for legislative changes. Because the Basic Agrarian Law (UUPA) of 1960 was never repealed but simply ignored under President Suharto, activists demand that it now be implemented. The agrarian movement has been split over this issue. Some activists from urban-based NGOs, especially those in the KPA, were willing to work with bureaucrats and elected officials to gain support for agrarian reform even if the communist-associated UUPA was to be put aside and replaced with new laws (Fauzi 1999). Other activists, mostly leftist academics and leaders of farmers' unions under the FSPI, rejected any changes to the UUPA (Bey 2002). The efforts of the first camp resulted in a Parliament decision in 2001 (People's Consultative Assembly Decree No. IX/2001 or TAP MPR No. IX/2001) that promised agrarian reform but that failed to mention the UUPA. The second camp, which protested the decision on the day it was passed, viewed this legislation as serving only the interests of NGOs and not those of farmers (Lucas and Warren 2003). The differences in outlooks and strategies between the KPA and FSPI, the two leading groups in the movement, are sometimes portrayed as coming from their social bases: KPA members are mostly urban NGOs, whereas FSPI members are mostly farmers' unions (ibid.). Yet both share many members, and KPA leaders have denied that the differences are significant (Fauzi and Bachriadi 2006).

Struggles over natural resources overlap those over land but primarily involve communities on the outer islands who rely on both forest resources and (often swidden) agriculture. For this reason, the cause was sponsored first by NGOs working on environmental issues, such as WALHI (Moniaga 2007). Essentially these struggles centre on claims based on customary rights to land or resource uses. Disputes between indigenous communities and state agents over land and natural resources go back to colonial times, but took shape as a national movement only in the 1990s with the help of NGOs which framed the issue in terms of *masyarakat adat*, the rights of indigenous communities.

Since the concept of 'indigenous communities' was first approved in 1993 by the NGOs involved, there have been two national congresses in 1999 and 2003 that gathered representatives from numerous communities to display solidarity, formulate a vision, coordinate action, and consolidate the movement (ibid.). The movement has achieved some success. In a dispute over a government plan to build a hydroelectric power station in the Lore Lindung area of Central Sulawesi, local protests and NGO pressure led to its cancellation (Sangaji 2007). NGOs have assisted many communities in mapping the territories that their customary rights cover (Peluso 2003). These efforts have allowed these communities to challenge the state or its agents when there were disputes. An example is the conflict concerning the Lore Lindung National Park where a local community, Katu, was allowed to use some land in the park based on its arguments of indigenous rights (ibid.). Elsewhere, in Sosa, North Sumatra, farmers' protests under the banner of 'indigenous rights' similarly forced a state plantation company to offer more fair compensation for their lands (Afiff and Lowe 2007).

Similar to the UUPA issue that split agrarian reform activists into two camps, the *masyarakat adat* (indigenous communities) movement is controversial. The *adat* (tradition or custom) concept is criticized because it is 'overly idealistic and does not adequately reflect empirical realities', assuming characteristics of *adat* groups to be static (Sangaji 2007: 321). There is also considerable social stratification within each community, and guaranteeing *adat* rights does not ensure equality. In areas with large migrant populations, *adat*-based struggles often pit one community ('indigenous') against another ('settlers') (Li 2007; also compare with the chapter by Dressler in this volume). Finally, local elites have sought to manipulate the movement to their own political ends. Violent communal conflicts among ethnic Dayaks, Malays and Madurese in Kalimantan were caused or exacerbated by urban Dayak elites who manipulated landless Dayak resentment to advance their political interests (Van Klinken 2006; Davidson 2008).

Besides land and indigenous rights, protests against free trade are another major activity of farmers' groups in Indonesia but have received less attention from academics. Four kinds of activity can be discerned. First are actions to protest specific government decisions or legislation such as the import of rice or the 2007 Bill on Foreign Investment. Second are rallies to commemorate certain dates which represent nationalistic symbols such as the Day of National Awakening (28 January 1908) and the Africa–Asia Conference in Bandung (24 April 1955, the closing day of the conference). These events are linked to activists' demands for agrarian reform or food sovereignty. Third, movement leaders organize conferences scheduled to occur at the same time as major events held by international organizations such as the Food and Agriculture Organization (FAO) and the WTO, whether in Indonesia or abroad. The organizers and participants in these events do not seek access to the events held by those international organizations. Rather, these parallel conferences (also noted in Caouette's chapter) are to raise public concerns about issues important to farmers and to present alternatives to official policies. The events, especially the demonstrations, are also to display popular support for the causes embraced by protesters. Fourth and finally, some organizations are active abroad, participating in protests to strengthen international solidarity with the worldwide anti-globalization movement.

The FSPI has played a central role in most activities. In April 2005, it helped found the umbrella group *Gerakan Rakyat Lawan Nekolim* (People's Movement to Oppose Neo-colonialism and Neo-imperialism or *Gerak Lawan*).[5] Other members of this group include WALHI, *Aliansi Buruh Mengugat* (Alliance of Critical Workers), *Koalisi Anti Utang* (Anti-Debt Coalition), *Front Perjuangan Pemuda Indonesia* (Youth Front for Struggle), *Lingkar Studi-Aksi untuk Demokrasi Indonesia* (Academic-Activist Circle for Democracy), *Komite Mahasiswa Anti-Imperialisme* (Student Committee against Imperialism), *Kesatuan Aksi Mahasiswa LAKSI 31* (United Action for LAKSI 31), and *Perhimpunan Bantuan Hukum dan Hak Asasi Manusia Indonesia* (Legal Aid and Human Rights Association). Not all NGOs and farmers' unions have joined *Gerak Lawan*. The KPA, which is active on land issues, has rarely participated in anti-trade activities.

To recap, the agrarian movement in Indonesia has experienced considerable growth and transformation since 1998. It is increasingly diversified, both in organization and in issues. Existing accounts have focused mostly on land disputes and protests involving natural resources. Anti-trade activities are more recent and have not yet been analysed. Missing from the literature are not only these activities, but also the discourses of the movement.[6] What are the world views of activists? What concepts, images and arguments do they use in their struggles and different forms of resistance?

Agrarian movement discourses [7]

Discourses constitute a major part of any social movement. Consisting of words, arguments, images and symbols, discourses not only express movement visions, goals and strategies, but also serve to connect members and facilitate communication with others. In this section I analyse the anti-capitalist ideology that is deeply held and broadly shared among many agrarian activists in Indonesia. This ideology is expressed in their profound hostility toward capitalism and the pillars of the global 'capitalist system'. Targets of their harsh and frequent denunciations include global trade, foreign investment, specific capitalist countries, especially the US, and the international organizations such countries dominate. Some activists have more nuanced views than others, but most tend to share basic assumptions about capitalism, as will be shown in the following analysis.

Agrarian activists in Indonesia commonly view capitalism as an unjust socio-economic system. Wiradi, an early advocate of agrarian reform and a senior adviser to the KPA, writes that the capitalist mode of agrarian transformation historically involved the creation of large-scale agribusinesses that 'swallowed almost all the small farmers' (Wiradi 2000: 64). The result was a process by which land control was concentrated in the hands of a few while small farmers were turned into workers or tenants. In New Order Indonesia, this unjust process triggered numerous land disputes (ibid.).

Noer Fauzi (1996: online), former director of the KPA, opposes the land administration project funded by Australia because he thinks farmers would not benefit from such a single land management system: 'Having a certificate put [farmers] into the capitalist arena. But [they] will be weak participant[s], and could be worse off than before.' Instead, Fauzi predicts that (further) unequal land distribution would result. This belief in capitalism as unjustly favouring the strong is also shared by Saragih of the FSPI, who criticizes the World Bank for promoting 'market-assisted land reform' (cited in Netto 2006: n.p.). Saragih believes that this kind of land reform would lead to the privatization of land and the creation of land markets. In these markets the rich who are able to pay would accumulate land. Agribusinesses would become more powerful while farmers would have less access to land (ibid.).

Many agrarian activists in Indonesia also challenge the ideological and philosophical bases of 'capitalism', namely classical liberalism and neoliberalism. They associate these '-isms' with 'colonialism', 'imperialism' and 'individualism', concepts carrying strong negative connotations in a country which was once colonized and whose culture is often touted for valuing family spirits and communal collaboration. Idham Samudra Bey, who directs the Center for National Democracy Studies, writes that colonialism and imperialism were 'born from the womb of classical liberalism which is based on an individualistic philosophy' (Bey 2002: online). Neoliberalism, he maintains, is based on the same philosophy and is thus only the continuation of classic liberalism. Anti-colonialism and anti-imperialism were at the foundation of the UUPA, and Bey was adamant that the Land Reform law be implemented unchanged.

Being hostile to capitalism, many activists view the world in structural terms: divided between rich/advanced/industrialized countries (*negara industri maju*); as compared to poor/less advanced/developing countries (*negara sedang berkembang*). Advanced countries are targets not of emulation but of denunciation. Indonesia's rural activists frequently argue that there are many mechanisms through which developing countries and their people are exploited in a structurally asymmetric world. The first mechanism is through loans promoted or arranged by international organizations such as the World Bank and the International Monetary Fund (IMF). These activists often voice visceral hatred toward these organizations. As Dani, the speaker representing *Koalisi Anti Utang* (Anti-Debt Coalition), argued at a rally in front of the Japanese and several Western embassies in Jakarta on 5 September 2006, '[through their loans] the World Bank and the IMF have committed crimes against humanity for the interests of the advanced countries' (*Federasi Serikat Petani Indonesia* 2006a: online). The loans are similarly argued to have benefited foreign investors at the expense of 'the people's welfare' (*Federasi Serikat Petani Indonesia* 2006b: online). Likewise, activists highlight that even though more than 150 out of 184 members of the World Bank are developing countries, 67 per cent of votes are controlled by 34 'advanced countries', with the largest numbers of votes held by the US, Japan, France, the UK and Germany.

To agrarian movement activists, 'free trade' can be another means of exploitation. They argue that free trade hurts farmers in importing countries because the advanced countries can produce goods at cheaper prices and often subsidize their producers (see Smeltzer's chapter for similar standpoints in Malaysia). The giant transnational companies present in Indonesia such as Monsanto (agrochemical), Freeport MacMoran (mining), Cargill (agriculture) and Charoen Pokphand (agriculture) are accused of 'flooding the markets of poor and developing countries' with their 'super-cheap commodities that harm the small rice farmers' (*Gerak Lawan* 2007: online).[8] Rice imports are said to have turned Indonesian rice farmers into non-agricultural workers, migrants or the unemployed (ibid.). Finally, activists argue that free trade causes Indonesia to depend on the international market and impinges upon national sovereignty. Some activists stress that they do not advocate a complete ban on food trade, but the needs of domestic families and local people must be given priority, and agriculture must be based on sustainable small-scale household production (Ikhwan 2007).

Due to activists' animosity toward trade, the WTO has received particularly vicious attacks from them. Calling this trade organization 'the enemy of the Peasant', the declaration of the FSPI-hosted Dili conference of *Via Campesina* accused the WTO of creating poverty and hunger while causing the exploitation of natural resources and environmental destruction worldwide (*Federasi Serikat Petani Indonesia* 2000). Other international organizations are not so bitterly opposed. The United Nations and its agencies such as the FAO are not targets of protest, even though Western nations in some sense also dominate these organizations. When the FAO organized the International Conference on Agrarian Reform and Rural Development (ICARRD) in Brazil, 7–10 March 2006, the KPA and its two senior advisers, Sediono Tjondronegoro and Gunawan Wiradi, met with several government ministries to form a joint delegation (Consortium for Agrarian Reform 2006). At the same time, the KPA joined the FSPI and others in a joint position paper to demand, among other items, that the Indonesian government boycott the ICARRD if the conference approved the programme of land registration sponsored by the World Bank (*Federasi Serikat Petani Indonesia* 2006c).

Activists have protested against rice imports and unfair trade practices not only on the streets but also at the conceptual level. 'Food Sovereignty' (*kedaulatan pangan*) is a concept aggressively promoted by the movement to counter the FAO's concept of 'food security'. The FSPI/*Via Campesina* organized a conference on food sovereignty in Jakarta in May 2006 that gathered representatives of farmers' organizations from Japan, Korea, the US, India and other Asian nations. Food sovereignty includes at least three demands. First, as organizers explained:

> FAO's 'food security' concept only relates to food availability, access to food and food safety. It does not take into consideration where the food comes from and how it is produced . . . This is why we are promoting food sovereignty that also encompasses issues such as land distribution, farmers' control over water, seed biodiversity and technology.
>
> (*Federasi Serikat Petani Indonesia* 2006d: online)

Activists thus see the hunger problem as involving more than simply ensuring that there is sufficient food on every family's table. In this view hunger is not solved unless farmers have full control over inputs (seeds, water, land and technology) and the production process.

Second, it is argued that there is more value and meaning assigned to food than simply something to eat, and for activists the problem of food goes beyond hunger. Muhammad Nuruddin, the Secretary General of the Indonesian Alliance of Farmers (*Aliansi Petani Indonesia*: API) elaborates:

> Food is a basic need of humankind. Because of this, the food problem relates to the individual, household and society as a basic human right. Food sovereignty is the right of a nation and monopoly of its availability is a form of colonization through food and clearly violates Human Rights.
>
> (Nuruddin 2007: online)

To activists like Nuruddin, control over food production and consumption is a basic human and national right; hence the term 'sovereignty'.

Third, because the Jakarta Conference on Food Sovereignty focused on the Asia–Pacific region where rice is commonly the main staple food, activists gave special attention to rice. This conference declared: 'Rice is not only a commodity; it is life, culture and dignity!' This slogan suggests that the problem perceived by activists is not limited to hunger, human rights and national sovereignty, but encompasses also moral and cultural preservation; at least as far as rice is concerned. The free trade of rice or food threatens not only food availability but also the very foundation of societies in Pacific Asia.

Investment is another mechanism that activists argue is used by advanced countries to exploit developing countries. It is through their investment that transnational companies are 'colonizing' (*jajah*), 'sucking' (*hisap*) and 'absorbing' (*serap*) Indonesia (*Federasi Serikat Petani Indonesia* 2007a: online). Statements made at various events commonly recite a litany of damages that foreign investment causes to Indonesia. For example, one statement at the protest against the draft Bill for Foreign Investment read:

> Foreign investment makes the people poorer and more marginalized. Women are even more marginalized and lose access and control over natural resources. [Foreign investment causes] imbalances in the production and distribution of necessities for the people's livelihood. Eventually this will cause disasters such as agrarian conflicts and violations of human rights as is happening in Indonesia now.
>
> (*Federasi Serikat Petani Indonesia* 2007a: online)

Some acknowledge that Indonesia may still need foreign capital for the time being, but call for the protection of 'people's rights' (*hak-hak rakyat*) when engaging with such capital (Wiradi 2000: 178).

With their hostilities toward capitalism, trade and foreign investment, it is not surprising that many activists feel apprehensive about globalization. Wiradi (2000) defines globalization as essentially the movement of international capitalism. He argues that agribusinesses are simply a part of this movement. These companies represent 'efforts to acquire the use and benefits of land in developing countries for the interests of owners of international capital through the help (*nebeng*) of the governments of advanced countries' (ibid.: 177). While globalization generates economic growth, it also creates economic and social inequalities and increases the dependency of developing countries on advanced nations. Wiradi (2000) thus sees globalization as a threat (*ancam*), not an opportunity for developing countries, and agrees with the well-known Indonesian agronomist, Mubyarto, that Indonesia must be 'extra-vigilant' about globalization, and its impacts on agrarian livelihoods. Usep Setiawan, Deputy Secretary General of the KPA, explains in detail what he perceives as the negative consequences of globalization. He argues that first, the process makes farmers become 'objects driven in the interests of capital' (Setiawan n.d.: online). Second, there is no substantial protection for farmers to maintain stability and security. Third, subsidies for farmers are discontinued, which makes it difficult for governments to help them. Fourth, imported products 'crush the competitiveness of Indonesian farmers' products', and fifth, agriculture only serves the elites while accelerating urbanization and proletarianization (ibid.). The bottom line of Setiawan and others' argument is the same: globalization is believed to cause the destruction of (small-scale) agriculture and the 'proletarianization' of farmers.

It needs to be pointed out that an irony exists in some activists' attitudes toward the state. While farmers are said to have suffered tremendously under Suharto's repressive developmental state, many activists still trust the state to provide protection for farmers. An often-heard criticism of globalization is that it weakens the power of the state in developing countries. Although these activists must be well aware of how corrupt BULOG was under Suharto, they still defend the agency vigorously in the face of IMF and World Bank pressure on the Indonesian government to make BULOG a state-owned corporation rather than a state agency. The discrepancy among activists in their attitudes toward the state is a major cause of the disagreement over TAP MPR No. IX/2001. The UUPA entrusts the state with the control of all land, and this clause is the main reason why many activists in the KPA want this law to be revised (Fauzi 1999). With their memories of Suharto still fresh, these activists emphasize that the control of land must rest with the people, not the state. This may also be the reason why the KPA has not rallied to defend BULOG as the FSPI does.

Discourse formation among Indonesian agrarian activists is sometimes inspired by activities occurring in Latin America. *Alternativa Bolivariana para las Américas* (ALBA), the Latin American alternative trade alliance in opposition to US domination, is viewed as an attractive approach (Ikhwan 2007). This organization was founded in 2004 by Hugo Chavez (Venezuela) and Fidel Castro (Cuba). Although most Indonesian activists admire these Latin American figures, they have different ideas about foreign models. Henry Saragih, of the FSPI, once expressed his pride that the Bandung Conference in 1955 had inspired Latin American populist leaders such as Hugo Chavez and Evo Morales (Bolivia) (*Federasi Serikat Petani Indonesia* 2007b). He believed that it was right for Indonesians, in turn, to be inspired and to learn from these leaders, but that Indonesians ought to develop their own solutions based on their own country's history. Noer Fauzi shares the same belief. Asked whether there is any possibility for Indonesia to develop a situation similar to Venezuela, where the military supports a 'progressive government' under Hugo Chavez, Fauzi responded that Indonesians could learn from them, but should not consider Latin American models as ideals to emulate (Fauzi 2007). Instead, Fauzi argued that Indonesians should learn from the models of their own Communist Party (PKI)'s programmes such as the 'Go Down' campaign to create stronger links between activists and farmers through educational activities (Fauzi and Bachriadi 2006).[9]

Rejecting neoliberalism, activists advocate many alternatives, ranging from a 'People's economy' (*ekonomi kerakyatan*), to an 'economy complying with *Pancasila* principles' (*ekonomi Pancasila*),[10] to 'neo-populist' agrarian reform. Wiradi proposes neo-populism as an alternative to capitalist and socialist approaches. This approach aims for an agrarian transformation that preserves the agricultural activities of small-scale farmers rather than moving them out of agriculture to make way for large-scale agribusinesses. *Via Campesina's* Conference on Food Sovereignty produced a list of demands grouped under four areas: land, water and seeds; rice production systems; post-harvest activities and processing; and trade. The first includes calls for 'land to the tiller' and communal or public ownership of water and seeds. In the second, activists condemn the Green Revolution and advocate organic and natural farming. In the third and fourth areas, it is demanded that processing and local trade be managed by small family units. The government is asked to abolish all export subsidies while giving subsidies to small farmers who produce for domestic needs. Domestic production should be regulated to prevent surpluses and rice imports should be banned.

Explanations for Indonesia's agrarian movement

There have been few efforts to explain the rise of the contemporary agrarian movement in Indonesia. Yet analysts have begun to highlight five sets of explanatory factors, including farmers' grievances; expanding political opportunities; the dissemination of progressive ideas; leadership and organization; and changes in civil society under Suharto. Although discussed in turn here, these are by no means mutually exclusive (see also Caouette and Turner, this volume).

Grievances

Analyses of particular cases, sometimes by activists themselves, often focus on farmers' grievances (Stanley 1994; Lucas 1997, 1998; Warren 1998a, 1998b). Under Suharto, numerous farming communities were dispossessed of millions of hectares that were expropriated, often with little compensation and through intimidation, for plantations or other development projects.

Such actions were the direct cause of farmers' grievances and the majority of land disputes. Many land protests occurred under the Suharto regime and the farmers who participated in these protests risked arrest and death. A deep discontent over the annexation of farmland was clearly behind the land reclamation movement, a movement that peaked within a few years of the collapse of Suharto's New Order regime. In some cases grievances were inherited: the farmers who seized land from Suharto's family ranch in Tapos after he resigned were children of the same farmers whose lands were taken to create the ranch decades beforehand (Bachriadi and Lucas 2001).

Yet such grievances with the state over land ownership are not sufficient to explain many of the protests focused on the agricultural sector. While rural grievances were widespread under Suharto, they did not cause as many open conflicts as they do now. In addition, college students from the urban middle-class working for NGOs have joined the farmers in their protests. These students often have broader motivations, and use the cause of environmental issues to contribute to a wider fight for greater political freedom (Warren 1998a: 230, citing G. Aditjondro). In the last few years, there have been massive demonstrations on the streets of Jakarta against the WTO that similarly do not stem from any specific instance of land grievances.

Political opportunities

The expansion of political opportunities since 1998 has catalyzed a surge of agrarian protests (Fauzi and Bachriadi 2006). The collapse of the New Order regime immediately removed people's fear of repression, amply demonstrated by the farmers who seized Suharto's ranch within days of his resignation. At the same time, subsequent free elections opened up space for political entrepreneurs and groups to organize (Di Gregorio 2006). Decentralization now offers farmer groups new avenues for resistance and new ways of influencing politics, in particular by enabling them to elect their leaders to local offices (Fauzi and Bachriadi 2006).

The structure of political opportunity for Indonesian activists has been influenced not only by domestic political change, but also by a major shift in the global political climate (Uhlin 1995). As the Cold War drew to a close in the late 1980s, Western allies of the Suharto regime became more forthcoming in their criticisms of the regime's poor human rights record. These criticisms hurt the legitimacy of the government while emboldening domestic activists. Political opportunities, however, require that people seize them, regardless of the risks involved, which brings us to the third explanation.

Dissemination of progressive ideas

A third explanation for the agrarian movement is the dissemination of democratic progressive ideas such as human rights in Indonesia since the 1980s.

Western models of NGOs, adopted by organizations such as the Legal Aid Society and the Indonesian Environmental Forum (WALHI), have been vehicles for these internationally supported norms, and have indeed played decisive roles since the beginning of the contemporary agrarian movement. Activists fighting for agrarian justice have found the ideas and discourse surrounding democracy such as the rule of law, human rights, indigenous rights and protection of the environment to be useful tools for their struggle. These progressive ideas allow them to frame demands in ways that do not draw comparison or association with communism so as to avoid repression. This enables them to join a community of activists elsewhere in Asia (especially the Philippines and South Korea), Latin America and Europe.

Democratic activists in Indonesia have also adopted ideas from beyond the West, drawing on cases of authoritarian collapse around the world: Iran in 1979, the Philippines in 1986, South Korea in 1987 and the Soviet Bloc in 1989 (Uhlin 1995). However, one must also note that while democratic ideas may help to explain the rise of urban activism, they do not necessarily account for protests by farmers, who are motivated mostly by the direct injustices they have suffered. I would argue that the dissemination of elite ideas about human rights and democracy is a lengthy process and does not necessarily explain the growth pattern of the agrarian protest movement in Indonesia. In addition, foreign ideas, however relevant, need cultural interpreters to resonate with Indonesians.

Leadership and organization

Following from this last point above, the fourth explanation for the agrarian movement stresses factors of leadership and organization. As such, it could be argued that Indonesian intellectuals interpret and elaborate Western ideas to affirm their applicability in Indonesian cultural and social contexts (Uhlin 1995). An example of a cultural entrepreneur is Abdurrahman Wahid, a Muslim democrat who would later become President of Indonesia (1999–2001). In responding to criticisms of (Western) democratic ideas from Islamist groups, Wahid pointed out Islamic and Hindu traditions that corresponded to basic principles of (Western) democracy such as the rule of law and basic human rights. Other activists reached back into history to demonstrate that authoritarian culture was not culturally rooted in Indonesia any more than democracy was. In the same vein, environmental issues were reframed in terms of basic human rights and became politicized during the 1990s thanks to the efforts of democratic activists (Nomura 2007).

Cultural entrepreneurs must operate alongside political ones. While the former expand the cultural resources deployable in conflicts and resistance actions, the latter seize political opportunities and turn them into political events. An example of this is the training organized in the 1980s by some advocacy NGOs for student activist groups to raise awareness on issues of development, authoritarianism and methods of people mobilization. This training has been credited for keeping the movement alive at a difficult time (Fauzi and Bachriadi 2006). Seizing or expanding opportunities often involves selecting appropriate tactics and strategies (Di Gregorio 2006). The campaign for agrarian reform led by the KPA during the period from 1999 to 2001 is an example of adopting the right tools to take advantage of different opportunities. Initially, the KPA sought to create dialogues with major political parties, but to no avail (Rosser *et al.* 2005). In 2001, the KPA changed its strategy and tried to 'socialize' the issue of land reform among parliament members while maintaining popular pressure through street protests. They also expanded opportunities by finding allies among sympathetic officials and by exploiting differences among ruling elites and state agencies (Afiff *et al.* 2005). Despite the fall of Suharto, there remained strong, entrenched interests in the political system and the hard work of activists was required for the parliament to pass a decision on agrarian reform.

Changes in civil society under Suharto

The four explanatory factors discussed thus far rely on social movement approaches and concepts (also noted by Caouette and Turner in this volume). These factors are not mutually exclusive but are in fact complimentary. In the Indonesian case, grievances motivate farmer protests, which are connected regionally and nationally by networks of urban NGOs. The activists directing the efforts of these NGOs are influenced by progressive ideas, and at the same time interpret them and transform them into culturally appropriate resources that can be applied to further their cause. *Reformasi* has expanded the structure of political opportunities, and activists as well as disaffected farmers have seized these openings to demand social justice. Yet social movement concepts do not capture the whole picture, and broader forces at work in civil society also need to be considered.

Under military rule from 1966 to 1998, Indonesia's society witnessed considerable change.[11] The success of the authoritarian state in establishing its dominance profoundly restructured civil society. This can be observed by comparing land conflicts in the early 1960s to those in the late 1980s and 1990s. Land conflicts in the former period were within village society, occurring between local landlords and farmers who were members of the PKI (Huizer 1980). In contrast, those in the late 1980s and 1990s pitted entire rural communities against either the state or its capitalist agents (Aspinall 2004) such that by the mid-1990s, horizontal conflicts had been replaced by vertical ones. Social activism and agrarian protests were mostly directed against the state, not for the purposes of waging a social revolution, as they were in the 1960s, but rather to win policy concessions and to limit the arbitrary power of the state.

Under the New Order regime, radical and polarizing organizations such as the PKI were suppressed but some moderate social organizations such as the *Nahdlatul Ulama* (NU) and certain newly created NGOs were tolerated

(Aspinall 2004). The combination of toleration and repression meant that moderate organizations and ideas were promoted while radical ones were 'weeded out'. The moderation of civil society was further carried forward by a small but vocal minority of a growing urban middle class that emerged due to rapid economic development under the Suharto regime. This new group sought to connect their interests in greater political freedom to the desires of dispossessed farmers for social justice (ibid.). Civil society, in this context, became the vehicle for the dissemination of moderate middle-class values among the lower classes.

While existing explanations have offered valuable insights into the causes of the contemporary agrarian movement in Indonesia, there has been a lack of attention to and a failure to anticipate the growth of radical groups in recent years. Despite the increasing access to numerous policy-making channels, groups such as the FSPI still reject taking advantage of such access points.[12] Their rhetoric borders on promoting revolution against the global capitalist system which they view as fundamentally unjust. We have also seen the puzzling return of old anti-colonial and Cold War ideological themes. Although there are obvious links between the contemporary agrarian movement and the PKI of the 1960s, the roots of the movement may extend further back to colonial times. Finally, if the central motif of conflict underlying today's agrarian movement is between the state and society, as Aspinall (2004) argues, it is difficult to explain why many activists desire a strong state that can 'protect the people'. As noted earlier, by protesting against rice imports, the FSPI demands the return of the state in the form of a powerful BULOG that can maintain adequate supplies and affordable prices for all. As such, I argue below that a better understanding of this movement can be gained by examining the evolution of anti-capitalism in Indonesia's modern history.

The discursive approach: the ideological genealogies of the agrarian movement

What is the history of anti-capitalism in Indonesia? How did it survive 30 years of rapid capitalist development under Suharto? In this section I sketch the evolution of anti-capitalism in Indonesia from its birth in the 1920s, its consolidation during the revolution, its embattled position in the 1960s, and its decline under the New Order regime. This review of the historical development of anti-capitalism, I argue, offers many insights into the current agrarian movement.

Anti-capitalism in Indonesia was the child of the marriage of Marxism and nationalism.[13] Dutch socialists and labour organizers introduced Marxist ideas to the Dutch Indies in the mid-1910s with the creation of the Indies Social Democratic Association (*Indische Sociaal-Democratische Vereniging*: ISDV), which was the forerunner of the PKI. This was a decade before a nationalist group first used the term 'Indonesia' in the name of their party.[14] Until then (1925), the term used by all political organizations to indicate today's Indonesia was still the Dutch Indies (*Hindia Belanda*). In other words, the 'Indonesian' political activists of the second decade of the twentieth century had known Marx before they started calling themselves 'Indonesians'.

By 1918, Marxist discourse, including themes of class struggle, anti-capitalism and world revolution, was popular not only among radical circles and political organizations but also in the moderate press outside Java (McVey 1965). The dominance of Marxism in the indigenous intellectual discourse at the time was due in part to the rapid ascendancy of the ISDV/ PKI. Within a few years of its birth, communist members successfully persuaded the Islamic League (*Sarekat Islam*: SI) to let them join. Communist *Sarekat Islam* members soon formed a significant faction in both the top leadership and local branches of the organization (ibid.). *Sarekat Islam* was founded originally in 1912 as an association of Muslim traders. In its first constitution, the promotion of commerce, Muslim brotherhood, progress and religion were declared to be the goals of the organization (Noer 1973). A decade later this was no longer the case. Under pressure from communist members, *Sarekat Islam* leader H.O.S. Cokroaminoto came out forcefully in 1917 to declare his opposition to capitalism (Shiraishi 1990).

It was this particular environment that nationalist ideas faced when they arrived in the Indies in the 1920s. Hostilities toward nationalism came from both communists and Muslims. To communists, nationalism was a nineteenth-century, European phenomenon and not a real issue in the Dutch Indies (McVey 1965). The PKI struggled for a world proletarian revolution, not for national independence (ibid.). Nationalism also met with resistance from conservative Muslim leaders who believed in Pan-Islamism. In their view, 'the nation' (*bangsa*) and 'homeland' (*tanah air*) were simply the masks of chauvinism that led countries to fight each other (Sukarno 1964: 109–14, citing H. A. Salim). Islam, they argued, did not recognize national boundaries.

Whether out of conviction or mere convenience, young nationalists such as Sukarno and Hatta sought to justify nationalism with socialist concepts. Marxist terms peppered their discourses. Most nationalists of this period, whether secular or Muslim, claimed they were socialists. Sukarno did not simply preach nationalism since he believed that the concept by itself was inadequate. Instead he called for '*sosio-nasionalisme*' (Sukarno 1964: 187–91). In Sutan Sjahrir's vision (Indonesia's first prime minister and a key nationalist organizer), an independent Indonesia would be a country where the ownership of the means of production was socialized (Sjahrir 1947).[15]

Yet the emerging nationalist discourse was no longer Marxist: rather, the discourse was only strongly coloured by it. Visceral anti-capitalist sentiments replaced class analyses. Rather than promising a utopian classless society or calling for a violent class struggle as communists did elsewhere, Indonesian nationalists preferred to spend their energies on attacking capitalism, namely its exploitative and oppressive character (Sukarno 1964; Hatta 1976). In an influential thesis that sought to unify nationalist, Marxist and Islamic groups, Sukarno argued that these groups should unite because they all shared the same enemy: Western capitalism (Sukarno 1964). Like Marxists, nationalists naturally opposed the forces of Western capitalism which had colonized Indonesia. For Muslims, Westerners were infidels and Islamic teachings of wealth-sharing and injunctions against usury meant that capitalism must be opposed. Anti-capitalism, not class struggle, was promoted as the common denominator of all three ideologies.

If the PKI had *not* been crushed in their failed rebellion during 1926/7, or if Marxism had arrived concurrently with nationalism as in China or Vietnam, anti-capitalism may not have been born. Yet once born, anti-capitalism became the dominant force thanks to the ability of anti-capitalist formulations to accommodate different ideologies, from Islam to communism, to the central roles that its progenitors (Sukarno, Hatta, Sjahrir and others) played in the fight against the Dutch for national independence, and to the politics of accommodation during state formation (Vu Tuong 2007).

In the last months of the Japanese occupation in 1945, the Japanese government allowed Indonesian nationalists to form a committee to prepare for independence. As chair of this committee, Sukarno proposed five main principles called '*Pancasila*' for the future Indonesian state (Yamin 1959). These five principles included 'nationalism' (a unified nation), 'internationalism' (respect for the family of nations and for humanity), 'democracy' (based on representation and consultation for consensus), 'social justice' (prosperity and welfare for all) and 'belief in God' (God of any religions). One could argue that the first two combined would be nationalism without chauvinism; and the third and fourth principles taken together would be representative democracy without capitalist exploitation. Anti-capitalism was thus codified as a foundation of the Indonesian state. Anti-capitalism was also embedded in several clauses in the 1945 constitution. For example, Article 33 called for government ownership and supervision of all important industries, presumably to protect 'the people' from capitalist exploitation.

The coalition led by Sukarno faced and fought many challenges from both left and right. During the struggle against the Dutch (1945–9), nationalist leaders had to pledge to respect the interests of Western capital in Indonesia in return for diplomatic recognition. Tan Malaka, a former PKI leader, almost toppled the Sjahrir cabinet in early 1946 by challenging the compromise it had made with Western capitalists. When the Cold War started, Musso, who led the PKI for a few months before being killed in a failed coup in late 1948, demanded that the government join the Soviet Union to fight imperialism. To both Malaka and Musso, Sukarno-style anti-capitalism was unsatisfactory since it did not make real commitments to class struggle and world revolution, the key tenets of communism at that time.

Still, anti-capitalism was powerful throughout the 1950s. 'Large foreign capital' (*modal besar asing*) was a favourite target of denunciation for leftist politicians in parliamentary debates. Advocates for the nationalization of foreign assets launched frequent and virulent attacks on foreign capitalists, condemned as 'shrewd and dangerous' 'criminals' who 'would be tortured in hell under the law of Allah' (Vu Tuong 2008: 297–300). Anti-capitalist discourses directly challenged the policies to develop a capitalist economy promoted by several post-independence cabinets led by men such as Mohammad Natsir and Wilopo. These conservative Muslim leaders promoted rapid economic growth, welcomed Western investors back into the country, banned labour strikes, and sought relationships with Western powers. Yet these pro-capital governments soon collapsed in the face of harsh criticisms against capitalism and imperialism and, in the 1950s, Indonesia nationalized most foreign assets. These assets were placed under state management to make sure their profits went to 'the people'. Anti-capitalist sentiments, and the political coalitions that promoted them, succeeded in pushing for the promulgation of UUPA in 1960 and other progressive agrarian reform measures.

The mid-1960s witnessed the rapid rise of the PKI and the radicalization of Indonesian politics. The removal of conservative leaders and technocrats such as Natsir, Sjafruddin Prawiranegara and Sumitro Jojohadikusumo from the political stage contributed to this trend.[16] As Indonesia challenged Western powers in the West Irian conflict and in the campaign against Malaysia, anti-colonialism and anti-imperialism brought Sukarno closer to the PKI (Mortimer 1974). These themes had also been part of 'anti-capitalism', but with the PKI now on board, the discourse had latent communist tones. In late 1963, PKI leaders openly urged farmers to take unilateral action to implement the UUPA, pushing class struggle one step further (Huizer 1980). The PKI stressed the need for the working classes to fight 'feudalism' and 'imperialism' as well as capitalism (Mortimer 1974: 314).

After the PKI-inspired coup in October 1965 was crushed by a counter-coup by Suharto, the military regime under Suharto destroyed the PKI, overthrew Sukarno, banned communism, and made 'development' (*pembangunan*) the new national creed. Yet this regime never had the strength, confidence or capacity to completely erase the legacies of anti-capitalism. In part this was because the generals themselves had come of age during the struggle for independence and considered anti-capitalism part of their political belief.[17] Internationally, while Suharto welcomed Western investment and formed close relationships with Western powers, he never supported the American war in Vietnam as South Korea or Thailand did. Domestically, he kept the 1945 Constitution and forcibly imposed *Pancasila*, Sukarno's brainchild, as the official state doctrine. All social organizations were now forced to accept *Pancasila* as their ideology while students and bureaucrats were made to study *Pancasila* in specialized indoctrination programmes.

Carol Warren (1990: 191) reported that she frequently encountered what she called 'vocabularies of modern critical discourse' during her fieldwork in rural Bali, suggesting the resilience of anti-capitalism under Suharto. Words

such as *kesadaran* (consciousness of collective goods), *pemerataan* (equaliza-
tion of economic benefits), *sosial* (socially-committed) and *piodal* (feudal),
commonly found in the discourses of the 1950s and 1960s, did not disappear
under Suharto as one might expect. Others have noted that the New Order
regime, especially in its first two decades, never called itself 'capitalist' or even
'free enterprise', while government propaganda in the 1980s still described its
strategy of development as 'taking the middle path between capitalism and
socialism' (Lane 1982 cited in Warren 1990: 192).

While the above review is preliminary, several core elements stand out.
Parallels between the discourse of the contemporary agrarian movement and
the pre-New Order anti-capitalist discourse are hard to miss. Today, there are
strong anti-capitalist sentiments mixed with anti-colonialism and anti-
imperialism, as there also were decades ago. Striking continuities can be discerned in the deep mistrust among activists of foreign trade, foreign capital
and international financial organizations. There is an obsession with rice as a
symbol of social justice, a phenomenon that emerged during the struggle
against the Dutch between 1945 and 1949 (Vu Tuong 2003). Finally, Sukarno's
nationalist symbols such as *Nekolim* and the National Day of Awakening
have been revived to serve new purposes.

One may argue that today's anti-capitalism is only a reaction to capitalist
development under Suharto, not owing anything to what preceded him. It is
not possible to say exactly whether contemporary groups really find in the
Constitution, the UUPA and Sukarno's other formulations the same ideas
that they fundamentally believe in, or if they merely seek to manipulate these
political tools. Still, it is difficult to dismiss such a rich past that left so many
legacies in today's discourses and that was never completely subdued under
Suharto.

Conclusions

Geographically, nowadays the struggles over land and trade policy are most
intense on Java, where most Indonesians live. This contemporary agrarian
movement began in the 1980s and has grown rapidly since the end of the New
Order. It is composed of spontaneous actions by farmers at the grassroots
level on the one hand, and organized efforts by urban NGOs with extensive
transnational links on the other. At the discursive level, leaders of the movement are profoundly influenced by the anti-capitalist ideology rooted in
Indonesia's struggle for independence from colonial rule. The moderates and
the radicals in the movement may disagree over strategies but they share
fundamental assumptions about capitalism as an exploitative and inhumane
system.

Existing explanations for the evolution of the Indonesian agrarian movement have focused on factors such as grievances, political opportunities,
ideas, leadership and organization, and changing state–society relations. By
analysing movement discourses, I have added a more nuanced perspective. In

particular, I have endeavoured to show how the current movement has ideological genealogies in the longstanding anti-capitalist movement in Indonesia. While existing accounts show some continuity between the current movement and the PKI's agrarian mobilization efforts in the 1960s, I have demonstrated that one can go back much further to the birth of anti-capitalism in the 1920s.

The agrarian movement in Indonesia adds an interesting twist to the thoughts of Polanyi (1944, 1957), while Gramsci (1971) gives us some clue about the direction in which it may be heading. First, activists not only agree with Polanyi that land cannot be made a commodity; they go further to demand that rice should be similarly treated. This demand suggests that the meanings of labour, land and food may differ across societies and change over time.

Second, Gramsci's concept of 'passive revolutions' may be more appropriate in Indonesia than his better-known concept of 'hegemony'.[18] As anti-capitalism has evolved in Indonesia since the 1920s, no hegemonic ideas or classes have emerged. There was a revolution (1945–9) and a counter-revolution (1965–6), but the winners emerging from these critical events never succeeded in establishing complete hegemony. Gramsci offers two possible scenarios for countries like Indonesia that have experienced 'passive revolutions' but not class hegemony (Cox 2005). One is caesarism, or the emergence of a strong man, and the other is *trasformismo*, or the rise of a broad movement that incorporates lower classes into a corporatist system. In Gramsci's Italy, *trasformismo* would develop into fascism. Both scenarios are not too far-fetched in the Indonesian context. Sukarno and Suharto arguably represented some combination of caesarism and *trasformismo* at different points. Sukarno's Guided Democracy began as caesarism but increasingly displayed characteristics of *trasformismo* with his *Nasakom* government.[19] Suharto's New Order was clearly caesarism.

Gramsci's pessimistic predictions for countries with passive revolutions seem relevant to conditions in Indonesia today. If Aspinall (2004) is right in arguing that moderation trends contributed to the rise of civil society in Indonesia in the 1980s, recent trends in Indonesian and global politics suggest that polarization has returned. From a class perspective, the transition of power in 1998 did not overthrow the ruling elites; it only removed Suharto and rearranged the relative positions of various elite factions (Hadiz 2003). The regime remains essentially capitalist and is arguably more integrated into the international capitalist system than ever before. Social inequalities appear to have increased under *Reformasi*, in part because of the impact of the 1997 financial crisis (Breman and Wiradi 2002). With a weak central authority and corrupt local governments, one wonders how effective programmes of poverty reduction can be implemented (Aspinall and Fealy 2003). Under a weak state, conflicts within society – whether of an ethnic, religious or class nature – seem to have increased (Bertrand 2004; Sidel 2006). Internationally, despite (premature) declarations about 'the end of history', the early years of the twenty-first century have witnessed the consolidation of an anti-globalization movement that emerged barely a decade ago. Although one may dismiss Hugo Chavez as pompous, or Osama bin Laden as a terrorist, they do attract numerous admirers, including many Indonesian radicals, simply for standing up to the US. There is thus some possibility that Indonesian civil society and the now-moderate agrarian resistance may turn 'uncivil' again if polarizing trends continue in the future.

Notes

1 The Asia Research Institute, National University of Singapore provided generous financial support for the research to write this paper. I am indebted to a travel grant from the US-Indonesia Council and to helpful comments from Dominique Caouette, Jamie Davidson and Sarah Turner.
2 BULOG is a state-owned company that manages food distribution and controls specific prices.
3 'Originally, the law had two key purposes: first, to create a single land law applicable to all citizens of Indonesia, thereby replacing the legal pluralism of colonial law in which racial categories and regional status determined which legal systems (customary, commercial, civil) would be applied in adjudicating or resolving land disputes. The second purpose was to require land reform through the imposition of ceilings on private landholdings, both owned and controlled' (Afiff *et al.* 2005: 3).
4 The plantation originally was leased to an agricultural enterprise during the colonial era but was taken over by a state plantation company at independence. Villagers' ownership rights to this land are not well established in this case, as in most other cases.
5 *Nekolim* is an acronym created in the 1960s by Sukarno.
6 A few exceptions are Warren (1998a, 1998b), Peluso (2003), and Afiff and Lowe (2007). Uhlin (1995) offers a good analysis of the early discourses of democratic activists, of whom agrarian activists were a part.
7 Due to space constraints, I do not aim to provide a comprehensive analysis of its discourses here. In addition, the subject of analysis is limited to elite discourses, not those of the masses. Geographically, the analysis is focused mostly on Java, where anti-capitalism has been most intense and where most Indonesians live.
8 Charoen Pokphand is actually a Thai company which is one of the largest multinational investors in Asia.
9 The PKI's 'Go Down' campaign was borrowed from Chinese Communists' 'Xiafang' campaign (Mortimer 1974: 278–81).
10 *Ekonomi Pancasila* was first developed by Mubyarto. For various expositions of current thinking on *Pancasila* economy, see the online journal *Ekonomi Rakyat* (www.ekonomirakyat.org).
11 This section draws on Aspinall (2004).
12 FSPI seems to have an Islamic equivalent in the Hizbut Tarir, a radical Muslim group, which has rejected participation in democratic activities such as elections.
13 The discussion of Indonesia's anti-capitalism throughout the 1950s is abridged from Vu Tuong (2008).
14 This group was PI or *Perhimpunan Indonesia* (Ingleson 1975). PKI was founded in 1920 – five years earlier than PI – but its name then was *Perserikatan Komunist di India* (McVey 1965).
15 Sutan Sjahrir was Indonesia's Prime Minister from late 1945 to mid-1947 and led the difficult negotiations with the Netherlands for Indonesia's independence.

16 These leaders joined the failed regional rebellions in 1957 and were later either imprisoned or sent into exile.
17 Suharto, for example, was born in 1920 and was thus only 25 in 1945.
18 Cox (2005: 39) argues that this notion of 'passive revolutions' is particularly appropriate in industrializing Third World countries.
19 *Nasakom* stands for nationalism, religion and communism.

References

Aditjondro, G. (1998) 'Large dam victims and their defenders: the emergence of an anti-dam movement in Indonesia', in P. Hirsch and C. Warren (eds) *The Politics of Environment in Southeast Asia: resources and resistance*, New York: Routledge, 29–55.

Afiff, S. and Lowe C. (2007) 'Claiming indigenous community: political discourse and natural resource rights in Indonesia', *Alternatives*, 32: 73–97.

Afiff, S., Fauzi, N., Hart, G., Ntsebeza, L. and Peluso, N. (2005) 'Redefining agrarian power: resurgent agrarian movements in West Java, Indonesia', working paper, Ford Foundation Crossing Borders project: University of California at Berkeley. Online. Available HTTP: <http://repositories.cdlib.org/cseas/CSEASWP2-05> (accessed 20 February 2009).

Aspinall, E. (2004) 'Indonesia: transformation of civil society and democratic breakthrough', in M. Alagappa (ed.) *Civil Society and Political Change in Asia*, Stanford: Stanford University Press, 61–96.

Aspinall, E. and Fealy, G. (eds) (2003) *Local Power and Politics in Indonesia: decentralization and democratization*, Singapore: Institute of Southeast Asian Studies.

Bachriadi, D. and Lucas, A. (2001) *Merampas Tanah Rakyat: kasus tapos dan cimacan* (Expropriating People's Lands: The Cases of Tapos and Cimacan), Jakarta: Perpustakaan Populer Gramedia.

Bertrand, J. (2004) *Nationalism and Ethnic Conflict in Indonesia*, New York: Cambridge University Press.

Bey, I.S. (2002) 'Menyelamatkan semangat UUPA 1960 dari Kepungan neoliberalisme' ('Rescuing the spirit of the UUPA 1960 from the siege of neoliberalism'), *Kompas*, 30 October. Online. Available HTTP: <http://www.unisosdem.org/article_detail.php?aid=774&coid=2&caid=2&gid=1> (accessed 20 February 2009).

Breman, J. and Wiradi, G. (2002) *Good Times and Bad Times in Rural Java*, Singapore: Institute of Southeast Asian Studies.

Consortium for Agrarian Reform (KPA) (2006) 'Progress report: establishing a platform for undertaking agrarian reform. December 2005 to March 2006'. Online. Available HTTP: <http://www.landcoalition.org/pdf/ICARRD_KPA_pr_May06.pdf> (accessed 20 February 2009).

Cox, R. (2005) 'Gramsci, hegemony and international relations', in L. Amoore (ed.) *The Global Resistance Reader*, New York: Routledge, 35–47.

Davidson, J. (2008) *From Rebellion to Riots: collective violence on Indonesian Borneo*, Madison: University of Wisconsin Press.

Di Gregorio, M. (2006) 'The influence of civil society organizations on forest tenure policies in Indonesia: networks, strategies and outcomes', paper presented at the IASCP Eleventh Biannual Conference, Bali, Indonesia, 19–23 June 2006.

Eldridge, P. (1995) *Non-Government Organizations and Democratic Participation in Indonesia*, Kuala Lumpur: Oxford University Press.

—— (2007) 'Non-government organizations and democratic transition in Indonesia', in R. Weller (ed.) *Civil Life, Globalization, and Political Change in Asia*, New York: Routledge, 148–70.

Fauzi, N. (1996) 'We promote community-based land mapping', interview, *Inside Indonesia*, 47. Online. Available HTTP: <http://insideindonesia.org/content/view/935/29> (accessed 20 February 2009).

—— (1999) *Petani dan Penguasa: dinamika perjalanan politik agraria Indonesia* (*Farmers and Rulers: dynamics of implementing agrarian reform in Indonesia*), Jakarta: INSIS Press and KPA.

—— (2003) 'The new Sundanese Peasants' Union: peasant movements, changes in land control, and agrarian questions in Garut, West Java', University of California, Berkeley: Center for Southeast Asian Studies.

—— (2007) 'Gerakan Tani Harus Berjaringan dengan Kekuatan Lokal' ('Farmers' movement must create links with local authorities'), interview, 18 July. Online. Available HTTP: <http://indoprogress.blogspot.com/2007/07/noer-fauzi-gerakan-tani-harus.html> (accessed 20 February 2009).

Fauzi, N. and Bachriadi, D. (2006) 'The resurgence of agrarian movements in Indonesia: scholar-activists, popular education and peasant mobilization', paper presented at the international conference hosted by the Institute of Social Studies, The Hague, 9–10 January 2006.

Federasi Serikat Petani Indonesia (FSPI) (2000) 'Ten years of the WTO is enough! Defense sovereignty and expelling WTO', Dili Declaration, May. Online. Available HTTP: <http://www.viacampesina.org/main_en/index2.php?option=com_content&do_pdf=1&id=380> (accessed 20 February 2009).

—— (2006a) 'Puluhan aktivis demo kedutaan Jepang, Inggris dan Jerman' ('Dozens of activists demonstrated at Japanese, British and German embassies'), 5 September 2006. Online. Available HTTP: <http://www.fspi.or.id/index.php?option=com_content&task=view&id=327&Itemid=41> (accessed 20 February 2009).

—— (2006b) 'Bank Dunia dan IMF Harus Dibubarkan' ('World Bank and IMF must be dissolved'), 5 September 2006. Online. Available HTTP: <http://www.fspi.or.id/index.php?option=com_content&task=view&id=337&Itemid=41>   (accessed 20 February 2009).

—— (2006c) 'Position paper of People Organization toward the Agrarian Reform', 20 February. Online. Available HTTP: <http://fspi.or.id/en/content/view/62/1> (accessed 20 February 2009).

—— (2006d) 'Rice and food sovereignty in Asia Pacific', May. Online. Available HTTP: <http://www.viacampesina.org/main_en/images/stories/2006_07_13_Rice_and_Food_Sovereignty_in_Asia_Pacific.pdf> (accessed 20 February 2009).

—— (2007a) 'Batalkan Pengesahan RUU PM' ('Reject the Draft Bill on Foreign Investment'), 28 March. Online. Available HTTP: <http://www.fspi.or.id/index.php?option=com_content&task=view&id=456&Itemid=37> (accessed 20 February 2009).

—— (2007b) 'Ekonomi Kerakyatan harus digali kembali untuk mencari alternatif dari model ekonomi neoliberal' ('People's economy must be rediscovered to become an alternative to the neoliberal model'), 8 June. Online. Available HTTP: <http://www.fspi.or.id/index.php?option=com_content&task=view&id=476&Itemid=1 > (accessed 20 February 2009).

Gerak Lawan (Opposition Movement) (2007) 'Tolak upaya menghidupkan kembali WTO' ('Reject the effort to revive the WTO'), 19 February. Online. Available

HTTP:<http://www.fspi.or.id/index.php?option=com_content&task=view&id= 427&Itemid=1> (accessed 20 February 2009).

Gramsci, A. (1971) *Selections from the Prison Notebooks of Antonio Gramsci*, trans. and ed. Q. Hoare and G. N. Smith, New York: International Publishers.

The Guardian, '50 people who could save the planet'. Online. Available HTTP: <http:// www.guardian.co.uk/environment/2008/jan/05/activists.ethicalliving> (accessed 20 February 2009).

Hadiz, V. (2003) 'Reorganising power in Indonesia: a reconsideration of the so-called 'Democratic Transition'', *The Pacific Review*, 16 (4): 591–611.

Hatta, M. (1976) *Kumpulan Karangan (Collection of Papers)*, v. 1, Jakarta: Bulan Bintang.

Huizer, G. (1980) *Peasant Movements and their Counterforces in Southeast Asia*, New Delhi: Marwah Publications.

Ikhwan, M. (2007) 'Forum kedaulatan pangan: cerita dari Nyeleni 2007' ('Forum on food sovereignty: story from Nyeleni 2007'), 31 March. Online. Available HTTP: <http://indoprogress.blogspot.com/2007/03/forum-kedaulatan-pangan.html> (accessed 20 February 2009).

Ingleson, J. (1975) *Perhimpunan Indonesia and the Indonesian nationalist movement, 1923–1928*, Melbourne: Centre of Southeast Asian Studies, Monash University.

Lane, M. (1982) 'Voices of dissent in Indonesia', *Arena*, 61: 110–28.

Li, T. (2007) 'Adat in Central Sulawesi: contemporary deployments', in J. Davidson and D. Henley (eds) *The Revival of Tradition in Indonesian Politics*, New York: Routledge, 337–70.

Lucas, A. (1997) 'Land disputes, the bureaucracy, and local resistance in Indonesia', in J. Schiller and B. Martin-Schiller (eds) *Imagining Indonesia: cultural politics and political culture*, Athens: Ohio University Center for International Studies, 229–60.

—— (1998) 'River pollution and political action in Indonesia', in P. Hirsch and C. Warren (eds) *The Politics of Environment in Southeast Asia: resources and resistance*, New York: Routledge, 181–209.

Lucas, A. and Warren, C. (2000) 'Agrarian reform in the era of Reformasi', in C. Manning and P. van Diermen (eds) *Indonesia in Transition: social aspects of Reformasi and crisis*, Singapore: Institute of Southeast Asian Studies, 220–38.

—— (2003) 'The state, the people, and their mediators: the struggle over Agrarian Law Reform in Post-New Order Indonesia', *Indonesia*, 76: 88–126.

McVey, R. (1965) *The Rise of Indonesian Communism*, Ithaca: Cornell University Press.

Moniaga, S. (2007) 'From Bumiputera to Masyarakat Adat: a long and confusing journey', in J. Davidson and D. Henley (eds) *The Revival of Tradition in Indonesian Politics*, New York: Routledge, 275–94.

Mortimer, R. (1974) *Indonesian Communism Under Sukarno: ideology and politics 1959–1965*, Ithaca: Cornell University Press.

Netto, A. (2006) 'World Bank profits from poor countries – report', *Interpress Service*, 19 September: no page.

Noer, D. (1973) *The Modernist Muslim Movement in Indonesia 1900–1942*, Singapore: Oxford University Press.

Nomura, K. (2007) 'Democratisation and environmental non-government organisations in Indonesia', *Journal of Contemporary Asia*, 37 (4): 495–517.

Nuruddin, M. (2007) 'Hak atas pangan: memahami situasi' ('Food rights: to understand the situation'), Jakarta: Aliansi Petani Indonesia, 9 November. Online. Available HTTP: <http://api-indonesia.blogspot.com/2007/11/oleh-muhammadnuruddin-efleksi-tentang.html> (accessed 20 February 2009).

Peluso, N. (2003) 'Territorializing local struggles for resource control: a look at environmental discourses and politics in Indonesia', in P. Greenough and A. Tsing (eds) *Nature in the Global South: environmental projects in South and Southeast Asia*, Durham: Duke University Press, 231–52.

Polanyi, K. (1944) *The Great Transformation. The political and economic origins of our time*, Boston: Beacon Press.

—— (1957) 'The economy as instituted process', in K. Polanyi, C.M. Arensberg and H.W. Pearson (eds) *Trade and Market in the Early Empires: economies in history and theory*, New York: Free Press, 243–70.

Rosser, A., Roesad, K. and Edwin, D. (2005) 'Indonesia: the politics of inclusion', *Journal of Contemporary Asia*, 35 (1): 53–77.

Sangaji, A (2007) 'The Masyarakat Adat Movement in Indonesia', in J. Davidson and D. Henley (eds) *The Revival of Tradition in Indonesian Politics*, New York: Routledge, 319–36.

Setiawan, U. (n.d.) 'Pertanian di Era Globalisasi' ('Agriculture in the Age of Globalization'). Online. Available HTTP: <http://www.unisosdem.org/article_detail .php?aid=5062&coid=1&caid=24&gid=5> (accessed 20 February 2009).

Shiraishi, T. (1990) *An Age in Motion: popular radicalism in Java, 1912–1926*, Ithaca: Cornell University Press.

Sidel, J. (2006) *Riots, Pogroms, Jihads: religious violence in Indonesia*, Ithaca: Cornell University Press.

Sjahrir, S. (1947) *Pikiran dan Perjuangan* (Thoughts and Struggle), Jakarta: Pustaka Rakyat.

Stanley (1994) *Seputar Kedungombo* (About Kedungombo), Jakarta: Elsam.

Sukarno (1964) *Dibawah Bendera Revolusi* (Under the Revolutionary Flag), v. 1, Jakarta.

Uhlin, A. (1995) *Indonesia and the 'Third Wave of Democratization'*, Richmond: Curzon.

Van Klinken, G. (2006) 'The forest, the state, and communal conflict in West Kalimantan, Indonesia', in H. Nordholt and I. Hoogenboom (eds) *Indonesian Transitions*, Yogyakarta: Pustaka Pelajar, 163–204.

Vu Tuong (2003) 'Of rice and revolution: the politics of provisioning and state-society relations on Java, 1945–1949', *South East Asia Research*, 11 (3) (November): 237–67.

—— (2007) 'State formation and the origins of developmental states in South Korea and Indonesia', *Studies in Comparative International Development*, 41 (4, Winter): 27–56.

—— (2008) 'Accommodation vs. Confrontation: state formation and the origins of Asia's developmental states', unpublished book manuscript.

Warren, C. (1990) 'Rhetoric and resistance: popular political culture in Bali', *Anthropological Forum*, 6 (2): 191–205.

—— (1998a) 'Tanah Lot: the cultural and environmental politics of resort development in Bali', in P. Hirsch and C. Warren (eds) *The Politics of Environment in Southeast Asia: resources and resistance*, New York: Routledge, 229–61.

—— (1998b) 'Symbols and displacement: the emergence of environmental activism in

Bali', in A. Kalland and G. Persoon (eds) *Environmental Movements in Asia*, Copenhagen: Nordic Institute of Asian Studies, 179–204.

Wiradi, G. (2000) *Reforma Agraria: perjalanan yang belum berakhir* (Agrarian Reform: the journey continues), Jakarta: INSIST Press.

Yamin, M. (ed) (1959) *Naskah Persiapan Undang-Undang Dasar 1945* (Documents Related to the Preparation of the 1945 Constitution), v. 1, Jakarta: Yayasan Prapanca.

10 Paradigm shift: The 'September Thesis' and rebirth of the 'Open' peasant mass movement in the era of neoliberal globalization in the Philippines

Jennifer C. Franco and Saturnino M. Borras Jr

Introduction

Nearly twenty years after his seminal study of the Huk Rebellion, Kerkvliet turned to look at 'everyday politics' in a Central Luzon village in the Philippines, questioning the conventional view of politics as limited to 'certain behaviour that is clearly related to matters of governance for an entire society' (Kerkvliet 1991: 9). According to the latter view, he noted that '[w]hat happens elsewhere is [considered] politically relevant only insofar as it affects or, as in organized protest or rebellion, challenges these society wide policies' (ibid.). One implication is that 'what goes on in, say, church organizations, labor unions, universities, corporations, or villages is not considered political unless it bears on elections, the government, or the ability of public officials and institutions to govern' (ibid.). Another implication 'is that politics is something optional. A person can jump into or out of the "political arena" ' (ibid.). By contrast, he argued that 'everyday politics' entails 'antagonism among people along class and status lines' (ibid.: 15), which in turn often involves 'contending claims about what constitutes a just use and distribution of resources' (ibid.: 17).

Kerkvliet (1991) and Scott (1985) have shown how the countryside spawns various kinds of everyday forms of resistance, through long-standing or well-established practices among peasants, such as harvest-sneaking (*palusot*), foot-dragging, and so on. Such individual, clandestine acts are best understood as responses by less powerful peasants to relationships and arrangements with landlords that they perceive as exploitative and unjust but with little or no hope of being changed. This is often because of the effective absence of the state in many parts of the countryside and a near complete default on its responsibility to enforce national laws and policies that could make a difference in peasants' everyday lives. In such settings, where peasant household subsistence is either threatened or uncertain, everyday forms of resistance are often as much acts of desperation as they are acts of defiance. It bears stressing that the targets of such actions are most frequently landed families and other politically powerful people whose near-total socio-economic and political control over peasants' lives is permitted to flourish partly because of the continued relative absence of state authority.

In looking at the Philippines, our chapter aims to highlight an important shift in approach in rural organizing that began in the late 1980s, with lasting repercussions. This shift was perceived as paradigmatic by its inventors, and came to be known among its adherents as 'the paradigm shift'. This paradigm shift occurred when an intermediate organ of the underground Communist Party of the Philippines (CPP), the National Peasant Secretariat (NPS), undertook a major rethinking of party policy on organizing in the country-side. The party's existing policy hinged on the orthodox Maoist framework of a 'protracted people's war' (PPW); the NPS rethinking flowed from a shared conviction that the PPW was falling short of what was needed – and indeed possible – to alter the status quo in the countryside. The resulting change in the orientation and approach to resistance, at least among the party's organizers responsible for 'white areas' (that is, geographic areas not under the effective control of the communist guerrillas), made a huge impact in prying open large areas of the countryside that had previously been closed to democratization pressures.

Many rural areas had been closed to change due to entrenched authoritarian–clientelist holds on them by landed elites who had never been challenged by any of the main contending political movements calling for social change. As will be seen, the paradigm shift initiated a major rural turning point by targeting such 'hard case' areas for change, while other important contending rural organizing paradigms – from the more centrist social democrats to the leftist national democrats – left them out. The paradigm shift also laid the groundwork for a national turning point by sparking new momentum for land redistribution via the government's agrarian reform programme beginning in the late 1980s. Given that one of the main targets of neoliberalism has been to (re)orient national land policy towards a market-based property rights regime, the paradigm shift also contributed to building peasant resistance to neoliberalism. The paradigm shift in rural organizing thus warrants much closer attention than it has been given to date.

Background

Philippine agriculture

The development of capitalism in Philippine agriculture has been highly uneven over time, and much has been written about this process elsewhere (see Ofreneo 1980; McCoy and de Jesus 1982; Tadem *et al.* 1984; David *et al.* 1983; Putzel 1992; Boyce 1993; Rivera 1994; Aguilar 1998; Borras 2007a). In brief, colonial and post-colonial processes historically transformed the country's agrarian structure into one marked by the persistence of land monopoly, impoverishment of peasants, highly skewed share tenancy arrangements that were 30:70 in favour of landlords, and widespread practices of usury, among others. This type of agrarian structure enabled the landed classes to control the nature, pace, direction and disposition of surplus farm production, leading to widespread poverty and inequality in the countryside. This agrarian structure also shaped the character of the Philippine state, with the land-owning classes deeply entrenched in political support (see discussions by Hawes 1987; Anderson 1988; Hutchcroft 1991; Putzel 1992; McCoy 1993; Rivera 1994; Abinales and Amoroso 2005). After the 1986 regime transition, 'local authoritarian enclaves' persisted below the level of the central state (Fox 1994; see also Franco 2001a; Wurfel 1988). Even today, local bosses, most of them landed (Anderson 1988), continue to use violence to impose (in)formal authority in their 'territories' (Sidel 1999).

Beginning in the 1980s, a regimen of structural adjustment was introduced that was aimed at restructuring the country's economic policies to align them towards the free-market framework (Broad 1988; Bello and Gershman 1992; Boyce 1993). The Structural Adjustment Programs were initiated in an attempt to 'alter the balance between the market and the state in the Philippine economy in order to promote economic efficiency' (Bello *et al.* 2004: 12). According to Bello *et al.* the programme 'unfolded in roughly three phases':

> . . . the first from 1980 to 1983, when the emphasis was placed on trade liberalization; the second, from 1983 all the way to 1992, when the focus shifted to debt repayment; and the third, from 1992 until the end of the decade, when all-sided free-market transformation marked by rapid deregulation, privatization, and trade and investment liberalization was the order of the day.
>
> (ibid.)

The adjustment in agriculture involved the uneven withdrawal of state subsidies from agricultural inputs, including credit and price supports for farm products. Particularly affected was the state-owned National Food Authority, mandated to buy food grains at high prices and to sell the resulting stocks at low prices. Under structural adjustment, production costs escalated, while farm gate real prices plummeted, adversely affecting small grains producers and rural labourers linked to this sector, as explained by Borras (2007a). Overall, the adverse effects were felt mainly in the 'traditional sector' of rice, corn and coconut, where most poor peasants' livelihoods are concentrated.

Skewed land distribution

The country's agrarian structure has long been marked by the economic and political dominance of the landowning classes, often in alliance with transnational agribusiness capital. In 1988, the year the landmark Comprehensive

Agrarian Reform Program (CARP)[1] began, the Gini coefficient for land ownership was at 0.64, suggesting a high degree of inequality in the distribution of ownership and control of resources (Putzel 1992). Twenty years on, CARP has continued to be the compromise programme it started out as, accommodating demands from the landowning classes and agribusiness, as well as the peasantry under certain conditions. In the context of Philippine agrarian politics, this 'compromise' programme nonetheless offered progressive potential via redistributive 'pressure points' embedded in it. It was not until CARP was implemented that officially mandated agrarian reform in the Philippines began to include *all* croplands and farm systems, while opening up the real possibility of expropriation, and setting low retention limits. The programme thus opened what had been previously closed political–legal space on the agrarian front, to be exploited or not, depending on opportunity, perception and means.

From 1988 to 1993, the CARP process was dominated by anti-reform policy currents and marked by nepotism, corruption, repression and the non-participation of several rural social movements. Predictably, the results of land redistribution in terms of the quantity of land redistributed and the number of households who received land was well below public demand and government claims. Yet the situation changed after 1992, when the leadership of the Department of Agrarian Reform (DAR) shifted to reformists. The new leadership sought out rural social movements, which for their part had tentatively decided to link up with state reformers to try to maximize the programme's potential. The improved climate lasted roughly eight years until 2000. This was CARP's golden era, where a dynamic state–society pro-reform alliance served to push forward the land reform process (Borras and Franco 2005). Two-thirds of the total reported output (measured as redistributed land) achieved over CARP's nearly 20-year lifespan can be attributed to this eight-year reformist period (Borras 2007b).

To be sure, this view of CARP's accomplishments in land acquisition and distribution has been disputed by several groups with competing ideological agendas, including some sections of the Philippine elite, the CPP-tied national democratic movement and the World Bank (Borras 2007b). Ironically, the overall impact of these groups – despite drawing upon different sources of inspiration, but nonetheless sharing the same scepticism of CARP in the 1990s – was to bolster a World Bank-led neoliberal incursion onto the agrarian field in the form of the so-called 'willing seller–willing buyer' market-assisted land reform model.

Neoliberal incursions

In 1996, World Bank representatives attempted to recruit the Philippine government to their market-led agrarian reform model, at the same time suggesting a halt to the implementation of CARP in small- to medium-size farms (meaning the 5- to 24-hectare farm-size category). In their view, CARP was 'distorting' the land market and was fiscally expensive (World Bank 1996; Reyes 1999; Borras *et al.* 2007). The DAR leadership at the time rejected the proposal and allied with rural social movement organizations to defend CARP's redistributive components and discredit the World Bank's initiative through public protests. The Bank retreated. Yet three years later Bank officials were back with a new plan and under different circumstances. By 1999 DAR was facing a shortage of public funds for CARP. At the same time, programme implementation was heating up in two of the most contentious categories: commercial banana farms and large private landholdings (Franco 1999a). Meanwhile, civil society groups associated with the broad non-governmental organization named Caucus of Development NGO (CODE-NGO), announced their openness to the idea of market-assisted land reform as a way to lessen the resistance of landlords to land reform. This 'warming up' to the idea of the market on the part of some NGOs was reflected in a new series of public consultations held by the World Bank at this time (Franco 1999a).

In this changed atmosphere, a new DAR leadership agreed to a small pilot project-cum-feasibility study to explore the World Bank's 'market-assisted' approach to land reform, repackaged as 'complementary' to CARP and rechristened as the Community-Managed Agrarian Reform and Poverty Reduction Project (CMARPRP). Not long after, the sitting national government was overthrown and a new political configuration led by Gloria Macapagal-Arroyo assumed power, which led to a more systematic incursion of a neoliberal agenda into agrarian matters. Whatever positive momentum remained in CARP-sponsored land redistribution after the Estrada government was overthrown in early 2000 ground to a halt by mid-year as the Macapagal-Arroyo administration settled in and state pro-reform currents dried up. Since then, anti-reform manoeuvres by landlords via market-oriented land transfer modes, ironically part and parcel of CARP policy since its inception, have expanded and accelerated (Franco 2008). This trend has coincided with other developments on the agrarian front that seem to be moving in one basic direction: the displacement of state-led expropriatory land reform by neoliberal land sales schemes as the country's main land policy (Borras and Franco 2005).

Contemporary rural activism

We now turn to examine how 'peasant resistance' has unfolded over the same period and the forms this resistance has taken. The countryside has always attracted competing perspectives in rural organizing, both within and across specific historical junctures. Ever since the Philippines was created in the crucible of colonialism, a steady and varied stream of agents have sought to 'form' the countryside, including those from the central state, the institutional churches and other non-state political and civil society elites. One important source of social change activism has been the broad 'Left'. As early as the

1920s, left-leaning political movements went to the countryside, hoping to enlighten, liberate, harness, unleash, sow, harvest, tap into and mobilize the potential wealth of mass power in a large, oppressed and often restive peasant class. This is not to say that the countryside lacks its own history (or histories) of innovation in organizing and resistance as shown by Scott (1985) and Kerkvliet (1991). Bringing their ideological perspectives (and biases) to the countryside, leftist organizers have indeed encountered, ignored, dismissed, embraced, colonized or respected local peasant political cultures and action repertoires. At other times they have contributed to elaborating new repertoires of peasant action and resistance.

The post-Marcos challenge

The Marcos dictatorship had a unifying impact on broad opposition in Philippine civil society in the 1970s and 1980s.[2] However, its collapse and overthrow removed this force, and civil society became more differentiated in terms of agenda and strategy. While many civil society activists felt that

> the task awaiting [them during the post-Marcos years] was not simply the restoration of democracy, but more importantly, its 'deepening' . . . The task of looking into issues of social justice and equity was left largely in the hands of the Left.
>
> (Abao 1997: 274)

As the new era of 'democratic deepening' beginning in the late 1980s unfolded, two broadly distinct currents emerged, reflecting contending views of the challenge of democratization in a formal liberal-democratic setting dominated by entrenched authoritarian elites – a truly 'flawed democracy'.

First, a political-electoral reform-oriented stream viewed civil society as a democratizing national political force whose main raison d'être was to seize state power by wrestling it from selfish and corrupt 'traditional politicians' through political-electoral means, particularly by organizing alternative political parties to compete in elections. Second, a more social reform-oriented stream saw civil society as the seedbed of empowered, locally rooted social movement actors whose main objective was to exercise citizenship power in order to win redistributive gains by engaging the state bureaucracy and making it accountable to traditionally excluded social groups. Stepping back, together these two streams reflect a chicken-and-egg dilemma: in flawed, inequitable settings such as the Philippines, which comes first: more political democracy or more economic redistribution? In this case, both streams sought a significant redistribution of power to traditionally excluded social groups; but their preferred means differed, bringing them, at times, into conflict with one another (see Franco 2004).

The paradigm shift of the 1980s, introduced at the start of this chapter, grew out of the second current, which included individuals and organizations long involved in rural organizing work within the CPP-led national-democratic movement. On numerous occasions since the 1970s they had tried to introduce and legitimize within the underground movement the unlikely concept of an autonomous open peasant mass movement, with mixed results (see Franco 2001b). For the CPP, the Maoist 'Protracted People's War' or 'PPW' framework determined the form and parameters of rural organizing. In practical terms this meant 'solid organizing' – that is, step-by-step, slow, usually clandestine – in support of armed struggle and the establishment of guerrilla zones in remote interior areas of the countryside (as seen in Figure 10.1). From the start, the CPP leadership kept rural organizing within the limits set by the PPW framework – except when it was not. Let us explain.

The CPP-led movement became known as the National-Democratic movement, or 'Nat-Dem' or 'ND', because of its programme of a two-stage revolution (that is, first achieve 'national democracy' by overthrowing imperialism, feudalism and bureaucrat-capitalism; then move on to the second stage, the socialist revolution). The principal form of struggle was armed, patterned after the Maoist dictum of 'wave by wave, surround the cities from the

Figure 10.1 New People's Army, the Philippines, taking a rest from training exercises.
Photo credit: Dominique Caouette

countryside' within the politico-military strategy of a 'protracted people's war'. The ND movement subordinated all other forms of struggle (for example, legal and electoral) to armed struggle. It identified the 'proletariat' as the 'leading force' and the peasantry as the 'main force' (Guerrero 1970; see also Putzel 1995; Caouette forthcoming). The ideological, political and organizational make-up of the legal ND organizations including the *Kilusang Magbubukid ng Pilipinas* (KMP), or Peasant Movement of the Philippines, formally launched in 1985, was influenced by this orientation. Two aspects warrant reiteration: 'genuine agrarian reform' could only be achieved after victory of the revolution; yet while the revolution was being waged, partial and selective implementation of revolutionary agrarian reform could be carried out. Included in the 'minimum' programme was the New People's Army's (NPA) *tersyung baliktad* campaign, the terms of which are similar to CARP's leasehold. *Tersyo* literally means 'a third', pertaining to the usual share of the peasants in 67:33, or more commonly 70:30 share, tenancy arrangements. Inverting (*baliktad*) in favour of the peasants has been a powerful rallying campaign that involved tens of thousands of peasants across the country in the 1970s and 1980s (Padilla 1990).

The theory was clear, but reality was always more complicated, and the movement was contested from within as movement activists assigned to do the work found themselves having to respond to everyday dynamics and the complexities of discrete situations as they unfolded (see Franco 2001b). As it turns out, many party cadres assigned to rural work had trained in community organizing methods at the Philippine Ecumenical Council for Community Organizing (PECCO), the pioneer in this field in the late 1960s and early 1970s.[3] Although the CPP rejected community organizing as being reformist in nature, many PECCO graduates who were part of the movement continued to draw on their experiences there in carrying out their work as party cadres. Throughout the 1970s and 1980s, they quietly sought to carve out small 'free spaces' within the limits of the underground party, where they could experiment with blending community organizing methods – (1) undertaking swift and complex collective action on the basis of pressing local issues, and (2) paying systematic attention to winning tangible gains and non-tangible outcomes – into the larger framework of revolution. When the collapse of the Marcos regime opened up new space for innovation and experimentation, many of these now veteran rural organizers found themselves clustered around the National Peasant Secretariat (NPS).

The paradigm shift

In the late 1980s and early 1990s the NPS launched a fundamental rethinking of its work, partly in response to changes in the larger socio-economic and political situation, and partly in response to the devastating impact of the counter-insurgency strategy of 'low intensity conflict', which had been launched by the first post-Marcos government of Corazon Cojuangco

Aquino. Between 1987 and 1989, the Aquino administration launched its 'total war' policy against the communist insurgents. Most of the victims of the military's indiscriminate bombings and arrests were peasants and peasant leaders who were broadly associated with the ND rural social movement.

Hard hit by the counter-insurgency campaign were the land occupations that had been undertaken by the KMP in the fluid months after Marcos's overthrow. In the aftermath of the dictatorship, the Congress for a People's Agrarian Reform (CPAR), a centre-left coalition of peasant organizations, had been formed to push for a new redistributive land reform law. Although a member of the new coalition, KMP 'never believed that a meaningful land reform policy could be enacted by a national legislative body overwhelmingly dominated by big landlords' (Borras 1999: 54). Instead, its main concern was 'to expose the "anti-land reform character" of the Aquino regime and at the same time put forward the alternative of a radical version of land reform' (ibid.). Hence, KMP had

> intensified its national campaign for widespread peasant occupation of idle and abandoned lands and Marcos crony-owned lands in order to project the land reform issue politically, more than to secure and consolidate actual lands to address the peasants' pressing needs.
>
> (ibid.)

Thousands of hectares of lands were occupied, but only barely secured. As a result, when the counterinsurgency campaign hit, the peasants' hold on the land soon fell away.

> In many cases, the KMP conducted its land occupations with the direct participation of the NPA. In other cases, areas that were projected as KMP-occupied lands were the same communities that had in fact earlier been subjected to the CPP's 'agrarian revolution' programme. In still other cases, local peasants had occupied lands and later sought assistance from the KMP. But most, if not all, of these land occupations were not sustained.
>
> (ibid.: 55)

The KMP land occupation campaign, driven by underground forces and oriented to the PPW framework, soon collapsed under the combined pressures of intense militarization and lack of socio-economic preparation, and support to make lands that were held productive and enable peasants to start building viable livelihoods (see Borras 1999: 55–6).

Some of the local peasant leaders were driven off contested land to emerge later as leaders of KMP at the national level. Other local peasant leaders did not escape alive. Many ordinary peasant participants abandoned the occupation and went elsewhere. Many also left the movement completely. In some cases, for instance in the Langkaan case in Dasmarinas, Cavite, the local KMP chapter collapsed when the land case got stuck in the Supreme Court and members scrambled to reconstruct their lives and livelihoods.[4] In other cases, the land occupation ended when local leaders and ordinary participants entered into (sometimes separate) settlement agreements with companies wanting to buy the land, poignantly revealing a potential divergence of interests between a movement's national political leadership and its grassroots peasant base.

At the local level, the KMP-affiliated organizations almost completely disappeared while trying to evade harassment from Aquino's military (1987–92). Participation in the KMP's mobilizations dwindled dramatically, not only due to fears of military reprisal. Most KMP leaders reported that ordinary peasants persistently complained about purely political 'agitprop' (agitation-propaganda) campaigns that were without any concrete, especially immediate, socio-economic objectives and gains. As a popular saying among agrarian activists goes: '*Pudpod na ang tsinelas namin sa kama-martsa, pag-uwi namin sa bahay, wala pa ring mai-saing*' [Our slippers were already worn out amid so many marches that we attended, but when we came back to our homes, we still had nothing to cook]. This became a popular sentiment among the ND-influenced peasant communities, and it slowly trickled into the sympathetic consciousness of cadres within the KMP and its non-government organization (NGO) allies.

It was in this context that the idea of a paradigm shift was born. Alarmed at the situation, the NPS prescribed a massive reinvigoration of the 'open peasant mass movement'. In their view, the peasant movement was falling to its knees at the very moment when more strength was needed to push the government to implement the progressive components of the new agrarian reform programme CARP. The devastating effects of deregulation of farm inputs also demanded intensified mobilization. The movement had reached a critical ebb when what was needed was a vigorous flow. A plan for how to reverse the tide was unveiled in an internal paper entitled 'The September Thesis' (so named because it came out in the month of September). The plan, detailed in Textbox 10.1, challenged the most basic tenets of the PPW framework, which the NPS nonetheless hoped to stretch as far as possible in order to respond to the urgent new realities on the ground.

Textbox 10.1 Highlights of the September Thesis

1. *Open* forms of collective action/mobilization: the need to engage the state on specific issues cannot be done effectively if the form of collective action is 'underground' or clandestine;
2. Rural *plains* as the key site of struggle: the more populous plains are needed as 'pace-setters' in (re)launching the open peasant mass movement toward another possible people's uprising (see point #4

below); this is in contrast to PPW's concentration on upland, remote areas;

3. Systematic revival of basic community organizing principles through Fast-track, Issue-based, Sweeping Organizing (FISO): there are pressing concrete issues affecting rural communities now (underground ignores these), which require fast action (underground is too slow), which in turn requires organizers to cast the net widely and then identify and test possible leaders and collective working relationships through mobilization (departure from underground criteria for identifying leaders and members and building organizations);

4. *Peasant uprising*: What is needed is to build up the peasant component of a new popular uprising that would complete the unfinished 'people power revolution' of 1986 that overthrew the Marcos dictatorship.

Source: CPP (1988)

The basic 'thesis' to be tested, according to Esteban Guerrero, then head of the NPS, was the 'relatively even' setting of the peasant struggle.[5] The main target was no longer solely found at the village or municipal levels, but also at the higher district, provincial, regional and even national levels. Take the 'rice and corn cartels'. These cartels manipulated not only farm gate prices of farm produce like rice and corn, but also the marketing of these products at the consumer end as well. Such power blocs could only be confronted at the level where their power was most concentrated, which in turn meant that the rural social movement had to match the necessary scale and scope of struggle as well, that is, also at the district, provincial, regional and national levels. The 'relative evenness' of the rural setting in this sense, and its implications for the scale and scope of peasant struggle, also called for a new kind of peasant movement organized along territorial and crop lines.

To be sure, official party approval of the new rural organizing plan was not a foregone conclusion. It was a daring initiative by one relatively minor organ (in terms of political influence) of the underground party, that is, the NPS. Its basic assumptions were still untested, and its ideological moorings still had to be evaluated by party elites. Nonetheless, by 1992 implementation of the new approach was under way in many 'white areas' (that is, areas not controlled by the CPP/NPA). While awaiting official approval by party higher-ups that might never come, the NPS quietly deployed cadres to negotiate space for the new initiative *within* the movement. NPS cadres entered guerrilla territory to sell the September Thesis to sceptical front commanders and powerful party secretaries, or at least to persuade them to permit NPS organizers to deploy in areas adjacent to those under their control. Some were received warmly;

others were not. But at least some party higher-ups agreed that a new approach was needed (even if only temporarily).

The NPS's main vehicle for implementing the new approach was a national NGO called PEACE (Philippine Ecumenical Action for Community Empowerment), which had to undergo its own process of reorientation as well. PEACE set up new 'Training-Organizing Laboratories' (TOLS) to reorient its own trainers and organizers, while testing the Fast-track, Issue-based, Sweeping Organizing (FISO) approach (as outlined in the September Thesis) through integrated socio-economic work and local mass struggles. The idea was precisely to help convince the unconvinced that the FISO approach can work. Compared to the solid, but slow and silent, organizing approach associated with the PPW framework, FISO was a radical departure implying the organization of the greatest number of people based on commonly-felt problems, in the shortest period possible. Advocates of the new strategy were pressed to prove that it could really work. 'Countryside Teams' (CS Teams) of community organizers trained in the new approach were deployed to facilitate contact between PEACE and regional underground authorities in areas where recovery efforts were most needed, and to initiate actual recovery work using the FISO method (Franco 2001b).

The new method spawned a number of breakthroughs across the country. In Nueva Ecija, located in the Central Luzon region, FISO helped communities mobilize around land issues in the sprawling Fort Magsaysay military reservation. In Laguna, communities got organized around land issues in the newly conceived CALABARZON (Cavite, Laguna, Batangas, Rizal, Quezon) region slated for fast-track industrialization. In different parts of the Visayas, FISO helped to mobilize communities to demand the dismantling of military detachments. In Cebu, it was communities threatened with land use conversion and affected by militarization; while in South Cotabato, FISO served to revive the open peasant mass movement through a massive mobilization of rice farmers to assert their right to benefit from government price subsidies through *tambak palay* (rice-dumping) at the region's National Food Authority (NFA) warehouse (Franco 2001b).

FISO was also applied to 'land tenure improvement' (LTI), in an effort to explore the possibilities for real land redistribution under CARP. This delicate process was still unfolding when a dramatic event intervened to alter the situation for ever. In December 1992, a major ideological debate erupted within the CPP that soon engulfed the larger ND movement, and eventually led to a full-blown split. Over several months, numerous segments of cadres split away from the party, including the NPS. Both the debate and subsequent split were complex and profound processes; we do not pretend to do them justice here (see Rocamora 1994; Caouette forthcoming). What merits stressing here is that the split finally unleashed, as it were, the NPS and the network of activists and legal organizations associated with it. With the split behind them, they were now basically free to pursue a new course. Key in this pursuit was the Partnership for Agrarian Reform and Rural Development Services

(PARRDS), a new coalition that the now-defunct NPS, through its allied organization PEACE, helped to co-found.

In addition to the split in the ND movement, the early 1990s brought several events that combined to alter the larger political dynamics around agrarian reform. First, the election in 1992 of a new president, former military general and defence secretary Fidel Ramos, also brought new leadership to the Department of Agrarian Reform when a former NGO social reform activist, Ernesto Garilao, was appointed to head the department. After convincing President Ramos to abandon his plan to raise the retention limit, Garilao reached out to agrarian reform activists in civil society. Second, there was the break-up of CPAR, also in 1992, and prompted in part by the coalition's failure to unite behind a single candidate during the election, leaving a vacuum in agrarian reform advocacy. Third, there was the birth of PARRDS. PARRDS, mainly through PEACE, went on to fill the vacuum left by CPAR's collapse, and to breathe new life into CARP by helping to reorient it toward social justice (see Franco 1999b).

'Bibingka *strategy*'

As early as 1989, PEACE began exploring how positive provisions of the new agrarian reform law could be maximized to affect the redistribution of land ownership in commercial farms and to challenge the evasive stock distribution path in Hacienda Luisita.[6] This was also the time when a new wave of peasant-initiated land occupations was carried out (with direct and substantial PEACE involvement) in such places as Bukidnon and South Cotabato, Negros and Mindoro, Cavite and Isabela – as yet another effort to test CARP's potential to respond to rural poor people's interests. In addition, CARP's leasehold provision was studied closely, then carefully explained and consciously propagated within the underground movement by the NPS as superior even to *tersyung baliktad*, the tenancy sharing formula advocated by the New People's Army (NPA).

One of the earliest 'land tenure improvement' breakthroughs came in Sitio Poultry, Jaen, Nueva Ecija, where peasants used land occupation to win the land (see Borras 1999). The case involved a 49-hectare landholding that 39 tenant households had been cultivating for years and for which the tenants were trying to secure CARP coverage. The landowner had been trying to get a ten-year deferment and retention rights. In early 1992, the tenants linked up with PEACE. By August 1992, they decided to occupy the land in order to put pressure on the DAR to decide the case in their favour. The Sitio Poultry case was where they first tested the FISO approach (open-legal) against the traditional underground (armed) method in land occupation as a step towards redistribution. The eventual success of the Sitio Poultry tenants in winning CARP coverage helped to convince them of the value of the new strategic ideas, leading to an expansion of efforts nationwide. The approach eventually came to be known as the '*bibingka* strategy'. Drawing on Fox's

(1993) concept of 'sandwich strategy' in the context of rural Mexico, Borras explains that

> *bibingka* is a native Filipino rice cake baked in a homemade oven of two layers, with charcoal smolders in each layer, on top of and underneath the cake ... [highlighting] the situation that the state and society are marked by often heated simultaneous conflicts between pro- and anti-reform forces at different levels.
>
> (Borras 1999: 8)

Through PEACE-sponsored efforts alone, a total of 196,873.21 hectares of land was re-assigned between 1992 and 1998, benefiting nearly 80,000 peasant households, although this figure includes the 9,139-hectare DOLE-DARBCI (Dole Philippines Agrarian Beneficiaries Cooperative, Inc.) plantation in South Cotabato that was redistributed in 1989, while an additional 11,082.307 hectares was redistributed between 1998 and 2000 (see Franco 2001b). By virtue of the *bibingka* strategy, the period from 1992 to 2000 thus ended up being the golden years of CARP implementation. These golden years were not without conflict, yet there persisted a positive interaction of pro-reform allies consisting of the state bureaucracy at the top and social pro-reform forces at all levels, including on the ground. The combined efforts of these different actors contributed to the redistribution of hundreds of thousands of hectares of land to hundreds of thousands of poor peasant households.

Contemporary resistance

This 'golden era' ended after a non-constitutional overthrow of the popularly-elected Estrada government brought Gloria Macapagal-Arroyo to power. Since then, the rural social movement engaged in agrarian reform has become increasingly radicalized under the combined pressures of a deteriorating human rights situation in the countryside and the (re)consolidation of anti-reform forces inside the state, especially at the top. In response, some local peasant groups have adopted an alternative strategy akin to what O'Brien (1996) has called 'rightful resistance' in an effort to confront intensified resistance to agrarian reform and to reset the playing field by forcing shake-ups at the DAR. O'Brien's study of peasants' 'rightful resistance' against abusive local party officials in rural China revealed how ordinary poor rural peasants exercise citizenship power to redefine their relationships with public authorities. The study highlighted how peasants used central state law as leverage in their face-to-face struggles against local official corruption, thereby drawing an analytic distinction between this kind of resistance and the more individual and clandestine type of rural 'everyday' resistance emphasized by Scott (1990) and Kerkvliet (1991) in the Philippines. Here, the role of collective and militant *rights-based* peasant mobilization in potentially pushing processes of democratization is stressed. The immediate goals of rightful resistance, in this case, are to bring pro-reform actors back into the state bureaucracy at the highest levels and to insulate the current state land-related policy-making process from neoliberal pressures.

Underlying the new wave of mobilization in the 1990s was also a certain kind of overall historical–institutional logic. Persistent rural protest over the last century had helped to 'ratchet up' the content of organized societal demands for agrarian justice, and also to change the nature of the state's response to these in terms of official declarations, legal measures, policy prescriptions and programmed mechanisms. One finds a gradual shift over time, from mobilization around relatively simple demands for tenancy reform in rice and sugar in the 1930s, to relatively more complex demands for far-reaching land reform in all crop and farm systems by the 1980s. Yet, with every new state response to demands for agrarian justice, there were 'unkept promises', which discouraged some from further action, while prompting others to sharpen their policy advocacy and strategies of engagement over time (Putzel 1992; Herring 2003).

Significantly, the new more localized forms of militant action (rights-based land occupation, share boycotting and harvest seizures) have been combined with a variety of other, more open forms as well, in an effort to expand and extend the reach of peasant pressure and political impact. Mass direct action at the landholding level has been increasingly calibrated and combined with mass actions at 'higher' levels of the political system and state bureaucracy (see Figure 10.2). For example, 'camp-outs' at DAR's regional or central offices by members of local peasant organizations claiming specific land-holdings under CARP became an important part of the new repertoire of collective action since regional and national officials take many crucial decisions on specific land reform cases and are vulnerable to landlord pressures.

In addition to serving notice to public officials that they will be held accountable for their decisions, such actions have served to bring local conflicts into the public eye along with taking grounded peasant collective actions out of their isolation. This has brought maximum pressure to bear on relevant government agencies and officials to act in favour of petitioning peasants. Even reformist allies within the state should not be assumed automatically to be reliable allies when landlord pressure is a factor. As such, it should be emphasized that in practice, under the new paradigm, these pressure tactics have been tightly calibrated to the local struggles wherever they were situated in the CARP implementation process pipeline. Other types of this kind of action include highly purposive 'sit-ins' at government offices and at times even militant 'takeovers' of key government offices and buildings.

More recently, peasant land claimant groups have also been engaging in what are referred to as 'legal offensives', collective actions specifically targeting the legal system, particularly regional and municipal trial courts and local law enforcement which, historically, have been a reliable weapon for landlords

Figure 10.2 'Struggle of the masses: change the elitist system', the Philippines.
Photo credit: Saturnino M. Borras Jr.

to use against peasants seeking justice, in this case claiming land rights under state law. The most prominent example so far has involved the mass surrender to national police authorities in 2003 of more than a hundred peasant land rights petitioners from Bondoc Peninsula facing trumped-up criminal charges previously filed by landlords. Those who surrendered were CARP petitioners; and all the charges they faced (from qualified theft to attempted murder) stemmed from ongoing land conflicts under CARP coverage. The regular judicial system is barred from accepting agrarian-related cases, by order of the Supreme Court. Yet many local judges tied to the landlord class accept them nonetheless. The mere filing of such charges makes the peasants acutely vulnerable to harassment by police, in addition to landlords' private armies and the military. In collectively surrendering to the authorities, the peasants were aiming to break the historical link between legal and judicial authorities and landlords; it remains to be seen whether this 'break' has been achieved.

New repertoires of resistance intended to radicalize and implement the government land reform programme have provoked stiff anti-reform actions from landlords and their allies in both the state and society. The human rights of peasant land claimants have increasingly been violated by a combination of state, non-state and anti-state military forces – namely local military and police units, regional landlords and their private armies, and local units of what are now various guerrilla movements, respectively. Unfortunately, the fact that various 'non-state' actors (rather than state actors) are the main perpetrators of violence against organized peasants and CARP petitioning communities has been an obstacle to effective human rights work in many of these cases. This situation has begun to change recently, partly because the number of incidents has increased so dramatically that it is hard to ignore.

The affected peasant communities face a serious dilemma. Living under constant harassment and death threats, in settings where the state is either 'captured' by the local landed elite or absent altogether, organized peasant land rights petitioners have been compelled to turn to collective self-defence in order to deter and defend against further attacks. At times, self-defence has served to offset landlord might, leading to a reduction of attacks; in others, it has contributed to a spiral of violence. Such action by peasant communities seeking to avail of their legal and constitutional rights would presumably not be necessary if the state would step in to protect, defend, and fulfil those rights under state law. The fact that the state fails to do this, but instead cedes power to local authoritarian elites, has created the conditions where active self-defence by rural citizens is seen as the only logical recourse.

Conclusions

In the new resistance paradigm in the Philippines, the most basic site of struggle is at the grassroots, in and around contested farms or landholdings, such as banana plantations and coconut haciendas.[7] It is in relation to specific pieces of land where peasant claims to land rights are made, that national policy advocacy proceeds. The farm and its environs are the main locus and orientation of struggle: from the process of informing potential petitioners of their rights under the law and building alternative organizations, to imagining an alternative system for farming once possession of the land is secured, to actually gaining and sustaining physical possession of the land. All of these elements of the struggle tend to take place under hostile socialpolitical conditions, as well as in conditions of chronic poverty. The Philippine experience of land reform implementation over the past twenty years shows that peasants must win their struggle for land reform both on paper in the halls of government *and* on the ground in specific contested landholdings. Moreover, in order to struggle effectively against specific land policies, it is not enough to denounce the scheme at rallies in Manila. Instead, one must first be physically present inside and around the places where it matters most, that is the contested landholdings. For example, to struggle effectively against the stock distribution option scheme of CARP, one must organize and build 'upward' political pressure from inside the most prominent places where it is implemented, like Hacienda Luisita in Central Luzon (Borras, Carranza and Franco 2007). This is the logic that has led rural organizers to go to not only Hacienda Luisita, but also to the DOLE-DARBCI plantation in South Cotabato, and many others throughout the country (De la Rosa 2005).

In sum, as Kerkvliet (1991) noted, the rural political arena is not something that peasants can climb into or out of at will. It is the formal and informal institutional milieu within which peasants are embedded, and within which they necessarily construct their economic livelihoods, social relationships and political perceptions (as noted in the chapter by Caouette and Turner in this volume). However, in the process of carrying out these everyday life activities, even amid landlord coercion and state militarization, they make choices. The national democratic movement 'paradigm shift' vis-à-vis rural organizing in the 1980s and 1990s reveals just how much ideology, imagination and the perception of what is possible (or not) have shaped – and at times unnecessarily limited – the aspirations and choices that people make in the rural political arena. Interestingly, radical direct actions by peasants that have not been planned and organized by the Communist Party of the Philippines tend to be dismissed or denigrated by the Party members and supporters as 'spontaneous', rather than understood as 'peasant agency'. At least part of the story, then, of peasant mobilization and resistance in the Philippines since the 1980s is the story of continuing struggle against, and partial liberation from, the confines of instrumentalist thinking within the political Left, and movement towards relatively more vigorous assertion of peasant political agency.

Notes

1 The Comprehensive Agrarian Reform Program (CARP) was a land reform law mandated by Republic Act No. 6657. It was signed by President Corazon Aquino on 10 June 1988. Its original land redistribution scope covered all 10.3 million hectares of agriculture lands, both privately and publicly owned.

2 Ferdinand Emmanuel Edralín Marcos (11/9/1917–28/9/1989) was President of the Philippines from 1965 to 1986.

3 PECCO closed down in the mid-1970s, but its graduates went on to participate in the broad anti-dictatorship movement – and many of these as members of the CPP-led underground guerrilla movement.

4 This agrarian case involved a piece of land owned by a government-owned corporation that was sold to a Japanese investor to be converted into an industrial complex despite its highly agricultural character. Peasants living in the area protested, supported by powerful allies from civil society. The case captured the attention of the mainstream media for a while.

5 Panel presentation, Asian Rural Economy Consultation, Nov. 5–9, 1992, where Franco was present and tape-recorded some of the discussions.

6 Hacienda Luisita is a 6,400-hectare sugarcane plantation owned by the family of former president Corazon Aquino. It employs 4,000 farmworkers.

7 The 'verticalization' of struggles to span local, national and transnational spaces is also a feature of this new paradigm, but this is not elaborated here; instead refer to Borras and Franco (2008).

References

Abao (1997) 'Dynamics among political blocs in the formation of a political party', in M.C. Ferrer (ed.) *Philippine Democracy Agenda: civil society making civil society*. Quezon City: Third World Studies Center, 45–63.

Abinales, P. and Amoroso, D. (2005) *State and Society in the Philippines*, Manila: Anvil.

Aguilar Jr., F. (1998) *Clash of Spirits: the history of power and sugar planter hegemony on a Visayan island*, Honolulu: University of Hawaiʻ Press.

Anderson, B. (1988) 'Cacique democracy in the Philippines: origins and dreams', *New Left Review*, 169: 3–29.

Bello, W., Docena, H., de Guzman, M. and Malig, M. (2004) *The Anti-Development State: the political economy of permanent crisis in the Philippines*, Quezon City: University of the Philippines Press.

Bello, W. and Gershman, J. (1992) 'Democratization and stabilization in the Philippines', *Critical Sociology*, 17 (1): 34–56.

Borras Jr., S. (1999) *The Bibingka Strategy in Land Reform Implementation: autonomous peasant movements and state reformists in the Philippines*, Quezon City: Institute for Popular Democracy.

—— (2007a) ' "Free Market," export-led development strategy and its impact on rural livelihoods, poverty and inequality: the Philippine experience seen from a Southeast Asian perspective,' *Review of International Political Economy*, 14 (1): 143–75.

—— (2007b) *Pro-Poor Land Reform: a critique*, Ottawa: University of Ottawa Press.

Borras, S., Carranza, D. and Franco, J. (2007) 'anti-poverty or anti-poor?: the world bank's experiment in market-led agrarian reform in the Philippines', *Third World Quarterly*, 28 (8): 1557–76.

Borras, S. and Franco, J. (2005) 'Struggles for land and livelihood: redistributive reform in Philippine agribusiness plantations,' *Critical Asian Studies*, 37 (3): 331–61.

—— (2008) 'The national land reform campaign in the Philippines', 'Citizens' Participation in National Policy Processes Project' of the Institute of Development Studies (IDS), Sussex, and the Ford Foundation.

Boyce, J. (1993) *The Political Economy of Growth and Impoverishment in the Marcos Era*, Quezon City: Ateneo de Manila University Press.

Broad, R. (1988) *Unequal Alliance: the world bank, the international monetary fund and the Philippines*, Berkeley: University of California Press.

Caouette, D. (forthcoming) *Persevering Revolutionaries: armed struggle in the 21ˢᵗ century, exploring the revolution of the communist party of the Philippines*, Manila: Ateneo de Manila University Press.

CPP (1988) 'September thesis of the national peasant secretariat', NPS-CPP: internal document.

David, R., Rivera, T., Abinales, P. and Teves, O. (1983) 'Transnational corporations and the Philippine banana export industry', in R. David, T. Rivera, P. Abinales and O. Teves (eds) *Political Economy of Philippine Commodities*, Quezon City: Third World Studies Center, University of the Philippines. 1–34.

De la Rosa, R. (2005) 'Agrarian reform movement in commercial plantations: the experience of the banana sector in Davao del Norte', in J. Franco and S. Borras (eds) *On Just Grounds: struggling for agrarian justice and exercising citizenship*

Rights in the Rural Philippines, Quezon City: Institute for Popular Democracy; Amsterdam: Transnational Institute, 45–82.

Fox, J. (1993) *The Politics of Food in Mexico: state power and social mobilization*, Ithaca: Cornell University Press.

—— (1994) 'The difficult transition from clientilism to citizenship: lessons from Mexico', *World Politics*, 46 (2): 151–84.

Franco, J. (1999a) 'Market-assisted land reform in the Philippines: round two – where have all the critics gone', *Conjuncture*, 11(2): 1–6.

—— (1999b) 'Between uncritical collaboration and outright opposition: an evaluative report on the partnership for agrarian reform and rural development services, PARRDS', *IPD Occasional Papers* No 12, Quezon City: Institute for Popular Democracy.

—— (2001a) *Elections and Democratization in the Philippines*, New York: Routledge.

—— (2001b) 'Building alternatives, harvesting change: PEACE network and the institutionalization of bibingka strategy', Quezon City: PEACE Foundation.

—— (2004) 'Philippines: fractious civil society, competing visions of democracy', in M. Alagappa (ed.) *Political Change in Asia: the role of civil society*, Stanford: Stanford University Press, 97–137.

—— (2008). 'Making land rights accessible: social movements and political-legal innovation in the rural Philippines,' *Journal of Development Studies*, 44 (7): 991–1022.

Guererro, A. (pseudonym) (1970) *Philippine Society and Revolution*, Oakland, CA: International Association of Filipino Patriots.

Hawes, G. (1987) *The Philippine State and the Marcos Regime: the politics of export*, Ithaca: Cornell University Press.

Herring, R. (2003) 'Beyond the political impossibility theorem of agrarian reform', in P. Houtzager and M. Moore (eds) *Changing Paths: international development and the new politics of inclusion*, Ann Arbor: University of Michigan Press, 58–87.

Hutchcroft, P. (1991) 'Oligarchs and cronies in the Philippine state: the politics of patrimonial plunder', *World Politics*, 43 (3): 414–50.

Kerkvliet, B. (1991) *Everyday Politics in the Philippines: class and status relations in a Central Luzon village*, Berkeley: University of California Press.

McCoy, A. (ed.) (1993) *An Anarchy of Families: state and family in the Philippines*, Madison: Center for Southeast Asian Studies, University of Wisconsin Press.

McCoy, A. and de Jesus, E.C. (eds) (1982) *Philippine Social History: global trade and local transformations*, Manila: Ateneo de Manila University Press.

O'Brien, K. (1996) 'Rightful resistance', *World Politics*, 49: 31–55.

Ofreneo, R. (1980) *Capitalism in Philippine Agriculture (Updated Edition)*, Quezon City: Foundation for Nationalist Studies.

Padilla Jr., S. (1990) *Agrarian Revolution: peasant radicalization and social change in Bicol*, Manila: Kalikasan Press.

Putzel, J. (1992) *A Captive Land: The politics of agrarian reform in the Philippines*, London: Catholic Institute for International Relations; New York: Monthly Review Press; Quezon City: Ateneo de Manila University Press.

—— (1995) 'Managing the "Main Force": the communist party and the peasantry in the Philippines', *Journal of Peasant Studies*, 22 (4): 645–71.

Reyes, R. (1999) 'Market-assisted land reform: an indecent proposal', Online. Available HTTP: <http://www.philsol.nl/D-RicReyes-WB-mar99.htm> (accessed 4 March 2009).

Rivera, T. (1994) *Landlords and Capitalists: class, family, and state in Philippine manufacturing*, Quezon City: University of the Philippines Press.

Rocamora, J. (1994) *Breaking Through: the struggle within the communist party of the Philippines*, Manila: Anvil.

Scott, J. (1985) *Weapons of the Weak: everyday forms of peasant resistance*, London: Yale University Press.

—— (1990) *Domination and the Arts of Resistance: hidden transcripts*, New Haven and London: Yale University Press.

Sidel, J. (1999) *Capital, Coersion and Crime: bossism in the Philippines*, Stanford: Stanford University Press.

Tadem, E., Reyes, J. and Magno, L.S. (1984) *Showcases of Underdevelopment in Mindanao: fishes, forests, and fruits*, Davao: Alternate Forum for Research in Mindanao (AFRIM).

World Bank (1996) *Philippines: strategy to fight poverty*. Washington DC: World Bank.

Wurfel, D. (1988) *Filipino Politics: development and decay*. Ithaca: Cornell University Press.

11 Is rice non-negotiable? Malaysian resistance to free trade with the United States

Sandra Smeltzer

What we seek is fair trade, not free trading that is blatantly lopsided. Though economic progress is crucial to the nation's development, it is only part of the catalyst for sustainable growth. The welfare of the people and the livelihood of various communities, such as farmers and HIV patients, are of equal importance.

(Cheah Chee Ho, Federation of Malaysian Consumers
Associations 2007: online)

In this chapter I discuss the potential ramifications of a Malaysia–United States (US) Free Trade Agreement (FTA) on Malaysia's rice sector and national food sovereignty. While domestic resistance to the agreement may at first glance appear non-existent, a growing number of civil society agents in Malaysia have employed a range of overt and covert mechanisms to question and challenge the agreement and its negotiation process. Though they often focus on different sections of the agreement, these citizens' groups have uniformly called for greater transparency, and public and parliamentary consultation about the negotiations. This chapter takes a critical look at these resistance efforts, examining which groups are – and are not – involved in the process, and highlights both the challenges they face and the limitations to their success. The discussion that follows is based, to a large extent, on semi-structured and unstructured interviews conducted in July and August 2007 with Malaysian civil society agents, political party members and local media practitioners; as well as an extensive review of domestic media sources.

The road to a Malaysia–US FTA

Since 2004, Malaysia's Ministry of International Trade and Industry (MITI) has entered into a growing number of bilateral and regional free-trade agreement negotiations. In addition to a bilateral agreement with Japan, MITI has signed a trade pact with Pakistan and is expected to conclude trade talks with Australia and India by the end of 2009, and is (at the time of writing) in negotiations with New Zealand, Chile, Korea and the EU.

Malaysia is also a member of the Association of Southeast Asian Nations (ASEAN) Free Trade Area, the ASEAN–China Free Trade Area, and the Trade Preferential System-Organization of Islamic Conference (TPS-OIC). As well, Malaysia has ratified the Developing Eight (D-8) Preferential Tariff Agreement (which includes Bangladesh, Egypt, Indonesia, Iran, Nigeria, Pakistan and Turkey) and is expected to take part in both the EU-ASEAN regional FTA and the ASEAN + 3 (China, Japan and South Korea) Free Trade Area (Ramasamy and Yeung 2007; bilaterals.org 2008; MITI 2008).

Malaysia's rapidly expanding network of trade agreements is part of a global trend toward bilateral and regional trading relationships. This widespread shift away from a multilateral negotiating framework is, in part, a response to the collapse of the World Trade Organization's (WTO) Doha and Cancún talks. To secure trading relationships that are in its best interest, the US (along with many other developed countries) has actively circumvented the WTO and instead sought out agreements with key trading partners. As the 'world's largest agricultural exporter' (USDA 2008: online), the US is particularly keen to further open up foreign markets for its agricultural goods. Malaysia, the tenth largest trading partner of the US, represents a key destination for these goods. According to the United States Trade Representative, a Malaysia–US FTA will also 'provide US companies with a gateway to the dynamic South East Asian region – a market approaching $3 trillion' (USTR 2006: online). As well, Malaysia plays a politically strategic role for American interests: as a capitalist country with a large Muslim population, relative political stability, and a government willing to support the US 'war on terror', Malaysia is critical for the US in furthering its political involvement in Southeast Asia.

On the other side of the bilateral bargaining table, many developing and newly industrializing countries hope to gain access to US markets and fear the economic repercussions of being left out of preferential deals. Malaysia's government, for example, is very clear about its expectations: 'In the ear [*sic*] of globalization, Malaysia has taken the initiative to negotiate Free Trade Agreements (FTA) in order to seek better market access and enhance the competitiveness of Malaysian exporters' (Government of Malaysia 2007: online). As international political economy scholar Eul-Soo Pang writes, 'after Doha and Cancún, bilateral FTAs proliferated, and even Malaysia dropped its vehement opposition to cross-regional bilaterals for fear of "missing out" ' (2007: 14). With an increasing number of their regional neighbours negotiating trade agreements with the US,[1] many Malaysians are interested in establishing stronger economic ties with their number one trading partner.

The activists described in this chapter, however, feel quite differently about a Malaysia–US FTA, viewing it as a neocolonial tool of exploitative hypercapitalism that will further entrench trading practices that benefit few and negatively impact the majority (see Vu Tuong's chapter in this volume for similar sentiments in Indonesia). Given former Prime Minister Mahathir's[2] history of vocal opposition to unfair multilateral trade policies, many Malaysian activists find it deeply ironic and troubling that Malaysia has entered negotiations to establish even greater trade liberalization than that mandated by the WTO.

Trade talks between Malaysia and the US first kicked off in March 2006, with both countries hoping to reach a deal before the July 2007 deadline to fast-track agreements through US Congress (via President George W. Bush's Trade Promotion Authority). They did not, however, reach a deal in time and subsequent rounds of talks have since taken place. Although the global economic crisis may delay negotiations, the 2008 US Presidential election helped renew the Malaysian government's faith in the potential for a positive outcome from the process. As Prime Minister Badawi stated post-election: 'I am confident that with Barack Obama as president, we will have an easier time negotiating a better trading deal compared with the current administration' (quoted in Atan 2008: online).

Against the grain: is rice non-negotiable?

Of particular interest to this book is that the protection of Malaysia's food sovereignty and agricultural sector often tops activists' lists of priorities vis-à-vis the proposed Malaysia–US FTA. In comparison to many other Southeast Asian countries, Malaysia has transitioned away from its agrarian roots. Less than 10 per cent of the country's Gross Domestic Product (GDP) now comes from agriculture, and export crops (rubber, palm oil and cocoa) represent 76.6 per cent of the country's cultivated land (Southeast Asian Council for Food Security and Fair Trade (SEACON) 2005: 40). By comparison, rice, which is grown almost exclusively for domestic use, comprises only 11.6 per cent of Malaysia's cultivated land (ibid.).

Rice is, however, a staple crop in Malaysia in terms of both consumption and production. Malaysians consume about 2.4 million tonnes of rice per year (*New Straits Times* 2007) and rice production is an important part of local rural incomes. While export-oriented crops tend to be managed by companies – often in association with multinational corporations – rice tends toward small-scale production, therefore impacting a larger number of farmers (SEACON 2005). Though Malaysia's rice sector is relatively small compared to many of the other countries in the region, 'some 296,000 farmers depend on rice for their livelihood, with 116,000 farmers exclusively involved in the cultivation of padi' (Third World Network (TWN) 2007a: 15). Rice is also an important symbol of Malaysia's food sovereignty with a particularly 'close cultural connection between traditional Malay *kampung* life and padi production' (Pletcher 1990: 327). As a salient example, the crop is centrally featured in the flag of Kedah, a key state in the 'rice bowl' of Malaysia.

Concerns about rice, thus, revolve around both the assurance that

Malaysians have enough rice for their domestic food requirements and the need to protect local livelihoods. As Sudha Narayanan and Ashok Gulati argue, in assessing the impact of any trade liberalization, 'both the *consumption* and *production* of the commodity in question [must] be considered' (2002: 20). Although rice – and Malaysia's agricultural sector in general – may not contribute much to the country's GDP, its importance in terms of rural livelihoods and cultural currency means that the crop/food staple carries significant political weight and, therefore, plays a central role in trade negotiations (Pasadilla 2006).

Although the Malaysian government has historically been 'very protective of the rice industry' by subsidizing farm equipment, fertilizer, irrigation, and the like (Consumers International 2002: online), its most significant tariff reductions since the early- to mid- 1990s have been in the country's agricultural sector (Jomo and Tan 2006: 232).[3] Local farmers and other activists are concerned about the implications of this trend continuing. In 2010, the current 40 per cent import tariff on rice, for example, will drop to 20 per cent within the ASEAN Free Trade Area. If tariffs are subsequently eliminated under a Malaysia–US FTA, American rice, which is *heavily* subsidized by the US government (see James and Griswold 2007),[4] will flood the market and further damage local livelihoods. The US agricultural subsidization campaign is acutely problematic for 'poorer countries, which rely more on tariffs and can less afford subsidies' (Anderson 2006: 252).

In response to concerns about the rice issue, Assistant US Trade Representative for Southeast Asia and the Pacific, Barbara Weisel, argues that Malaysia already imports 30 per cent of its rice (primarily from Thailand) of which only a small fraction comes from the US. Therefore, Weisel contends, rice 'needs to be included in the talks. We do not believe that inclusion of rice in the FTA would pose a threat to Malaysian farmers' (quoted in *Business Times* 2007: online). However, Malaysia's tariffs are precisely one of the primary reasons why so little US rice has, up until now, been imported. Removing this protection would also fly in the face of the Ninth Malaysia Plan – the country's national budget for 2006–10 – which set a target annual padi growth rate of 5.9 per cent (Government of Malaysia 2006: 91). According to Chapter 3 of the plan, 'production of *padi* will be increased to meet the target of self-sufficiency level of 90 per cent', up from 72 per cent in 2005 (ibid.: 90, 93).[5]

Weisel's reassurances also appear to contradict a 2005 survey of 147 small-scale Malaysian rice farmers conducted by the Southeast Asian Council for Food Security and Fair Trade (SEACON) to assess the impact of trade liberalization in the region. According to the survey, which took place *before* the Malaysia–US talks were initiated, 'for those who reported decreases in the prices of their crops, most reasons cited were the increased [*sic*] of imports of products that are also locally-produced such as rice . . . the low prices set by traders . . . and poor government policy on prices' (SEACON 2005: 49). SEACON also argues that smallholder farmers will be the ones negatively affected by even greater trade liberalization, while importers, exporters and rice processors will likely benefit the most.[6]

More recently, concerns about a global food crisis have made both the consumption and production sides of the agricultural sector even more vulnerable. During the 2008 food price crisis when many Southeast Asian countries banned the export of rice, the Malaysian government struggled to secure enough rice from international suppliers to ensure a sufficient stockpile for domestic consumption. The extent of this struggle is evidenced by the Minister for Plantation Industries and Commodities's announcement that Malaysia would trade its palm oil for rice with any willing country (Lewis 2008). As Malaysia continues to shift away from its agrarian roots toward strengthening its manufacturing and high-tech industries, it has become increasingly dependent upon outside sources for staple foodstuffs. The livelihoods of local farmers are, however, in greater jeopardy: even with government subsidies, they must absorb the costs associated with producing rice, including rising fuel prices, fertilizer and transportation (Rajoo 2008). Escalating rice prices have also stretched the budgets of many Malaysians reliant on this essential food crop.

Unfortunately, and despite the Malaysian government's hopes to the contrary, a bilateral agreement with the US will not necessarily result in increased exports of such agricultural products to American markets. As signatories of a January 2007 Press Statement by the Malaysian-based Committee Against the US FTA (discussed below) argue,

> Malaysian farmers are unlikely to be able to export more to the US as the US markets are protected by tariffs which the USTR (US Trade Representative) has no power to give concessions on and subsidies which would be impractical for the US to remove.
>
> (FTA Malaysia 2007: online)

As well, the USTR has made it very clear that the goal of the bilateral agreement is to open up markets for American products, not the other way around: 'Because most Malaysian products and services already enter the US market duty-free, an FTA will level the playing field' (USTR 2006: online).

Other bumps along the FTA road

Notwithstanding the importance of Malaysia's agricultural sector, the most contentious issue slowing down the negotiation process is the Malaysian government's procurement procedures. The US wants Malaysia to open government contracts to bidding by American companies, a move that would significantly impact Malaysia's affirmative action policies that privilege *Bumiputra* companies in government tenders, thereby spelling political suicide for the ruling United Malays National Organisation (UMNO) party.[7]

Activists are also concerned about intellectual property rights as, historically, the US has pressured countries to introduce protection measures extending beyond those of the WTO agreement on Trade-Related Aspects of Intellectual Property Rights (TRIPS) (Arnold 2006; Choudry 2007). These stringent patent protection regulations could compromise Malaysia's control of its own genetic resources, including access to essential and affordable generic medicines (Choudry 2006; L.L. Lim, pers. comm., 2007; L.C. Lim, pers. comm., 2007; E. Low, pers. comm., 2007; C. Santiago, pers. comm., 2007; Smeltzer 2008a). Additionally, activists worry that the investment liberalization section of the Malaysia–US FTA will negatively affect small- and medium-sized companies as well as Malaysia's financial services sector. They are also concerned about potential threats to local employment security and labour benefits. As demonstrated below, these issues continue to drive the direction of resistance efforts against the Malaysia–US FTA.

Resistance from the grassroots, industry and opposition parties

At the outset, it is important to emphasize that Malaysia does not have a cohesive anti-FTA movement in terms of either focus or methods of resistance. While some individuals and groups want the government to completely cease negotiations, others have focused their attention on specific sections of the agreement that they consider particularly problematic (namely, rice, food sovereignty, government procurement and access to essential medicines). At this point, a total withdrawal from the process seems unrealistic given the time, energy and finances already dedicated to negotiations, and the government's obvious desire to negotiate a deal. It is unlikely that Prime Minister Badawi and his MITI Minister will simply walk away from the bargaining table, particularly as many of Malaysia's regional neighbours cum competitors are also in the process of inking deals with the US. By focusing only on specific issues, however, activists may give the government room to solve one 'problem' in exchange for greater overall public support of the agreement. If, for example, the US relents on Malaysia's rice tariffs, the rest of the agreement would likely gain more widespread support and the government would have demonstrated its commitment to protecting farmers, a staple crop and national sovereignty. Although this would be a positive achievement for resistance efforts – especially for farmers – there are other important and problematic elements of the proposed agreement that may end up being overlooked.

The size and scope of the proposed agreement also makes it difficult for activists to mount an effective resistance campaign. To grab citizens' attention and attract media coverage, activists often concentrate on particularly salient and easy-to-understand issues such as rice and food sovereignty. At the same time, they also want to convey the range of possible negative implications of the agreement, some of which may be more difficult to explain. Finally, the focus of resistance efforts is not always entirely clear; targets can include the Prime Minister, the MITI Minister, the government as a whole, and/or the US administration and its 'intimidatory tactics' (Santiago 2007: online).

Despite these limitations, three primary and overlapping coalitions of FTA resistance exist in Malaysia. The first is the Coalition on the US–Malaysia FTA, which includes 38 groups representing 'people living with HIV/AIDS, consumers, workers, farmers, health activists, human rights groups' (TWN 2006: online). Leading the coalition are three well-established non-govern-mental organizations (NGOs): Third World Network (TWN), *Sahabat Alam Malaysia* (Friends of the Earth Malaysia: SAM), and the Consumers' Association of Penang (CAP). Drawing on evidence from US FTAs signed with other countries, these NGOs inform both their coalition counterparts and other Malaysian citizens about the possible ramifications of the agreement.

Some of the groups in this first coalition also belong to a second move-ment: the People's Anti-USA–Malaysia FTA Coalition (also referred to as the People's Coalition Against Malaysia–US FTA). This coalition brings together 40 NGOs, activist organizations and opposition political parties. It includes TWN, *Parti Sosialis Malaysia* (Socialist Party of Malaysia: PSM), *Parti Keadilan Rakyat* (People's Justice Party: PKR), the Positive Malaysia Treatment Access and Advocacy Group, the Malaysia Youth and Students Democratic Movement, and *Jaringan Rakyat Tertindas* (the Oppressed People's Network: JERIT) (Y. Kohila, pers. comm., 2007; E. Low, pers. comm., 2007; A. Sivarajan, pers. comm., 2007). The Malay Businessmen and Industrialists Association of Malaysia, the Malaysian Organisation of Pharmaceutical Industries and the Malaysian Trade Union Congress – all members of this second coalition – have also voiced particularly strong opposition to specific sections of the proposal (such as government procure-ment regulations, intellectual property provisions and labour rights, respectively).

The third coalition is the Action Committee against the US FTA (Northern Region), also known as the Anti-US FTA Action Committee for the Northern Region. This group represents farmers, fisherfolk, rural citizens and NGOs from the northern states of Kedah and Penang (TWN 2007b: online), two important rice-producing states.[8] With help from CAP and the community-based organization, *Teras Pengupayaan Melayu* (Malay Empowerment Group: TERAS), SAM is the key coordinator of this third coalition. Not surprisingly, and of particular relevance to this discussion, members of the Northern Region coalition have focused much of their energy on issues related to rice. Organizers have collected thousands of signatures – primarily from Malay citizens in rural regions – to petition Prime Minister Badawi and the MITI Minister to cease negotiations with the US. Although the petition's actual impact on the government is difficult to ascertain, these signatories represent an important segment of UMNO's voting base and live in states with a strong *Parti Islam SeMalaysia* (Pan Malaysian Islamic Party: PAS) presence. Although PAS is not officially part of this northern coalition, some party leaders from Kedah and Penang have become involved in the campaign to support their constituents' livelihoods (M.N. Mahshar, pers. comm., 2007). Moreover, as a Malay-centred party, PAS is also reticent to support an agreement that could jeopardize *Bumiputra* policies.

PAS's involvement with this third coalition offers a useful example of how domestic opposition political parties have helped raise awareness of the proposed agreement and pressured Prime Minister Badawi and MITI to be more public about their negotiations. As Meredith L. Weiss has argued, this type of political party/civil society partnership in Malaysia 'makes political reform far more feasible than otherwise, particularly when economic or political crises motivate a broader than usual swathe of the public to seek change' (Weiss 2003: 59). The Democratic Action Party's (DAP) Lim Kit Siang has been particularly vocal about the Malaysia–US FTA. On his blog and in parliament, Lim has pushed for a cost–benefit analysis of the agreement and questioned why the Ninth Malaysia Plan 'devotes no more than a passing paragraph' to something as 'vital and important' as bilateral agreements (Lim 2006: online).

While the *Parti Keadilan Rakyat* (People's Justice Party: PKR) is part of the People's Anti-USA-Malaysia FTA coalition, it appears to have taken a rather ambivalent stance on the issue. Some party members support the idea of an agreement, albeit with reservations and demands for greater transparency; others primarily or completely oppose it. This ambivalence may, in part, be attributed to PKR's Anwar Ibrahim,[9] who has historically supported free trade and trade liberalization while also advocating for the abolishment of the New Economic Policy that underpins *Bumiputra* policies. Some party members would, therefore, be more likely to support an agreement that dismantles government procurement mechanisms.

Although not a registered political party (as the government has continually denied it official party status), the *Parti Sosialis Malaysia* (Socialist Party of Malaysia: PSM) has voiced the strongest opposition to the agreement and is the only party to formally denounce the negotiations. Former Prime Minister Mahathir, who has historically accused Western countries – especially the US – of using multilateral trading mechanisms to recolonize Malaysia (see, as examples, Khoo 2002; Mahathir 2003; Welsh 2004), has also strongly chastised his successor for courting an agreement that would grant the US even greater control over the country (*Malaysiakini* 2006: online). Within the ruling *Barisan Nasional* (BN) coalition, Khairy Jamaluddin – Deputy Chief of the UMNO Youth wing and Prime Minister Badawi's son-in-law – has also expressed particularly strong reservations about the FTA.

Malaysia's domestic media also play an important role in raising awareness of the proposed FTA and advancing critical discussion of its benefits and drawbacks. To this end, mainstream media have offered some coverage of trade negotiations – rather surprisingly, considering the government's myriad hegemonic, regulatory and coercive mechanisms to control the press. Though not overly critical or in-depth, this coverage has helped push the issue more into the public eye. Most FTA activists interviewed for this research indicated that they focus the majority of their efforts on attracting mainstream media coverage, even if it is just descriptive, in order to reach the widest audience possible.

While the mainstream press should, ideally, support civil society, alternative media are usually considered more centrally involved. Malaysia's alternative media, for example, include political bloggers, websites of critical NGOs, and the web-based newspaper *Malaysiakini*. These media operate separately from, and often in resistance to, both the government and mainstream media, tending to be oriented more toward improving democracy than making a profit (although these two goals are not mutually exclusive). As a result, the government publicly censures, harasses and threatens these media practitioners, especially if it thinks they wield political influence within the country (see Smeltzer 2008b). Alternative media coverage of the FTA has, however, been relatively sparse. This limited coverage may be attributed to numerous causes, including a range of other serious domestic issues that also deserve discussion and debate, a difficulty in acquiring accurate and up-to-date information about the ins-and-outs of trade talks, and a lack of recognition of the agreement's importance to Malaysia's future.

Although they may focus their resistance efforts on different aspects of the proposed agreement, the activists and politicians described above are particularly concerned by the lack of transparency, public discussion and parliamentary debate about the process. In response to demands for a cost–benefit analysis, however, then MITI Minister Rafidah Aziz replied that the government had done its 'arithmetic and its [*sic*] very clear the benefits far outweigh the costs that Malaysia and the US will have to face' (Aziz quoted in Lim 2006: online). This conclusion is far from convincing to those engaging in resistance to the FTA, the tactics of whom are detailed below.

Forms and methods of resistance

While some Malaysian civil society agents take a more confrontational approach in their dealings with the government, others operate in various roles *within* the system to affect change. This dual-pronged approach is par for the course in Malaysia's civil society. As Weiss contends, local activists 'simultaneously proffer an alternative ideological grounding for politics' that critiques and opposes the status quo; others 'work within the prevailing framework to alter policies' (Weiss 2004: 259). Each of these methods of resistance is of a very different nature than James C. Scott's 'weapons of the weak'. Scott focused his Malaysian fieldwork on 'infrapolitics' – micropolitical, everyday forms of individual and class resistance against domination rather than open opposition to authority. These types of resistance are, Scott writes, 'the ordinary weapons of relatively powerless groups . . . [that] require little or no coordination or planning' (Scott 1985: xvi). In the case of FTA resistance, however, organized and primarily overt forms of opposition are carried out by citizens with varying levels of power – from rural Malay farmers to middle-class urban Indian NGO workers to the Chinese leader of a major opposition party. Everyday forms of hidden resistance would, quite simply, be ineffective for amassing the kind of opposition necessary to encourage the government to reconsider negotiating a bilateral agreement with its largest trading partner.

Consequently, activists have organized *modest* demonstrations during major rounds of the trade talks held in Malaysia and coordinated smaller protests targeting specific sections of the agreement (see Figure 11.1). They have also linked up with an anti-Iraq war protest outside the US Embassy in Kuala Lumpur. Knowing the mainstream media would cover a government-sanctioned protest,[10] activists focused on the anti-American element of the FTA, chanting: 'Get out of Iraq! Stop the FTA!'. Various groups and coalitions have held workshops with local communities throughout Peninsular Malaysia to raise public awareness and inform citizens about the FTA. They have also mounted fax and petition-writing campaigns, targeting MITI and the Prime Minister's Office. JERIT organized a leafleting campaign about the agreement, distributing thousands of leaflets at state and federal government buildings and in key urban locations throughout Peninsular Malaysia.

Figure 11.1 Protests against the US–Malaysia Free Trade Agreement.

Photo credit: Third World Network (reproduced with permission)

Specific NGOs and activist groups have also tried to make inroads toward effectuating change by working within the government system, leveraging their expertise on committees, acting as consultants to ministries, and, perhaps most importantly, informing members of parliament and civil servants about how US FTAs have affected other countries and the potential implications for Malaysia.

Rough road ahead: the hard work of resistance

Although relatively limited in number, FTA-oriented activists in Malaysia include a relatively diverse group of Malaysians, cutting across ethnic, regional and class lines. While the inclusive nature of these efforts is positive, organizing advocacy campaigns and creating a unified front becomes more difficult when individuals and groups have different priorities and expectations of how resistance should be engendered. Activists working on democratic reform writ large and/or advocacy work on specific issues must also balance their existing responsibilities with this new free-trade beast that requires cooperation within a heterogeneous civil society and political landscape. It is also difficult for activists to convince fellow citizens to turn possible concerns about a Malaysia–US FTA into action. Potential government backlash – in the form of general harassment, fines, and even imprisonment – limits the number of people willing to be involved in more overt displays of resistance (Hilley 2001; Hassan 2002; Heryanto and Mandal 2003). As Saliha Hassan writes, the government's control mechanisms 'regulate, monitor, depoliticize and if necessary, eliminate critics of government, especially since their opposition is regarded as a disruption of established political and development agendas' (2002: 201). When JERIT, PSM and TWN extended their leafleting campaign into the home constituency of then MITI Minister Rafidah, for example, their actions were met with a fairly serious response from the authorities. Members of the coalition were prevented from further distribution, threatened with imprisonment, and some were escorted to the local police station for questioning.

Fear of government reprisals also helps to explain why there is an absence of large-scale demonstrations on the streets of Kuala Lumpur. Citizens are more likely to weigh the potential risks involved with overt resistance when deciding whether to become involved. If citizens *do* choose to take to the streets, they may direct their energies toward what appear to be bigger issues (such as electoral reform, which was at the heart of the November 2007 BERSIH rally).[11] Without such public protest, however, it becomes more challenging to make other citizens aware of the importance of the agreement to Malaysia.

As the discussion above illustrates, there is indeed resistance to the proposed Malaysia–US FTA. This opposition is not, however, concentrated and, as of late 2007, resistance efforts have started to wane. This was particularly as the political fall-out from the BERSIH rally for fair elections and the

HINDRAF (Hindu Rights Action Force) demonstration in Malaysia captured much of the attention of civil society and local media.

For FTA activists, the most encouraging development thus far has been that the FTA agreement negotiations missed the fast-track deadline. As one coalition organizer commented: 'Definitely, the anti-FTA demonstrations has [*sic*] forced Malaysia to miss the deadline. It is a victory for now' (Kohila quoted in *Malaysiakini* 2007: online). It is difficult to know, however, how much the missed deadline can be attributed to such resistance efforts or to other political and economic issues, especially disagreements between the two countries over rice and government procurement procedures. A bilateral agreement with the US could also 'generate a backlash from the Muslim world', particularly considering Malaysia's heavy involvement in the Organisation of the Islamic Conference (Pereira and Ahmad 2006: 12). Interministerial conflicts (for example, between MITI and the Ministry of Natural Resources and Environment, the Ministry of Health and the Ministry of Agriculture) and political jousting between Prime Minister Badawi and ex-Prime Minister Mahathir may have also, to some extent, hindered the talks.

There are also factions within Malaysia that are either apathetic about the agreement or very much in favour of it. As Charles Santiago argues, it would be a mistake to focus solely on the neo-colonialist actions of other countries; rather, we must also examine the 'social and political forces inside ASEAN member-states who themselves are pro-actively pushing for precisely these kinds of agreements' (quoted in Aziz 2007: online). For instance, many local manufacturers have supported stronger trading ties with the US, hoping that an agreement will prise open American markets for their export goods. Due to Malaysia's rampant cronyism (cf. Gomez and Jomo 1999; Milne and Mauzy 1999; Fraser *et al.* 2006; George 2006; Case 2008), politically well-connected and wealthy individuals control considerable chunks of the local economy. These economically powerful figures also tend to gravitate toward supporting a Malaysia–US FTA because their sizeable companies will likely fare better against international competition than their small and medium-sized domestic counterparts.

Many non-*Bumiputra* Malaysians are also in favour of negotiating an agreement – whether with the US or another foreign country – that could help repeal an affirmative action policy that is not to their benefit. As Saliha Hassan and Carolina López explain, 'although dissent may not surface overtly, since citizens are forbidden to discuss the issue . . . privileging one ethnic group over the others has long met with a degree of discontent and resistance from non-Malay citizens' (2005: 115) and is a key factor behind the brain drain out of Malaysia (see Bunnell 2002; Jussawalla 2003). Indeed, numerous interviewees expressed frustration with attempts to convince non-Malay Malaysians, eager to abolish the *Bumiputra* policy, that a US FTA would negatively impact the vast majority of Malaysians regardless of whether the affirmative action policy were to be revoked.

Interviewees also expressed frustration that many citizens they talked to about the agreement assumed that increased trade with the US and its massive market would automatically be good for Malaysia's economy. This is particularly true of middle-class, urban Malaysians. Free trade, however, is not necessarily fair trade. An FTA with the US is not about promoting trade so much as it is about *controlling* trade. This is a message activists are at pains to get out and one that seems to have found greater resonance with marginalized Malaysians. Some interviewees suggested that these citizens recognize the impact a bilateral agreement with the US will have on their lives and livelihoods. By comparison, much of Malaysia's growing urban middle class may not realize what lies ahead with the agreement, or see how it will personally affect them. With its relative political apathy, combined with a general preference 'to celebrate . . . private or personal achievements, measurable in terms of family expansion, career advancement and material purchases' (Case 2003: 47), the middle class can be a tough sell for activists concerned about a trade agreement with the US. As Francis Loh Kok Wah has argued, the comfortable lifestyle enjoyed by Malaysia's growing middle class is often viewed as being contingent on the political stability offered by the political status quo, the BN coalition. The coalition's politics of 'developmentalism', rather than ethnicism or 'Asian values', has also played an important role in stymieing widespread political action in Malaysia (Loh 2002: 21).

Conclusions: back to the negotiating table?

FTA activists had hoped that the government's poorer than expected showing in the March 2008 federal elections would prompt Prime Minister Badawi to shift his focus away from the Malaysia–US FTA and toward other domestic priorities. When Badawi appointed former Agriculture Minister Muhyiddin Yassin to replace Rafidah as MITI Minister and Chief Trade Negotiator, activists were also hopeful that agriculture would be protected in any and all trade agreements. Muhyiddin has, however, indicated that he will continue where Rafidah left off and attempt to conclude negotiations with the US under President Obama's administration.

Activists are also worried about power imbalances in the negotiation process; the US team has significantly more experience and resources to secure a deal in its best interests. Minister Muhyiddin's relative lack of experience in negotiating at an international level could, they fear, further tilt the balance of power toward the US. As well, in late 2008, Malaysia's Deputy Prime Minister and Minister of Finance, Najib Razak, started to take a more active role in the country's trade issues. While Najib is a more seasoned and experienced politician than Muhyiddin, he is strongly in favour of free trade and neoliberal principles (see Kamil 2008) and, more problematically, may not negotiate in the best interest of all Malaysians (for a critical discussion of Najib's recent political history, see Case 2008). As Badawi has chosen Najib as his successor for the country's top position, the Deputy Prime Minister will continue to play a central role in shaping Malaysia's future trade relationships for the foreseeable future.

On a more positive note, in May 2008, Muhyiddin publicly declared that

> the agriculture sector is important to the country and we will not compromise if we feel that any agreement is likely to negatively affect farmers ... This is the reason why we did not agree to include the planting of padi (for example) in the negotiations.
>
> (AFP 2008: online)

Whether rice is actually excluded from the negotiations remains to be seen, especially considering that the US has recently intensified its pressure on other trading partners to accommodate American agriculture products. The US Food, Conservation, and Energy Act of 2008 (also known as the 2007 US Farm Bill), for example, promises American farmers greater access to foreign markets, while also maintaining its substantial domestic agricultural subsidies.

The increased political presence of opposition parties in parliament may result in more serious discussions about the Malaysia–US FTA, as well as future bilateral and multilateral trade agreements (including the EU–ASEAN agreement). Though the three main opposition parties – DAP, PAS and PKR – have not categorically opposed bilateral and multilateral trading relationships, they have all signed a memorandum calling on the government to stop negotiations with the US (even though the agreement was not a significant issue in the March 2008 federal election). Activists must continue the hard work of pressuring political figures in these parties, and in the ruling BN coalition, to seriously examine the potential implications of this agreement and encourage them to walk away from the negotiating table if, *and when*, the deal is not in the best interest of the majority of Malaysians.

Notes

1 In Southeast Asia, the US currently shares an FTA with Singapore and South Korea, and is engaged in ongoing talks with Thailand.
2 Dr Mahathir bin Mohamad served as Malaysia's Prime Minister from July 1981 to October 2003, but remains active in domestic politics.
3 For a useful history of Malaysia's rice sector, see the work of John Overton (1999).
4 From 2000 to 2003, 'the cost of production and milling of milled rice was 41 US cents ... per kilo while the export price was 27 US cents per kilo' (Idris 2007: 29), creating an artificially cheap export product.
5 In summer 2007, Prime Minister Badawi launched the multi-billion ringgit Northern Corridor Economic Region (NCER) strategy to boost economic prosperity in the states of Penang, Kedah, Perlis and the north of Perak, specifically targeting increased padi production. While the NCER plan has the potential to benefit rural Malaysians, it must ensure small-scale farmers receive adequate protection and support as the government pushes for farming to be scaled up to commercial levels.

6 See also the work of the Save Our Rice Campaign of the Penang-based Pesticide Action Network (PAN) Asia and the Pacific. Online. Available HTTP: http://www.panap.net/217.0.html (accessed 23 February 2009).

7 *Bumiputra* (also referred to as *Bumiputera*), or 'sons of the soil', is a term used throughout Malaysia. It encompasses ethnic Malays, Javanese, Minang, Bugis, and other ethnic groups such as the Orang Asli in Peninsular Malaysia, and groups indigenous to East Malaysia. Under the Federal constitution, however, the Orang Asli are not considered *Bumiputra* and are thus ineligible for the government's preferential policies.

8 Kedah and Penang were also early adapters of Green Revolution technology at the beginning of the region's agrarian transition. In particular, Malaysia's Muda irrigation scheme did not increase productivity, failing to provide a useful and consistent source of water for farmers; see, for example, Clare L. Johnson (2000).

9 Anwar re-entered Malaysian politics in early 2008 after being removed from the office of Deputy Prime Minister by former Prime Minister Mahathir, charged with corruption and sodomy, and serving nearly six years in jail. As leader of PKR, Anwar is the official opposition leader of Malaysia's lower house of parliament.

10 Despite its willingness to support the US in its 'war on terror', Malaysia has officially supported a US withdrawal from Iraq.

11 BERSIH is a coalition of domestic NGOs and opposition political parties working toward electoral reform in Malaysia. On 10 November 2007, the coalition organized a demonstration of an estimated 40,000 citizens calling for fair and democratic elections. The event was met with a harsh response from the authorities, including the use of water cannons and arrests.

References

AFP (Agence France-Presse) (2008) 'Malaysia won't compromise farmers in FTA with US: Minister', 26 May. Online. Available HTTP: <http://afp.google.com/article/ALeqM5hLWRnCLkqrL2GNnaQoFFeGRx4-EQ> (accessed 23 February 2009).

Anderson, T. (2006) 'Globalization and agricultural trade: the market access and food security dilemmas of developing countries', in B.N. Ghosh and H.M. Guven (eds) *Globalization and the Third World: a study of negative consequences*, Basingstoke: Palgrave Macmillan, 251–64.

Arnold, C.M. (2006) 'Protecting intellectual property in the developing world: next stop – Thailand', *Duke Law & Technology Review*, Rev. 10., no page numbers. Online. Available HTTP: <http://www.law.duke.edu/journals/dltr/articles/pdf/2006DLTR0010.pdf> (accessed 23 February 2009).

Atan, H. (2008). 'PM hopes to see fairer trade ties with US', 7 November. *New Straits Times Online*. Online. Available HTTP: <http://www.nst.com.my/Current_News/NST/Friday/Frontpage/2395650/Article> (accessed 23 February 2009).

Aziz, F.A. (2007) 'Local interest blocs behind FTA drive?', *Malaysiakini*, 7 July. Online. Available HTTP: <http://isarawak.com.my/cmsis/index.php?option=com_content&task=view&id=295&Itemid=37f> (accessed 25 February 2009).

bilaterals.org (2008) 'Malaysia'. Online. Available HTTP: <http://bilaterals.org/rubrique.php3?id_rubrique=112> (accessed 25 February 2009).

Bunnell, T. (2002) 'Multimedia utopia? a geographical critique of IT discourse in Malaysia', *Antipode*, 34 (2): 265–95.

Business Times (2007) 'Washington wants rice included in FTA talks with KL', 9 June. Online. Available HTTP: <http://www.twnside.org.sg/title2/FTAs/info.service/fta.info.service102.htm> (accessed 25 February 2009).

Case, W. (2003) 'Thorns in the flesh: civil society as democratizing agent in Malaysia', in D.C. Schak and W. Hudson (eds) *Civil Society in Asia*, Aldershot: Ashgate, 40–58.

—— (2008) 'Malaysia in 2007: high corruption and low opposition', *Asian Survey*, 48 (1): 47–54.

Cheah, C. H. (2007) 'Take a hard look at it', *New Straits Times*, 12 December 2007, Local: 26.

Choudry, A. (2006) 'Bilateral free trade and investment agreements and the US corporate biotech agenda', *bilaterals.org*. Online. Available HTTP: <http://www.bilaterals.org/article.php3?id_article=4861> (accessed 23 February 2009).

—— (2007) 'Not under the same sky: bilateral free trade agreements (FTAs), agriculture and food sovereignty', Pesticides Action Network Asia-Pacific. Online. Available HTTP: <http://www.panap.net/uploads/media/SR_3_inside_pages.pdf> (accessed 23 February 2009).

Consumers International (2002) 'Food security in Asia: Malaysia'. Online. Available HTTP: <http://www.consumersinternational.org/Templates/Internal.asp? NodeID =93305> (accessed 23 February 2009).

Fraser, D. R., Zhang, H. and Derashid, C. (2006) 'Capital structure and political patronage: The case of Malaysia', *Journal of Banking & Finance*, 30 (4): 1291–308.

FTA Malaysia (2007) 'Press statement by the Committee Against the US FTA', 10 January 2007. Online. Available HTTP: <http://www.ftamalaysia.org/article. php?aid=125> (accessed 23 February 2009).

George, C. (2006) *Contentious Journalism and the Internet: towards democratic discourse in Malaysia and Singapore*, Singapore: Singapore University Press.

Gomez, E.T. (2003) 'Politics of the media business: the press under Mahathir', in B. Welsh (ed.) *Reflections: the Mahathir years*, Washington DC: Johns Hopkins University Press, 475–86.

Gomez, E.T. and Jomo, K.S. (1999) *Malaysia's Political Economy: politics, patronage and profits*, 2nd edn, Cambridge: Cambridge University Press.

Government of Malaysia (2006) 'Ninth Malaysia Plan (2006–2010)', *Economic Planning Unit, Prime Minister's Department*. Online. Available HTTP: <http://www.epu.jpm.my/rm9/html/english.htm> (accessed 23 February 2009).

—— (2007) 'Malaysia and free trade agreements', *myGovernment: The Malaysia Government's Official Portal*. Online. Available HTTP: <http://www.gov.my/MyGov/BI/Directory/Business/BusinessByIndustry/BusinessAndEBusiness/BusinessAndAgreement/MalaysiaandFTA> (accessed 23 February 2009).

Hassan, S. (2002) 'Political non-governmental organisations: ideals and realities', in F. Loh Kok Wah and B.T. Khoo (eds) *Democracy in Malaysia: discourses and practices*, Richmond, Surrey: Curzon, 198–217.

Hassan, S. and López, C. (2005) 'Human rights in Malaysia: globalization, national governance and local responses,' in F.K.W. Loh and J. Öjendal (eds) *Southeast Asian Responses to Globalization: restructuring governance and deepening democracy*, Copenhagen: Nordic Institute of Asian Studies, 110–37.

Heryanto, A. and Mandal, S.K. (2003) 'Challenges to authoritarianism in Indonesia and Malaysia,' in A. Heryanto and S. K. Mandal (eds) *Challenging Authoritarianism in Southeast Asia: comparing Indonesia and Malaysia*, London and New York: Routledge Curzon, 1–23.

Hilley, J. (2001) *Malaysia: Mahathirism, hegemony and the new opposition*, London: Zed Books.

Idris, S.M.M. (2007) 'Keep rice out of the deal', *New Straits Times*, 15 June 2007, Local: 29.

James, S. and Griswold, D. (2007) 'Freeing the farm: a farm bill for all Americans', Center for Trade Policy Studies, CATO Institute. Online. Available HTTP: <http://www.freetrade.org/files/pubs/pas/tpa-034.pdf> (accessed 23 February 2009).

Johnson, C.L. (2000) 'Government intervention in the Muda irrigation scheme, Malaysia: "actors", expectations and outcomes', *The Geographical Journal*, 166 (3): 192–214.

Jomo, K.S. and Tan, E.C. (2006) 'External liberalization, economic performance, and distribution in Malaysia,' in L. Taylor (ed.) *External Liberalization in Asia, Post-Socialist Europe, and Brazil*, Oxford: Oxford University Press, 232–66.

Jussawalla, M. (2003) 'Bridging the 'Global Digital Divide', in M. Jussawalla and R.D. Taylor (eds) *Information Technology Parks of the Asia Pacific: lessons for the regional digital divide*, Armonk, NY: M.E. Sharpe, 3–24.

Kamil, M. (2008) 'Najib: Malaysia wants an open global trading system', *New Straits Times*, 22 November, Local, 6.

Khoo, B.T. (2002) 'Nationalism, capitalism and "Asian values" ', in F. Loh Kok Wah and B.T. Khoo (eds) *Democracy in Malaysia: discourses and practices*, Richmond, Surrey: Curzon, 51–73.

Lewis, G. (2006) *Virtual Thailand: the media and cultural politics in Thailand, Malaysia and Singapore*, London: Routledge.

Lewis, L. (2008) 'Food crisis forces Malaysia into barter: palm oil for rice', 14 May. *Times Online*. Online. Available HTTP: <http://business.timesonline.co.uk/tol/business/industry_sectors/natural_resources/article3930237.ece> (accessed 23 February 2009).

Lim, K.S. (2006) 'Parliament and private sector NGOs should be fully concepted in FTA negotiations with United States: Speech (9) on the Ninth Malaysia Plan'. Online. Available HTTP: <http://www.dapmalaysia.org/english/2006/april06/lks/lks3861.htm> (accessed 23 February 2009).

Loh, F.K.W. (2002) 'Developmentalism and the limits of democratic discourse', in F.K.W. Loh and K.B. Teik (eds) *Democracy in Malaysia: discourses and practices*, Richmond, Surrey: Curzon Press, 19–50.

Mahathir, M. (2003) 'Federal Budget 2004'. Online. Available HTTP: <http://www.kit.sabah.gov.my/budget/2004enn.htm> (accessed 23 February 2009).

Malaysiakini (2006) 'FTA with US may harm economy, warns Dr M'. Online. Available HTTP: <www.malaysiakini.com/news/48705> (accessed 25 February 2009).

—— (2007) 'Activists celebrate as FTA deadline expires' *Malaysiakini*, 2 April. Online. Available: <www.malaysiakini.com/news/65344> (accessed 23 February 2009).

Milne, R.S. and Mauzy, D.K. (1999) *Malaysian Politics Under Mahathir*, London: Routledge.

MITI (Ministry of International Trade and Industry Malaysia) (2008) 'Free Trade Agreement: Malaysia's FTA involvement'. Online. Available HTTP: <http://www.miti.gov.my/cms/content.jsp?id=com.tms.cms.section.Section_8ab556937f00 0010-72f772f7-46d4f042> (accessed 24 February 2009).

Narayanan, S. and Gulati, A. (2002) 'Globalization and the smallholders: a review of issues, approaches, and implications', International Food Policy Research

Institute, Markets and Structural Studies Division, Discussion Paper No. 50. Online. Available HTTP: <http://www.ifpri.org/divs/mtid/dp/papers/mss-dp50.pdf> (accessed 23 February 2009).

New Straits Times (2007) 'Bernas ordered to create emergency rice stockpile', *New Straits Times*, 12 July, Local, 8.

Overton, J. (1999) 'Integration or self-sufficiency? Peninsular Malaysia and the rice trade in Southeast Asia', *Singapore Journal of Tropical Geography*, 20 (2): 169–80.

Pang, E.S. (2007) 'Embedding security into free trade: the case of the United States–Singapore Free Trade Agreement', *Contemporary Southeast Asia: A Journal of International and Strategic Affairs*, 29 (1): 1–32.

Pasadilla, G.O. (2006) 'Preferential trading agreements and agricultural liberalization in East and Southeast Asia', *Asia-Pacific Research and Training Network on Trade*, Working Paper Series, No. 11, April 2006. Online. Available HTTP: <www.unescap.org/tid/artnet/pub/wp1106.pdf> (accessed 23 February 2009).

Pereira, D. and Ahmad, R. (2006) 'Malaysian "dithering" over FTA worries US: KL may be wary of negative Muslim views and unequal trade benefits', *The Straits Times*, 18 September: 12.

Pletcher, J. (1990) 'Public interventions in agricultural markets in Malaysia: rice and palm oil', *Modern Asian Studies*, 24 (2): 323–40.

Rajoo, D.A. (2008) 'Malaysia delays buying rice for stockpile', *Bernama*, 11 October. Online. Available HTTP: <http://www.bernama.com/bernama/v3/news_lite.php?id=363885> (accessed 23 February 2009).

Ramasamy, B. and Yeung, M.C.H. (2007) 'Malaysia – Trade Policy Review 2006', *The World Economy*, 30 (8): 1193–208.

Santiago, C. (2007) 'Malaysia–US FTA: what's at stake?', FTA Malaysia, 17 April. Online. Available HTTP: <http://www.ftamalaysia.org/article.php?aid=170> (accessed 23 February 2009).

Scott, J.C. (1985) *Weapons of the Weak: everyday forms of peasant resistance*, New Haven: Yale University Press.

The Southeast Asian Council for Food Security and Fair Trade (SEACON) (2005) 'Regional report on the impact of trade liberalization on small scale producers in South East Asia – a cause for concern'. Online. Available HTTP: <http://www.seacouncil.org/seacon/images/stories/publications/1033-regional_report_on_trade_liberalization.pdf> (accessed 23 February 2009).

Smeltzer, S. (2008a) 'The message is the market: selling biotechnology and nation in Malaysia', in J. Nevins and N. Peluso (eds) *Taking Southeast Asia to Market: commodifications in a neoliberal age*, Cambridge: Cornell University Press, 191–205.

—— (2008b) 'Blogging in Malaysia: hope for a new democratic technology?', *Journal of International Communication*, 14 (1): 28–45.

TWN (Third World Network) (2006) 'Coalition on the US–Malaysia Free Trade Agreement memorandum to the Government of Malaysia'. Online. Available HTTP: <http://www.twnside.org.sg/title2/FTAs/info.service/fta.info.service014.htm> (accessed 23 February 2009).

—— (2007a) 'Proposed Malaysia–United States Free Trade Agreement (MUFTA): Implications for Malaysian Economic and Social Development'. Online. Available HTTP: <www.twnside.org.sg/title2/par/MUFTA.doc> (accessed 23 February 2009).

—— (2007b) 'Cabinet ministers urged not to rush to conclude US FTA without public disclosure and consultation' Online. Available HTTP: <http://

www.twnside.org.sg/title2/FTAs/info.service/fta.info.service102.htm> (item 2) (accessed 25 February 2009).

USDA (United States Department of Agriculture) (2008) 'Frequently asked questions about agricultural trade', Foreign Agricultural Service. Online. Available HTTP: <http://www.fas.usda.gov/itp/Policy/tradeFAQ.asp> (accessed 23 February 2009).

USTR (Office of the United States Trade Representative) (2006) 'Free Trade Agreement: U.S. – Malaysia: key player in Southeast Asian market'. Online. Available HTTP: <http://www.ustr.gov/assets/Document_Library/Fact_Sheets/2006/asset_upload_file510_9123.pdf> (accessed 23 February 2009).

Weiss, M.L. (2003) 'Civil society and political reform in Malaysia', in D.C. Schak and W. Hudson (eds) *Civil Society in Asia*, Aldershot UK: Ashgate, 59–72.

—— (2004) 'Malaysia: construction of counterhegemonic narratives and agendas', in M. Alagappa (ed.) *Civil Society and Political Change in Asia: expanding and contracting democratic space*, Stanford: Stanford University Press, 259–91.

Welsh, B. (ed.) (2004) *Reflections: the Mahathir years*, Washington DC: SAIS.

12 Scaling up rural resistance globally

Dominique Caouette [1]

Introduction

While other chapters in this book have tended to adopt a local or national lens to look at different forms of resistance, many have also alluded to the international connections that exist, whether through resistance to different food products, land conversion for export crops, market integration, or commoditization of local knowledge. Unsurprisingly, rural resistance is increasingly organized transnationally in Southeast Asia (Piper and Uhlin 2004). One could further argue that this tendency accelerated following the 1997 Asian Financial Crisis. In a context where one can witness the multiplication of transnational organizations, ranging from large multinational enterprises to small non-government organizations (NGOs), I examine here how transnational advocacy networks engage in debates on agrarian processes and offer support to peasant and rural-based movements, in particular looking at how transnational advocacy networks can link local-level rural concerns and struggles with global processes.

This chapter examines four transnational organizations, namely the Asian Regional Exchange for New Alternatives (ARENA), formerly based in Hong Kong; Third World Network (TWN), established in Penang (Malaysia); Focus on the Global South, headquartered in Bangkok (Thailand); and the Asia-Pacific Research Network (APRN), with its secretariat in Manila (Philippines). These four transnational activist organizations are involved in research and policy advocacy. My focus is on how these four link local rural concerns to global advocacy claims. To do so, I first discuss the growing importance of transnational activism in the region, then trace the genealogy of each organization, before reviewing how each create these 'glocal' (that is, global–local) connections. The methodologies and processes of these organizations are key variables that allow them to make these links and connections genuine and significant. The examination of these cases reveals that local rural issues and struggles are processed by these regional organizations into global frames that can be understood and that resonate among a range of civil society actors. This process of framing involves counter-discourse production, which allows for the framing of issues into calls for collective action.[2] Where these organizations differ is in their methodologies and approaches to social change and how they construct these counter-frames to dominant discourses. As will be reviewed, the more decentralized the transnational network is, the more possibilities there are for representing the views and concerns of local communities, and making their voices heard. This examination also reveals the increasing importance of global processes, not only economic but also normative, that delineate the contours of social protest and mobilization in rural Southeast Asia.

The 'emergence' of transnational activism

While it is impossible to identify a single event or an historic landmark for the emergence and accelerated growth of current forms of transnational activism,[3] it is important to recognize that such forms of activism have been present for quite some time. In fact, their intensification and geographic spread appear to be characteristic of the post-Cold War era.

For example, the extent and the size of the peace mobilizations of early 2003 to oppose the US-led invasion of Iraq was unprecedented in history. The 15 February 2003 peace rallies around the globe represented the 'single largest international demonstration in history' (Della Porta and Tarrow 2005: 227). Social movement analysts have noted that we might have entered an era marked by transnational forms of contention increasingly intertwined with state-centric movements (ibid.). According to Della Porta and Tarrow (2005), attention to three types of changes in the international environment can help in developing an understanding of this transnationalization of collective action: first, the end of the Cold War with the breakdown of the socialist bloc and the implosion of the USSR that 'encouraged the development of forms of non state action' that were previously difficult to organize; second, the rapid expansion of 'electronic communications and the spread of inexpensive international travel' that allowed movements and organizations that were previously isolated to move and 'to communicate and collaborate with one another across borders'; and third, the increasing role of international and multilateral actors as illustrated in particular 'by the growing power of transnational corporations and international institutions and events, like the global summits of the World Bank, the Group of Eight, and especially the World Trade Organization' (ibid.: 7–8). In rural Southeast Asia, such changes are being experienced as agricultural production and rural markets are increasingly integrated into global commodity production chains (Nevins and Peluso 2008) or captured in global narratives on environment and economic development (Forsyth and Walker 2008).

However, these changes are not sufficient in themselves to explain the transnationalization of resistance and social protest. Two other types of change are essential. The first is 'cognitive change'. Social movements and activists are 'reflective' social actors and, as a result, their international experiences are constantly analysed and critically assessed, and often 'tactics and frames that appear to succeed in more than one venue have been institutionalized' (Della Porta and Tarrow 2005: 8). The second important change is relational: with the acceleration of globalizing processes, especially economic ones, there are growing possibilities to identify common 'vertical' targets such as international institutions and in turn organize the 'horizontal' formation of transnational coalitions that can result in the 'growth of common identity and therefore reduces national particularism' (ibid.: 10). This is the point from which the present chapter starts, as the intent here is to explore how four transnational organizations and networks involved in advocacy and research are trying to weave local expressions of rural resistance into regional and global campaigns. By dwelling on this specific component of various social movement analysts, I wish to show that there is nothing automatic or simple in globalizing local concerns and echoing local rural resistance (Wood 2003).

Transnational activism in Southeast Asia

Before turning to the process that links local rural resistance to global advocacy, it is useful to underline the specific context in which these four different networks emerged. Transnational activism emerged in Southeast Asia as a response to socio-economic and political processes (many of which have direct ties to the agrarian transition) associated with globalization, as well as being a consequence of the relative and limited political liberalization that has characterized some Southeast Asian countries (see Caouette 2006).[4] Unsurprisingly, transnational activist organizations established themselves in countries where relative political space existed, or at least allowed, for regional and global organizing.[5]

These organizations intervene in the realm of ideas, knowledge production and alternative discourse, and act primarily at the regional and global level. Indeed, they could be considered the 'think tanks' of civil society. What makes them transnational is that, on the one hand, the knowledge they produce seeks to explain regional and global processes, and on the other, this knowledge nurtures and sustains collective action nationally and regionally. In fact, each of the four organizations offers a collective action framework that challenges not only nation states but also the very regional and global processes represented by, for example, the Asia-Pacific Economic Cooperation (APEC), the Association of Southeast Asian Nations (ASEAN) and the World Trade Organization (WTO). Bilateral processes, such as the signing of free trade agreements, are also challenged, as shown in Figure 12.1. Underlying their activities is the idea that it is essential to create and disseminate knowledge that can be used and acted upon by social actors to challenge the dominant order.

The four organizations studied here are connected to various international formations around international development issues, global financial architecture, global social justice and food sovereignty. While they may be part of the same international networks, they are recognized as distinct actors with

Figure 12.1 Protests in Pattaya, Thailand to oppose the US–Thailand Free Trade
Agreement negotiations in 2005.

Photo credit: FTA Watch Group, Thailand.

their own specificities. The four emerged at different times, and their 'repertoire of collective action', their linkages with social movements, and their
interactions with government authorities vary. All four networks have
expanded since their formation, especially in the 1990s at a time when Southeast Asia was becoming increasingly linked to the global economy, and when
various social sectors (labour, farmers, migrant workers, women and students)
were increasingly organizing and seeking alternative knowledge to the dominant export-oriented paradigm. As noted above, this expansion was most
significant in the year that followed the 1997 Asian Financial Crisis.

Although these four different networks were initially organized in different
periods, all four became key transnational nodes for knowledge and discourse
in the 1990s (Prokosh and Raymond 2002; Loh 2004). In Southeast Asia,
they are important components of the 'altermondialiste movement' because
they engage in the counter-hegemonic discourse seeking to connect a variety
of forms of resistance and specific issues into alternative narratives. This
undertaking enables more collective action-oriented movements such as *Via
Campesina* (Borras 2004, 2008; Desmarais 2007) or the Jubilee Movement to
put forward such analyses in their training and mobilization.[6]

Asian Regional Exchange for New Alternatives (ARENA)

ARENA is the oldest transnational organization among the four examined here. It was established in 1980 and its secretariat is located outside Southeast Asia, previously in Hong Kong and now in Seoul. ARENA was formed following an initial consultation organized by the Christian Conference of Asia (CCA) that brought together 'progressive scientists and church people' who recognized at the time that it was not possible to undertake critical research in mainstream universities (Nacpil-Manipon and Escuetas, pers. comm. 1998). At the time, the CCA was very active in the region, helping to set up various regional organizations, including the Asia Monitor Resource Center (AMRC), the Committee for Asian Women (CAW), the Asian Human Rights Commission and later on the Asian Migrant Center (AMC) (Cheong n.d.; Escuetas, pers. comm. 2005). During its first decade, the Christian Conference of Asia[7] played a central role in supporting the network; fellows helped identify other fellows and their works focused mostly on research and advocacy while providing a certain degree of protection for those scholars living in repressive contexts (Nacpil-Manipon and Escuetas, pers. comm. 1998). ARENA's initial location in Hong Kong was not by chance; in the early 1980s, many Asian countries were under dictatorship or under semi-authoritarian rule that constrained the possibility of setting up an organization such as this (Cheong n.d.; Tadem, pers. comm. 2005).

Since its formation, ARENA has sought to develop an Asia-wide approach and striven to bring together 'intellectual activists' to produce conceptual works that would be relevant to social movements in Asia, while building a community of concerned Asian scholars.[8] In fact, this precise constituency is a key feature of the organization: 'ARENA is a unique NGO because it has chosen to focus on the concerned Asian scholars as its immediate constituency, believing that this sector can play a vital role in the process of social transformation' (ARENA 2005: online).[9] It seeks to strengthen and sustain civil-society organizations by providing knowledge and research that can be acted upon, recognizing that these organizations 'play an important role in the process of social transformation and the search for peace and social justice' (ARENA n.d.: online).

Until 1992, the network grew slowly, gathering about twenty individuals into its Council of Fellows, who were left-wing academics; many were concerned with human rights and linked with various social movements, including anti-dictatorship movements, such as in the Philippines. Following a five-year evaluation, ARENA became more formalized in 1992–3, with the establishment of the Hong Kong secretariat that assumed greater responsibilities as programme coordinator. At the same time, ARENA began expanding rapidly, with its number of fellows eventually reaching sixty, the establishment of an executive board, and the greater inclusion and participation of women fellows (Pagaduan, pers. comm. 2005). As explained by Eduardo Tadem, ARENA's coordinator between 1993 and 1997, once ARENA had secured a more solid base of funding and was able to launch various research initiatives, it became a way to enlarge and build a community of fellows (Tadem, pers. comm. 2005). Beyond funding availability, there was also a shared understanding that ARENA needed to develop a genuine community of scholars, since many ARENA members had been handpicked by ARENA's first coordinator. The appointment of women coordinators from 1989 was also a positive factor in terms of establishing a greater gender balance and bringing on board a clearer feminist perspective among some members.[10] At the moment, ARENA has over seventy fellows based mostly in East, Southeast and South Asia[11] with a small number based in Australia, the US and the UK.

Third World Network (TWN)

TWN describes itself as 'an independent non-profit international network of organizations and individuals involved in issues relating to development, the Third World and North South issues' (TWN website, www.twnside.org.sg, accessed 24 February 2009). Its international secretariat is based in Penang, Malaysia where it was first established in November 1984.[12] The history of TWN goes back to the early 1980s. Martin Khor, who was working as Research Director with the Consumers' Association of Penang (CAP), along with other Penang-based activists, organized a conference in 1984 on development issues that would lead to the creation of TWN with the goal to 'link the local problems of communities in the South to the global policy-making arenas' (Commonwealth Foundation n.d.: online). The formation of TWN took place well before the latest wave of transnational social movement activism referred to as the anti-globalization movement. As two programme officers from Inter Pares, a Canada-based social justice organization and one of the first supporters of TWN, noted, 'the creation of TWN emerged from the process of taking a broader view at consumerism linking issues of public health, environment to North–South relations' (Seabrooke and Gillespie, pers. comm. 2005). This orientation towards international advocacy was not a coincidence; it was partly a reaction to blocked channels of political expression at the national level, but also a direct consequence of Malaysia's rapid integration in the global economy (Verma 2002; Loh 2004, 2005; Weiss 2004).

What distinguishes TWN from the other organizations examined here is TWN's explicit commitment to working when possible with government officials to affect public policies. Over the years, the TWN network has been regularly involved with multilateral processes such as the United Nations Development Program (UNDP) and ASEAN. Beyond participation in official and parallel summits, TWN produces a wide range of publications (two magazines, its monthly *Third World Resurgence* and its bimonthly *Third World Economics*, books and monographs, and occasional briefing papers), many circulated on the internet. Its website has become its primary portal for the dissemination of materials and analysis. TWN is also playing an important role in supporting and advising trade negotiators from the South around WTO issues, and it has been active with regards to the Biosafety Convention and the World Summit on Sustainable Development.

Focus on the Global South

Conceived in 1993 and 1994 by its first two co-directors, Kamal Malhotra and Walden Bello, Focus on the Global South (hereafter referred to as Focus) was officially established in Bangkok, Thailand in January 1995 (Malhotra and Bello 1999). In many ways, the two represent archetypes of transnational activists: Bello, a Filipino political economist, had lived in the US for years, where he was very active in the anti-Marcos dictatorship struggle and the international Third World solidarity movement. He had also worked with a Northern NGO, the Institute for Food and Development Policy/Food First. Malhotra, from India, had been involved for years with an international NGO, Community Aid Abroad (CAA – Oxfam Australia) and many other local NGOs. As noted in its first external evaluation, the two agreed on a common set of ideas, including that it was important to move beyond the existing North–South paradigm. In fact, they sought to offer an alternative conception to the North–South divide since 'North and South' were being re-conceptualized to distinguish between those who are able to participate in and benefit from globalized markets and those who are excluded and marginalized from them. (Kaewhtep 1999: 45). They were also 'skeptical about mainstream economic analysis and the economics-culture-politics methodology' and thought that it was essential to strengthen the links between micro and macro perspectives (ibid.: 45). At the same time, they thought it important to bridge activists mobilizing on the ground with progressive researchers and scholars. As explained in its initial concept paper, 'Focus does not see itself as just another think tank but as engaged enterprise, where analysis is meant to inform activism and vice-versa' (Focus 1997).

The reputation, track records and networks of its two co-directors helped the organization become established with a set of funding agencies committing to support it. Thailand's relative political stability and the possibility of being associated with the Chulalongkorn University Social Research Institute (CUSRI) were two key factors which led to locating the Focus head office in Bangkok. Beginning with a small staff (six in 1996), the Focus team expanded rapidly; by 1999, it already had close to 20 staff members and about 25 by 2005. It also opened two national offices, one in India and one in the Philippines. One reason for such successful expansion was the Asian financial crisis that began in Thailand before spreading throughout the region. During and following the crisis, Focus analyses and staff were in high demand.[13] Over the years, Focus staff have been involved not only in the production of research and policy analysis but have played a central role in organizing civil society networks within the region around a range of issues such as food security, APEC, ASEAN and Asia–Europe Meeting (ASEM). They have also been closely involved in many global processes, such as the World Social Forum, anti-WTO coalitions (for example, the *Our World is Not for Sale* campaign) and the peace movement (Banpasirichote *et al.* 2002). Within a few years, Focus became a key reference point for civil society organizations not only in Southeast Asia but also within the broader anti-globalization movement.[14]

Asia-Pacific Research Network (APRN)

The fourth organization examined here is the Asia-Pacific Research Network (APRN). Established in 1999, it was the product of a two-year process of consultation and exchanges of materials among organizations from the Asia Pacific region involved in research and documentation efforts. Spearheaded by a Manila-based research and data-banking centre, IBON (especially Antonio Tujan, its director), APRN's initial objectives were to: 1) build the research capacity of selected Asian NGOs; 2) identify and strengthen one organization in each target Asian country that can act as the research-information and data banking provider for local organization; 3) propose common research strategies by sharing experiences while enhancing capacities; and 4) 'develop capacity and common research platform [*sic*] to support social movements in their respective countries in the emerging issues related to the WTO Millennium round, the IMF and the APEC' (APRN 1999: 3). Its first Annual Conference, organized around the theme of trade liberalization, brought together 85 individuals from 50 organizations located in 11 different countries and included 10 of the 17 founding organizations of the network (CI-ROAP 1999). Following the conference, a workshop identified specific future activities for the Network.[15]

Through a grant from a Northern funding agency, APRN established a small secretariat located in the IBON office in Manila, responsible for communications among network members, developing and maintaining a website and an email list, and coordinating the publication of the *APRN Journal* (APRN 2000). In late 1999, APRN helped organize the People's Assembly, a parallel summit held during the WTO Third Ministerial meeting in Seattle. Early in 2000, it conducted a series of workshops on information, documentation and research training with regards to women and globalization, food security and the Agreement on Agriculture (AoA) of the WTO. In the following years, APRN continued to organize annual conferences that were co-hosted by at least one of the network members. Its sixth Annual Conference, held in Dhaka in 2004, focused on the theme of agriculture and food sovereignty, and the organizers sought to transform 'the APRN conference from a purely research and academic conference to a more open and public gathering of research institutions and people's organizations' (APRN 2004a: 1). Well attended with over 500 participants from more than 30 countries, this resulted in the adoption of the People's Convention on Food Sovereignty as well as a People's Statement (APRN 2004b).

Beyond its annual conferences, APRN organized a range of research activities. For example, during its 2002 General Council meeting, APRN members agreed to 'embark on coordinated researches as originally envisioned at the start of the network in Manila' (APRN 2002: 3). Instead of financing individual research conducted by APRN members, research would be conducted jointly. In recent years, APRN has participated in the formation of *The Reality of Aid – Asia* network, thereby establishing an Asian counterpart to the initial *Reality of Aid* network based in Europe and North America that is aimed at monitoring and documenting international development assistance programmes and projects. APRN has also continued to be involved in other global and regional activities, including a policy workshop on regional cooperation and human rights in Asia in June 2004, an international conference to commemorate the 50th anniversary of the 'Bandung Conference' in April 2005, and a range of consultations and parallel forums on ASEAN and the WTO. After more than ten years in existence, APRN has established itself as a key research and advocacy network; primarily in Southeast Asia, but also within the broader Asia-Pacific region (Tujan, pers. comm. 2005). In doing so, it has expanded from 17 to 50 member organizations based in 19 different countries (APRN website, www.aprnet.org, accessed 24 February 2009).

Connecting local resistance and global advocacy?

It is now possible to reflect on how each of these networks operates to connect rural local claims to global advocacy. As described earlier, these four organizations aim at building and developing advocacy platforms that echo grassroots demands, while also informing local mobilization. Interestingly, each one attempts to do so through different methodologies.

In the case of ARENA, the main mechanism has been through gatherings and consultations among its members who are activist intellectuals located within the region, either in universities, progressive think tanks or, in some cases, NGOs. As reported in an unpublished document tracing the history of the organization, ARENA's initial principle was 'to uphold the unity of intellectual and organizing work and reject attempts at driving a wedge between the two' (*ARENA History Project*, ARENA n.d.: 1). The assumptions underlying such an approach are that fellows, as 'activist intellectuals', are connected to local struggles and processes.

Through research efforts deployed in their own local contexts, ARENA fellows attempt to bring forward the grassroots' perspectives. Through a generic notion of organic intellectuals, ARENA envisions that its mandate will be carried out via the principled commitment of its fellows (Pagaduan, pers. comm. 2005; Tadem, pers. comm. 2005). However, the links between ARENA and local struggles and dynamics remain fragile, as no clear line of accountability or mechanisms for validation were necessarily defined as part of the modus operandi. While progress could be achieved as long as the lead fellow was willing to invest his or her time and energy, the design and implementation of specific research topics were contingent on a large and encompassing commitment to empowerment at the grassroots. Since early 2000, there have been attempts to link together local activists among themselves and with ARENA fellows. One model has been through 'regional alternative schools' that aim to 'engage Asian scholars and scholar-activists in critical reflection on emerging issues, discourses, and alternative praxis' (ARENA 2000: 18). The first of these was held in the Philippines in October 1998 and brought together sixty participants for a two-week regional workshop, followed by a smaller gathering in Indonesia. More recently, ARENA carried out a *Regional School on Marriage Migration in Asia: A Platform for Research and Action* in November 2007 in the Philippines, and, even more recently, in August 2008, organized a Summer Regional School on 'Rural Regeneration in Asia' as part of a Master of Arts in Inter-Asia NGO Studies (MAINS) (ARENA 2008). A 'night university' was also organized in Northern Thailand targeting rural activists, while further examples include the participation and involvement in a variety of people's alliance such as the Asian Peace Alliance (2003). These cases illustrate attempts that were made to develop greater capacity at the more local and grassroots level, with the explicit objective of training and developing a new generation of intellectual activists who were products of local struggles, rather than from mainstream university institutions. Such an orientation had been defined in the 1997–2000 Three-Year Plan that identified the support of people-to-people alliances as a key element of programming (ARENA n.d).

Yet, by mid-2000, there were increasing questions within the network about how ARENA might be able to bring a specific contribution to the growing numbers of regional networks and organizations that were involved in organizing and policy advocacy. As noted in an external evaluation completed in 2004, 'successful regional groups . . . are often involved in advocacy and resistance actions where their skills and alliance work and coalition building are sometimes more critical than the intellectual input that they bring into these processes' (Dias and Francisco 2004: 19).

With the multiplication of regional networks and coalitions often dealing with specific themes and issues, including rural and agrarian, ARENA is faced with the challenge of more clearly locating its specific niche in facilitating transnational linkages and fostering regional resistance. As pointed out by Dias and Francisco, 'ARENA must ask itself: how much does ARENA systematically link with other groups outside of its fellowships? How far and wide and fast do your analytical debates with one another reach others in the external environment' (ibid.). As identified in its 2003–6 Three-Year Plan entitled 'Hope Amidst Despair: Resistances and Alternatives to Hegemonies' (ARENA 2003), the issue of strengthening and reflecting on resistance remains at the core of ARENA's mission. As examined here, developing global–local connections with rural resistance is done through regional schools and linking intellectuals, scholars and students with rural activists.

In the case of the second oldest network, Third World Network, its methodology has been characterized essentially by the formation of expert knowledge to provide alternative analysis and policy discourse on issues of the day for many Third World activists and even government officials. With its long tradition of analyses and its range of publications established in the mid-1980s, TWN developed significant expertise in trade negotiations, especially with regards to the Agreement on Agriculture (AoA) and the WTO processes (TWN website). Its process of linking local processes to global advocacy has been through the organization of consultations between researchers and activists to document specific experiences on various global concerns linked to global economics, including the role of TNCs, trade regimes and intellectual property rights. Increasingly, its contribution to activism has been through its various publications. Moreover, TWN seeks to bring local concerns, broadly defined as Southern, to a more global scale by participating in international gatherings sponsored by multilateral agencies or by certain governments. For example, a survey of the various Annual Reports produced by TWN between 1993 and 2003 revealed an amazing increase in its participation in international and regional events. TWN's participation in civil society activities and government and multilateral organizations' meetings increased threefold from 50 in 1993 to 158 by 2003. In fact, throughout the period, TWN consistently participated in UN-sponsored processes, often at the request of the UN itself.[16]

As TWN expanded, its publications also multiplied. Its key publication, *Third World Network Features* (*TWNF*), has been published at a rate of about 150 issues per year.[17] In its 1993 Annual Report, TWN specifies that *TWNF* dealt with 'environment, economics, health, human rights, biotechnology, development and many other issues affecting the Third World' (TWN Annual Report 1993: 5). Ten years later, while producing approximately the same number of issues per year (155 in 2003), the themes covered included 'terrorism, the Iraq crisis, health, safety, poverty, hunger, agriculture, human rights, finance, economics, globalization, development, war, environment, ecology, biotechnology, genetic engineering, information technology, human rights, etc.' (TWN Annual Report 2003: 2). In its other publications, the *South–North Development Monitor* (*SUNS*), *Third World Economics* (*TWE*), and *Third World Resurgence*, dominant topics have centred around 'economic-related themes' (TWN Annual Report 1993: 24), especially the General Agreement on Tariffs and Trade (GATT), the International Monetary Fund (IMF), the World Bank (WB), the WTO, transnational corporations, trade, environment and development.

This focus on economics and global economic institutions has been consistent, and TWN has repeatedly given 'high priority to economic related activities' (TWN Annual Report 1995: 30). This priority became all the more central following the establishment of the WTO, the proposed Multilateral Agreement on Investment (MAI), and the Asian Financial Crisis in 1997. As described by TWN (Annual Report 1996: 35), 'the year 1996 saw a great expansion in TWN's activities related to the WTO and related trade and development issues', especially around the time of the WTO Ministerial Meeting Conference held in Singapore in December 1996.

As the years passed, the TWN website became a key component of its dissemination of information. In 2003, it recorded a total of 8.2 million hits, an increase of 5 per cent compared to 2002 (7.8 million hits), and almost twice as much as 2001 (4.8 million hits): 'among the top ten most requested web pages ... were web pages on trade/WTO issues, women's rights, the World Bank/IMF, the financial and economic crisis, biotechnology/biosafety and the TWN Online bookstore' (TWN Annual Report 2003: 36). Another means of disseminating knowledge and expertise for TWN has been through its participation in various international gatherings, conferences and workshops.

In terms of micro processes, it appears that local voices are brought forward indirectly, that is, through the specific perspective that TWN offers on global processes. The role of its main investigators is central as these individuals act as interpreters of local realities as well as translators, deconstructing global processes to make them intelligible not only to Southern government officials but to social movements as well.[18]

Focus, from its early days, sought to combine analyses of the workings and impacts of regional and global economic processes with studies of local resistance and initiatives through its two main programmes: policy-oriented research and analysis of critical regional and global socio-economic issues (the Global Paradigms Program); and documentation, analysis and dissemination of 'innovative civil society, grassroots, community-based efforts in democratic, poverty reducing and sustainable development' (the Micro–Macro Paradigm Program) (Kaewhtep 1999: 46). In many ways, Focus is similar to TWN since it is partly through its analysis and research that links between local and global processes are made. Through maintaining direct contacts with social movements, Focus seeks to bring forward local voices. As noted in a review by Banpasirichote *et al.*: 'Linked by intensive networking to social movements, progressive local and international NGOs, southern governments and activists around the world, Focus organizes its activities in an interactive and creative process of research/analysis, advocacy and campaign, capacity and movement building' (2002: 2). Nevertheless, the same authors also note that 'Focus doesn't pretend to represent anybody except itself but it finds its legitimacy and credibility in the role Focus plays in the global movement against neoliberalism, providing analysis, ideas, strategies and capacity building' (ibid.: 2).

As the years have passed since its establishment, Focus has become increasingly involved in global advocacy and activism, in particular in response to economic processes. Not only working to make global processes understandable (via forms of translation and interpretation), Focus staff are also trying to act as bridges, facilitating the creation of linkages across social movements: 'Focus's role of facilitating linkages between various grassroots social movements, as well as facilitating their access and participation in international forums and venues, has been much appreciated by grassroots NGOs and social movements' (ibid.: 3). As noted by one staff member, Focus often chooses to work through coalitions rather than taking the lead position (Chanida Bamford, pers. comm. 2005). The effort to remain rooted in local and national processes is illustrated by Focus's move to set up offices in the Philippines and in India. Lately, and similarly to ARENA, Focus has developed a programme of international courses for activists seeking to enhance their understanding of global processes. Similar to its 2007 programme, its 2008 International Course, held in Bangkok at the Chulalongkorn University Social Research Institute, was entitled 'Globalization and Social Transformation', aimed at 'those who have at least 2 years of involvement in any social movement and volunteer work or work experience in NGOs' (Focus 2008: online). With the recent food crisis, Focus has also worked intensively to produce analyses that can be used by local rural coalitions for advocacy (ibid.). In terms of micro processes, like the previous two organizations, its 'glocal' connections operate through the production of knowledge and framing of issues, especially in framing global processes in order to make them understandable not only for grassroots activists, but also for international networks and NGOs. Complex processes such as WTO negotiations, the AoA, or the food crisis and the 2008 economic downturn are explained and linked to global advocacy platforms and coalitions.[19]

For its part, since its founding, APRN has emphasized the consolidation of research skills and documentation at the local level. This has been very much the rationale for its creation: the establishment of a network of research and data banking organizations (in theory, one per country) to strengthen the capacity of social movements to document their local struggles (APRN 1999: 1; see also CI-ROAP 1999). In the case of APRN, accountability to social movements is often direct as many of APRN's members are social movement activists or sympathizers directly linked to certain social movements. In terms of micro processes, beyond interpreting and translating local realities within a global framework, APRN acts as a bridge and organizer for various cross-national initiatives. In fact, during the last WTO ministerial meeting in December 2005, APRN acted as an organizer for marches and protests, thus amplifying its role as a movement organizer that is able to act as a gathering force (Tujan, pers. comm. 2006).

APRN has also placed a strong emphasis on developing a genuine research institution that can feed national and local social movements. Nevertheless, as its membership expands, the challenge is to ensure that coordinated research projects are genuinely collective efforts, bringing together the perspectives of a variety of local social movements. Its peculiar niche as a network that strengthens the capacities of people's organizations to undertake documentation and research linked to concerns on the ground certainly constitutes an advantage of APRN in terms of its capacities to link local struggles to global advocacy. However, much energy in the past has been placed around organizing annual conferences. With a growing membership and a new willingness to act as a social movement organizer, the challenge in the coming years will be for ARPN itself to remain conscious of its particular contribution to strengthening and scaling up local research efforts. With the People's Convention on Food Sovereignty and new research with the Coordinated Research Conference on Agrarian Reform (APRN 2005, 2006), the network maintains its commitment to root capacity and skills within research organizations linked closely to rural movements. As specified in the description of the above conference, one of its objectives is to 'bring together researchers and peasants around Asia-Pacific who are interested in participating in a coordinated research effort on the theme' (APRN 2005: online). At the same time, overall, as one can observe with Focus, there is a growing desire to act as a social movement organizer, such as during the WTO ministerial meetings held in Hong Kong and more recently during the Bali Climate Change meetings, where APRN, along with IBON, Aid Watch and Indonesian grassroots organizations organized 'protest actions' and campaigns in favour of a People's Protocol on Climate Change (APRN 2007: 6). Similarly to TWN (also a member of APRN) and Focus, APRN also engages in framing local issues into broader masterframes, people's food sovereignty being an example as well as the concept of a 'people's protocol on climate change'.

Conclusions

Findings from these four cases largely confirm those of Della Porta and Tarrow (2005) that transnational activists are very seldom working at the transnational level exclusively.[20] Instead, they tend to be rooted at the local and national levels, engaging different institutions and social movements simultaneously. Whether it is the staff from Focus and TWN or APRN member organizations, they all came to transnational activism after local- and national-level advocacy. Many remained rooted in their own national struggles, arguing that advocacy and policy engagement at one level does not deter activism at another level. In most cases, transnational activists are capable of and interested in creating linkages and coalitions among various types of actors operating on different levels (local, national, regional, international) in order to respond to various political contexts, each offering a different range of political opportunities. As the work of Focus and TWN reveals, specific and localized rural concerns are woven together around the theme of resistance to neoliberal globalization and the need for global social justice.

Interventions have focused around resistance to global economic processes through an aggregation of local demands and global calls to oppose and resist the WTO or new forms of multilateral or bilateral processes that are perceived as exclusionary in terms of civil society participation, in particular peasant and farmer organizations. Rural struggles have become framed at the global scale within struggles for food sovereignty and resistance to corporate control (McMichael 2008) and more broadly woven with the global justice movement.

However, this weaving is more problematic than usually described. As the above analysis reveals, there are a number of dilemmas and choices when transnational networks seek to bring local perspectives to the regional and global levels. As the Southeast Asian rural sector continues its integration into the global political economy, transnational advocacy will likely expand. Exploring further the micro processes at work when local issues and struggles become part of regional activism will remain a key analytical challenge. Such linkages between local and global scales become all the more complex as cyber activism now forms one of the modalities by which local networks can disseminate globally (Bob 2001, Bennett 2003). In the case of the four organizations analysed here, websites and mailing lists have been key tools for disseminating research and policy advocacy platforms. Yet these do not replace the need for direct encounters and gatherings, as well as the need for public mass mobilizations.

One key challenge is how to ensure that those directly affected at the local scale are able to access and use these new technologies. Unsurprisingly, there have been various methods to enlarge participation and render such tools more widely accessible for activism. One method has been through training and capacity building such as that provided by APRN to its members, another method has been the production of popular education videos and downloadable materials such as the series on the WTO produced by Focus, and through the regular updating of websites as resource sites and the use of mailing lists, the latter undertaken almost daily by TWN.

Another analytical challenge is how to trace the policy influence of such global activism. Transnational advocacy networks help produce shared identities and a common understanding of issues (Caouette 2006, Singh 2008), and they generate common campaigns and proposals that can be put forward during regional and international gatherings and implemented at both the regional and national levels. In some cases, transnational activism can influence the dominant discourse and force its tenants to defend and justify their positions. As the study of TWN demonstrates, reformist policy-makers interested in developing alternative proposals to a more orthodox neoliberal agenda may seek the expertise and knowledge generated by transnational networks. Finally, by connecting community organizations and local NGOs' struggles to a broader set of issues and struggles, transnational activists are able to amplify and enrich both the work being conducted at the very local level, and the advocacy and policy work conducted regionally and globally.

What do we learn, though, from this discussion in terms of rural resistance? The first is that the regional networks examined here place an important emphasis on organized forms of resistance, either through protest action or meetings with state officials or representatives of global institutions. Secondly, all four act as both interpreters and knowledge producers and thus engage in what Forsyth and Walker describe as 'narratives' (2008: 228). In many ways, the knowledge and the advocacy platforms produced, whether by ARENA fellows or members of the three other organizations, position themselves as counter-hegemonic narratives, with equal claims to scientific knowledge. As such, they constitute politicized knowledge, and, as underlined by Forsyth and Walker, 'understanding and overcoming the problem of narratives requires a more complex and approach than the belief that scientific research is somehow independent of politics and that policymakers will always listen to its finding' (ibid.: 228–9).

With regards to the four case studies above, advocacy and knowledge are closely intertwined with consideration of responding to multilateral and inter-state conferences, meetings and forums, somehow reminiscent of Jepperson's metaphor used by Tarrow of a coral reef 'helping to form horizontal connections among activists with similar claims across boundaries' (Tarrow 2001: 15). However, in such processes of narrative and claim-making, one might wonder if such aggregative and normative undertakings are not in the end contributing to a further encroachment of market relations and commodity logic into rural areas, as illustrated by various contributors in Nevins and Peluso (2008). In this process, other narratives and more subtle forms of resistance, especially at the local level, are overlooked or bypassed, not intentionally, but constrained by the logic of global resistance and the pursuit of building transnational rural movements. Recent analyses and discussions around *Via Campesina*, a transnational peasant movement (Desmarais 2007; Borras 2008), might bring more nuances to what Rosenau (2003) described as 'distant proximities' to illustrate the contradictory and intertwined dynamics of these 'glocal' connections. Understanding resistance on multiple scales might require breaking away from easily understood and usual dichotomies – local versus global, open versus hidden, inclusionary versus exclusionary, private versus public, and so on. As observed by O'Riordan and Church: 'Local perceptions are shaped by global influences, the combinations of which process local actions. These in turn are fuelled by local aspirations, many of which are the product of global images and expectations' (2001: 3).

Notes

1 Parts of this chapter were initially published in *Kasarinlan: A Philippine Quarterly of Third World Studies*, Manila (Philippines), vol. 21, no. 2 (2006): pp.3–33 and in *Pacific Focus: Inha Journal of International Studies*, vol. 22, no. 2 (Fall 2007): pp. 141–66. A first version of the chapter was presented during the 5th EuroSEAS Conference held at the University of Naples, 'L'Orientale', 12–14 September 2007, and I thank all participants of Panel 10, 'Transnational Activism in Southeast Asia', in particular its organizers Michèle Ford and Lenore Lyons, for their questions, comments and suggestions. All shortcomings and errors are, however, my sole responsibility.
2 By framing, I refer to what Noakes and Johnston describe thus: 'In the simplest of terms, framing functions in much the same way as a frame around a picture : attention gets focused on what is relevant and important and away from extraneous items in the field of view. . . . Moreover, collective action frames not only must indicate what is going on and why it is important, but must do it in a convincing

way. Successful frames must not only analyze events or identify who is responsible but also ring true with an audience – or resonate' (2005: 2).

3 A useful historical treatment of this question can be found in Hopkins (2002).

4 As Loh and Öjendal note, 'although the Southeast Asian countries enjoyed unprecedented high rates of economic growth in the 1980s and 1990s, and experienced pluralisation of their societies, nonetheless, the state authorities continued to dominate over their societies' (2005: 3). See also Taylor (1996) and Singh (2008).

5 In her study of six regional NGOs based in Hong Kong, Soo-Bok Cheong (nd: 1–5) proposed a similar argument emphasizing the importance of these two variables, naming them 'globalization and industrialization' and 'authoritarianism and democracy'.

6 Jubilee 2000 was an international campaign that took place in over forty countries. Members called for cancellation of Third World debt by the year 2000.

7 The Christian Conference of Asia (CCA) is a regional ecumenical organization now comprising sixteen national councils and over one hundred churches/ denominations in the Asia Pacific area. It was first established in 1957 and was quite active in the 1970s, supporting regional gatherings including regional meetings of the Rural Youth Programme that helped foster links among those who eventually formed ARENA (ARENA n.d.).

8 ARENA defines itself as an 'interdisciplinary programme for Asian studies and research cooperation', and a regional network 'of concerned Asian scholars – academics, intellectuals, activists, researchers, writers and artists – which aims to contribute to a process of awakening towards meaningful and people-oriented social change' (ARENA 2005: online).

9 In ARENA's view, concerned scholars are: '[I]ndividuals capable of conceptualising, theorising, analysing, interpreting and articulating issues and concerns as direct participants of or in support of struggles for social transformation in the interests of disadvantaged peoples' (ARENA 2000: 9).

10 These changes were also supported by the results of the first ARENA evaluation conducted in the early 1990s.

11 In East Asia (Beijing, Hong Kong, Taiwan, Korea and Japan), Southeast Asia (Indonesia, Malaysia, Philippines, Singapore, Thailand and Vietnam), and South Asia (Bangladesh, India, Nepal, Pakistan and Sri Lanka).

12 At the moment, TWN has offices in Delhi, Montevideo, Geneva and Accra and affiliates in India, the Philippines, Thailand, Brazil, Bangladesh, Malaysia, Peru, Ethiopia, Uruguay, Mexico, Ghana, South Africa and Senegal.

13 As one of the external evaluators noted, 'the Asian financial crisis and the role of the international financial institutions have undoubtedly become the burning issues of the day' (Sta. Ana III 1999: 24).

14 In its 2003–5 Work Plan, the organization recognized such a position: 'Focus has also traveled considerably from its starting point. It is today widely considered a "key player" in the global movement for a different and better world. Its analyses of global developments are extensively consulted, as are its suggestions for structural changes' (Focus 2003: 3).

15 These included 'common and/or coordinated research projects', 'training in research and related technologies' and 'publications' (APRN 1999: 4). Common research areas were: government transparency; the impact of globalization on workers' rights and labour migration; the impact of globalization on food security; and, finally, the impact of the GATT agreement on agriculture.

16 Details sourced from TWN archives, TWN office, Penang (consulted May 2005).

17 Through the years, *TWNF* issues have been sent to over fifty regional and international newspapers, and to another fifty magazines and newsletters, the remainder going to radio stations, press and news agencies, NGOs, journalists and individuals. Published originally in English, several of the *TWNF* issues are

translated every year into Chinese and Bahasa Malaysia by the Penang office, into various Indian languages by the Goa and Delhi Offices, into Spanish by the Montevideo office, and into Bahasa Indonesia at the Jakarta office. By 1993, these features began to be posted on 'electronic mail' (TWN Annual Report 1996: 3).

18 For example, the Minister of Industry and Commerce of Zimbabwe wrote to TWN in 1996 following a seminar organized by TWN prior to the Singapore meeting: 'Thank you for all the excellent work you did to educate some of us on the issues before the Singapore meeting. Because of that work, it was possible to have some issues deferred' (TWN archives, Penang).

19 See Singh (2008) for a rich and detailed analysis of these framing processes, especially in relation to global trade agreements.

20 This was also a key observation of Keck and Sikkink (1998), who described the combination of forms of activism insightfully.

References

Asian Peace Alliance (2003) 'Kalinaw: Asia people speak up for peace' (Proceedings of the Asian Peace Alliance – Inaugural Assembly), Hong Kong: APA Secretariat, ARENA Archives.

Asian Regional Exchange for New Alternatives (ARENA) (2000) 'Reimagining "Asia": redefining "human security" and "alternative development"; movements and alliances in the twenty-first century', *Communiqué*, Issue 55–6: 4–31.

—— (2003) 'Resistances and alternatives to hegemonies', *Communiqué, Special Issue: ARENA Three-Year Plan (2003–2006)*: Special Issue: 2–19.

—— (2005) 'ARENA online: what is ARENA'. Online. Available HTTP: <www.arenaonline.org/content/view/17/54/> (accessed 24 February 2009).

—— (2008) '2007 regional school on marriage migration in Asia'. Online. Available HTTP: <http://www.arenaonline.org/content/view/357/157/> (accessed 5 March 2009).

—— (n.d.) *ARENA History Project: General Mapping of Major Events*, unpublished document, ARENA Archives (consulted in May 2005).

Asia-Pacific Research Network (APRN) (1999) 'Narrative report,' Unpublished Report (September), Inter Pares Archives.

—— (2000) 'Project accomplishment report – Asia-pacific research network – 2nd annual conference (August 21–23) / business meeting (August 24) / training on information documentation', Unpublished Reports, (November), Inter Pares Archives.

—— (2002) 'Project accomplishment report / Asia-Pacific research network / 4th annual conference', Unpublished Report, Inter Pares Archives.

—— (2004a) 'The people's convention on food sovereignty' and 'people's statements of the Asia Pacific convention on food sovereignty'. Online. Available HTTP: <www.aprnet.org/conferences-a-workshop/44-food-sovereignty/187-the-peoples-convention-on-food-sovereignty> and <www.aprnet.org/conferences-a-workshop/44-food-sovereignty/188-peoples-statement-of-the-asia-pacific-convention-on-food-sovereignty> (accessed 5 March 2009).

—— (2004b) 'Asia Pacific convention on people's food sovereignty,' Unpublished Report (June 15), Inter Pares Archives.

—— (2005) 'Coordinated researches: APRN coordinated conference on agrarian reform' (Concept Paper – 22 September), Online. Available HTTP: <http://

www.aprnet.org/coordinated-researches/35-agrarianreformconference/52-concept-paper> (accessed 5 March 2009).

—— (2006) *Neoliberal Subversion of Agrarian Reform*, Manila: APRN – IBON Books.

—— (2007) 'People and planet over profits: conference on people's sovereignty on natural resources,' Conference Report, Online. Available HTTP: <http://www.aprnet.org/conferences-a-workshop/peoples-convention-on-natural-resources/214-conference-report-people-and-planet-over-profits-conference-on-peoples-sovereignty-on-natural-resources> (accessed 5 March 2009).

Bamford, C. (Focus on the Global South Staff), 25 May 2005, Bangkok. Personal Communication.

Banpasirichote, C., Singh, R. and Van der Borght, D. (2002) 'Report of the review: focus on the global south', unpublished report, Focus Archives.

Bennett, W. L. (2003) 'Communicating global activism : strengths and vulner-abilities of networked politics', *Information, Communication & Society*, 6 (2): 143–68.

Bob, C. (2001) 'Marketing rebellion : insurgent groups, international media, and NGO support', *International Politics*, 38 (3): 311–34.

Borras, S. (2004) 'La via campesina: an evolving transnational social movement', *TNI Briefing Series*, No. 2004/6, Amsterdam: Transnational Institute.

—— (2008) 'La via campesina and its global campaign for agrarian reform', *Journal of Agrarian Change*, 8 (2–3): 258–89.

Caouette, D. (2006) 'Thinking and nurturing transnational activism in Southeast Asia: global advocacy through knowledge-building', *Kasarinlan: a Philippine quarterly of third world studies*, 21 (2): 3–33.

Cheong, S.-B. (n.d.) *Six Asian Regional NGOs and the Formation of Social Actors*, unpublished documents, ARENA Archives (consulted May 2005).

CI-ROAP (Consumers International – Regional Office Asia-Pacific) (1999) 'First conference of the Asia Pacific research network (APRN)', *The AP Consumer*, isue 18 (December).

Commonwealth Foundation (n.d.) 'Connecting people – Dr. Martin Khor (Inter-view); creating change by making people's voices heard'. Online. Available HTTP: <http://www.commonwealthfoundation.com/news/news/detail.cfm?id=48> (accessed 5 March 2009).

Della Porta, D. and Tarrow, S. (2005) 'Introduction: transnational processes and social activism: an introduction' in D. Della Porta and S. Tarrow (eds) *Transnational Protest and Global Activism*, Lanham: Rowman and Littlefield: 1–17.

Dias, C.J. and Francisco, G.S. (2004) 'Final external ARENA evaluation report,' (July 24), ARENA Archives.

Desmarais, A. (2007) *La Via Campesina: globalization and the power of peasants*, Halifax: Fernwood Press.

Focus on the Global South (1997) 'A program of development policy research, analysis and action', unpublished brochure.

—— (2003) 'Work plan 2003–2005', unpublished document, Focus Archives.

—— (2008) 'Focus on the global south international course 2008 "Globalization and Social Transformation", Online. Available HTTP: <http://focusweb.org/focus-on-the-global-south-international-course-2008.html?Itemid=146> (accessed 24 February 2009).

Forsyth, T. and Walker, A. (2008) *Forest Guardians, Forest Destroyers: the politics of environmental knowledge in Northern Thailand*, Seattle: University of Washington Press.

Hopkins, A.G. (ed.) (2002) *Globalization in World History*, London: Pimlico.

Kaewhtep, K. (1999) 'A program and organizational assessment of focus on the global south', in *Focus on the Global South: an external assessment*, unpublished document, Inter Pares Archives.

Keck, M. and Sikkink, K. (1998) *Activists Beyond Borders*, Ithaca: Cornell University Press.

Loh, F. (2004) 'Les ONG et les mouvements sociaux en Asie du Sud-Est', in L. Delcourt, B. Duferme and F. Polet (eds) *Mondialisation des résistances: l'état des luttes 2004*, Paris: Éditions Syllepse, 41–55.

—— (2005) 'National security, the police and the rule of law: militarisation by other means', *Asian Exchange* (special double issue on 'Militarising state, society and culture in Asia: critical perspectives'), 20 (2) and 21 (1): 179–208.

Loh, F. and Öjendal, J. (2005) 'Introduction', in F. Loh and J. Öjendal (eds) *Southeast Asian Responses to Globalization: restructuring governance and deepening democracy*, Singapore: NIAS Press and ISEAS Publications, 1–16.

Malhotra, K. and W. Bello (1999) 'Background and rationale', *Focus on the Global South: an external assessment* (Final Draft), unpublished document (July), Focus Archives.

McMichael, P. (2008) 'Peasants make their own history, but not just as they please . . .', *Journal of Agrarian Change*, 8 (2 –3): 205–28.

Nacpil-Manipon, J. (Executive Director) and Escuetas, T. (Program Officer) 5 December 1998, ARENA, Hong Kong. Personal Communication.

Nevins, J. and Peluso, N. (eds) (2008) *Taking Southeast Asia to Market: commodities, nature, and people in the neoliberal age*, Ithaca: Cornell University Press.

Noakes, J.A. and Johnston, H. (2005) 'Frames of protest: a road map to a perspective', in H. Johnston and J.A. Noakes (eds.) *Frames of Protest: social movements and the framing perspective*, Lanham: Rowman and Littlefield Publishers, 1–29.

O'Riordan, T. and Church, C. (2001) 'Synthesis and content', in T. O'Riordan (ed.) *Globalism, Localism and Identity: fresh perspectives on the transition to sustainability*, London: Earthscan, 3–24.

Pagaduan, M. (ARENA Fellow), 20 May 2005, Manila. Personal Communication.

Piper, N. and Uhlin, A. (eds) (2004) *Transnational Activism in Asia: problems of power and democracy*, London: Routledge.

Prokosh, M. and Raymond, L. (eds) (2002) *The Global Activist's Manual: local ways to change the world*, New York: Thunder's Mouth Press / Nation Books.

Rosenau, J.N, (2003) *Distant Proximities, Dynamics Beyond Globalization*, Princeton: Princeton University Press.

Seabrooke, K. and Gillespie, P. (Program Officers) 1 March 2005, Inter Pares, Ottawa. Personal Communication.

Singh, J. (2008) *Framing Processes in Transnational Activist Networks: the case of anti-free movements in Southeast Asia*, unpublished MA thesis: Lund University, Sweden.

Sta. Ana III, F. (1999) 'Executive summary of assessment', *Focus on the Global South*, (Final Draft), unpublished document (July), Focus Archives.

Tadem, E. (ARENA Fellow), 18 May 2005, Manila. Personal Communication.

Tarrow, S. (2001) 'Transnational politics: contention and institutions in international politics', *Annual Review of Political Science*, 4: 1–23.

Taylor, R.H. (ed.) (1996) *The Politics of Elections in Southeast Asia*, Cambridge: Cambridge University Press.

Third World Network – Annual Reports, (1993–2005), 'Annual reports', TWN Archives.

Tujan, T. (Chairperson) 12 May 2005, APRN, Manila. Personal Communication.

Verma, V. (2002), 'Debating rights in Malaysia: contradictions and challenges.' *Journal of Contemporary Asia*, 32 (1): 108–29.

Weiss, M.L. (2004) *Protest and Possibilities: civil society and coalitions for political change in Malaysia*, Stanford, Stanford University Press.

Wood, M. (2003) 'Deconstructing rural protest: the emergence of a new social movement', *Journal of Peasant Studies*, 19: 309–25.

13 The persistence of resistance: Analysing responses to agrarian change in Southeast Asia

Tim Forsyth

As this book demonstrates, the diversity of activities within the rubric of resistance, and the manner in which academic debates about resistance take place, have changed over time. This final chapter revisits the concept of resistance, and draws conclusions about how this book has furthered our understandings of responses to agrarian change across scale, in the Southeast Asian realm.

Initial perspectives suggested that resistance emerged through opposition to market forces (Polanyi 1944), but also in opposition to the creation of hegemonies by the state and elites (Gramsci 1971). Since the 1970s, however, a variety of analysts have proposed that the relationships between those who are dominating and powerful, and those who are being dominated, are multifaceted and far more complex than first conceptualized. James Scott's work (1985, 1990) has assessed the local 'infrapolitics' of how subordinated classes respond to the state and to elites, likewise Ben Kerkvliet (1990, 2005). Social movement theorists have also considered how political action may transcend localities and even operate globally, as discussed by Caouette and Turner in Chapter 2 of this volume (cf. Della Porta and Tarrow 2005). This book's conceptual viewpoint is launched from wishing to bridge the divide between such approaches, with a focus on analysing resistance across scales.

In Scott's *Domination and the Arts of Resistance* (1990), resistance is best summarized by his concept of 'hidden transcripts', or what he defines as 'a critique of power spoken behind the back of the dominant' (Scott 1990: xii). Yet owning such transcripts does not simply equate to the act of resistance. Dominators too have their hidden transcripts, which they use to justify the practices and claims of their rule, but which cannot be declared openly. As noted in several chapters in this volume, including those by Dressler, Potter, Tran, Turner and Michaud, and Walker, people who commonly find themselves in a subordinate position may use their transcripts in the rumours, gossip and jokes familiar in *Weapons of the Weak* because they allow an anonymous criticism of power. Scott (1990: xiii) calls these the 'infrapolitics of the powerless'.

Yet hidden transcripts also have a dynamic role. Scott argues that hidden transcripts may often emerge in response to 'public transcripts', or the discourses that reinforce hegemonies. He writes: 'the public transcript will typically, by its accommodationist tone, provide convincing evidence for the hegemony of dominant values' (Scott 1985: 4). These are, says Scott, drawing on Foucault, 'technologies of domination' (ibid.: 20).

Analysing hidden transcripts may allow us to understand how subordinate groups might be socialized into accepting hegemonic views, or how these provide a space where alternative visions may be voiced. Optimistically, if these voices become more common and more powerful, the cumulative effect may be to reduce the influence of the hegemony. In turn, this may lead to that moment of 'political electricity' where a hidden transcript becomes no longer hidden, and the subordinated speaks directly to the powerful (Scott 1990: 223).

The beauty of Scott's work lies in demonstrating that resistance and domination need not be a zero-sum game: they co-exist, and resistance may gain in momentum. Scott also shows that subordinated people may have more agency in resisting hegemony as argued historically by Gramsci, or that hegemony may not always exist as a uniform acceptance of elite agendas. In this way, Scott's work forms part of the post-structuralist thinking in development studies seeking more optimistic outcomes about social and political relations than those posed under structural Marxism (see Chapter 1).

Yet Scott is not always clear about how local hidden transcripts can 'grow legs', or how they transcend their localities and become powerful enough to change hegemony. Scott's prime focus is on hidden transcripts within localities. Thus contributors to this book have turned to later scholars' work to analyse resistance at larger spatial scales, or to assess how hidden transcripts actually do 'grow legs' to become politically contentious through organized collective action (for example, the chapters by Franco and Borras, Kuhonta, Potter and Smeltzer).

Assistance and resistance

Transcending spatial scales is not simply a matter of hidden transcripts becoming public. It is often linked to other political processes of social activism, social movements, and alliances between different social groups and actors. Questions must then be raised about the politics of these alliances and political movements. Moreover, we need to consider questions of knowledge, or how activists understand each other and the normative basis for political intervention. Indeed, the social movement theorist Sydney Tarrow has defined transnational activism as 'the political processes that activists trigger to connect their local claims to those of others across borders and to international institutions, regimes and processes' (2005: 11) (see also the chapters by Caouette and Turner, and Caouette).

Transnational activism may depend upon resource mobilization and the strategies adopted by activists to achieve their objectives. At the same time, these optimistic accounts of transformative politics need to be questioned alongside the more hidden politics of how less powerful actors may be affected or represented in this process. For example, Nancy Peluso's *Rich Forests, Poor People* (1992) discusses peasant resistance to state forestry in Indonesia, but also adopts post-structuralist insights into how history, language and culture affect resistance. Peluso (1992: 16) writes that 'cultures of resistance – consisting of ideology, local social structure, and history – are contextual configurations of common peasant responses to external controls and state appropriation of resources'. Further illustrations of these configurations are provided in this volume with regards to oil palm plantations in Indonesia in the chapter by Potter, regarding conservation efforts in national parks in the Philippines (Dressler), and in the ethnically complex milieu of Vietnam's northern highlands (Turner and Michaud).

Resistance and forces of domination cannot be assessed independently. Peluso accordingly explains resistance as part of a long-term process of how the state and its allies have defined what are appropriate or inappropriate forest uses. In Indonesia's case she argues that notions of appropriate forest use date from long-term capitalist exploitation, and the 'legitimizing ideology of scientific forestry under the colonial state in Java' led to the 'progressive criminalization of customary rights of forest access' (Peluso 1992: 236). The result of these processes was a range of legal instruments to restrict agriculture and settlement in forest zones. State agencies were created to regulate and generate knowledge about appropriate forest uses. Middle-class and international non-governmental organizations (NGOs) would occasionally ally with the state in supporting some forms of forest restrictions. Yet various peasants would resist these restrictions through settlement and agriculture in state-claimed forest zones and by engaging in unsanctioned forest use. The parallels here with Dressler's chapter are evident.

In Scottian terms, these historic beliefs about the criminalization of peasant activities or the appropriate uses of forests are the public transcripts that legitimate the subordination of peasant forest users. If we are to understand how these transcripts – or discourses – emerged it is therefore important that we look historically at who created them, the role of state agencies in generating authoritative knowledge, and the supplemental role played by alliances with other political actors such as international NGOs. Hajer (1995) uses the term 'discourse coalitions' to refer to how different political actors may reinforce fixed visions of forests or other physical artefacts even if the political actors may disagree about other topics.

A further implication of taking a historically rooted, post-structuralist approach is that we need to ask how far the very roles ascribed to peasants have been created by these public transcripts or discourses. As this book has made clear, resistance and the presumed causes of subordination are mutually constitutive. Dominating discourses may therefore carry with them definitions by which social groups or citizens may be considered appropriate or not (Agrawal 2005). Consequently, we cannot essentialize resistance by poor peasants without considering the normative basis by which we evaluate their acts as either emancipatory or disobedient.

Perhaps most controversially, this book has shown that there is also a need to consider how far extending resistance across spatial scales might actually further disempower subordinated groups. Giving hidden transcripts 'legs' by linking the transcripts to social movements or international resistance movements might empower vulnerable groups by increasing public attention or placing more pressure on oppressors, but what happens if old public transcripts are replaced by new public transcripts that are nationally or internationally accepted and promoted but oppressive locally, as illustrated in Dressler's and Kuhonta's chapters? This could easily become the case for the Hmong discussed in Turner and Michaud's chapter as well.

One possible means of excluding poor peasants is to portray them in overly romanticized or 'traditional' settings that deny them access to new commercial activities. Rangan (2000), for example, argues that the history of the Chipko conservationist movement in northern India has been improperly portrayed as examples of villagers adopting 'green' environmental philosophies when, in fact, many villagers were seeking to assert their own uses of forest resources. Instead, she argues that the original activists found themselves benefiting from the publicity attracted by the campaign, but also increasingly disempowered as more powerful actors portrayed the campaign in terms that suited them, rather than reflecting the diversity of local opinions.

Clearly, commercialization and rapid environmental change can carry negative impacts, and many poor people are relatively powerless to resist these. Yet outsiders' well-meaning intent needs to be tempered with concern for how far new public transcripts of resistance might be based on their own histories and contexts that do not necessarily reflect local hidden transcripts. As Emery Roe once noted, 'crisis narratives [or discourses] are the primary means whereby development experts and the institutions for which they work claim rights to stewardship over land and resources they do not own' (Roe 1995: 1066). Can this problem be avoided?

Resistance is fertile, perhaps too fertile?

As this book demonstrates, resistance is a heuristic concept for analyzing contemporary rural dynamics in Southeast Asia. The editors note in Chapter 1 that a diverse and healthy literature exists on opposition and dissent towards overarching changes that control or affect rights and livelihoods. Building on this literature, the studies presented in this volume range from 'everyday forms of peasant resistance' at local levels, to more transnational and organized protest linked to the globalization of agriculture and food production. As this book affirms, resistance occurs when people feel disposed, threatened or subordinated. Yet, as the editors also note, resistance – as a process in its own right – cannot exist without understanding the structures that trigger it. We cannot study resistance without also asking: resistance to what? In turn, we must also ask who resists, and what is the rationale behind identifying some activities as resistance.

Resistance, therefore, may be more widespread than is obvious at first blush because it can take many guises, be caused by multiple changes, and be difficult to see because those who are resisting may take care not to make it apparent. At the same time, one must remain careful in trying to identify the various forms, shapes and scales of resistance given that the temptation could be to fall into a 'resistance mentality'; that is, *assuming* state–society relations are those organized by notions of resistance, or that certain groups are unwilling to accept changes, or that change must necessarily instil resistance. If rural resistance and dominance are mutually constitutive, we need to ask how we identify and evaluate these forces. Why do we assume that greater commoditization and reach of capitalist markets cause resistance? Whose viewpoints are we assessing? Are we beginning to essentialize the responses to change – and assume they are resistance – without also asking why is it we expect to find resistance? Are we making assumptions about both the nature of changes and people's responses that might oversimplify current social and economic processes? These are the sorts of questions that the contributors in this book have attempted to keep at the forefront of their analyses.

The contributions of this book

The diverse case studies in this book present rich examples of different forms of resistance in Southeast Asia in the context of the contemporary agrarian transition. Yet the arguments put forward by the different contributors do not suggest that there is a uniform relationship between commercialization and resistance; far from it. Turner and Michaud's chapter on Hmong trading in northern Vietnam argues that members of this ethnic group are resisting both commercialization and the state by selectively engaging in trading cardamom in conjunction with other livelihood activities, such as part-time textile production. Even so, according to the approach suggested by Walker, perhaps we should see this activity as economic opportunism, or a healthy engagement in (rather than resistance to) new commercial opportunities. Yet Turner and Michaud contend that these activities can be considered a subtle form of resistance because they allow the Hmong autonomy from hegemonic dependency on the market, or reliance on state-led development initiatives. In this respect, Turner and Michaud are demonstrating Scott's infrapolitics of the powerless, illustrating how the Hmong find ways to reach some level of autonomy despite being affected by both state and market.

Walker's discussion of contract farming in northern Thailand raises further questions that challenge a 'resistance mentality'. He suggests that contract farming has – apparently – been welcomed in many villages for adding additional income sources to diverse portfolios. Nevertheless, contract farming has had a chequered reputation for allegedly diminishing farmers' rights and for causing environmental degradation resulting from agrochemical use. Walker argues that the low-key sources of resistance that do occur – such as one eggplant farmer aiming a punch at a company representative, or harvesting crops in ways that maximize their weight – come from how the contracts are arranged and honoured, rather than from an overarching, and essentially oppressive, impact of commercialization.

Dressler's chapter on Palawan, the Philippines is all the more revealing of the complicated issue of representation. Here he argues that conservationists implementing devolved conservation have misrepresented upland indigenous farmers in overly traditional terms, restricting their livelihood options. As a result, current discourses of community-based natural resources management have reinforced social divisions and exacerbated local inequalities rather than assisted poor upland communities. The Tagbanua, reflecting on their marginal position, have come to articulate their ethnic identity as a marker of difference in opposition to those who subordinate them.

Potter's chapter similarly concentrates on rural-based relationships that raise questions around ethnicity and identity, this time focusing upon the replacement of the Dayak's traditional swidden-based mixed farming in Kalimantan, Indonesia, with large oil palm plantations, on which the Dayak sometimes become smallholders. Evident here are differing forms of resistance, from very local, everyday forms – including unexpected reactions when plantation managers' wives invited local Dayak women to dine together (the Dayak women immediately left with the food in a symbolic representation of the unsanctioned seizure of their land) – to violent local-level protests, and to those incorporating the activities of local and national non-governmental organizations. Particularly of note here is the range of resistance forms apparent, all occurring at a fairly local scale.

Still other chapters point further to the complicating impacts of political alliances and contested representations of subordinated people. Kuhonta, in his discussion of the conflict over the Pak Mun Dam in eastern Thailand, argues that development in Thailand has 'steamrollered' the peasantry. Yet the chapter also points to the divisions in Thai society about the ethics of this dam and its protest. It also highlights how middle-class academics engaged in new statistical analyses in order to shift government and public thinking (or public transcripts) away from the view that any source of energy was acceptable in industrializing Thailand.

The chapters by Tran on Vietnam, Vu on Indonesia, and Franco and Borras on the Philippines lead us to more national-scale discussions over how comprehensive programmes of agrarian change and the introduction of market forces have resulted in numerous shapes and forms of resistance by landless, or smallholding, peasants. Here again specific political-economic features and historical characteristics are vital to our understanding of present-day resistance. These chapters reflect how resistance is linked to different elements of the agrarian transition, including changes for peasants from subsistence to market-based economies, and from general self-reliance to dependency on the market and the state (see also Rigg 2005).

For Tran, everyday forms of resistance in Vietnam during the central planning and collectivization period from the early 1960s to the early 1980s have been replaced, since the 1980s, by a more sporadic resentment of the uneven impacts of economic liberalization. Yet these contemporary open and collective protests remain localized and small-scale, rarely spreading beyond district or provincial boundaries, and, especially rarely, targeting the central government.

Since 1998, Vu notes that Indonesia has seen the birth of hundreds of farmers' unions, and other forms of covert and overt resistance to land control disparities. Behind such behaviour, he argues, is an anti-capitalist ideology that is broadly shared among many Indonesian agrarian activists. This ideology is expressed in a profound hostility toward capitalism, which also unites such locals and activists with a broader range of other social organizations throughout the country.

Franco and Borras, writing on the Philippines, point to the 1986 rejection of President Marcos as allowing for the formation of a 'paradigm shift' in resistance by creating new political spaces for open and legal rural social movements. Yet this change in political governance also ushered in an era of neoliberalism that has changed relations between farmers and the market, making traditional forms of political opposition less attractive, while new forms of rural organizing, reflecting peasant political agency, are developing.

The final two case study chapters move us across the scale again. Smeltzer's chapter discusses how Malaysian civil society groups have organized and used primarily overt forms of activism to demonstrate their resistance to a planned Free Trade Agreement between Malaysia and the US that would, among other things, directly impact upon rural livelihoods. This political activism includes a relatively broad cross-section of the population, cutting across ethnic, regional and class lines. It appears to be giving hidden transcripts 'legs' by linking peasant groups to national activists, and possibly 'wings' too by linking them internationally, via both overt and covert mechanisms such as the internet.

In the penultimate chapter, Caouette discusses the role of regional transnational activism and organizing, which has led to the growth of important development-oriented NGOs as forms of resistance in Southeast Asia, such as the Third World Network (based in Kuala Lumpur) or Focus on the Global South (Bangkok). These 'think tanks of civil society' provide key strategies and resources for resistance, processing local rural issues and struggles into global frames that can be appreciated among a broad range of civil society actors. Emphasizing again the importance of a multi-scalar approach, these transnational activists seldom work at the transnational level exclusively, tending instead to be rooted at the local and national.

In total, these chapters reveal a number of elements not previously articulated in the literature on rural resistance. First, there are parallels in these discussions of resistance with the long-standing debate about capitalism as either a means of production (with its implicit assumptions of surplus extraction and inherent inequality) or as a means of organization. If economic growth was organized in accessible ways then perhaps it could be empowering to poorer farmers, and we should not see it as necessarily oppressive. A second theme – well expressed by Anderson (1977) – is that resistance is not always specifically about the economic changes wrought by markets, but also about the identities of the actors linked to these changes. As noted in several chapters, legitimacy of the state, and its legal processes, and of the economic changes taking place, can sometimes influence resistance just as much as wider economic change.

Persisting with resistance but cautiously

As Walker has noted in this volume, there is a danger of adopting a 'resistance mentality' in which all overarching changes in society are viewed in terms of how they will create resistance. Doing this excessively will essentialize resistance, without considering how changes and responses are linked, or how pre-existing assumptions may shape how we see resistance. It is important to differentiate between broader socio-economic shifts and hegemonic frames. If we adopt a hegemonic frame uncritically, we risk misplacing social or economic activities into pre-defined narratives of resistance that might overlook positive opportunities for poor groups, or misread impacts of economic change (Sivaramakrishnan 2005; Forsyth and Walker 2008).

Nonetheless, it is clear that forms of resistance continue to exist in response to a variety of dominating structures. Sometimes these causes can be related to sudden economic change. The transitions in Vietnam following economic liberalization are an example. Similarly, the immense political reforms and changes in investment regimes following the falls of Suharto in Indonesia and Marcos in the Philippines have had widespread impacts on peasant farmers and resistance practices. These impacts are related partly to changing economic circumstances, but also to the perceived legitimacy and inclusiveness of the state. Different social groups or individuals are choosing their own infrapolitics, or more overt methods, to address these impacts.

Part of the agrarian transition taking place now in Southeast Asia involves changes that are occurring to the nature of the state, and to the manner in which the state is perceived by its citizens. Actions by the state are increasingly affected by changes in international markets. States no longer have the autonomy to set the rules, and citizens are presented with a more complex interaction between states and markets as sources of authority. James Rosenau refers to this process as 'glocalization' (Rosenau 2003). Consequently it is not surprising that farmers and peasants may choose to engage partially or wholeheartedly with resistance, and involve both state and market processes. Similarly, it is not unusual that researchers might wrestle with new ways of conceptualizing resistance when the scales and objectives of resistance are so obviously in flux.

As these chapters have shown, resistance now connects different spatial scales, and involves actors of varying resources and viewpoints. Transnational social movements have power; they can provide 'legs' to so-called local hidden transcripts. Yet while transnational resistance can empower peasants and farmers, we should not assume that national or international advocacy coalitions necessarily produce an unprejudiced or neutral form of empowerment. The only way to address this concern is to think critically about how we make assumptions about distant places and people, to consider how political alliances and activism (mis)represent different groups, and to ask – again – if the focus on change is hampered by an overarching hegemonic frame.

Conceptualizing resistance as a known process, with known causes and outcomes, should be avoided; rather, as revealed throughout this volume, resistance should be conceived as a diverse process where peasants engage in long-standing and evolving negotiation and opportunism. Resistance should be about how deprivation occurs and is responded to, rather than about enforcing a fixed view about resistance itself. This book, by moving across scales, by diversifying the means and objectives of resistance, and by emphasizing the broad range of actors involved, each with their own agency, histories and politics, advances debates about how farmers try to shape their lives. The authors have expanded our understandings of local, national and regional-level resistance measures to agrarian change in Southeast Asia, with all their diversity and nuances. Positively, this resistance has, at times, created opportunities that allow resistors to maintain some control over their identities and livelihoods. Still, as the case studies demonstrate, it is important to focus on the underlying transitions and impacts as well as the contextually constituted meanings of resistance and domination, rather than remain wedded to a specific theory or explanation of resistance itself.

References

Agrawal, A. (2005) *Environmentality: technologies of government and the making of subjects*, Durham: Duke University Press.

Anderson, B. (1977) 'Book review: *The Moral Economy of the Peasant: rebellion and subsistence in Southeast Asia* by James C. Scott', *Journal of Asian Studies*, 37 (1): 172–4.

Della Porta, D. and Tarrow, S. (2005) 'Transnational processes and social activism: an introduction', in D. Della Porta and S. Tarrow (eds) *Transnational Protest and Global Activism*, Lanham: Rowman and Littlefield: 1–17.

Forsyth, T. and Walker, A. (2008) *Forest Guardians, Forest Destroyers: the politics of environmental knowledge in northern Thailand*, Seattle: Washington University Press.

Gramsci, A. (1971) *Selections from the Prison Notebooks of Antonio Gramsci*, trans. and ed. Quintin Hoare and Geoffrey Nowell Smith, New York: International Publishers.

Hajer, M. (1995) *The Politics of Environmental Discourse*, Oxford: Clarendon Press.

Kerkvliet, B.J.T. (1990) *Everyday Politics in the Philippines: class and status relations in a central Luzon village*, Berkeley: University of California Press.

—— (2005) *The Power of Everyday Politics: how Vietnamese peasants transformed national policy*, Ithaca, NY: Cornell University Press.

Peluso, N. (1992) *Rich Forests, Poor People*, New Haven: Yale University Press.

Polanyi, K. (1944) *The Great Transformation. The political and economic origins of our time*, Boston: Beacon Press.

Rangan, H. (2000) *Of Myths and Movements: rewriting Chipko into Himalayan history*, London: Verso.

Rigg, J. (2005) *Living with Transition in Laos: market integration in Southeast Asia*, London and New York: Routledge.

Roe, E. (1995) 'Except Africa: postscript to a special section on development narratives', *World Development*, 23 (6): 1065–9.

Rosenau, J. (2003) *Distant Proximities: dynamics beyond globalization*, Princeton: Princeton University Press.

Scott, J.C. (1985) *Weapons of the Weak: everyday forms of peasant resistance*, New Haven: Yale University Press.

—— (1990) *Domination and the Arts of Resistance: hidden transcripts*, New Haven: Yale University Press.

Sivaramakrishnan, K. (2005) 'Some intellectual genealogies for the concept of everyday resistance', *American Anthropologist*, 107: 346–55.

Tarrow, S. (2005) *The New Transnational Activism*, Cambridge: Cambridge University Press.

Glossary

absen   absent (Indonesia)[1]
adat   traditional law; tradition or custom (Indonesia, Malaysia)
Aliansi Buruh Mengugat   Alliance of Critical Workers (Indonesia)
api   to oppress, bring about shame (the Philippines)
baht   Thai currency
banig   sleeping mat woven out of *pandan* (the Philippines)
bersih   translates as 'clean' in *Bahasa Malaysia*. Also name of the *Gabungan Pilihanraya Bersih dan Adil* (Coalition for Clean and Fair Elections) (Malaysia)
Bumiputra (or **Bumiputera**)   'sons of the soil' (Malaysia)
bupati   district head (Indonesia)
các dân tộc thiểu số   minority nationalities (Vietnam)
camat   subdistrict head (Indonesia)
dao krachai   'scattered star': a strategy of staging protests at multiple sites rather than at one major location (Thailand)
Dayak   generic term given to indigenous groups on the island of Borneo
diwan   foreigner, outsider; used in reference to migrants (the Philippines)
đổi mới   economic renovation (Vietnam)
đồng   Vietnamese currency
dusun   sub-village (Indonesia)
ekonomi kerakyatan   people's economy (Indonesia)
Front Perjuangan Pemuda Indonesia   Youth Front for Struggle
gaharu   a valuable perfumed wood ('eaglewood', *Aquilaria spp*) (Indonesia)
Gerakan Rakyat Lawan Nekolim   People's Movement to Oppose Neo-colonialism and Neo-imperialism or *Gerak Lawan* (Indonesia)
Gini coefficient   used as a measure of inequality of income or wealth distribution. Defined as a ratio with values between 0 and 1, a low Gini coefficient indicates more equal income or wealth distribution, while a high Gini coefficient indicates more unequal distribution.
hak-hak rakyat   people's rights (Indonesia)
inti   core (Indonesia)
Jaringan Rakyat Tertindas   The Oppressed People's Network (Malaysia)
kaingin   shifting agriculture (swidden) (the Philippines)

kamnan   sub-district leaders (Thailand)
kampung   village (Indonesia, Malaysia)
kapling   a two-hectare plot of oil palm (Indonesia)
katutubo   innateness, concept connected with indigenous self-identification (Philippines)
kedaulatan pangan   food sovereignty (Indonesia)
Kesatuan Aksi Mahasiswa LAKSI 31   United Action for LAKSI 31 (Indonesia)
khoán hộ   household contracts (Vietnam)
Kinh   lowland Vietnamese
Koalisi Anti Utang   Anti-Debt Coalition (Indonesia)
Komite Mahasiswa Anti-Imperialisme   Student Committee against Imperialism (Indonesia)
lahan tidur   sleeping land (Indonesia)
Lingkar Studi-Aksi untuk Demokrasi Indonesia   Academic-Activist Circle for Democracy (Indonesia)
mae krua yai   female group leader in charge of logistics during demonstrations (Thailand)
masyarakat adat   the rights of indigenous communities (Indonesia)
nay ampoe   district officer (Thailand)
nii mul wian   rotating debt (Thailand)
padi   paddy, often refers to land in which rice is grown, or threshed unmilled rice (Indonesia, Malaysia)
padi pulut   sticky rice (Indonesia)
Pancasila   official ideological foundation of the Indonesian State introduced by President Sukarno in 1945
Parti Islam SeMalaysia   Pan Malaysian Islamic Party (Malaysia)
Parti Keadilan Rakyat   People's Justice Party (Malaysia)
Parti Sosialis Malaysia   Socialist Party of Malaysia
pembangunan   development (Indonesia)
Perhimpunan Bantuan Hukum dan Hak Asasi Manusia Indonesia   Legal Aid and Human Rights Association, Indonesia
Perkebunan Inti Rakyat   estate + smallholder production system (Indonesia)
pho khrua yai   male group leader (Thailand)
phra mae khongkha   goddess of the river (Thailand)
plasma   smallholder plot (Indonesia)
puu yai baan   village headman (Thailand)
rai   unit of measurement equivalent to 0.16 hectares (Thailand)
Reformasi   reformation period or post-1998 era (Indonesia)
ringgit   Malaysian currency
rupiah   Indonesian currency
Sahabat Alam Malaysia   Friends of the Earth Malaysia
(kelapa) sawit   oil palm (Indonesia)
Serikat Petani Kelapa Sawit   Organization of oil palm farmers (Indonesia)
sitio   small village / territorial enclave (the Philippines)

tembawang communal fruit groves (Indonesia)
Teras Pengupayaan Melayu Malay Empowerment Group (Malaysia)
tuak rice wine (Indonesia)
tubigan rainfed paddy rice (the Philippines)
Việt Minh (*Việt Nam Độc Lập Đồng Minh Hội*) League for the Independence of Vietnam
yantok rattan (*Calamus spp.*) (the Philippines)

Note

1 The national languages of Indonesia and Malaysia, respectively *Bahasa Indonesia* and *Bahasa Malaysia*, are very similar. The country named after each entry in this glossary relates to the location in which the term is predominantly used in this book, not to the language.

Index

CPSIA information can be obtained at www.ICGtesting.com
Printed in the USA
LVOW072133111011

250053LV00006B/17/P

9 780415 681957